Membership-Based Organizations of the Poor

This important and new volume grows out of a conviction that membership-based organizations of the poor (MBOPs) – organizations whose governance structures respond to the needs and aspirations of the poor because they are accountable to their members – are central to achieving equitable growth and poverty reduction.

Some MBOPs have been remarkably successful, while others have failed. What structures and activities characterize MBOPs? What is meant by success? What factors account for success? In particular, what are the internal (governance structure and leadership) and external (policy environment) factors that account for success? Are these factors replicable across countries or even within countries? What are the constraints to successful MBOPs expanding, or to new ones being formed? What sort of policy environment enables the success of MBOPs and the formation of new MBOPs? What types of institutional reforms are needed to ensure the representation of the poor through their own member-based organizations (MBOs)? All these questions are considered in this highly topical volume, which includes contributions from researchers from both developed and developing countries.

Martha Chen teaches at the Kennedy School of Government, Harvard University, and is Coordinator of the global policy research network Women in Informal Employment: Globalizing and Organizing (WIEGO). **Renana Jhabvala** is the National Coordinator of SEWA and the Chair of SEWA Bank, Ahmedabad, India. **Ravi Kanbur** is T.H. Lee Professor of World Affairs at Cornell University, USA. **Carol Richards** is an advisor to foundations, universities and NGOs regarding programs in human development.

Routledge studies in development economics

Membership-Based Organizations of the Poor

Edited by Martha Chen,
Renana Jhabvala, Ravi Kanbur and
Carol Richards

Routledge
Taylor & Francis Group

LONDON AND NEW YORK

First published 2007
by Routledge
2 Park Square, Milton Park, Abingdon, Oxon OX14 4RN

Simultaneously published in the USA and Canada
by Routledge
711 Third Ave, New York, NY 10017

Routledge is an imprint of the Taylor & Francis Group, an informa business

Typeset in Baskerville by Wearset Ltd, Boldon, Tyne and Wear

British Library Cataloguing in Publication Data
A catalogue record for this book is available from the British Library

Library of Congress Cataloging in Publication Data
A catalog record for this book has been requested

First issued in paperback in 2013

ISBN13: 978-0-415-74859-9 (pbk)
ISBN13: 978-0-415-77073-6 (hbk)

Contents

Illustrations

Figures

Tables

Boxes

Contributors

Vivi Alatas is an Economist with the World Bank in Indonesia.

Ruth Alsop is the Task Team Leader for Empowerment in the World Bank's Poverty Reduction Group. She has worked for international NGOs, bilateral agencies and in British academia.

Stephan Baas is Sustainable Rural Development Officer at the Food and Agriculture Organization of the UN, working principally on participatory processes, local institutions, pastoral development and disaster risk management in agriculture. He holds degrees in geography and social anthropology.

Sharit K. Bhowmik is Professor of Labour Studies at Tata Institute of Social Sciences, Mumbai. He has degrees from the University of Mumbai and the University of Delhi. He has served as Member (Expert) on the National Task Force on Street Vendors, Ministry of Urban Development, Government of India and is one of the founding members of the National Alliance of Street Vendors of India.

Tessa Bold is a researcher at the Economics Department of the University of Oxford. Her current research focuses on the theoretical modelling of informal insurance groups.

Maria A. Bouquet is a Rural Development Specialist at the World Bank. Since 2002, she has worked in Community Driven Development and Land Administration projects in Latin America, Eastern Europe and Central Asia. She holds degrees from the University of Buenos Aires and the University of California, Berkeley.

Edward W. Bresnyan is an Agricultural Economist on staff at the World Bank. Since 1997, he has worked in implementing both rural poverty reduction and natural resource management projects, primarily in Northeast Brazil. He holds a PhD from the University of Florida.

Martha Chen teaches at the Kennedy School of Government, Harvard University, and coordinates the global policy research network on the informal economy (WIEGO). She has a PhD in South Asia Regional Studies from the University of Pennsylvania.

Eve Crowley is Senior Officer for Rural Livelihood Strategies and Poverty Alleviation at the Food and Agriculture Organization of the UN. Focusing now on rural institutions, land tenure and sustainable development, she holds degrees from Yale University and Smith College.

Celine D'Cruz helped found the Society for the Promotion of Area Resource Centres (SPARC), an NGO working in more than 40 Indian cities and towns to build the capacity of urban poor organizations. Since 1998, Celine has also been coordinator of Slum Dwellers International (SDI).

Arjan de Haan is at the UK Department for International Development and, during 2005–2006, on special leave at the University of Guelph.

Stefan Dercon is the Professor of Development Economics at the University of Oxford, based at the Department of International Development (Queen Elizabeth House), and a fellow of Wolfson College. Formerly he taught at the Economics Department and Jesus College, Oxford as well as the Catholic University of Leuven.

Joseph Devine is a lecturer of International Development at the University of Bath (UK). At the moment, he is also the Bangladesh country coordinator for the ESRC Research Group on Wellbeing in Developing Countries.

Joachim De Weerdt is the Research Director of EDI (Economic Development Initiatives), a research house based in Bukoba, Tanzania.

Geneviève Dionne is a consultant for the Livelihood Support Programme at the Food and Agriculture Organization of the UN and is a PhD candidate in Anthropology, McGill University (Montréal, Canada).

Renana Jhabvala is an activist with SEWA for over 25 years. She is the National Co-ordinator of SEWA, the Chairperson of SEWA Bank and the President of the National Federation, SEWA Bharat. She holds degrees from Harvard and Yale.

Ravi Kanbur is T.H. Lee Professor of World Affairs at Cornell University. He has served on the staff of the World Bank, including as the Chief Economist for Africa. He holds degrees from Cambridge and from Oxford.

Themrise Khan is a freelance social development consultant based in Islamabad, Pakistan. She also writes on development issues for the media and has graduated from York University in Toronto, Canada, and the London School of Economics and Political Science.

Brett Matthews is a specialist in community-based microfinance with Mathwood Consulting Co. He has served in management roles at Oxfam America and at Toronto's Metro Credit Union. He holds an MBA (finance) from the Schulich School of Business.

John D. McCarthy is Professor of Sociology at the Pennsylvania State University. He previously taught at the Catholic University of America and Vanderbilt University. He received his PhD from the University of Oregon.

Martin Medina has collaborated with the World Bank, the United Nations and other organizations on community-based solid waste systems in Africa, Asia and Latin America. He holds degrees from Yale University and the University of North Carolina.

Diana Mitlin works at the International Institute for Environment and Development where she focuses on issues related to poverty reduction in urban areas. She is also a staff member at the Institute for Development Policy and Management (University of Manchester).

Alula Pankhurst is Associate Professor at the Department of Sociology and Social Anthropology at Addis Ababa University.

Pamela Pozarny is the Land Tenure and Rural Development Officer in the FAO Regional Office for Africa. She holds a PhD in Anthropology from the University of Florida, Gainesville, and has lived and worked in Africa for over 15 years.

Lant Pritchett is currently Lead Socio-Economist in the New Delhi regional office of the World Bank. From 1998 to 2000 he lived in Indonesia and worked in the Social Development group of the World Bank.

Pun Ngai is Assistant Professor at Division of Social Science, Hong Kong University of Science and Technology. She is the author of *Made in China: Women Factory Workers in a Global Workplace* (Duke University Press and Hong Kong University Press, 2005) and, with Agnes Ku, *Remaking Citizenship in Hong Kong: Community, Nation and the Global City* (RoutledgeCurson, 2004). Her current interests include global production, gender and labor in China. She is also the President of the Chinese Working Women Network (www.cwwn.org).

Carol A. Richards is an advisor to foundations, universities and NGOs on human development and economic justice. Memberships include WIEGO and the Pacific Council on International Policy. She holds degrees in Anthropology from the University of California, Los Angeles.

Sally Roever is Visiting Professor of Public Administration at Leiden University (Netherlands). She earned a PhD in political science from the

University of California, Berkeley in 2005. Her dissertation is entitled "Negotiating Formality: Informal Sector, Market, and State in Peru."

John Rouse, former Senior Officer, Cooperatives and Rural Organizations Group at the Food and Agricultural Organization of the UN and Coordinator of its People's Participation Programme, is now an international consultant on rural organization development based in Rome.

Francesca Russo is a lecturer on cultural anthropology at the University of Modena. Since 2002 she has been working as a consultant for the World Bank on environment- and community-driven development, primarily in Central America. She holds a PhD in human geography from the University of Trieste (Italy).

Samita Sen is Professor of History, Calcutta University, and holds a PhD degree from Cambridge University.

Paola Termine is Sustainable Agriculture and Rural Development Officer at the Food and Agriculture Organization of the UN. Holding a PhD in economics, she focuses on rural institutions and sustainable development, with special interest in agricultural labour and rural employment.

Sarojini Ganju Thakur is a civil servant who belongs to the Indian Administrative Service. She is currently on secondment to the Commonwealth Secretariat, London, where she works as Adviser (Gender), with a focus on gender, poverty eradication and economic empowerment.

Jan Theron is a practising labour lawyer and co-ordinates a research project on labour standards and development based in the Law Faculty at the University of Cape Town. He was formerly general secretary of a prominent affiliate of the trade union federation COSATU.

Anand Mohan Tiwari is a civil servant belonging to the Indian Administrative Service. He is currently working with the Government of Gujarat as Commissioner of Geology and Mining. He has earlier worked in rural development and microfinance sectors at the national and state levels.

Edward T. Walker is a doctoral candidate at the Pennsylvania State University. His work on poor people's movement organizations (with John McCarthy) appeared in *Nonprofit and Voluntary Sector Quarterly*. His research on grassroots lobbying was awarded an NSF Dissertation Grant.

Anna Wetterberg was the director of the Local Level Institutions II study in Indonesia and is now completing her PhD in sociology at the University of California, Berkeley.

Acknowledgements

The editors acknowledge the financial support of the Broad Reach Foundation and Cornell University. They also thank SEWA organizers and members of the Exposure and Dialogue program that preceded the conference and acknowledge the excellent organizational arrangements for the conference by the staff of SEWA Academy and WIEGO. For help with preparation of the volume, thanks are due to Sue Snyder of Cornell University.

Part I

Introduction and overview

1 Membership-based organizations of the poor

Concepts, experience and policy

Martha Chen, Renana Jhabvala, Ravi Kanbur and Carol Richards

Introduction

This volume grows out of a conviction that membership-based organizations of the poor (MBOPs) – organizations whose governance structures respond to the needs and aspirations of the poor because they are accountable to their members – are central to achieving equitable growth and poverty reduction. The literature on civil society organizations generally focuses on non-governmental organizations (NGOs), which are treated as a broad category thought to cover all the ways that people get together and act together. However, an MBOP is to be distinguished from a conventional NGO, which, however well intentioned, operates as an outside entity that does not have a membership base of the poor. Political parties are membership-based organizations (MBO), but are not exclusively concerned about the welfare of the poor. Trade unions are membership based, but only some of them are directly concerned with advancing the cause of the working poor. Cooperatives are classic MBOs, but again not all of them are focused on the poor, and some of them have elements of formal contractual obligations that make them akin to private sector firms.

The leading example we have in mind when we talk of MBOPs is that of SEWA, the Self-Employed Women's Association in India.[1] SEWA is governed by its members – working poor women in the informal economy whom SEWA serves through a range of activities. As an MBOP, SEWA acts as a channel for carrying the voice of its members to policy makers and in turn helps to transmit the benefits of poverty-focused government projects and programs to its members. Its twin pillars are economic activities to enhance income earning opportunities and organization to enable its members to claim and exercise their rights in the economic, legal, and social spheres.

What structures and activities characterize MBOPs? What is meant by success? What factors account for success or failure? What are the challenges faced by MBOPs? How can policy best help MBOPs? Answers to such questions were sought at a conference organized by SEWA, the WIEGO network, and Cornell University in Ahmedabad, India, in January

2005.[2] Papers covering experiences from around the world were presented and discussed. The presenters included economists, sociologists, anthropologists, representatives of aid agencies, and MBOPs. The papers presented at the conference were then revised by way of peer review, and have been brought together in this volume.[3]

This introduction to the volume provides an overview of the issues and of the papers. Section 2 addresses the conceptualization and definition of MBOPs. Section 3 turns to the definition of MBOP success, the determinants of this success, and the challenges faced by MBOPs. The lessons learnt from the evidence presented in the papers are reviewed in this section. Section 4 discusses policy towards MBOPs. Section 5 concludes.

Conceptualizing and defining MBOPs

NGOs, MBOs, and MBOPs

There is growing recognition of institutions that straddle and interact with, but are distinct from the market and the state. This domain has been described under various labels – the third sector, civil society, non-governmental organizations, and so on. It covers a large variety of institutions, ranging from the family and the extended household, through community management arrangements to trade unions and political parties. Our focus in this volume is on an important slice of this institutional terrain – MBOPs. MBOPs are a subset of MBOs. We define MBOs as those in which the members elect their leaders and which operate on democratic principles that hold the elected officers accountable to the general membership. MBOPs are MBOs in which the vast majority of members are poor, although some non-poor persons may also be members. The form that MBOPs take – whether legally registered or not – may range from trade unions and cooperatives to funeral societies and self-help groups (SHGs). They have, in common, a commitment to collective action to change the conditions of their poor members.

It is useful to first distinguish MBOs from other NGOs, then MBOPs from other MBOs, and finally one MBOP from the other. MBOs are different from other NGOs. The democratic governance structures of MBOs are intended to provide both internal accountability (leaders are elected) and external legitimacy (leaders represent their constituency), characteristics not shared by other NGOs. While this basic distinction is central to our argument, there can of course be intimate relationships between NGOs and MBOs. Often, MBOPs are created by actions of NGOs, whereby the NGOs help the local community to organize their own MBOPs. In many cases, NGOs offer services such as finance, education or health services to MBOPs. Many MBOPs enter strategic partnerships with NGOs that provide services, join in advocacy efforts, and otherwise help mediate the external environment.

Turning now to MBOPs as a subset of MBOs, we have considered several alternative terms to try to capture what we had in mind, namely, that the poor need to be organized, need to be recognized, and need to have a "seat at the (policy) table." We finally settled on "membership-based organizations of the poor," putting an emphasis on *of* (not for) and *the poor* (not the non-poor).[4] But what are we to make of the fact that some MBOPs like SEWA itself include non-poor members? Our response is based on our view that SEWA is an MBOP because the management and governance structures of the organization are *predominantly* comprised of working poor women. Hence our conclusion that MBOPs are membership-based organizations in which the vast majority of members are poor and the organization is accountable to the poor.

A related theme then is the role of the non-poor in MBOPs. The non-poor in MBOPs can play two broad types of roles: internal and external. In terms of internal roles, some MBOs are self-started while others are started by non-poor outsiders while still others, like SEWA, are started by the poor with the help of one or more sympathetic non-poor persons already known to them. Also, some MBOs remain small and internally focused, and devise their own self-government and self-management structures. Others, especially those that grow in scope and size, often rely on non-poor members to provide technical and managerial support (for a classification along the lines of funding and organizational support, see Chapter 2). In terms of external roles, non-poor members of MBOPs help raise external funds, frame issues, generate policy-relevant information, leverage policy reform, and otherwise mediate the external environment. Sympathetic non-poor members can help leverage contacts, power, and influence. The challenge is to ensure that the non-poor members do not dominate the poor members or control the organization as a whole.

Another related issue is that of finance. At an abstract level, the test for an MBOP is that whether it is responsive to the needs of its poor members. An intermediate test is that whether the governance structures are such as to be responsive in this way, a key indicator being the role of poor members in various executive and governing functions. In principle, these structures could be in place and work well even when the members of an MBOP do not contribute financially or in kind to the operation of its activities – indeed, existence of many excellent NGOs that are *non-*membership-based organizations *for* the poor is an indication of this possibility. However, while it is difficult to specify the exact amount in advance, we believe that at least some contribution to the organization from its members is a *sine qua non* of an MBOP. Otherwise, if all of the funding comes from outside, the interests of its members are at risk of being subverted to the interests of the donors, which, however laudable in principle, may not accord with the felt interest of the members, expressed through the organization. For small MBOPs like funeral associations (see Chapter 9), membership contribution is built into the very *raison d'être* and structure of the organization. For these and larger organizations like waste picker cooperatives or street trader associations (see Chapters 6 and 14), contributions come in cash and in kind. It is when organizations grow and take on external sources of funding for projects that extra vigilance is needed in ensuring that the organization still remains an organization *of* the poor.

Consider the case of SEWA. It is an MBOP in that working poor women represent the vast majority of its members and form the majority of its governance and management structures. Clearly, non-poor members have played key roles in the formation, growth, and overall effectiveness of the organization. Equally clearly, SEWA has worked systematically from its formation more than three decades ago to build a whole set of membership-based organizations that can assume, over time, the governance and management of its many institutions and activities. Working poor women represent the majority of members in the executive committees and the governing bodies of the SEWA Union and its sister MBOs such as the SEWA Bank, the various cooperatives, and the cooperative federation. While there is significant external funding for projects run by SEWA, all members pay financial dues and contribute in kind, and the working poor women represent the vast majority of the decentralized management teams that implement and oversee its integrated activities on the ground.

Crowley *et al.* (see Chapter 2) propose the following criteria for identifying MBOPs:

- MBOPs are defined as organizations that poor members control and partially or fully finance, and whose membership exhibits the following characteristics.
- The majority are poor.
- They have joined on a voluntary basis.
- They have developed, agreed upon, and engage in their own decision-making structures.
- They provide contribution, financial or in kind, as a condition of membership.

Theron (Chapter 13), also develop a related set of "six characteristics of any organization that aspires to be an MBOP," based on the traditions of trade unions and cooperatives, including,

1   [its] primary objective is to cater for the socio-economic needs of its members;
2   a well-defined constituency from which membership is drawn;
3   the organization is financed by its members;
4   the highest decision making structure is (or should be) the most representative forum of members;

5   a strongly developed sense of ownership of the organization by the members, and of accountability of the leadership to the membership;
6   embody values of cooperation and solidarity.

Thus, while there may be specific differences of detail between different authors in this volume and in the literature, there appears to be a broad consensus on the key characteristics that define an MBOP.

Types of MBOPs

Within this broad framework, there is a wide range of MBOPs:

- trade unions;
- cooperatives of various kinds: production, service, marketing, credit, bank;
- worker committees;
- savings and credit groups/SHGs;
- community-based finance institutions;
- funeral associations;
- informal insurance institutions;
- producer groups;
- village or slum associations;
- community-based organizations, some of which represent traditional social groupings (based on kinship, caste, patron–client relationships);
- clubs: youth, recreational.

For example, the types of organizations discussed in this volume include:

- informal workers' committees in China (Ngai);
- committees formed to manage specific projects in Brazil (Bresnyan *et al.*);
- trade unions (de Haan and Sen, Theron);
- cooperatives (Medina in South America, Bhowmik in India, Matthews in Cambodia);
- small self-help groups in Africa (De Weerdt *et al.*) and in India (Tiwari and Thakur, and Alsop);
- street vendor organizations in Peru (Roever);
- community-based organizations (Khan in Pakistan, Devine in Bangladesh, Theron in South Africa).

In addition to this range of primary groups, there are various organizations through which the primary groups link to each other through federations and issue-based coalitions or networks, both secular and religious (d'Cruz and Mitlin).

Formal legal recognition of MBOPs appears to happen through two main channels – trade union legislation and cooperatives legislation. Formal registration is often required when certain thresholds (on numbers or type of activity) are crossed. Though such registration can bring constraints through regulation, it benefits through legal protection, access to formal channels, and facilitation of expansion. Other forms, not always legally recognized, include producer groups of various kinds, worker committees (as in the case of the migrant women workers in south China described by Ngai, Chapter 5), and coalitions of worker organizations such as StreetNet (the international coalition of street vendor associations) and HomeNet South Asia and South East Asia (regional coalitions of home-based worker associations). Other themes related to the issue of trade unions and other MBOs of workers that emerge from the discussions in this volume include:

- Trade unions of formal sector workers have only just begun to reach out to organize informal sector workers.
- Organizing in the informal economy requires different strategies and approaches than organizing workers in a large formal factory or firm.
- Trade unions of informal workers often take an integrated approach that goes beyond just collective bargaining. For instance, SEWA takes an integrated approach that involves the joint action of trade unions and cooperatives or, as SEWA puts it, the combined strategies of "struggle" and "development." SEWA is a registered union but many of its sister institutions such as the SEWA Bank are cooperatives.

The above suggests that a useful criterion to distinguish one MBOP from another is whether it organizes the poor around their identity as workers and around work- or livelihood-related issues or it organizes the poor around other issues. Organizing the poor around their identity as workers has several advantages: it helps focus policy attention on the poor as economic agents – as contributors to the national economy. It also helps minimize other identities which are often used by politicians to divide people based on caste or religion. Finally, it helps bring together people around two common basic needs – the need to earn a living and the need for a sense of dignity. Most of the cases considered in this volume focus on MBOPs that organize around economic issues. However, as the paper by Alatas *et al.* (Chapter 17) shows, organizations built around social, religious, or cultural issues can also have a significant impact on external governance, and thus, in turn, on economic outcomes for the poor.

Successes and challenges

Defining success

We are interested in identifying the determinants of successful MBOPs. But, first of all, what is "success"? Crowley *et al.* (see Chapter 2) define success in terms of four criteria:

1 [A successful MBOP] achieves the objectives agreed upon by the members.
2 [It] retains or expands its membership.
3 [It] shows progress towards financial and managerial self-reliance, inspiring members to maintain their equity stake in the organization.
4 [It] brings improvement to the self esteem, economic, and social well-being of its members.

Roever (Chapter 14) divides indicators of success into two categories. In the "internal dimension" are included: building individual capacity, fostering expression and debate, and carrying out concrete projects. In the "external dimension" are included: gaining access to policy discussions, achieving favorable policy, and representing voices of the excluded. Roever's characterization of success thus looks beyond the narrow confines of outcomes for members, given the existing external policy environment; it also looks for success in changing these policies through coordinated collective action. Roever's discussion also emphasizes process as much as outcome. Thus, the fostering of expression and debate is rated as an internal success indicator, and carrying out concrete projects and representing the voices of the excluded are considered as external success indicators, as achieving favorable policy.

In our view, the criteria for success of an MBOP have to be context specific, paying attention to the objectives of the organization. Thus, it would be inappropriate to classify as failure an MOBP that does not manage to change a policy because (after having calculated that it cannot influence that policy) it does the best for its members, given the policy. On the other hand, all MBOPs know that their ability to help their members is determined significantly by the external environment, and some of them, especially as they scale up, do become involved in national and even international policy dialogue. Even here, given the multitude of forces operating on policy making at the macro-level, care is needed in attributing either success or failure in policy change to a particular MBOP or a group of MBOPs.

We are on somewhat surer ground when success is measured by the improvement in well-being (as defined in the objectives of the organization) of the members of the organization, drawing on elements from Crowley *et al.* and Roever definitions. Even here, there are two issues.

The first is again the attribution issue; although the more concrete the assessment, the easier it is to identify specific causality to the MBOP itself, rather than other interventions or general trends in the economy. The second touches on the process versus outcome issue mentioned here. Although it is difficult to delineate precisely, process matters such as "fostering of expression and debate" and strengthening the ability of the poor to speak out, should also be categorized as success indicators.

While success can be measured for specific outcomes or specific projects, Crowley *et al.* propose two general indicators, which are in one sense, the result of an aggregation of a series of specific successful outcomes. These indicators are retention and expansion of membership, and maintenance by members of their "equity stake in the organization." An interesting research agenda is opened up by these considerations. Empirically, we need information not only on membership numbers but also on membership fees as a percentage of total core running expenses of the organization. An organization which expands the former without reducing the latter, in these terms, is doubly successful. And, presumably, this success would not come unless concrete dimensions of well-being were improving for the members as a result of their membership in the organization.

An extreme case of failure is when an organization simply stops existing. The flip side of this – survival and longevity – seems to accord with the Crowley *et al.* indicators discussed here. While it is of course true that "longevity is not necessarily a good indicator of success, as an MBOP can be highly successful and then dissolve when it has met its objectives," (Crowley *et al.*, Chapter 2), for most organizations dealing with the needs of the poor in general, with careful interpretation, survival could be interpreted as an indicator of success (just as membership expansion is interpreted as an indicator of success). This is the line of argument developed by Walker and McCarthy (Chapter 3). Using the files of a donor agency funding social movement organizations in the US, they analyze the survival of organizations over a period of 12 years and attempt to statistically identify the causal factors behind survival versus demise.

Determinants of success: lessons from papers

The case studies and arguments in the chapters in this volume provide a rich source of empirical evidence on the determinants of success in MBOPs and of the challenges they face. We begin with a review of the findings of the papers presented in the conference, which also provides an opportunity for a brief overview of each paper. The volume is divided into six sections after this introduction and overview:

1   General principles: survival and success
2   Trade unions

3   Cooperatives
4   Small self-help groups
5   Campaigning organizations
6   Local power structures and MBOPs.

We take up the papers in each of these sections, in turn, focusing on the lessons for determinants of success of MBOPs.

Crowley *et al.*, in their "Organizations of the poor: conditions for success," develop a typology of organizations, metrics for success, and conditions for success, based on a review drawn from United Nations (UN) reports and from the field experiences of the staff of the Food and Agricultural Organization (FAO) of the UN. We have already seen their definition of MBOPs and their definition of success. They derive conditions for success along two dimensions – internal and external. Among the internal factors is composition of membership. While having some non-poor members is helpful, having a predominantly poor membership is important for MBOPs to keep their focus on the poor, and having a relatively homogeneous membership in terms of socio-cultural and economic conditions, particularly occupation, helps to unify interests. Another factor is governance structure, including whether members pay significant financial or in-kind dues, and whether poor members are adequately represented in management structures. Finally, "an explicit code of moral conduct," exemplified by SEWA's Gandhian roots, is also argued to be a key determinant of success. On external factors, Crowley *et al.* highlight the role of external donor support, which becomes important as an MBOP grows from perhaps a small grouping to a larger organization. They are generally negative about the impact of this interaction because of external influence through finance and undermining of local dynamism and interest. They also highlight the role of government policies in setting the broad environment, in which MBOPs can either thrive or wither.

As noted earlier, Walker and McCarthy, in "The influence of organizational structure, membership composition and resources on the survival of poor people's social movement organizations," conduct a statistical analysis of survival patterns of a class of rights-based MBOPs over a 12-year period in the US. They test a number of hypotheses and find in particular that diversity of funding sources increases chances of survival, as does the age of an organization when funding is first received. They also find that individual-membership-based organizations are more likely to survive than coalitions of rights groups, although this may be because the former organizations are older in their sample (see finding on age and survival).

The chapter by de Haan and Sen, "Working class struggles, labor elites, and closed shops: the lessons from India's trade unions and experiences of organization," looks at the history of trade unions of unskilled labor in India. These arose at a time when the workers were poor and the colonial regime did not look kindly upon organizations of workers. And yet, they now have the classic image of the "labor aristocracy," with little regard for the poorest workers in the informal sector, particularly for women who work in the informal sector. The authors then relate this historical discussion to current concerns about success conditions for organizations of the poor, particularly, in terms of the debate on how civil society "thickens." This can happen through "state–society convergence" (where the state facilitates emergence of such organizations), external and local civil society coalitions, and "bottom-up mobilization." A key factor running through the story in India, according to de Haan and Sen, is that unions have not been "able to incorporate the interests of women as workers" and this is closely related to the need for formal sector unions to become representative of the informal economy, in which 90 percent of workers in countries like India operate. From our point of view, de Haan and Sen emphasize both internal governance factors (development of the "labor aristocracy" and unwillingness to look beyond the narrow formal sector in the case of the unions) and external factors (help from the state, or enlightened officials of the state) to explain the successes and failures of these, admittedly exclusive, unions.

Ngai describes the work of the Chinese Working Women Network (CWWN) in her chapter, "China as a world factory: new practices and struggles of migrant women workers." CWWN is a Hong Kong-based NGO that works with migrant female labor in Guangdong Province of China. The basic problem is the lack of corporate accountability for exploitative labor conditions, established by multinational corporations in this economic enterprise zone. The NGO is not of course an MBOP itself. Rather, it supports women's organization in factories. It conducts training workshops on labor rights. Ultimately, it is the women's groups in the factories that are a nascent form of MBOP. What is needed for these nascent organizations to grow and succeed? Ngai's case study demonstrates the possibility of organizing poor workers even where the legal and political space for new forms of organization is very narrow. NGOs can bring a human rights component to the development of MBOPs, even where state and corporate power combine to limit collective action. Returning to the observation in de Haan and Sen, industries and governments are not monoliths; there are ways of finding entry points, especially if there are individuals within corporations and states who are willing to help.

It is well known that garbage picking is a major form of survival for the desperately poor in developing countries. They work in hazardous conditions, and when they work as individuals they are exploited by middlemen. In Chapter 6, "Waste picker cooperatives in developing countries," Medina draws together the lessons from successes and failures with these organizational forms in Latin America and in Asia. He emphasizes internal capacity and governance issues – lack of education and business expertise, and "cheating and unscrupulous leaders." As external factors, sympathetic mayors (especially at times of change in administration) and NGOs who can help in organization and initial operation of cooperatives are emphasized.

Bhowmik's Chapter 7, "Co-operatives and the emancipation of the marginalized: case studies from two cities in India," links interestingly to the chapter by de Haan and Sen since it is a case study of cooperatives founded by trade unions in the two cities – Ahmedabad and Calcutta – in response to the closure of industrial units due to economic policies. The role of the external political environment is highlighted. In Calcutta, the intricate relations between the cooperative, the union that founded it, and the (Communist) state government are a central part of the story. In some cases, the relationship was supportive; in other cases it was disruptive. In Ahmedabad, the case study is that of SEWA and the waste picker cooperatives it founded. The help that SEWA's collective influence gave to the fledgling cooperatives is emphasized.

Matthews (see Chapter 8) focuses on internal capacity issues in Community Finance Institutions (CFIs) in Cambodia, in situations of low literacy. His "Literacy and internal control of community finance institutions in Cambodia" defines a CFI as "an institution that specializes in delivering financial services and is owned and controlled by its members within a local community." However, standard financial control techniques will not work in communities where literacy levels are very low. He calls for "contextually sensitive tools" relying on "symbols, relational formatting, group transparency, and collective memory." The point that Matthews is making is a general one on internal capacity building – this needs to be done in a way that does not privilege a few educated or better-off members of the organization.

De Weerdt *et al.* (Chapter 9) study "Membership-based indigenous insurance associations in Ethiopia and Tanzania." Their definition is as follows: "A membership-based indigenous insurance scheme is a locally initiated association of people, who have voluntarily entered into an explicit agreement to help each other when well-defined events occur." These associations offer insurance primarily for funeral and hospital-related expenses, with the larger goal of helping households absorb financial shocks, which would otherwise propel them into poverty.[5] The researchers find these associations to be broadly successful. They are self-grown and self-managed, and they are broadly inclusive. They seem to fill the niche between the state and market very well. Perhaps in this case, non-interference from the state has been a boon. The external cloud on the horizon, however, is HIV/AIDS. This may lead to increased premiums, and thus to the exclusion of the poorest members of the community.

Self-help groups are now part of the discourse on development, especially in microfinance, and are an important type of MBOP. These are studied by Tiwari and Thakur in Chapter 10 "SHG-based microfinance programmes – can they remove poverty?" They look at several examples of SHGs from Gujarat state in India. The chapter raises an issue that recurs in this volume – how sustainable is an SHG if it is founded for a specific project? What happens after the life of the project? Can SHGs evolve to address another set of issues? Can they endure as part of the institutional landscape when the project that spawned them is over? Based on the findings of Tiwari and Thakur, the jury seems to be out on these questions.

Alsop's Chapter 11 "Community-level user groups: do they perform as expected?" looks at the operation of community-level user groups for three local resource management projects in India (land reclamation, forest management, and water), based on a survey of 2400 user group members and representatives. Members are disproportionately male. The basic finding is that while members seem satisfied with the immediate personal benefits from the project, they "demonstrated low levels of ownership of the user group and little interest in, or commitment to, the group as a mechanism for managing cooperation beyond the end of the project." This raises the same questions as in Tiwari and Thakur (Chapter 10). It suggests the difficulty of "kick starting" sustainable MBOPs with external finance and initiative.

D'Cruz and Mitlin study not an MBOP but an NGO, one that supports a network of MBOPs, in Chapter 12 "Shack/Slum Dwellers International: one experience of membership-based organizations to pro-poor urban development." Shack/Slum Dwellers International (SDI) is a network of national level federations of urban poor. Each federation is in turn composed of community organizations that, in some cases, are membership-based saving schemes in which women are the majority of participants. The experience of SDI, as in the experience of SEWA cooperatives, shows the power of federating MBOPs. Together, they have a collective power and voice that no single MBOP can muster. As D'Cruz and Mitlin note, the "process of federation building is to ensure that the voices of its members are heard and acted upon within agencies involved in local and international policy making." The key, of course, is true representativeness on the part of the federation to ensure that it does not itself represent an "MBOP aristocracy" in the way that trade unions might represent a "labor aristocracy."

As noted earlier in this introduction, in "Membership-based organizations of the poor: the South African tradition," Theron highlights the trade union and cooperative traditions of MBOPs in South Africa. We have already listed Theron's characterization of MBOPs based on this tradition. The chapter makes clear that these same characteristics can be used as criteria for determinants of MBOP success. He highlights, in particular, the central role of financial self-sufficiency – "there can be no true accountability in an MBO that is not sustained by the contributions of its members. . . . External funding, I have suggested, is one of the drivers of a top-down tradition of organization." Theron also highlights the legal framework in which MBOPs operate, noting two opposing arguments, namely that, on the one hand, absorption into a formal legal framework is problematic, while on the other hand, without such incorporation, sustainability and expansion may be in doubt.

Roever studies 12 street vending associations in Lima, Peru. Her chapter, "Informal governance and organizational success: the effects of noncompliance among Lima's street vending associations," "explores the possibility that organizations of informal workers experience only mixed success because the organizations themselves are run informally." She documents how these associations, although they are meant to be accountable to their members, do not, in fact, have democratic governance structures. The informal methods of control and management reduce the credibility of leaders as representatives of their poor members. The noncompliance referred to in the title of the chapter is this noncompliance with democratic governance procedures. These internal failures have significant impact on the abilities of these MBOPs to better the lives of their members.

In "Membership-based organizations as a reflection of power structures in rural 'community': experiences and observations from Sindh Province, Pakistan," Khan argues that it is naïve to think of NGOs, Community-based Organizations (CBOs), and MBOPs as abstracted from the local power structures. Focusing on CBOs, she argues that, "beneath it all, it is social and caste hierarchy that controls how members of CBOs interact with each other and those around them." Her study of CBOs in Sindh Province gives empirical content to these observations. For example, villagers who were not members of a CBO said "we were not asked to be members," "they belong to a higher caste," "they only associate with their own kind." Moreover, the CBOs studied were associated with one individual, rather than broadly membership based. Khan argues that this stands in the way of the potential of CBOs in poverty reduction, since many of them do have an appreciation of local complexities, and "as legally registered formal organizations, they can act as much needed intermediaries between their community members and those more powerful such as landlords, and even donors."

Devine emphasizes the "immediate relationships and social networks" in the everyday lives of the poor, and their role in managing a precarious existence. His chapter, "Doing things differently? The everyday politics of membership-based organizations," "rests on the premise that the relational milieu constitutes the primary cultural terrain upon which people construct their wellbeing." Thus, rather like Khan's argument for Pakistan, Devine's argument, based on evidence from Bangladesh, is that the operations of MBOPs cannot be analyzed separately from local social networks and power structures. Thus, he finds that the MBOP he studies has, alongside creating new opportunities for its members, also reproduced "patterns of dependency and clientelism." This highlights the central role of the community context in which the MBOP is situated, in determining whether it has been "successful," or even in specifying what is meant by "success": e.g. whether changing existing community relationships is feasible or desirable.

Chapter 17 by Alatas *et al.*, "Voice lessons: local government organizations, social organizations, and the quality of local governance," presents analysis based on an interesting data set which collected information on household participation in four categories of "social activity": sociability, networks, social organizations, and village government organizations. Information was also collected on participation in village decisions. Village government organizations are created by the central government and are dominated by retired military officers. A key finding is that, after controlling for household characteristics such as education and gender of the head, households that are not members of the village government organizations are increasingly excluded from participation in local decision making. While the focus of the analysis is not on MBOPs directly, the findings do highlight important spillover effects from social activities to participation in village decisions.

Community-driven Development (CDD) by Bresnyan *et al.* is the subject of the final chapter in this volume. The chapter, "Community-driven development and the Northeast Brazil rural poverty reduction program," looks in detail at a particular program supported by the World Bank. Over 50,000 small-scale community investments in rural electrification, water, and so on have been financed and implemented by 36,000 community organizations. The potential beneficiaries are 1.2 million households and 7 million individuals. The chapter examines, in particular, the role of community associations in this program. These are "groups of rural citizens with a common interest and organized into legally constituted civil organizations (as required under Brazilian law)." There is an analogy with community user groups studied in Alsop's chapter, and the same question is central – will the community associations last beyond the project? Bresnyan *et al.* are more optimistic for Brazil than Alsop is for India.

Internal and external factors and challenges

Let us begin with a broad overview of the key internal (to the MBOP) and external determinants of success or failure identified in the chapters in this volume. The internal factors are:

- democratic governance structures whose operation keeps leadership accountable to members;
- significant role of membership dues, in cash and kind;
- sufficiently homogeneous membership along key dimensions (poverty, occupation, gender, and so on);
- capacity to manage the running of the organization;

- the use of federated governance structures as the organization expands;
- a strongly internalized "code of moral conduct" that guides actions of the organization and of individuals in the organization.

The external factors are:

- supportive community power structures;
- a broadly enabling legal, political, and policy environment;
- sympathetic individuals in government and bureaucracy;
- external funding and support from NGOs and donors that does not subvert internal democratic procedures and the objectives of the organization;
- diversified sources of external finance.

Based on the above discussion, we can identify the following internal and external challenges that MBOPs face, especially as they expand to address the problems of a larger membership. The internal challenges are:

- maintaining the strong "code of moral conduct" in the midst of changing social and cultural norms;
- capacity of MBOPs to manage ever increasing complexity of operations, without creating a divide between professional managers and the membership;
- ability of MBOPs to sustain and strengthen the engagement of members, and to hold leaders accountable, as they scale up or begin to address a more complex range of issues.

The external challenges are:

- ensure a diversified source of external finance and support, in a manner that does not undermine the basic nature of the organization;
- changing the local-level power structures and networks that mediate the impact of the MBOPs' activities on its members;
- changing the mindset of mainstream planners, policy makers, and development thinkers about the role of MBOPs in development planning, policy making, and program implementation, so that a better-enabling legal, political, and policy environment for MBOPs can be put in place.

MBOP and policy

The individual chapters in this volume provide plenty of evidence on the major effect that the broad policy environment can have on the operation of MBOPs. In the case studies, this has ranged from supportive to neutral to downright hostile. The hostility is easy to understand. MBOPs often challenge existing power structures at the local level, and their ground-level perspectives may not fit conveniently into the macro-worldview of national or international policy makers. However, there are those in the policy world, a growing number, who recognize the valuable, indeed, central role that MBOPs can and do play in achieving equitable development. What guidance can we give to the policy community, based on the analysis and evidence in this volume? We propose five points for consideration.

- First and foremost, there is a need for continued deepening of recognition by the development community, at all levels, of the role of MBOPs in economic and human development as well as poverty reduction. It is particularly important for macro-level policy makers, at the national and international level, to change their mindset – to recognize MBOPs and to incorporate them into policy planning and discourse. One of the ways to do this is to identify the types and numbers of MBOPs that exist in the policy maker's own country and to assess their capacities and their needs.
- Second, there is a need in each country to conduct a thorough review of the legal and regulatory setting in which MBOPs operate. Typically, they fall under trade union legislation or cooperatives legislation (or civil organizations' legislation). As their activities expand and become more complex, they come into the orbit of other legislation and regulation, for example, on insurance or banking. Laws and regulations that impinge on MBOPs have not, in general, developed from a systematic view of the role of MBOPs in development and the best way to nurture their development and regulate their operations. Country-specific reviews would reveal the major legal and regulatory constraints faced by MBOPs, and these could then be addressed legislatively.
- Third, there is a need for financial and other support to MBOPs, as they scale up and gear up to address the complex issues faced by their members in a globalizing world – to strengthen the capacity, solidarity, and representative voice of MBOPs. This support can be given directly or indirectly through NGOs, who in turn support MBOPs. However, as noted repeatedly in this volume, such support has to be given with great care, otherwise it will end up debilitating or destroying the MBOPs it seeks to help.
- Fourth, specifically on capacity, there is a need to build linkages which would strengthen the operational and organizational capacities of MBOPs. Depending upon the situation, these capacity-building activities could take the form of training of various types, building linkages with financial institutions, helping the MBOP assess and take advantage of markets or helping them to build an understanding of laws and policies.
- Fifth, there is a need to provide MBOPs a seat at the national and international policy making and regulation-setting table. These efforts

can range from consultation to formal inclusion in relevant committees of the government and the bureaucracy. Such representation will typically happen through federations of MBOPs that represent them. As noted earlier, an internal issue for MBOPs is how to address their challenges of expansion, through forming federations to represent groupings of MBOPs. Many such federations now operate at the national and international level. Yet, their representation in the councils of policy making is minimal.

Conclusion

Let us return to the questions posed in the introduction to this chapter: what structures and activities characterize MBOPs? What is meant by success? What factors account for success or failure? What are the challenges faced by MBOPs? How can policy best help MBOPs?

Based on the analysis and evidence of the chapters in this volume, we hope to have provided the beginnings of answers to these questions. To summarize the detailed and nuanced argument developed in this chapter:

- MBOPs respond to the needs and aspirations of the poor because the governance structures are accountable to the members and because the vast majority of the members are poor.
- Success of MBOPs can be measured not only in terms of the direct impact on the well-being of their members, but also in terms of their impact on the wider policy environment.
- There are internal and external factors behind successes and failures. These include: functioning democratic structures; capacity to run the organization; a moral code that guides actions; an enabling legal, political, and policy environment; diversified sources of finance and support that do not themselves undermine the MBOP.
- The internal and external challenges that MBOPs face, as they scale up and face increasingly complex issues, include: enhancing management capacity, maintaining accountability of organization to members, ensuring an enabling rather than debilitating flow of external finance and support, changing the policy and regulatory environment so that it becomes more enabling of MBOP operations and of the members of MBOPs.
- The main policy recommendations that follow from the analysis include: a review in each country of legislation and regulation as it impinges on MBOPs, to develop proposals for reform that enable their operation and expansion; the purposive inclusion of MBOPs in councils of national and international deliberation and policy making; and financial and capacity-building support, directly and through NGOs, delivered in a manner that does not debilitate the organization itself.

Without their own MBOs, the poor will not be able to mediate the wider environment, turn it to their benefit and hold it accountable. Without MBOPs to put pressure and make demands, more powerful interests in the wider environment will not be responsive or held responsible. As the studies in this volume demonstrate, MBOPs are already playing a wide-ranging role across the globe, in different settings and contexts. Their presence and vitality attests to the need for them. But they face challenges, and need the support of policy and policy makers. We hope that this volume lays the basis for further conceptual, empirical, and policy analysis, which will help MBOPs in their task of mediating the processes of development and change, for the benefit of the poor.

Notes

1 www.sewa.org
2 The conference website is available online at: www.wiego.org/ahmedabad/.
3 Before the conference, paper presenters engaged in an "Exposure and Dialogue" program, where they stayed in the homes of SEWA members to understand better the impact of an MBOP on the lives of poor women. Their experiences have been brought together, available online at: www.arts.cornell.edu/poverty/kanbur/EDP05Compendium.pdf.
4 This is not the place to get into esoteric and technical discussions of the definition of "poor" and "poverty". In fact, most standard definitions (for example, those based on the Millennium Development Goals) will work well, with suitable local adaptation, for the cases we are considering.
5 In some societies, including India, mutual insurance is offered primarily for death ceremonies and marriages, more so than health or medical expenses.

Part II
General principles
Survival and success

2 Organizations of the poor
Conditions for success[1]

Eve Crowley, Stephan Baas, Paola Termine,
John Rouse, Pamela Pozarny and Geneviève Dionne

Introduction

Throughout history, four main strategies have been used to support the survival of the poor (Iliffe 1987: 7). First, charitable institutions motivated by religions and individual philanthropy have been created to care for the poor. Second, forced confinement has been used to contain the poor, particularly lepers and stigmatized groups. The efforts of the poor themselves, as individuals who strive to improve their own livelihoods, is the third and by far the most common strategy. Finally, organizations of the poor have been created to enable the poor to escape from poverty. It is this last strategy that is the focus of this chapter.

Under what conditions have organizations of the poor emerged and what are the main types? Who makes up their membership and how do they evolve over time? What are the internal and external factors that promote or inhibit sustained membership and effective impacts?

Based on an institutional review of member-based organizations of the poor (MBOP), drawn primarily from the field experiences of staff of the Food and Agriculture Organization (FAO) of the United Nations (UN) working with rural institutions in developing countries and a selection of project reports produced by UN agencies, the authors attempt to answer these questions to enable emerging organizations of the poor, or those who assist them, to recognize some of the elements critical for the effectiveness and sustainability of these organizations.

After providing a working definition of MBOPs and what is meant by "success", the chapter distinguishes several broad types of MBOPs along a continuum, based upon the processes by which they are formed and sustained. Following a summary of some of the external factors influencing the emergence of MBOPs, the chapter explores key internal factors in MBOP success. The chapter concludes by summarizing major findings and highlighting key factors affecting the ability of MBOPs to scale up.

Towards a working definition of MBOPs

Membership-based organizations of the poor are distinctive among membership-based organizations (MBOs) because they are controlled by, accountable to, and seek to fulfil the objectives of their poor members. The poor are those who live at or below subsistence level, under the national poverty line, and include those bereft of income, power, opportunity, and security. MBOPs are defined as organizations that poor members control and partially or fully finance and whose membership exhibits the following characteristics:

- The majority are poor.
- They have joined on a voluntary basis.
- They agree to work together to achieve collectively defined objectives that are important to their poor members (Tilakatatna 1980: 2).
- They have developed, agreed upon, and engage in their own decision-making structures.
- They provide a financial or in-kind contribution as a condition of membership.

Membership-based organizations of the poor (MBOP) are member-financed organizations[2] that have some measure of financial, administrative, and technical ability to operate independently and survive and sustain their activities in the long run. MBOPs are frequently referred to as "self-help groups" and "community-based organizations" in the rural development literature. But MBOPs can also take the form of labour-sharing and savings groups, street gangs, producer, religious, and ethnic associations, micro-enterprises, cooperatives, trade unions, federations, national apex bodies, networks, international alliances, and social and political movements. However, only when these organizations are controlled and at least partially financed by poor members themselves are they considered to be MBOPs.

Groups of people sharing an ascribed status, such as an age grade, tribe, clan, or caste, are not necessarily MBOPs, since members become part of these groups involuntarily or at birth. Membership in MBOPs is, by definition, achieved voluntarily, even if social pressure can sometimes be an incentive for people to join an MBOP. However, people of certain ascribed statuses, for instance the infirm, disabled, orphans, widows, out-castes, and victims of political insecurity and natural disasters, are often among the poorest members of society and sometimes choose to form MBOPs to improve their well-being.

What is success?

For the authors, "success" means sustained, rather than short-term, achievement.[3] An MBOP can be considered "successful" when it fulfils all the following conditions:

- achieves the objectives agreed upon by members;
- retains or expands its membership;
- shows progress towards financial and managerial self-reliance, inspiring members to maintain their equity stake in the organization;
- brings improvement to the self-esteem, and economic and social well-being of its members.

Types of organizations and external factors that influence success

A continuum of organizations of the poor

Along the continuum of MBOP types, two end points can be distinguished based on the conditions under which they form and on their degree of autonomy. At one end are self-organizations of the poor, which are autonomous, self-started organizations that subsist exclusively with internal support. At the other end are externally supported MBOPs, organized by external agencies and supported entirely by external funds. Most MBOPs, however, fall somewhere along the continuum between these two extremes (see Matrix 1).

It is common for organizations to shift across these different types over time in response to specific historical opportunities. For example, an organization established by a benevolent individual can, over time, become owned exclusively by poor members (Hanko and Chantrabumroung 2003; SEWA 2004a), just as self-organizations of the poor can become co-opted by non-poor individuals and organizations (Walhof 2003). Some MBOPs have proven to be remarkably resilient and durable, while others have disappeared (Matson 1990).

The way in which an MBOP is formed and its degree of access to, and dependence upon, external funding influences its success and survival. However, as Table 2.1 shows, the two end points of the continuum of MBOPs also tend to be characterized by differences in scale, autonomy, and focus. Although there are too many types to be covered comprehensively

Matrix 1 Organizations in the Poor

		Organized	
		Internal	*External*
Support/funding	Internal	Self-organizations of the poor	Hybrid: externally organized, internally supported
	External	Hybrid: internally organized externally supported	Externally supported MBOPs

Table 2.1 Summary of attributes of MBOP types

Attribute	Self-organized	Mixed	Externally supported
Scale/size	Restricted to those who know each other well	Highly variable, can be very large	Somewhat restricted, due to criteria of funding organization, instability over time
Membership composition	Defined by members, generally includes a majority of poor members	Diverse, majority of poor members with some "outsiders" or elites as organizers	Often biased towards entrepreneurial poor (and non-poor)
Membership stability/durability over time	Stable, but can be short-lived, vulnerable to absence of individuals	Variable, tending towards unstable	Unstable, subject to availability of funds
Context dependence	High	Medium to high	Medium to low
Source of funding	Internal, mostly member contributions	Mix of internal member contributions and external funding	External
Scope of activities	Limited to those possible with member contributions	Broad	Medium to broad, depending on type
Nature of activities	Self-help, labour/capital/service mobilization/generation	Self-help, labour/capital/service mobilization/generation, information/data collection, policy change/advocacy	Capital/service access/generation, often includes financial services
Leadership	Poor members themselves	Members plus "outsiders". Risk of greater influence by "outsiders" on organization's objectives and strategies	Follows external criteria (e.g. literacy), favours entrepreneurs/non-poor member
Responsiveness to member interests	High, objectives defined primarily in response to member interests	Medium, long-term success depends upon ability to maintain high responsiveness to members, but expansion and "outsider" influence can reduce responsiveness	Low, objectives defined mostly in response to donor interests, including short-term results, external targets, time frames

Dependency and susceptibility to cooptation	Low, due to autonomy and relative independence from outside influences	Medium to high, susceptible to use by political parties/campaigns and risk of dependency on external finances	High dependency on external finances and funding organizations, easily side tracked by external agendas
Ease of spontaneous creation, replication, innovation	High because depends upon resources and capacities available to poor people	Medium to low, unless apex organization adopts long-term strategy to replicate/expand through organizing, exposure, public awareness	Low, unless significant outside resources available
Documentation	Scarce, except to ensure integrity of financial contributions for members	Relatively well documented for external funders and political awareness	Relatively well documented for external funders
Capacity to transcend ethnic, social, religious, residential differences	Low, without assistance from outside intermediary	Medium to high, often functions best with mixed constituency but may require strong leadership, explicit moral code, and stable financial base; "outsiders"/"non-poor" can play important role	Medium to low, often functions best with homogenous constituency
Impact on other organizations when successful	Stimulates other self-organizations of the poor in the vicinity	Can provide indirect benefits to other poor who are not members and their organizations; can also crowd out self-organizations of the poor	Can crowd out self-organizations and mixed organizations of the poor in their vicinity
Impact on fundamental socio-economic change	Often limited due to restricted size/scale	Variable, can be high if large scale/size, long-lasting, and some emphasis on policy impacts	Often limited due to restricted duration
Longevity	Variable though often short, often dissolved at departure/death of member	Variable, but can be long (several decades or more)	Variable, but usually short and linked to availability of funding/external support

here, some examples can illustrate the range of MBOPs along this contin-uum and clarify some of the factors that influence their success.

Self-organizations of the poor are created, owned, and sustained by poor members and are present in all parts of the world in a variety of forms. Particularly common are the small, relatively informal, trust-based self-help groups, including savings clubs, funeral associations, water user groups, mutual aid societies, and village banks (Van Duuren 2003; IFAD 2000a: 7, 2000b: 16, 2004c; Marsh 2003; FAO 2002: 16; Crowley 1993). These are usually limited in size between five and 25 individuals, of which most are of a similar socio-economic status. Also included among self-organized MBOPs are the guilds of beggars and semi-criminal gangs of the Hausa of West Africa (Cohen 1969: 42–7), modern China (Lu 1999), and elsewhere that distribute begging activities, monopolize the industry in particular neighbourhoods, and provide mobility, security, and other services to their members. Self-organizations of the poor also include rural refuge communities, voluntary ethnic and mutual aid associations organ-ized in urban areas, and war-affected zones and refugee camps that offer food and care to sick members, provide jobs, encourage adoption of desti-tute children, and offer other services (Marsh 2003: Annex 9; Crowley 1990: 277–8; Iliffe 1987: 176–8, 263).

At the other end of the continuum are MBOPs supported almost entirely by external donors, whether charitable individuals, governments, non-governmental organizations (NGOs), or development agencies. These also assume various forms. They include the financially self-reliant groups of the rural poor created through an approach pioneered by FAO in the mid-1970s (Small Farmer Development Programme in Asia) and in the 1980s and 1990s (People's Participation Programme). Externally sup-ported MBOPs also include the new microfinance groups which inter-national institutions encourage the poor to create in order to facilitate the transfer of credit and services (IFAD 2000a, 2000b, 2000c), some of Kenya's Harambee groups (Thomas 1985), and the rural producer organi-zations and federations supported by Burkina Faso's Ministry of Agricul-ture, Hydraulics, and Water Resources.

Along the continuum of MBOPs are a number of hybrid examples, including organizations that receive partial support from external sources, either when self-organizations approach donors for financial support or when donors seek out existing organizations to support (Marsh 2003; Messer and Townsley 2003).

In ideal situations, the role of external donors becomes one of building "on the foundations of solidarity that keep the community social order functioning" (Lundin 1999: 13), by strengthening existing MBOPs through technical assistance such as capacity building, group savings, liter-acy, business management, and communication (FAO 1990, 1994, 1995, 1998, 2001, 2002; Ali and Baas 2004; Hanko and Chantrabumroung 2003; IFAD 2000a, 2000b, 2004a, 2004c). Such support also comes from NGOs and national governments, and sometimes enables existing MBOPs to become legally recognized by governments and to gain access to funds, services, and a place at the negotiating table (ARBAN 2004; Praxis 2004; RISE 2004; Marsh 2003: 40–6).

Some hybrid MBOPs are created through the stimulus of "outsiders", including trade union organizers, social reformers, and educated elites (de Haan and Sen 2005), are run by poor members, and rely upon a mix of internal and external contributions. One example is the *Movimento Sem Terra* (MST) in Brazil, which was founded in 1984 to promote agrarian reform for the benefit of four million landless rural families (Stedile 2002; Wolford 2003). It is a decentralized movement built upon diverse "actions" to occupy underutilized land. Not only do the members contribute at least 2 per cent of their production or the equivalent in labour to the movement, but the governments, the Catholic Church, the European Union, US businessmen, and others also provide financial resources (Stedile 2002). A second example is the Self-Employed Women's Association (SEWA), (SEWA 2002, 2004b) which was founded in 1972 as a trade union to support the self-employment of poor women workers in the informal sector in Ahmedabad, India. SEWA is owned and democratically run by self-employed women, and is aimed at their financial self-reliance. In 2002, SEWA received less than 3 per cent of its funds from its own members, with the remaining resources coming from "institutional donors" (SEWA 2004b).

External factors that influence emergence and success

Comparisons of these different types reveal some of the factors that influence success. Self-organizations of the poor are usually small enough for members to know each other well, have a sense of each others' actions outside of the group, and exercise peer pressure. Their objectives and activities are defined and limited by the interests, contributions, and governance capacity of their members, which makes them relatively autonomous. While self-organizations of the poor are easy to establish and replicate and can be long-lasting, many of them are short-lived because they are vulnerable to the presence or absence of particular individuals. They also frequently encounter difficulties in transcending ethnic, social, and religious differences in membership.

Compared to self-organizations of the poor, externally funded MBOPs tend to undertake a comparatively wider range of income-generating activities.[4] However, the supply-side targets of external funding organizations often take precedence over the effective demand for these financial resources or the capacity of MBOPs to prioritize, plan, manage, and monitor the funds or other assistance effectively. MBOP dependence upon external sources of support

- creates a market incentive for individuals to join together to access funds (IFAD 2004b, 2004d; Douglas and Kato 2004: 25, 55);
- undermines local incentives to save (FAO 2002: 3);
- distorts member investment behaviour, leading to investment in inappropriate technologies;
- supports rule-based rather than reputation-based financing (Marsh 2003: Annex 10: 5) thereby encouraging defaults;
- favours the entrepreneurial poor (and non-poor), rather than the poorest members of the community;
- creates dependency on external resources, causing organizations to dissolve once the funding ceases (Douglas and Kato 2004: 55; IFAD 2000a: 27).

As a result, these organizations are easily co-opted by external agendas. Even well-meaning donors may actively influence MBOPs in their choices of activities and in the ways they are governed, affecting the organization's pro-poor focus, or inhibiting members from identifying their own creative solutions to address new problems as they arise. Because the decisions taken are ultimately circumscribed by the priorities of external donors, such support may also hinder the development of a decision making capacity within MBOPs. Donor pressure to produce "visible" results also creates incentives to demonstrate short-term outputs rather than to ensure longer-term outcomes (IFAD 2000b: VII).

There is also some evidence that a policy of external support for the creation of MBOPs may diminish the local dynamics of the poor to organize themselves (Douglas and Kato 2004: 55). This occurs as a sort of crowding-out effect, as limited human resources are co-opted by the MBOPs with external funding; potential members come to expect this funding at the expense of poorer-resourced autochthonous efforts to organize. "Quick fix" interventions tend to encourage this "dependency culture" in poor communities, since they do not engage in the longer-term processes required to build local capacities, internal credibility of groups, and accountability to the poor.

Hybrid organizations are of particular interest because, in some cases, they combine the strengths of self-organizations of the poor and the advantages of externally supported organizations: a strong membership base and member equity contributions, combined with a capacity to expand membership and diversify activities through external funding. They also suffer from the vulnerabilities of both types. However, unlike externally supported MBOPs that are rarely effective in bringing about fundamental socio-economic changes (IFAD 2004a: 51, 2000b: xi; McGee 2002: 113), this combination of characteristics enables the larger of these hybrid organizations to have some impact on the policies and socio-economic conditions that perpetuate poverty. Over time and with support from a diversity of sources, some hybrid organizations have successfully expanded beyond their original locations and membership, particularly if an emphasis is placed on organizing, expansion, and policy impact. In the process, they sometimes succeed and sometimes fail in retaining a pro-poor focus.

Beyond how these organizations are conceived and supported, certain external conditions also appear to have an influence on MBOP formation and survival. In many parts of the world, MBOPs in the form of mutual assistance groups have emerged historically in the absence of formal safety nets or government programmes to cater to the basic needs of the poor. In some cases, the converse has also been true: strong public welfare systems have created disincentives for the poor to organize themselves.

The absence of informal safety nets also appears to play a role. Larger-scale MBOPs that transcend ethnic, religious, and social differences appear to emerge particularly where there are large numbers of poor people or where there are evident wealth disparities, situations which make collective action easier and less costly due to economies of scale. Volatile and transient contexts, such as emergency, post-conflict, and major migration zones, where customary social institutions are absent or incapable of caring for large numbers of the poor, also appear to be conducive to the emergence of MBOPs (Marsh 2003: 53, 62; Iliffe 1987).

Yet, government policies to improve access by the poor to basic services have provided an impetus for the creation of MBOPs. The 1940s' shift in colonial policies from improving the welfare of destitute groups to community development approaches, as the primary method to reduce poverty and support the poor, and the subsequent mainstreaming of participatory approaches in development practice in the 1970s and 1980s (FAO 1978/79, 1990; Cernea 1991; Chambers 1997; Grillo and Stirrat 1997; Huizer 1983, 1997; McGee 2002; van Heck 1989; Watt *et al.* 2000; Woost 1997) contributed to the creation, proliferation, and strengthening of MBOPs. Donor and government support for such organizations was further intensified in the 1990s, as the state withdrew from rural service provision, decentralization and privatization processes took hold, and the influence of civil society grew.

Militating against the emergence of MBOPs are traditional, socio-economic "levelling mechanisms", which tend to protect the privileged positions of local power holders. Open suppression by dominant political groups that view large groups of the poor as a threat to their own status and civil stability can also prevent the development of MBOPs. This is a common feature of dictatorial regimes where the rights of association are either absent or not respected (see examples in Stedile 2002; Marsh 2003: Annex 12). Public apprehension of the organizational efforts of the poor has often led them to organize under apolitical guises.[5] The absence of policies, and legislative and regulatory frameworks that uphold the rights of association, assembly, and freedom of expression can also stifle these efforts.

Internal factors influencing success

Objectives and improvements in well-being

Many MBOPs combine social, economic, and other objectives (Bonfiglioli 2003: 14–15) ranging from group savings to agrarian reform. Members assess the value of being part of an organization by its ability to achieve these objectives. Even the apparently simple act of affording members the opportunity to analyse their own problems and propose objectives implies a power to control one's own destiny and can be profoundly empowering (Ali and Baas 2004: 12). Many of the improvements in well-being that members report go far beyond the specific objectives of the MBOP and can be incentive enough for members to continue to participate in the organization. Poor members, and women in particular, report improvements in security, dignity, status, respect, confidence, sense of self-worth, decision-making power, and access to public services as benefits of participation in MBOPs and "in overall community development activities" (IFAD 2000b: v, 2000c: 16; Geran 1996). Furthermore, the benefits of group membership are not limited to members, since MBOPs have been known to produce shifts in community perceptions about the capabilities of the poor (Hanko and Chantrabumroung 2003: 28).

Composition of membership

Many MBOPs are not composed exclusively of the poor. Group composition is important because it affects the "process, potentials, and outcomes of the group experiences" (Kilavuka 2003: 10). Ensuring that a critical mass of members is poor appears to be important for MBOPs to remain centred on actions that benefit the poor. Some development agencies employ mechanisms to target poor households and to ensure a pro-poor composition in the MBOPs they support (Ali and Baas 2004).

These organizations of the poor tend to be more successful when members share one or several socio-economic conditions and are relatively homogenous. MBOPs whose members have common occupations, geographical residence, gender, language, or tribal, ethnic, religious, or caste affiliation appear to have some advantage in defining common objectives. Of these, occupational homogeneity is especially critical for providing a unifying set of interests and skills and clarity on the obstacles, policies, market chains, and relationships to be addressed, fostering group cohesion, and minimizing conflict (Ali and Baas 2004: 19; Crowley 1993: 53; IFAD 2000b; SEWA 2004b; Stedile 2002: 9–10). Occupational homogeneity can remain remarkably stable over time, and as the building blocks of larger scale MBOPs (e.g. SEWA 2002), appears to be a precondition for scaling up.

Nevertheless, it is common for MBOPs to include a few non-poor member elites, organizers, or "outsiders" who have literacy, organizational, and entrepreneurship skills that are not characteristic of the rest of the membership (de Haan and Sen 2005; IFAD 2000a; Kilavuka 2003: 16; Stedile 2002: 4–5). Non-poor members can play a critical role in the transfer of these skills to poor members (Ali and Baas 2004: 38). However, the presence of both poor and non-poor members in an MBOP contributes very little to removing the socio-economic disparities existing between them.

The advantages or disadvantages of mixed-gender membership are less clear. In Yemen, women's organizations have benefited crucially from the support of men in the communities (Ali and Baas 2004) and in Kenya and Uganda, mixed-gender MBOPs have been found to be effective (IFAD 2000c: 16; Kilavuka 2003). However, in contexts in which women's status is significantly lower than men's, mixed-gender MBOPs have difficulty in ensuring adequate women's influence over decision-making and women-only groups appear to be the best option (IFAD 2000c: 16; IFAD 2004d).

Development of governance structure

Governance structure and rules have a bearing on an MBOP's cohesion and achievement of its objectives. Although a vast subject, five factors particularly illustrate the impact of governance on MBOPs.

The first fundamental element of governance is the *equity stake* of members in the organization. "Equity stake" refers to the in-kind or financial contribution that members make to be part of the organization. There is a positive correlation between the weight of a member's equity stake and their interest in governing the organization so as to gain a just rate of return on that investment (Rouse 2001: 3; IFAD 2000b: xi).

A second factor affecting governance is *group size and structure*, the optimal forms of which vary depending upon the objectives of the organization. For informal savings groups, small numbers of members tend to work best (IFAD 2000a: 16; IFAD 2000b: 7), whereas for social movements seeking broader socio-economic reform, very large numbers of members can be essential (Stedile 2002). The optimal organizational structures, whether highly decentralized (Stedile 2002) or very hierarchical (Lu 1999), also vary depending on the objectives of the organization.

A third dimension of governance is *leadership*. Mechanisms for electing, rotating, and mentoring leaders are important for successful MBOPs. Weighted representation in management structures to include different socio-economic groups can promote cohesion in heterogeneous organizations (Kilavuka 2003: 12–17). Regular meetings between members and management help to maintain a shared vision. However, there is no hard and fast rule about the value of elite involvement. Some MBOPs create honorary advisory positions in their governance structures to accommodate traditional leaders, and active participation of such leaders serves as an incentive for members to participate and strengthens the credibility of the organization (Douglas and Kato 2004; Ali and Baas 2004: 31; IFAD 2004c). If not carefully managed, however, the involvement of local elites offers them an opportunity to take control of an MBOP legitimately (IFAD 2004c). Effective leaders hold themselves accountable to members and find solutions to their changing concerns (Kilavuka 2003: 32–41).

Fourth, *internal rules* to govern group operations (FAO 1995, 2002; IFAD 2000a, 2000b), which are consistently applied to all members, are valuable for ensuring that heterogeneous organizations do not fracture along the lines of socio-economic difference. Even for informal MBOPs, clear oral or written rules are the foundation for collective action. Internal regulations of successful MBOPs are developed and refined by the members themselves, fall within the parameters of national laws, and change over time. In later stages of MBOP development, the rules often become more complex and analogous to a charter. When MBOPs surpass a certain scale of membership, written constitutions can be helpful. The formal or informal status of the organization and its legal status are not clearly linked to MBOP success or sustainability. Rotating savings and credit associations, for example, have operated for centuries without formal status. On the other hand, formalization may bring some advantages to larger MBOPs, helping to reduce conflicts over internal rules, while clarifying responsibilities and profit sharing among members (Ali and Baas 2004).

A fifth characteristic of many successful larger-scale MBOPs, particularly those that resemble social movements, is an *explicit code of moral conduct.* Successful MBOPs often selectively adopt positive elements of customary practices into their governance structures as vehicles for development, conflict resolution, solidarity, and appropriate moral behaviour. Such codes define the ethics and value system to which members aspire and are sometimes modelled on religious or philosophical ideologies. In SEWA, these values "are explicitly reinforced many times a day, at the opening of every meeting, through a series of songs/chants making reference to Hindu, Muslim and Buddhist belief" (Crowley 2001: 3; SEWA 2002: 2–3) and have been successfully employed to breed inclusiveness of historically marginalized groups.

Scope and diversity of organizations' activities

Successful MBOPs select their activities based on membership demand, but the number and scope of activities undertaken largely depend on the resources available. Smaller-scale MBOPs that rely exclusively on their members' savings tend to engage in a more restricted range of activities. As MBOPs scale up, they flexibly incorporate a range of new self-help activities on demand, such as income-generating initiatives, vocational training, and literacy education. To be successful, however, MBOPs must ensure that they have reached a certain level of organizational maturity and membership participation before slowly diversifying their activities, taking care to monitor the process carefully (IFAD 2000b; Ali and Baas 2004; Crowley 2001).

A first set of core activities in most MBOPs relates to building members' capacities to run the organization themselves. Training helps to build the capacities of individuals to operate effectively in the organization, reduce isolation, identify their own priorities, and plan a way out of poverty. Some agencies consider that the capacity of members to manage their own organizations is of paramount importance for success, and dedicate time and energy to on-going training in group formation, enterprise development, financial management, and other skills (Ali and Baas 2004; Hanko and Chantrabumroung 2003; IFAD 2000a, 2000b, 2004c). Capacity building serves a dual purpose: it builds the skills of individuals and improves the effectiveness and sustainability of the organization as a whole.

A second set of activities relates to generating productive or financial capital to provide members with some type of financial security. The most common reason for members to join MBOPs is to build their savings or gain access to credit, insurance (such as SEWA's support for identity cards and unemployment benefits), employment, land, or other safety nets. MBOPs usually engage in at least one activity which significantly benefits poor members. Generating productive and financial capital appears to be especially important for externally-funded MBOPs.

A third set of activities has to do with lobbying for the influence and negotiation power of their constituency. Compared to poor individuals, organized groups of the poor have a better chance to improve their well-being, access information channels, "redress disparities in power and in the distribution of resources" (Thomas 1985: 4), "assert their right to a legitimate share of social resources" (Tilakatatna 1980: 3), and compel attention to their needs by local elites and policy makers (IFAD 2001: 11). By joining organizations, poor individuals gain access to a wider range of resources, skills, information, knowledge, experience, and assets, as well as to the power that their combined numbers represent. Creating an MBOP is fundamentally a political act.

MBOPs striving to achieve policy reform, such as SEWA and MST, give great importance to the numbers of their members. In order to convince government officials of the need to change particular policies, statistics on the numbers of poor who are affected by those policies are essential. Hybrid organizations occasionally have to conduct research and censuses on their constituencies to demonstrate the numbers who stand to benefit from policy reform (Crowley 2001: 2). MBOPs provide the poor with an entry point to negotiate with donors who would not, in other instances, consider individual requests and the leverage needed to negotiate with local authorities and to "face markets, state institutions and local structures of power that discriminate" against them (Hussain 2004: 2I).

Hybrid organizations also invest time in raising awareness, organizing, and recruiting new members. To expand an MBOP's influence beyond a specific locality, inter-group associations and horizontal networks that include other like-minded organizations can be helpful. Some cases reviewed demonstrate that MBOPs can afford poor women new physical mobility, expanded contacts with banks, NGOs, and district authorities, awareness of political and property rights, and increased confidence (IFAD 2000b), all of which are vital skills for negotiation. MBOPs have also negotiated successfully with project authorities to build new rural infrastructure (IFAD 2000b), governments and public services to establish pro-poor procedures, employers to improve employment conditions and reduce the vulnerability of workers and small-scale farmers, the judiciary to provide legal representation to their members, and traders and other middlemen to increase the prices they pay for the produce of the poor.

Scaling up and linking MBOPs with other institutions

In order to have some impact on the laws and policies that lock the poor into poverty, effective links with and impacts on other institutions are critical. Relationships with external organizations tend to be established through the individual contacts of members, whether planned or circumstantial. MBOPs that have developed enduring relationships with other organizations have done so by transforming personal contacts into broader institutional relationships.

Peaceful coexistence between MBOPs and governments is sometimes made possible by coordination and clarification of their distinct domains of activity, which enables MBOPs and local governments to recognize the value added of their differences and to define mutually supportive legal relationships. Some MBOPs have policy linkages with higher level governments that permit joint development planning, and others enjoy the support of local governments in the provision of various types of social infrastructure.

However, MBOPs that maintain relationships with organizations of the non-poor for policy and advocacy purposes also run the risk of losing their own pro-poor focus. This happens gradually, as the interests of even well-intentioned external policy advocacy groups, often dominated by powerful constituencies, overtake the primary economic services and concerns of the MBOP's internal constituency. Some MBOPs try to manage this risk by creating subcommittees within their own management structures to ensure that external policy advocacy and internal activities are managed separately (Ali and Baas 2004). Larger-scale MBOPs, such as SEWA and MST, consider their autonomy to be vital and invest time and resources to ensure that they remain independent from political parties and other external political and religious influences (Stedile 2002: 4).

Many experiences show that larger-scale, hybrid MBOPs, such as unions or social movements, tend to encounter greater resistance from governments than do less threatening, community-based MBOPs. There are also cases, however, in which MBOPs that are initially considered threatening gradually develop a more cooperative relationship with governments. In essence, acceptability of the organization within a larger social and political context does not necessarily influence an MBOP's success. While acceptance may facilitate an MBOP's work and longevity, some are effective particularly because they offer an alternative social model, which may appear at odds with the dominant political and social context.

Summary and conclusions: conditions for successful MBOPs

Given the diversity of MBOPs and the socio-economic, agro-ecological, legal, and regulatory and policy contexts in which they are found, no blueprint combination of characteristics can guarantee their success or failure. However, lessons on how MBOPs have tackled common problems and risks can be helpful to strengthen the capacities of organizations of the poor to achieve their objectives and to develop into sustained organizations. Responses to three questions provide a useful structure for summarizing the main points raised in this chapter.

What are the conditions that have given rise to organizations of the poor?

Organizations of the poor can be entirely organized and funded by the poor themselves, by an external organization, or by some combination of internal and external support and funding. How an MBOP is formed and its degree of access to and dependence upon external funding are important because they influence its success and survival over time. MBOPs appear to emerge in contexts where there is an absence of formal safety nets, and weak or nonexistent government and private welfare programmes catering to the basic needs of the poor. Contexts which contain large, concentrated numbers of poor people and where customary social and family support systems are absent are particularly favourable to MBOPs. MBOPs also appear to emerge in contexts where government policies promote access by the poor to basic services, where the state has withdrawn in favour of decentralized and privatized authorities, where the influence of civil society is strong, and where development partners offering financial or technical support use community development and participatory approaches as a means for poverty reduction. In contrast, traditional socio-economic "levelling mechanisms", open suppression by dominant political groups, and the absence of policies and legislative and regulatory frameworks that uphold the rights of association and freedom of expression hinder the emergence and development of organizations of the poor.

What are the internal factors that make for successful MBOPs?

A successful MBOP achieves collectively defined objectives, retains its membership, inspires members to maintain an equity stake in the organization, and improves the well-being of its members. Members have to feel that the organization is representative of their interests, as reflected in objectives and rules of governance that they have defined and in the organization's capacity to adjust to members' changing needs. While mixed skills and mixed gender within the membership can sometimes strengthen an MBOP's ability to achieve its objectives, maintaining a poor majority and some level of occupational homogeneity appear to be more important for the success of an MBOP. Well-trained leaders who possess some locally valued leadership qualities, a clear understanding of their responsibilities, and an ability to recognize emerging needs are also paramount. Regular elections or periodic confirmation of leaders, mentoring of future leaders, and safeguards to avert "take over" by local elites have also proven to be advantageous.

For MBOPs to be successful, members must consider that the benefits from cooperation exceed their investments. An appropriate size and structure of the organization in relation to the objectives it wishes to achieve can encourage effectiveness. Successful MBOPs usually support some activities to strengthen the capacities, incomes, and influence of their membership.

What factors affect the ability of MBOPs to influence others and to scale up?

The organizational types outlined in this chapter are helpful for understanding the limitations that MBOPs need to overcome in order to scale up. The restricted funding sources and membership base of self-organizations of the poor tend to limit their scale and diversity of activities, while externally supported organizations are often less stable over time, and run the risk of losing their pro-poor focus. Although they also suffer from the vulnerabilities of both of these types (see Table 2.1), hybrid organizations sometimes succeed in combining the strengths of self-organizations of the poor and the advantages of externally supported organizations, demonstrating responsiveness to their poor membership and the stability of member equity contributions, combined with a capacity to expand membership and to diversify activities. This combination provides hybrid organizations with a potential to scale up, to attract a broader constituency, and given sufficient time and numbers, to effect fundamental political, social, and economic changes.

To scale up effectively, MBOPs must reach a certain level of organizational maturity and only gradually expand their membership and diversify their activities. Beyond the internal mechanisms summarized in the previous section, MBOPs that wish to scale up need to build the capacity of new members regularly and ensure that their funding is stable and drawn from a diversity of sources. As MBOPs scale up, the internal rules often become more complex and analogous to a charter or constitution. Written rules, regularly disseminated through oral media in local languages, are important for maintaining the internal cohesion of MBOPs as they expand.

Mechanisms for obtaining new recruits are essential if an MBOP is to expand beyond its original location, while maintaining its pro-poor focus. However, a key challenge is to ensure that there is sufficient trust for members to engage in joint action. This is the critical factor limiting the size of self-organizations of the poor. Trust is particularly difficult to achieve in larger-scale organizations, but can be managed successfully through two mechanisms: expansion around occupationally or regionally focused trust-based groups and the establishment of an ethical or moral code of conduct within an MBOP's governance structure to reduce conflicts and promote solidarity.

Creating an MBOP is fundamentally a political act. Not surprisingly, larger-scale MBOPs that take the form of social movements tend to encounter greater resistance from governments than do less threatening community-based MBOPs. As an MBOP grows, its capacity to influence other organizations also increases, as does the tendency of it being seen as a challenge to other organizations and politically and economically dominant groups. Large-scale MBOPs are particularly susceptible to being co-opted by politicians and political parties as part of their campaigns and therefore may grow or decline in influence in keeping with political favour. Some MBOPs choose to remain independent from political and religious groups in order to maintain their autonomy. Many MBOPs have to tread a fine line between conformity and political pressure in order to bring about lasting improvements for their members.

Notes

1 The authors are grateful to a number of reviewers who contributed information and comments that greatly enriched the chapter. From FAO, these include Ian Cherrett, Janus Juhasz, Bernd Seiffert, Vladimir Evtimov, Leith Deacon, Calvin Miller, Maria Pagura, and Gerard Ciparisse. In addition, the authors would like to thank Robin Marsh, Kristen Appendini, Zarina Douglas, Paolo Silveri, Ashwani Muthoo, Pablo Eyzaguirre, the participants at the conference on Membership-Based Organizations of the Poor and SEWA members who provided comments on the ideas presented in this chapter.

2 MBOPs are "organizations" or structured sets of individuals who are assigned specific roles and responsibilities to attain certain collective goals. Organizations are distinguished from "institutions", which refer to definable sets of socially accepted rules that regulate social behaviour and govern different types of collective action. Thus, a football team is an organization, whereas the game, which follows a set of rules, is an institution.

3 However, longevity is not necessarily a good indicator of success, as an MBOP can be highly successful and then dissolve when it has achieved its objectives.

4 The potential uses that MBOPs have for micro finance is so varied that

international finance institutions commonly develop criteria or broad parameters only for how these funds are *not* to be used.
5 It is no coincidence, for example, that Nelson Mandela was part of a sports club,
the only permissible form of self-organization for urban black Africans during
the apartheid regime, and conducted his initial organizing there.

Bibliography

Ali, O. and Baas, S. (2004) *Lessons Learned and Good Practice: CBO in Yemen*, Rome:
   FAO.
Association for Realisation of Basic Needs (ARBAN) (2004) available online at:
   www.landcoalition.org (accessed4 November 2005).
Bonfiglioli, A. (2003) *Empowering the Poor: Local governance for poverty reduction*. New
   York: UNCDF. Available online at: www.uncdf.org/english/local_development/
   documents_and_reports/thematic_papers/empowering/empowering.pdf (acces-
   sed 4 November 2005).
Cernea, M.M. (1991) 'Knowledge from Social Science for Development Policies
   and Projects', in M.M. Cernea (ed.) *Putting People First: Sociological variables in
   rural development*, Oxford: World Bank and Oxford University Press.
Chambers, R. (1997) *Whose Reality Counts? Putting the first last*, London: Intermedi-
   ate Technology Publications.
Cohen, A. (1969) *Custom and Politics in Urban Africa: A study of Hausa migrants in
   Yoruba towns*, Berkeley and Los Angeles: University of California Press.
Crowley, E. (1990) *Contracts with the Spirits: Religion, asylum and ethnic identity in the
   Cacheu Region of Guinea-Bissau*, Ann Arbor, Michigan: University Microfilms.
Crowley, E. (1993) *Guinea-Bissau's Informal Economy and its Contributions to Economic
   Growth*, Report to the United States Agency of International Development and
   the Government of Guinea-Bissau, Agency for International Development Con-
   tract 657-0025-C-00-3078-00. Bissau: USAID.
Crowley, E. (2001) *Back to Office Report: Exposure and dialogue programme SEWA,
   Gujarat India, 18–28 July 1999*, Rome: IFAD.
de Haan, A. and Sen, S. "Working Class Struggles, Labour Elites and Closed Shops:
   The lessons from India's trade unions and experiences of organisation", paper
   presented at the SEWA/Cornell/WIEGO Conference on Membership-Based
   Organizations of the Poor, Ahmedabad, India, January 2005.
Douglas, Z. and Kato, R. (2004) *Institutional Analysis and Livelihood Profiling in
   Fishing Communities in Masaka District, Uganda*, Rome: FAO/FNPP.
FAO (1978/79) *Small Farmers Development Manual, Vol. I and II*, Bangkok: FAO
   Regional Office for Asia and the Far East.
—— (1990) *Participation in Practice – Lessons from FAO People's Participation Programme*, Rome: FAO.
—— (1994) *The Group Promoter's Resource Book*, Rome: FAO.
—— (1995) *The Group Enterprise Resource Book*, Rome: FAO.
—— (1998) *Agricultural Cooperative Development: A manual for trainers*, Rome: FAO.
—— (2001) *The Inter-Group Resource Book: A guide to building small farmer group associations and networks*, Rome: FAO.
—— (2002) *The Group Savings Resource Book*, Rome: FAO.
Geran, J. (1996) "Effect of group formation on rural women's access to services in

Western Province, Zambia", *SD Dimensions*, available online at: www.fao.org/sd/PPdirect/PPre0010.htm (accessed 4 November 2005).

Grillo, R.D. and Stirrat, R.L. (1997) *Discourses of Development: Anthropological perspectives*, Oxford: Berg.

Hanko, J. and Chantrabumroung, M. (2003) *Mushroom Training for Disabled People: Thailand*, Rome: FAO.

Huizer, G. (1983) *Guiding Principles for People's Participation Projects*, Rome: FAO.

—— (1997) "Participatory action research and people's participation: Introduction and case studies", *SD Dimensions*, Available online at: www.fao.org/sd/PPdirect/PPre0022.htm (accessed 4 November 2005).

Hussain, A. (2004) *Poverty in Pakistan: A new paradigm for overcoming poverty*, Available online at: www.unmc.edu/Community/ruralmeded/underserved/poverty_in_pakistan.htm (accessed 4 November 2005).

IFAD (2000a) *The Exclusion of the Poorest: Emerging lessons from the Maharashtra Rural Credit Project, India*, Rome: IFAD.

—— (2000b) *The Republic of India: Tamil Nadu Women's Development Project (240-N). Completion evaluation*, Rome: IFAD, Office of Evaluation Studies.

—— (2000c) *Gender Perspective-Focus on the Rural Poor: An overview of gender issues in IFAD-assisted projects*, Rome: IFAD.

—— (2001) *Rural Poverty Report 2001: The challenge on ending rural poverty*, Rome: IFAD.

—— (2004a) *Republic of Indonesia. Country Programme Evaluation. Evaluation Report (1523-ID)*, Rome: IFAD.

—— (2004b) *The Socialist Republic of Vietnam: Agricultural resources conservation and development project in Quang Binh Province. Interim Evaluation Report* (Report No. 1532-VN), Rome: IFAD.

—— (2004c) *EKSYST. Lessons Learned by Themes – Groups and Financial Intermediation*, Available online at: www.ifad.org/evaluation (accessed 7 December 2004).

—— (2004d) *EKSYST. Lessons Learned by Themes – Group Formation Criteria and SADC Countries*, Available online at: www.ifad.org/evaluation (accessed 7 December 2004).

Iliffe, J. (1987) *The African Poor: A history*, Cambridge: Cambridge University Press.

Kilavuka, J.M. (2003) *A Comparative Study of the Socio-Economic Implications of Rural Women, Men, and Mixed Self-Help Groups: A case of Kakamega District*, Ethiopia: OSSREA.

Lu, H. (1999) "Becoming urban: mendicancy and vagrants in Modern China", *Journal of Social History*, 33(1): 7–36.

Lundin, I.B. (1999) "As estruturas tradicionais nas politicas e programas de descentralização e na realidade rural em Moçambique", manuscript prepared for the HH-LI FAO study, translated shorter version as HH-LI WP Series #13, Rome: SDAR/FAO.

Marsh, R. (2003) *Working with Local Institutions to Support Sustainable Livelihoods*, Rome: FAO.

Matson, F. (1990) "The Dark Ages and the Dawn of Organization", in National Federation of the Blind, *Walking Alone and Marching Together*, Available online at: www.nfb.org/books/books1/wam03.htm (accessed 4 November 2005).

McGee, R. (2002) "Participating in Development", in U. Kothari and M. Minogue (eds) *Development Theory and Practice: Critical perspectives*, Houndmills: Palgrave.

Messer, N. and Townsley, P. (2003) *Local Institutions and Livelihoods: Guidelines for analysis*, Rome: FAO.

Praxis (2004) Available online at: www.praxisindia.org/vision.asp (accessed 4 November2005).

Rouse, J. (2001) *Empowering the Rural Producers Organizations in Remote Areas*, unpublished presentation document, Rome: FAO.

Rural People's Institute for Social Empowerment (RISE – Namibia) (2004) Available online at: www.hrds.unam.na/na_rise.htm (accessed 4 November 2005).

SEWA (2002) *Annual Report 2002*, Ahmedabad: Shri Mahila Sewa Trust.

—— (2004a) *Information Update 2003–2004*, Ahmedabad: Shri Mahila Sewa Trust.

—— (2004b) *Self-Employed Women's Association*, Available online at: www.sewa.org (accessed 4 November 2005).

Stedile, J.P. (2002) "Landless Battalions: the Sem Terra Movement of Brazil", *New Left Review*, 15, May–June 2002. Available online at: www.newleftreview.net/NLR24904.shtml (accessed 11 November 2005)

Thomas, B.P. (1985) *Politics, Participation, and Poverty: Development through self-help in Kenya*, Boulder, Colorado: Westview Press.

Tilakatatna, S. (1980) *Organization of the Poor: Lessons learned from Sri Lanka*, Available online at: www.caledonia.org.uk/siritila.htm (accessed 4 November 2005).

Van Duuren, B. (2003) *Draft Report: Consultancy on institutional analysis in Cambodia, for the FAO Netherlands Partnership Programme (FNPP), Food Security Sub-Theme 9: Enhancing the Livelihoods of the Poorest*, Rome: FAO.

Van Heck, B. (1989) *Draft Guidelines for Beneficiaries Participation in Agricultural and Rural Development*, Rome: FAO.

Walhof, R. (2003, first published 1981) "History of Organizations of the Blind", in *Vision Loss and Senior Citizens: Rights, resources, and responsibilities*, Baltimore: American Action Fund for Blind Children and Adults.

Watt, S., Higgins, C. and Kendrick, A. (2000) "Community participation in the development of services: a move towards community empowerment", *Community Development Journal*, 35(2): 120–32.

Wolford, W. (2003) "Families, field and fighting for land: the spatial dynamics of contentions in rural Brazil", *Mobilization: An International Journal*, 8(2): 201–15.

Woost, M.D. (1997) "Alternative Vocabularies of Development? 'Community' and 'participation' in development discourses in Sri Lanka", in R.D. Grillo and R.L. Stirrat (eds), *Discourses of Development: Anthropological perspectives*, Oxford: Berg.

3 The influence of organizational structure, membership composition and resources on the survival of poor people's social movement organizations

Edward T. Walker and John D. McCarthy

Introduction

The Citizens' Action Program (CAP), an organization founded with the intention of building cross-cutting alliances between various community and interest groups across Chicago, was the last organizing project started by Saul Alinsky before his death in 1972. The CAP, like many groups formed on the original model of the Industrial Areas Foundation (IAF), built alliances through thick organizing networks used to develop consensus on broad-based issues, which would unite diverse constituencies. Originally formed as the Campaign Against Pollution, the group fought and won in its early struggles for better air quality and better regulation. Becoming a city-wide organization with a focus on local community interests, the group restructured into the CAP, with the intention of mitigating the relative powerlessness of small, local organizations based primarily on face-to-face ties; such an organization would hold the promise of thick community networks tied to others and congealed into a larger organization more likely to offer substantial influence in city politics. However, the metropolitan structure of CAP was as much a liability as an asset, as it struggled not only to maintain the commitment of member groups, but also to retain individual members. Moreover, due to their multi-issue focus, member groups each focused on a single instrumental goal such as service provision or defeating a specific policy and often lost interest when CAP sought redress on larger issues such as structural inequality. The organization became increasingly detached from its constituents, a problem further exacerbated by its tendency to adopt forms of fundraising, which would not mobilize its membership through involvement in grassroots revenue-generating activities. CAP also faced another series of problems; several at the bottom and others at the top. First, potential member organizations often refused to join CAP out of fear that their group would be faced with pressures to give up autonomy, especially given the fact that some of the white working-class member organizations distrusted the often largely black and Hispanic members who made up other

CAP organizations. At the top of the organization, problems stemmed from CAP's relationship to the IAF. Although the IAF helped the organization to form, it did not entirely honor the autonomy of CAP, nor was it perceived to recognize the sorts of local issues CAP faced; this inspired resentment among the locally-developed leadership of CAP toward the IAF's professional staff. By 1975, the organization was in disarray. It disbanded shortly after (Reitzes and Reitzes, 1987: 83–9).

The case of the late CAP represents only one of many instances where poor people's SMOs[1] have collapsed under the weight of the multiple pressures they face: membership retention, leadership struggles, and contention over strategies, tactics, and focal issues. Small SMOs attempting to represent the unrepresented, in general, are more vulnerable to mortality than larger ones (Edwards and McCarthy, 2004), and this should be especially true in the case of poor people's social movements. In the present analysis, we hope to illuminate the internal and external conditions that shape the likelihood of survival of such organizations in the long term.

Factors such as the organizational structure, the racial and ethnic composition, and the proportion of indigenous members in a poor people's social movement organization should all, in theory, have some effect on an organization's ability to sustain itself over time. Existing analyses of social movement groups have shown that some of the best predictors of organizational mortality are having a small membership base, being an organizational "adolescent" (rather than very "young" or "old"), legitimacy of the organization in the community, and having a more informal structure, among others (see, for example, Edwards and Marullo, 1995; Edwards and McCarthy, 2004). Specifically, it has been demonstrated that start-up grants from foundations and other sources tend to support organizational survival (Walker, 1991), as do continued access to financial benefactors (Gamson, 1990). However, no existing analyses examine the factors that differentially affect the mortality of poor people's SMOs in particular; this is, in part, related to the relative scarcity of research on small advocacy organizations (but see Alter, 1998; Cress and Snow, 1996; Edwards and Marullo, 1995; Kempton *et al.*, 2001; Lofland, 1993; Martin, 1990; McCarthy and Wolfson, 1996).

Our research addresses this problem by developing a systematic analysis of the factors that help poor people's SMOs to not only continue to exist, but to grow and flourish, empowering ever larger numbers of poor individuals through creating organizations which are an autonomous and collective voice of their own rather than a voice offered *for them* by parties, interest groups, and elite-sponsored NGOs. We believe that the survival of poor-people's organizations is a pre-condition for gaining political voice for low-income communities, in the sense that the larger socio-political project of poor empowerment relies heavily on the survival of a population of such organizations.[2] Further, accompanying the trend toward neo-liberal state reconfiguration (Banaszak, Beckwith, and Rucht, 2003;

Campbell and Pedersen, 2001), it becomes an increasingly important question whether the organizations replacing former state functions are truly *membership-based* and participatory. Alternatively, such groups may represent another instance of what Arundhati Roy (2004) calls the "NGOization of resistance" in which formal organizations come to play a dominant role, and are more accountable to their funders than their claimed constituency.

In this analysis, organizational structure is the central criteria by which we differentiate types of membership-based organizations from one another. In earlier research (McCarthy and Walker, 2004), we found that the organizational structure of poor people's SMOs tends to have significant consequences for an organization's membership size, capacity for the development of leaders, and willingness to take on more radical efforts for social change. We contrast the following three organizational structures: *individual-membership organizations, coalitions of religious groups* (congregation-based organizations), and *coalitions of mostly secular organizations which include individual members*. Based on past research (McCarthy and Walker, 2004; McCarthy and Wolfson, 1996), we expect that an organization's structure will have an impact on the ability of that organization to sustain itself. In part, this results from the fact that an organization's structure has consequences for its membership size, its issue focus, its repertoire of tactical methods, and its overall ability to obtain financial and other types of resources.

In order to examine which factors have the greatest effect on organizational mortality, we use a unique data source based on the successful grant applications of 315 organizations that applied to a major US funding agency in the years 1990, 1991, and 1992. We attempted to track down each of these organizations in late 2004, employing a diverse set of sources in order to assess mortality. These sources included organizational websites, email and phone contacts, and interviews with key informants, knowledgeable about general trends in the non-profit and voluntary sector. This research design allows us to test several theoretical expectations about the consequences of organizational structure, funding sources and amounts, racial/ethnic composition, and various other factors in determining the survival of poor people's SMOs.

Assessing the survival of poor people's organizations

The question of organizing the poor has long been a relatively contentious one among both analysts of and activists in poor people's social movements. The foundational work in the US debate is Piven and Cloward's *Poor People's Movements* (1977), in which they take the somewhat heterodox position that creating and maintaining organizations is a far less effective political strategy for the poor than focusing on more disruptive, spontaneous forms of contentious claims-making. They argue that the question of organization implicates elites through two related processes: (1) elites will prefer to help the poor build organizations in lieu of carrying out disruptive actions. (2) It follows that elites will be more likely to respond to the threat of insurgency than the emergence of a formal organization. Largely endorsing the conclusions of Michels (1962 [1915], see Clemens and Minkoff, 2004), Piven and Cloward argue that organizing carries with it the opportunity cost of placing primary emphasis upon organizational maintenance and the search for resources rather than the manifest purpose for taking action, which is insurgency. The very existence of organizations over the long term requires poor communities to jettison, in large part, truly oppositional politics.

Contrarily, some analysts have noted that the very survival of poor people's movements as a whole may require formal organizations (Gamson and Schmeidler, 1984; Hobsbawm, 1979), in that more professionalized forms of organization often help to sustain movements through periods of decline and abeyance (Taylor, 1989), even providing new opportunities for civic engagement and open dialogue (Barasko, 2005). However, conclusions regarding the extent to which resource dependence promotes organizational conservatism remain equivocal (Cress and Snow, 1996; Jenkins and Eckert, 1986; Cress, 1997), although it is typically an asset for an organization to rely on resources drawn from a greater diversity of sources (Alexander, 1998; Powell, 1988). Regardless, the survival of SMOs is likely to help sustain the larger movement by providing networks for the diffusion of information (Soule, 2004), organizing structures and weak ties on which diverse constituencies can build (Meyer and Whittier, 1994; Oberschall, 1973), and templates for unmobilized constituencies seeking to promote participation (Keck and Sikkink, 1998). Movement survival, then, depends rather directly on organizational survival; it is therefore vital to investigate which factors are most influential in promoting the long-term survival of SMOs.

Studies of the survival of small SMOs have displayed mixed results about which factors are most influential. In their study of the viability of homeless SMOs, Cress and Snow (1996), using a detailed typology of potential resources for each organization, found that a key factor in sustaining an organization was the presence of a relationship with a single benefactor that supplied financial and other resources (such as assistance in leadership training, office space, and forms of moral support). Indeed, as Aldrich (1999) notes, the very existence of a patron often has more influence on an organization's survival than does the amount of that patron's contribution. Since the homeless organizations examined by Cress and Snow required, as do most protest organizations, sustained collective effort in order to keep their constituents mobilized, the presence of a benefactor was found to allow disruptive activity *alongside* organizational maintenance (Cress and Snow, 1996: 1103), rather than being an exclusive alternative to it. Although this finding undermines Piven and

Cloward's argument that organizational maintenance tends to draw participants away from collective action, it must be tempered by the common finding that patronage, nevertheless, tends to "channel" organizational activity toward more professionalized forms of political engagement (Cress, 1997; Jenkins and Eckert, 1986; for a contrasting opinion, see Chaves, Stephens, and Galaskiewicz, 2004).

Other analyses have found differential influences of patronage and resources on survival. In their recent analysis of the short-term survival of local Mothers Against Drunk Driving (MADD) chapters, Edwards and McCarthy (2004; see also McCarthy and Wolfson, 1996) found that two factors were central to organizational survival: a wide-ranging set of weak ties (Granovetter, 1973) in the community as well as financial patronage at the time of a group's founding. The finding about weak ties suggests that organizations with a larger "stock" of social capital are more likely to survive. But they qualify their conclusion by noting that the SMOs in their sample that emerged out of pre-existing groups as well as those with leaders previously tied through civic engagement were *less* likely to survive in cases where the group expended more effort in providing services to victims of drunk driving. The value of social capital is therefore "contingent," in that the groups that are most likely to survive are those that carefully utilize their available stock of "strong" and "weak" ties (see also Ganz, 2000).

Edwards and Marullo (1995) find that a more diverse group of factors assist in the survival of the US peace movement organizations they examined. Contrary to the expectations of analysts working in a population ecology framework (see e.g. Minkoff, 1997), they found that organizational "adolescence" was more of a liability to survival than being an "old" organization. Their primary findings showed that smallness, lack of wider organizational legitimacy, having a semi-formal structure, and having a narrow issue focus all strongly predicted mortality.

Based on the research and debate we have reviewed, we expect to find several distinct patterns in the present analysis. First, we expect that groups having a religious coalition organizational structure (see pp. 49–50 for further explanation on this type) will be more likely to survive than those having one based either on an individual membership or on secular coalition structure. Although the causal relationship between organizational structure and cultural factors such as organizing philosophy is debatable (McCarthy and Walker, 2004), for present purposes we conceptualize the process as cyclical: the choice of an organizational structure is shaped by the context and specific needs of the local community (Alinsky, 1971; Eisenhardt and Schoonhoven, 1990), but, once chosen, is tremendously influential in determining an organization's future strategy and opportunities (McCarthy and Walker, 2004; Bower, 1970) as well as its innovativeness (Ganz, 2000; Damanpour, 1991). For our present purposes, we compare the longevity of the three organizational types, each of which derives from a specific organizing philosophy: religious coalitions, individual membership organizations, and largely secular coalitions. We suspect that as a result of the consistent employment of both "strong" and "weak" ties as well as the broad-based focus of the religious coalitions represented in our sample, we will find that they are more likely to survive than the other two organizational forms. Groups with institutional linkages, it should also be noted, have been found to have dramatic advantages in rates of survival (Baum and Oliver, 1991).

In addition, as we noted in previous work (McCarthy and Walker, 2004; see also Warren, 2001a), religious coalitions utilize thick community networks in order to develop consensus on issues that find widespread community support. These networks, developing through the active dependence on already-existing community ties, are, we suspect, more likely to survive. Individual-membership organizations tend to take on the more contentious issues that are potentially divisive among community members, rather than ones characterized by a lowest common denominator of consensus. Secular coalitions, by their very nature, are often temporary and created for strategic short-term purposes, and are therefore expected to be the most likely to disband during the period under observation.

Second, we hypothesize that organizations having a more diverse set of funding sources will be more likely to survive than those relying on one or only a few benefactors. Groups having a more diverse set of funding sources are more likely to survive because they tend to be less reliant on any given funding source and therefore can be more autonomous, since, as we have noted, patronage is likely to "channel" an SMO's activities (Jenkins and Eckert, 1986). A more diverse set of resource providers allows a group to be not only more autonomous but also more open to the use of new strategies (Alexander, 1998; Ganz, 2000: 1017), which should make it more adaptable to the challenges and therefore more likely to survive.

Third, consistent with the findings of a large literature on organizations of all kinds, we expect an effect of organizational age on survival. Researchers of organizations similar to that on SMOs have found mixed results with respect to the relationship between organizational age and the likelihood of mortality. Scholars working within an organizational ecology framework (e.g. Hannan and Freeman, 1989; Minkoff, 1997) often find that older organizations tend toward inertia and are less able to adapt to their changing environment, thereby facing an increased likelihood of mortality, or a "liability of senescence" (Aldrich and Auster, 1986; Ganz, 2000). However, what is perhaps an even more common finding is that younger organizations face the "liability of newness" (Stinchcombe, 1965; Carroll, 1983), because even though groups tend to experience heightened levels of energy and enthusiasm at their founding which helps them to overcome stresses associated with heavy workloads (Wicker, 1979), channels for resource acquisition and membership retention are less likely to have adequately developed (Aldrich, 1999). Still others find that organizational adolescents are at highest risk of mortality, finding that it is during this point that initial enthusiasm wanes while the more banal aspects of organizational maintenance become central (Edward and Marullo, 1995). We expect that the second of these explanations is correct: that younger organizations will be the least likely to survive. Our expectation is based on the specific features of the present case, in that poor people's SMOs do not face a dramatically changing environment which would force them to adapt frequently, as there is not much competition between organizations seeking to organize the poor. Younger groups are also more likely, we suspect, to take on narrow issues that, once resolved, may cause an organization to rapidly disband.

Fourth, groups being composed of greater proportions of indigenous members will be more likely to survive than those with a lower proportion. Being MBOPs, such groups must promote an authentic, autonomous voice for their members and not simply operate as a professional group of advocates. We believe that the comparison between "membership-based" and "professionalized advocacy" organizations should be thought of as a continuum rather than a dichotomy, and that the best indicator of it is the proportion of the group's membership base that is poor; this may also be taken as a proxy for the organization's *claim to* legitimacy. We hypothesize that groups that have a higher proportion of poor members will be taken as more legitimate and therefore will be more likely to survive than those with a lower proportion of poor members.

Finally, we expect, *ceteris paribus*, the smaller organizations in our sample to be at a higher risk of mortality than those with a larger membership base. Larger groups are typically found to have much higher rates of survival (Minkoff, 1993), and membership size may be one of its best overall indicators (Edwards and Marullo, 1995).

A note on membership structure

Most analyses of advocacy groups tend to underestimate the variety of organizational forms in use, and often implicitly assume that individual membership structures are the near-universal form (see Lofland, 1996). However, among the more than 6000 community organizations estimated to be working toward empowering poor communities in the USA (Delgado, 1994), there exists quite a diversity of organizational repertoires (Clemens, 1993) for meeting these ends. Since the individual membership form of organization is common in nations around the world we will not elaborate its features further here (for additional discussion, see McCarthy and Walker, 2004). Here, however, a note on the religious coalition, a form idiosyncratic to the USA, is necessary.

Although we use the generic term "religious coalitions" here, we must make clear that we refer to a culturally and historically particular form of religious coalition, the *congregation-based* coalition. This particular organizational form was pioneered by the IAF after its re-alignment following the death of Saul Alinsky, and has been replicated by several other groups in the USA in recent decades (see McCarthy and Walker, 2004; Rooney, 1995; Shirley, 1997). Some of the most successful of these groups are the affiliates of the IAF network in Texas, including Communities Organized for Public Service (COPS), Allied Communities of Tarrant (ACT), and the El Paso Inter-religious Sponsoring Committee (EPISO), all of which were described in detail by Mark Warren (2001a) and are represented in the present sample of organizations.

The congregation-based form tends to bring with it an ideology of broad-based organizing (Rogers, 1990; Rooney, 1995), which stresses the bridging of differences in the religious background of constituent groups, although at the same time being careful not to let organizing activities get in the way of each congregation's manifest purposes (Wood, 2002). COPS, for example, includes members from San Antonio's large Catholic Hispanic population, but African-American Protestants, White Protestants, and Jewish congregations are also well represented (Warren, 2001b). These groups are membership based and heavily focused on indigenous leadership development, a far cry from the "organizations without members" described by Theda Skocpol and colleagues (see Skocpol, 1999, 2003; Skocpol, Ganz, and Munson, 2000). Religious traditions are melded with an Alinskyian ideology of organizing for power (Alinsky, 1971; Hart, 2001) in order to accomplish community goals. We should, however, note that these organizations nearly always *originate* as top-down projects of organizers from nationally federated networks such as the IAF (Warren, 2001a), the Pacific Institute for Community Organizing (PICO, see Wood, 2002), or the Gamaliel Foundation. There also exists the concern that building groups on a congregational base merely reinforces the traditional hierarchical structures of religious organizations (Robinson and Hanna, 1994) and does not empower the poorest of the poor (Delgado, 1994), who tend not to be members of religious congregations. Further, the present-day push to fund "faith-based initiatives" by the Bush Administration may promote service provision among religious coalitions while suppressing autonomous organization-building or advocacy efforts.[3]

Data and methods

Our analysis is based on a sample of poor-people's SMOs, which was collected by John D. McCarthy and Jim Castelli (see McCarthy and Castelli, 1994 for more detailed information), drawn from the successful grant applications of poor people's organizations to the Catholic Campaign for Human Development (CCHD). CCHD was formed in the late 1960s by the US Catholic Bishops to serve as a mechanism for attacking the structural sources of poverty. But rather than supporting services to the poor (which was the traditional role of US Catholic Social Services), CCHD was conceived as an agency that would, instead, provide support for groups that seek to empower the poor through community organizing. For more than 30 years CCHD has made annual grants to a diverse set of local community organizing projects, including individual membership groups, and religious and secular coalitions.

Before we discuss the structure of our data, we should make note of the fact that the original sample of grant applications represents only those organizations which were viable enough not only to make application to CCHD, but also to have that application accepted as worthy of funding. Because only those groups organized well enough to apply are included in the sample, one might be reasonably concerned about bias in the selection of cases in the direction of a high degree of survival. Thus, two concerns arise: one regarding selection at the level of *whether or not a group applies to CCHD in the first place*, and another with respect to *which groups CCHD selects for funding*. Although the former concern is more significant, we note that because CCHD is one of the few funders of poor people's organizations in the USA and is well known as such, a wide and diverse array of groups apply for funding, thus mitigating the selection effects of which groups apply in the first place (McCarthy and Walker, 2004). As for the CCHD selection process, when the groups that were offered grants in the 1988–89 funding cycle were compared with those not funded, very few differences were found between them in size, structure, or substantive focus (McCarthy and Shields, 1990). Thus, concerns over the selection of cases are mitigated both by CCHD's prominent position in the non-profit and voluntary sector and also by funding criteria which do not appear to discriminate significantly according to the viability of the recipient (ibid.).

Our first wave of data is based upon the groups that were granted support by CCHD in the years 1991, 1992, and 1993. During those years more than 600 groups applied for funds annually, and in each annual funding cycle, approximately 200 groups received grants that ranged between $35,000 and $50,000. Many of the groups that received support from CCHD did so for several consecutive years. All groups funded in 1991 were included in the sample, and each group that was newly funded in either 1992 or 1993 was added to the sample. This procedure yielded a total of 315 groups that were funded in at least one of the study years, although we do not consider 41 of them for the purposes of the present analysis, because, here we wish to contrast the organizational coalition forms with the individual membership form.[4] Of the included 274 groups, 80 groups were congregation-based coalitions, 118 were composed of individual members, and 76 were largely secular coalitions.

In a second wave of data collection in late 2004 we attempted to establish which of these groups survived over the intervening period of more than a decade. In order to ascertain survival, we used a triangulated method to make contact with each group in the original study. Based upon past research on similar groups, we anticipated a mortality rate of between 25 and 50 percent (Edwards and Marullo, 1995; Edwards and McCarthy, 2004). Our analysis of the mortality of these organizations followed a five-step approach:

1   Along with two research assistants, we first sought information through Internet searches for the websites of existing organizations. If an official website was found, we collected the following information for each group: their contact information, any evidence of organizational activity in the past two years (e.g. documentation of events and meetings, press releases, links to news articles, lobbying activity), as well as evidence of future meetings and events planned. If we were unable to locate an organization's official website, we searched the Web for reliable, alternative sources of contact information.
2   Then, for groups that did not demonstrate recent activity on their website, we attempted, using the contact information we found online, to contact the group by way of email and/or telephone.
3   Those groups that either did not respond to emails or were unable to be contacted by telephone were then searched in the national telephone listings (www.yellowpages.com). If there was a telephone number found in this database for the organization different than ones already attempted, we attempted to contact the group at this new number.
4   If the previous steps failed, we searched the groups again through online search engines, seeking alternative sources of organizational activity. If we found a news article or other web-based source reporting the activity of the group since the beginning of 2003, we took this as a case of survival.
5   Our final step was to attempt to contact the organization using the telephone number collected in wave one.

All groups that remained after we exhausted all five steps were considered effectively "dead" for the purposes of analysis, as well as those groups who reported mortality in telephone or email exchanges, or through other web-based sources indicating mortality.[5] In addition, groups that reported a name change or merger with another organization were considered effectively "dead" as well, following the standard convention in organizational research; however, these indictors of mortality may be interpreted as much as indicators of success as they are of failure (Carroll and Delacroix, 1982).

Measures and descriptive statistics

Organizational survival

Our examination of the survival of MBOPs yielded a number of possibilities concerning the present-day state of these groups. These were: mortality, survival, merger, organizational name change, and unable to be contacted. For purposes of the present preliminary analyses, any organization that changed its name, merged with another, or was unable to be contacted, was grouped with "dead" organizations. This variable is coded such that 1 = survival and 0 = mortality. We found that overall, 62 percent of organizations survived (see Table 3.1).

Structural variables

In earlier research, we found that the structure an organization assumes is consequential for its membership size, issue focus, and ability to garner resources. Dummy variables were created for each organizational type under consideration: individual membership, primarily religious coalition, and primarily secular coalition, each coded such that a 1 is assigned if the group is of that type and 0 otherwise. We also include a variable for whether the SMO is part of a national or regional organizing network, such that a 1 is assigned if they are, and a 0 if not.

General organizational variables

In line with our discussion of the factors expected to influence organizational survival, we developed measures of a number of important factors determined by each group's *grant application in 1990, 1991, or 1992*. These

Table 3.1 Descriptive statistics

	Mean	*Standard deviation*	N
Organizational survival	0.62	0.49	274
Organizational structure variables			
Individual membership group	0.43	0.50	274
Religious coalition	0.29	0.46	274
Non-religious coalition	0.28	0.45	274
Member of an organizing network	0.53	0.50	274
General organizational variables			
Non-Profit (501(c)3)	0.73	0.44	274
% poverty membership	0.61	0.51	274
% minority membership	0.72	0.31	274
Membership size (in thousands)	10.19	29.82	274
Organization 1–4 years old	0.35	0.48	274
Organization 5–9 years old	0.33	0.47	274
Organization 10+ years old	0.30	0.46	274
Resource variables			
1990 total income (in tens of thousands)	15.55	18.20	274
Grassroots funds (in thousands)	22.96	44.74	274
Diversity of grassroots sources	2.05	1.55	274

included whether the organization was an officially-recognized US non-profit organization or had applied to become one [501(c)3 in the US tax code], coded 1 if they were and 0 otherwise. Seventy-three percent of groups in the sample reported this status. We also included the proportion of the group's members reported to have been in poverty (on average, 61 percent); the membership size of the organization, in thousands of members (with a mean of 10,194 and a median of 1210 members); the proportion of an organization's membership reported to have been composed of minority members (on average, 72 percent); and the organization's age, broken down into three categories: 1–4, 5–9, 10+ years old as shown in Table 3.1.

Resource variables

An organization's ability to sustain itself has been found to be strongly shaped by its amount and diversity of resources (e.g. Cress and Snow, 1996). We consider a number of measures of both. As for resource *amounts*, we include measures of the organization's income in 1990,[6] in tens of thousands of dollars (with an average of $155,551 and median of $11,919); and the amount of grassroots funding raised by the group in the year prior to application, in thousands of dollars (with an average of $22,963, median of $8851). We measured resource *diversity* with the number of types of grassroots fundraising activities reported (e.g. canvassing, direct mail, donations, membership dues), with groups reporting no grant providers or grassroots fundraising coded as 0.

Results

Recall our central interest in the impact of organizational structure upon SMO survival. First, we note that the overall survival rate for all of the groups is greater than 60 percent over a period of more than a decade, which translates to an estimated 3.2 percent rate of mortality per year.[7] This compares very favorably with the annual mortality rates seen among peace movement groups at 8.75 percent (Edwards and Marullo, 1995) and anti-drunk driving groups 7 percent (Edwards and McCarthy, 2004). Table 3.2 shows that, contrary to our expectation, the individual membership groups are more likely to survive than either religious or primarily secular coalitions, although the difference in survival rate is relatively modest, one of approximately 10 percent over each type of organizational coalition.

We present a summary of our complete analysis which includes the organizational structure, general organizational and resource variables in Table 3.3. The figures included in the table are, in the first column, the zero-order effects of each variable on the likelihood of survival. That is, it presents the effects of each variable on its own, before considering

Table 3.2 Survival rates by organizational membership structure

		Religious coalition	Non-religious coalition	Individual membership	Overall
Mortality	Number	35	30	40	105
	Percentage	43.75	39.47	33.90	38.32
Survival	Number	45	46	78	169
	Percentage	56.25	60.53	66.10	61.68
Total	Number	80	76	118	274
	Percentage	100	100	100	100

Note
Chi-square: 2.017 ($p = 0.365$).

Table 3.3 Factors influencing chances of survival

	Zero-order effect	Effect on the odds of survival
Organizational structure variables		
Individual membership group	<u>1.52</u>	0.99 (−1.01)
Non-religious coalition[1]	1.19	0.93 (−1.08)
Member of an organizing network	1.28	1.45
General organizational variables		
Non-profit (501(c)3)	0.79 (−1.27)	0.81 (−1.23)
% poverty membership	1.37	1.16
% minority membership	1.41	1.62
Membership size (in thousands)	1.00	1.00
Organization 1–4 years old	0.75 (−1.34)	1.01
Organization 10+ years old[2]	<u>**3.07**</u>	<u>**2.60**</u>
Resource variables		
1990 total income (in tens of thousands)	<u>**1.04**</u>	**1.03**
Grassroots funds (in thousands)	<u>**1.02**</u>	1.01
Diversity of grassroots sources	<u>**1.25**</u>	**1.19**

Notes
Underlined figures indicate statistical significance at the $p < 0.20$ level.
Bold figures indicate statistical significance at the $p < 0.10$ level.
Bold and underlined figures indicate statistical significance at the $p < 0.05$ level.
Each column lists the amount by which the odds of survival are predicted to increase or decrease with a one unit increase in each variable. Figures in parentheses indicate the amount of decrease expected if the effect is less than 1. The left column shows the effect of that variable independently, whereas the right column shows the effect of each variable while holding the value of all other variables constant.
1 The odds for the membership type variables are compared with religious coalitions.
2 The odds for the age category variables are compared with organizations 5–9 years old.

whether its effect is canceled out by some other variable So, for example, the figure for organizations 1–4 years old tells us that these organizations have odds of survival that are 1.34 times lower than organizations aged 5–9; organizations aged 10+ years old have odds of survival 3.07 times greater than organizations aged 5–9. This is distinct from the right column in that the latter considers the effect of each variable *when all other variables are also included.* In the second column, effects can be interpreted as either the reduction in the likelihood of survival or the enhancement of the chances of survival of each organizational factor measured more than a decade ago and when all of the other factors are also taken into account.

When we look only at a group's organizational structure and whether or not it is a member of an organizing network, we find that both of these factors have a positive and relatively strong impact upon a group's chance of survival, as expected. Yet, when we take all of the other factors into account, these two factors become statistically insignificant predictors of survival.

The other factors that remain important in accounting for a group's survival are organizational age and two of the resource variables. Both very young (between one and four years of age) and adolescent (between five and nine years of age) organizations are less likely to survive. These are reasonably strong effects of age, in that once all other factors are taken into account, organizations that were age ten or older by the first wave of data collection were 2.6 times more likely to survive than younger groups. The greater the 1990 total income of a group was, the more likely it was to survive. For each increment of 10,000 dollars, a group's likelihood of surviving increases by just a little more than one (1.03), but this translates into an increased likelihood of survival of 1.34 for every \$100,000 increment in total income (1.03^{10}), a reasonably powerful effect. We also found that, the greater the diversity of sources of grass-roots income, the greater the likelihood that a group will survive. Each additional source increases the likelihood of survival by 1.19 times, such that adding four additional sources more than doubles a group's likelihood of survival.

Summary and discussion

We begin by recalling that, in context, the poor people's organizations we have analyzed here exhibit a very robust rate of survival. That resilience stems, we believe, in large part from the fact that the groups we study were ones that had already succeeded in achieving some minimal level of organizational structure and community legitimacy in order to be judged qualified to receive institutional financial support from CCHD. Having the time, energy, and information to fill out a grant application tends to filter out organizations with low viability (McCarthy and Walker, 2004). And, although we remind readers that these issues of case selection may have influenced our findings in the direction of higher rates of survival, we do not believe that alternative means of sampling would have dramatically influenced our results, as CCHD attracts applications from a wide range of organizations, and the ones selected for funding are relatively similar to ones that were not (McCarthy and Shields, 1990).

We began with very strong theoretical claims about the survival advantages of religious (congregation-based) coalitions over individual membership organizations. Yet, our findings suggest that, if there are survival advantages to any organizational form, it inheres rather in the individual membership form. This may be the result of the fact that organizational members of congregation-based groups may identify more strongly with their congregations than with the poor people's organizations they spawn; if and when member congregations must choose between their religious and poor-empowerment activities, they may be inclined to put aside the latter (Wood, 2002). However, we should note that when we include other factors believed important to survival in our analyses, we find that the apparent advantages of survival for individual membership organizations in this sample actually result from differences between the two sets of groups in age structure and resources. The religious coalitions in our sample were, on average, younger than the individual membership organizations, and, as we showed, younger organizations were quite a bit less likely to survive. We also found, in separate analyses (available upon request), that belonging to a national individual membership organizing network (e.g. ACORN) greatly increases odds of organizational survival.

As well, the individual membership organizations in our sample, by virtue of their larger total incomes, have a survival advantage. And finally, because our individual membership organizations also have an advantage in having developed more diverse sources of grassroots financial support,[8] they gain a survival advantage over groups of each kind of coalition type. Our findings suggest that older groups that have succeeded in generating larger resource bases that are derived from more diverse sources are the groups more likely to survive, and that organizational form (e.g. coalition versus individual membership) does not account for any additional survival advantage in these data. Overall, we found support for two of our hypotheses (that diversity of funding sources increase chances of survival, while being a younger group decreases it), evidence contradictory to one of them (that religious coalitions would be the most likely to survive), and null findings for the other two (that groups with a higher proportion of poverty members would be more likely to survive, as would larger organizations).

Although our core hypothesis on organizational structure was falsified as a direct predictor of survival, we suspect that a process of mediation may be taking place, in which organizational structure shapes an organization's ability to acquire resources, which in turn shapes the likelihood of survival. Elsewhere (McCarthy and Walker, 2004), we have argued that that the coalition form, especially the congregation based variety, provides poor people's groups the advantage of a more reliable funding base that can, as a result, free those groups to devote more effort toward social change and also release them from some of the pressure to constantly seek financial resources. Our evidence showed some support for that argument. On the other hand, the necessity for individual membership groups to seek more diverse sources of resources appears, when successful, to improve their chances of survival over religious coalitions that do not broaden the range of their fundraising efforts. Regardless of how much of an organization's total effort is devoted to goal accomplishment, organizational survival is necessary in order to mobilize and institutionalize an autonomous voice for the poor in local and national politics. Even if short-term goals of insurgency are accomplished by disruptive activity (Piven and Cloward, 1977), without organization, the poor will be taken as a mere temporary threat to be managed rather than a true contender for power.

One final note. The importance of a group's diversity of funding sources to survival provides strong support for the strategy of US institutional funders, in general, who commonly encourage groups they support to seek *diverse sources of funding*, and funders of poor people's groups, in particular, to seek *diverse grassroots sources*. Reliance on any single source for patronage can easily restrict the autonomy of an organization and thereby, may generate the liability of a few strong ties. More important, the mobilization of membership in grassroots fundraising can make up for the general lack of capital available to poor populations seeking to organize (Reitzes and Reitzes, 1987); in this sense, *resourcefulness*, in fact, may be much more influential than financial resources (Ganz, 2000).

Notes

1 We use the terms "poor people's social movement organizations" and "membership-based organizations of the poor" interchangeably. Because all of these organizations in their own way are working toward increased participation and representation for the poor, we believe that they share fundamental similarities with other types of social movement organizations.

2 This is not, however, to say that movement *success* is necessarily dependent on organizational survival, as success is highly contingent and relates to the particularities of each movement organization; as well, organizations often dispand after attaining their goals, thus making long term survival distinct from success (Carroll and Delacroix, 1982).

3 This possibility is suggested by Chaves, Stephens, and Galaskiewicz (2004).

4 These 41 cases consisted of 11 groups that were excluded because they were duplicate cases of the same organization applying to CCHD in separate years (the information from the older application was dropped, the newer kept), 28 cases excluded because they were not membership-based organizations of the poor (e.g. corporations, school boards, native American tribes, and churches), and two cases excluded because information about their membership structure was missing.

5 Although our methodology does not guarantee with absolute certainty that those groups we were unable to locate are, in fact, no longer in existence, this is less of a concern because potential members may have a similarly difficult time

locating the organization, thus suggesting that such groups – even if in a minimal state of survival – are effectively dead.

6 Although the first wave of data includes groups that applied in *either* 1991, 1992, or 1993, we consistently have data on each organization's income for the year 1990, regardless of the year of their grant application.

7 Because our data collection includes the years 1991, 1992, and 1993, we estimated mortality based on the central category, 1992, for 62 percent overall mortality over a 12 year span.

8 The sources include group activities, membership dues, donations from individuals, donations from organizations, donations from charity campaigns, donations from institutions, direct mail, telemarketing, canvassing, and ad sales.

References

Aldrich, H. (1999) *Organizations Evolving*, Thousand Oaks, CA: Sage.

Aldrich, H. and Auster, E. (1986) "Even Dwarfs Started Small: Liabilities of Age and Size and Their Strategic Implications," in B. Staw and L.L. Cummings (eds), *Research in Organizational Behavior*, Volume 8, Greenwich, CT: JAI Press.

Alexander, V.D. (1998) "Environmental Constraints and Organizational Strategies: Complexity, Conflict, and Coping in the Nonprofit Sector," in W.W. Powell and E.S. Clemens (eds), *Private Action and the Public Good*, New Haven, CT: Yale University Press.

Alinsky, S. (1971) *Rules for Radicals: A Pragmatic Primer for Realistic Radicals*, New York: Random House.

Alter, C. (1998) "Bureaucracy and Democracy in Organizations: Revisiting Feminist Organizations," in W.W. Powell and E.S. Clemens (eds), *Private Action and the Public Good*, New Haven, CT: Yale University Press.

Banaszak, L.A., Beckwith, K., and Rucht, D. (2003) "When Power Relocates: Interactive Changes in Women's Movements and States," in Banaszak, L.A., Beckwith, K., and Rucht, D. (eds), *Women's Movements Facing the Reconfigured State*, Cambridge: Cambridge University Press.

Barakso, M. (2005) "Civic Engagement and Voluntary Associations: Reconsidering the Role of the Governance Structures of Advocacy Groups," *Polity* 37: 315–34.

Baum, J.A., and Oliver, C. (1991) "Institutional Linkages and Organizational Mortality," *Administrative Science Quarterly* 36: 187–218.

Bower, J. L. (1970) *Managing the Resource Allocation Process: A Study of Corporate Planning and Investment*, Homewood, IL: Richard D. Irwin.

Campbell, J.L. and Pedersen, O.K. (2001) "The Rise of Neoliberalism and Institutional Analysis," in Campbell, J.L. and Pedersen, O.K. (eds), *The Rise of Neoliberalism and Institutional Analysis*, Princeton, NJ: Princeton University Press.

Carroll, G.R. (1983) "A Stochastic Model of Organizational Mortality: Review and Re-analysis," *Social Science Research* 12: 303–29.

Carroll, G.R. and Delacroix, J. (1982) "Organizational Mortality in the Newspaper Industries of Argentina and Ireland: An Ecological Approach," *Administrative Science Quarterly* 27: 169–98.

Chaves, M., Stephens, L., and Galaskiewicz, J. (2004) "Does Government Funding Suppress Nonprofits' Political Activity?" *American Sociological Review* 69: 292–316.

Clemens, E.S. (1993) "Organizational Repertoires and Institutional Change: Women's Groups and the Transformation of U.S. Politics, 1890–1920," *American Journal of Sociology* 98: 755–98.

Clemens, E.S. and Minkoff, D.C. (2004) "Beyond the Iron Law: Rethinking the Place of Organizations in Social Movement Research," in Snow, D.A., Soule, S.A., and Kriesi, H. (eds), *The Blackwell Companion to Social Movements*, Malden, MA: Blackwell.

Cress, D.M. (1997) "Nonprofit Incorporation among Movements of the Poor: Pathways and Consequences for Homeless Social Movement Organizations," *The Sociological Quarterly* 38: 343–60.

Cress, D.M. and Snow, D.A. (1996) "Mobilization at the Margins: Resources, Benefactors, and the Viability of Homeless Social Movement Organizations," *American Sociological Review* 61: 1089–109.

Damanpour, F. (1991) "Organizational Innovation: A Meta-Analysis of Effects of Determinants and Moderators," *Academy of Management Journal* 34: 555–90.

Delgado, G. (1994) *Beyond the Politics of Place: New Directions in Community Organizing in the 1990s*, Oakland, CA: Applied Research Center.

Edwards, B. and McCarthy, J.D. (2004) "Strategy Matters: The Contingent Value of Social Capital in the Survival of Local Social Movement Organizations," *Social Forces* 83: 621–51.

Edwards, B. and Marullo, S. (1995) "Organizational Mortality in a Declining Social Movement: The Demise of Peace Movement Organizations in the End of the Cold War Era," *American Sociological Review* 60: 908–27.

Eisenhardt, K.M. and Schoonhoven, C.B. (1990) "Organizational Growth: Linking Founding Team, Strategy, Environment, and Growth among U.S. Semiconductor Ventures, 1978–1988," *Administrative Science Quarterly* 35: 504–29.

Gamson, W.A. (1990) *The Strategy of Social Protest*, 2nd edn, Belmont, CA: Wadsworth.

Gamson, W.A. and Schmeidler, E. (1984) "Organizing the Poor: An Argument with Frances Fox Piven and Richard A. Cloward's *Poor People's Movements*," *Theory and Society* 13: 567–85.

Ganz, M. (2000) "Resources and Resourcefulness: Strategic Capacity in the Unionization of California Agriculture, 1959–1966," *American Journal of Sociology* 105: 1003–62.

Granovetter, M. (1973) "The Strength of Weak Ties," *American Journal of Sociology* 78: 1360–80.

Hannan, M.T. and Freeman, J.H. (1989) *Organizational Ecology*, Cambridge, MA: Harvard University Press.

Hart, S. (2001) *Cultural Dilemmas of Progressive Politics: Styles of Engagement among Grassroots Activists*, Chicago: University of Chicago Press.

Hobsbawm, E.J. (1979) "Should the Poor Organize?" *New York Review of Books*, March 23.

Jenkins, J.C. and Eckert, C.M. (1986) "Channeling Black Insurgency: Elite Patronage and Professional Social Movement Organizations in the Development of the Black Movement," *American Sociological Review* 51: 812–29.

Keck, M.E. and Sikkink, K. (1998) *Activists Beyond Borders: Advocacy Networks in International Politics*, Ithaca, NY: Cornell University Press.

Kempton, W., Holland, D.C., Bunting-Howarth, K., Hannan, E., and Payne, C. (2001) "Local Environmental Groups: A Systematic Enumeration of Two Geographical Areas," *Rural Sociology* 66: 557–78.

Lofland, J. (1993) *Polite Protestors: The American Peace Movement of the 1980s*, Syracuse, NY: Syracuse University Press.

Lofland, J. (1996) *Social Movement Organizations: Guide to Research on Insurgent Realities*, New York: Aldine de Gruyter.

McCarthy, J.D. and Castelli, J. (1994) *Working for Justice: The Campaign for Human Development and Poor Empowerment Groups*, Washington, DC: Life Cycle Institute, Catholic University.

McCarthy, J.D. and Shields, J. (1990) "A Comparison of Funded and Non-Funded CCHD Applicant Groups: Structure and Issues," Washington, DC: Life Cycle Institute, The Catholic University of America.

McCarthy, J.D. and Walker, E.T. (2004) "Alternative Organizational Repertoires of Poor People's Social Movement Organizations," *Nonprofit and Voluntary Sector Quarterly*, Supplement to 33(3): 97S-119S.

McCarthy, J.D. and Wolfson, M. (1996) "Resource Mobilization by Local Social Movement Organizations: Agency, Strategy, and Organization in the Movement Against Drinking and Driving," *American Sociological Review* 61: 1070–1088.

Martin, P.Y. (1990) "Rethinking Feminist Organizations," *Gender and Society* 4: 182–206.

Meyer, D.S. and Whittier, N. (1994) "Social Movement Spillover," *Social Problems* 41: 277–98.

Michels, R. (1962 [1915]) *Political Parties: A Sociological Study of the Oligarchical Tendencies of Modern Democracy*, New York: Dover.

Minkoff, D. (1993) "The Organization of Survival: Women's and Race-Ethnic Voluntarist and Activist Organizations, 1955–85," *Social Forces* 71: 887–908.

Minkoff, D. (1997) "The Sequencing of Social Movements," *American Sociological Review* 62: 779–99.

Oberschall, A. (1973) *Social Conflict and Social Movements*, Englewood Cliffs, NJ: Prentice Hall.

Piven, F.F. and Cloward, R.A. (1977) *Poor People's Movements: Why They Succeed, How They Fail*, New York: Vintage.

Powell, W.W. (1988) "Institutional Effects on Organizational Structure and Performance," in Zucker, L.G. (ed.), *Institutional Patterns and Organizations*, Cambridge, MA: Ballinger.

Reitzes, D.C. and Reitzes, D.C. (1987) *The Alinsky Legacy: Alive and Kicking*, Greenwich, CT: JAI Press.

Robinson, B. and Hanna, M.G. (1994) "Lessons for Academics from Grassroots Community Organizing: A Case Study – The Industrial Areas Foundation," *Journal of Community Practice* 1: 63–94.

Rogers, M.B. (1990) *Cold Anger: A Story of Faith and Power Politics*, Denton, TX: University of North Texas Press.

Rooney, J. (1995) *Organizing the South Bronx*, Albany, NY: SUNY Press.

Roy, A. (2004) "Public Power in the Age of Empire," speech delivered at the annual conference of the American Sociological Association, San Francisco, CA, August 16. Available online at: www.democracynow.org/static/Arundhati_Trans.shtml.

Shirley, D. (1997) *Community Organizing for Urban School Reform*, Austin: University of Texas Press.

Skocpol, T. (1999) "Advocates without Members: The Recent Transformation of American Civic Life," in Skocpol, T. and Fiorina, M.P. (eds), *Civic Engagement in American Democracy*, Washington, DC: Brookings Institution Press.

Skocpol, T. (2003) *Diminished Democracy: From Membership to Management in American Civic Life*, Norman, OK: University of Oklahoma Press.

Skocpol, T., Ganz, M., and Munson, Z. (2000) "A Nation of Organizers: The Institutional Origins of Civic Voluntarism in the United States," *American Political Science Review* 94: 527–46.

Soule, S.A. (2004) "Diffusion Processes Within and Across Movements," in Snow, D.A., Soule, S.A., and Kriesi, H. (eds), *The Blackwell Companion to Social Movements*, Malden, MA: Blackwell.

Stinchcombe, A. (1965) "Social Structure and Organizations," in March, J. (ed.), *Handbook of Organizations*, Chicago: Rand-McNally.

Taylor, V. (1989) "Social Movement Continuity: The Women's Movement in Abeyance," *American Sociological Review* 54: 761–75.

Walker, J.L. (1991) *Mobilizing Interest groups in America: Patrons, Professions and Social Movements*, Ann Arbor, MI: University of Michigan Press.

Warren M.R. (2001a) *Dry Bones Rattling: Community Building to Revitalize American Democracy*, Princeton, NJ: Princeton University Press.

Warren M.R. (2001b) "Building Democracy: Faith-based Community Organizing Today," *Shelterforce: The Journal of Affordable Housing and Community Building*, available online at: www.nhi.org/online/issues/115/Warren.html.

Wicker, A.W. (1979) *An Introduction to Ecological Psychology*, Monterey, CA: Brooks/Cole.

Wood, R.L. (2002) *Faith in Action: Religion, Race, and Democratic Organizing in America*, Chicago: University of Chicago Press.

Part III
Trade unions

4 Working class struggles, labour elites, and closed shops

The lessons from India's trade unions and experiences of organisation

Arjan de Haan and Samita Sen

Introduction

At a workshop on membership-based organisations of the poor hosted by the Self-Employed Women's Association (SEWA), it seemed appropriate to reflect on the role and history of India's trade unions. SEWA came up in the context of the decline of the textile industry, one of India's largest employers of non-agricultural labour of the twentieth century. This industrial employment and the working conditions gave rise to what at the beginning of the twentieth century seemed to be amongst the most important forms of organisation of the poor. Its history of organisation of 'informal sector' workers has been closely associated to the 'formal sector' trade union,[1] first as part of it, later in an ongoing struggle for recognition, as organisation, first of women workers, and second of workers outside the traditional terrain of trade union activity.

This chapter will reflect on the history of India's trade unions of unskilled labour, their origins under colonial rule, transformation during the first decades of independence, and decline with the crises of the old colonial industries. While referring to studies on trade unions elsewhere, the chapter will focus on the fate of trade unions in and around Calcutta (now called 'Kolkata'), particularly – drawing on historical and contemporary work by both authors – of the colonial jute industry and the industrial neighbourhoods in which large numbers of migrant workers from different parts of India came to work.[2]

The chapter will, in a way, aim to restore the image of trade unions in countries like India where only a small proportion of the population derives livelihoods from large-scale industries. While they have become increasingly associated with notions of a 'labour aristocracy', the trade unions emerged as major progressive forces with the rise of the industries at the end of the nineteenth and early twentieth centuries, under – as a rule – regimes that did not favour organisation of the poor. They were major parts of the independence movement, and often have played a progressive role against rising communalism. They were major forces in moderately enhancing the living standards of the mostly unskilled work-force and their families, many of whom stayed back in rural areas (and hence improvement of wages did benefit the relatively poor rural areas), and many of whom did settle in urban areas and have expanded their economic and educational opportunities.

Against that background, and based on archival and field research carried out by both authors in Calcutta (de Haan 1994, Sen 1999), the main aim of the chapter will be to draw lessons regarding the successes and failures of trade unions, in organising and representing the interest of a section of India's poor population. We do this through a description of a number of key themes in the development of trade unions and labour history, since the growth of the colonial industries, and discuss how these have contributed to the extent in which unions have been able to include and be representative of sections of the population. These relate to themes of 'outside intervention' in union organisation, the nature of recruitment of labour and unions' role, the evolvement of the labour market – and legislation – over the twentieth century, and the gradual exclusion of women from the workplace and implications for their representation in unions. The concluding section will bring the description back to thinking about conditions for organisations by and for the poor, reflecting on the work by Fox on the 'thickening' of civil society.

Growth and decline of colonial industries: trade unions and the role of outsiders

In current debates of Indian economic development, it is often forgotten that it has had a fairly illustrious industrial history.[3] While much of the traditional rural industry disappeared, India created, between 1850 and 1914, the world's largest jute manufacturing industry, the world's fifth largest cotton industry, and the world's third largest railway network – even though by the time of Independence, as today, India was still largely non-industrial. The industries were located near the continent's main ports, Bombay, Calcutta, Madras, and Karachi (the first three of which are now renamed 'Mumbai', 'Kolkata' and 'Chennai'). Total employment in Indian manufacturing grew from about 500,000 in 1900 to more than 2.5 million by the time of Independence.

Both the cotton and the jute industry underwent major expansion towards the end of the nineteenth century: cotton mills in Western India employed about 60,000 people in 1880 and 260,000 in 1913, while the jute industry, mostly near Calcutta, grew from around 40,000 jobs in 1880 to over 200,000 by 1910 (Table 4.1). Both have continued to be major employers of unskilled labour throughout the twentieth century, though with serious booms and busts, at different points of time, and in both cases a secular decline throughout the second half of the twentieth century.

Table 4.1 Employment in the jute industry, 1880–1988

Bengal	
1880	42,000
1900	111,000
1920	280,321
1930	328,177
1940	284,720
West Bengal	
1950	285,585
1960	208,000
1970	223,000
1980	246,529
1988	225,151

Source: Indian Jute Mills Association (IJMA), Annual Reports (see de Haan 1994).

Even though total employment in manufacturing even at the time of Independence amounted to only a few per cent of the Indian labour force, its growth has attracted a great deal of attention. The Government of India produced a major report on industrial labour about every decade since 1890, and the Government of Bengal published a similar report – initially with a concern whether sufficient labour was available, but soon to a large extent with worries about 'industrial unrest'. The growth of Indian industries attracted the interests of international trade unions, and employment practices were influenced greatly by ILO regulation.

And, of course, trade unions became a significant feature of industrial and political life. But from the early history, the nature of labour organisation was disputed. On the one hand, officials like the Bengal labour commissioner (in 1935), emphasising the concentration of 300,000 jute mill workers in a close stretch of 20 miles north and south of Calcutta, warned that '[n]owhere in the world are there better territorial conditions for labour organisation than round about Calcutta.'[4] Protests and strikes – and other forms of protest, including dilatory work behaviour, irregularity in attendance – were never absent in the jute mills, from the 1890s onwards as described by the pioneer of Bengal's labour history, the late Ranajit Das Gupta (1994), and by Amal Das for Howrah, the industrial town opposite the river from Calcutta (1999).[5] Waves of protest occurred during the Swadeshi movement in Bengal during 1905–8, and militancy appeared to be increasing during the 1920s. After Independence, militancy flared up from the mid-1960s onwards, while the industry went into crisis, and even around 1990, one could not but be impressed by vocal and influential trade unions organisations.

At the same time, militancy and frequent strikes were not necessarily accompanied by stable organisation. Numbers on membership of trade unions have been, and still are, notoriously unreliable: an inquiry in 1945 showed that about 18 per cent of workers were members of unions, and in

1952, the general secretary of the Bengal Chatkal Mazdoor Union warned that 95 per cent of jute mill workers were not organised (Chakrabarty 1989: 116). Many an observer, most notably Dipesh Chakrabarty (1989: Chapter 4), has concluded that there was a paradox of organisation: evidently, there has been great discontent among the workers, dissatisfaction often led to protests, and the Indian Jute Mills Association in the 1930s set up its own intelligence to be prepared, but this was not related – at least during the colonial period – to a form of stable organisation.[6]

After Independence, of course, the nature of organisation changed significantly. However, observations in the early 1990s (de Haan 1994) suggested that trade union/organisation remained fairly fluid – even though official figures confirmed by workers' testimonies, do show significant increases in trade union membership after Independence (de Haan 1994: Chapter 9). With the decline of the industries since the 1960s, the role of unions has changed drastically. During the 1960s, unions became, again, increasingly militant, but its nature was thoroughly political, fuelled by political party differences rather than – we would argue – workers' long-term concerns.[7]

Moreover, trade unions while increasing in numbers became increasingly powerless because of the emergence of the phenomenon of 'lock-outs' – the employers' strike in which factories were closed for extended periods of time. Sometimes, this was a reaction to emerging power of trade unions. Often, it was a covert means to respond to changes in the product market. While initially labour could be easily hired and fired (which in the early twentieth century was reflected in enormous labour turnover), from the 1950s, with increasing unionisation as well as 'modernisation' of labour relations,[8] employers had to resort to other means to adjust the volume of production to the fluctuations in the product market: 'lock-outs' became a common feature of the industrial landscape (and continued throughout the century). As a result, the power of unions was greatly undermined. Where the paradox of the beginning of the twentieth century had been militancy without stable organisation, the paradox at the end of the century was the large number of unions even within one factory, without concomitant ability to defend the interests of the workers.

One of the possible reasons for the specific form of workers' organisation may have been the role of outsiders in the trade unions, which has been extensively discussed in the historiography of labour and trade unions. This has included links with international trade union movements, including during the early part of the twentieth century, but has mainly consisted of a range of Indian middle class men, with a variety of backgrounds: social reformers who took the plight of poor workers against the conservative regime of mostly British employers and the colonial state, communists developing Indian chapters of the international workers' movements, and the nationalist movement that associated itself with or consisted of groups of industrial workers. In the case of the jute industry, it needs to be highlighted, particular circumstances shaped the nature of a possible 'outsider': capital was mostly foreign, either British (in fact, with lower management from Scotland) or 'Marwari' (i.e. from western India), while most of the workers (increasingly) were non-Bengali – the Bengali, educated middle class, the *bhadralok*, became an almost natural candidate for the role of outsider, typically distrusted by the colonial officials.

When the first signs of protests emerged, employers and officials alike blamed this on agitation by troublemakers and outside instigation.[9] Even though in many cases employers recognised workers' concerns, the legitimacy of organisation was disputed. A dominant view among employers was one of a relatively calm and satisfied (usually migrant, as discussed further) worker – an apparently orientalist and certainly paternalistic view that was carried forth well after Independence. Organised protest, so was the image, could only be the result of agitation by people who did not belong to the rank of the workers. And the colonial government made frequent use of Section 144 of the Penal Code to expel agitators.[10]

Much of the (radical) historiography has played down the role of outsiders. According to Ranajit Das Gupta (1994: 351), for example, reflecting on an official view (of a Deputy Inspector General of Police) of the possibility that agitators were present, 'may be incited to mischief by the native papers', highlighted that no evidence in support of the insinuation existed, that the vernacular press did not show much concern for the plight of the workers, and that even mill managers were aware of agitation arising within the ranks of workers. Das Gupta and others' description, moreover, highlighted the large number of reasons directly related to wages, work practices, and work and living conditions that were direct causes of forms of protest.[11] And the lack of sustained organisation could, at least in part, be attributed to a repressive political environment.

When reflecting on the lack of sustained workers' organisation, in the 1920s, reformist-minded officials like Gilchrist highlighted the lack of education and illiteracy among workers. Interestingly, this view was shared by some of the trade union leaders: K.C. Roy Chowdhury, a local labour union leader in the early 1920s, stated that 'constructive trade unionism will not take root . . . unless the soil is weeded and workers receive primary instruction' (Chakrabarty 1989: 128). The significance of this remark is not in its truth or falsehood, but in the fact that it came from a union leader, implying an assumed distance between the leader and the subject. For the more radical organisers, this concern obtained the form of 'political education' (including about the Russian revolution), but even Indrajit Gupta in the 1950s showed great concern for workers' 'cultural and social activity' (ibid.: 129–30).

While many radical historians, as described, have downplayed the role of outsiders, Dipesh Chakrabarty does find evidence of their pre-eminent role, but shifts the focus on the paradox to a deeper level, that of 'culture'. He neither sees a necessary contradiction between involvement of outsiders and sustained organisation, nor sees workers as passive instruments of the leaders' will, but highlights personalistic forms of leadership (sometimes couched in terms of 'zamindari' – landlord – control) and paternalistic – or in the case of Prabhabati Das Gupta during the 1929 strike, maternalistic – authority over the workers: 'I will insist that even these people [Bengali intellectuals, the *bhadralok*], for all their sacrifice, remained imprisoned in the *babu*–coolie relationship insofar as the nature of their contract with the working class is concerned' (Chakrabarty 1989: 150). An old worker we interviewed in 1991 still did remember Ms Das Gupta and the successful strikes she led – but not as part of sustained workers' organisation.

The extent and importance of outsiders in working class organisation may, and probably will, remain a matter of dispute. However, it is plausible that they played a crucial role – in fact, that the history of labour has continued to be written by outsiders may be seen as proof of their sustained importance (until today there are no known records or testimonies by workers). This is not to argue that this role has not changed (or that this is either good or bad). On the contrary, with the changed political circumstances of Independence, at least the Bengali middle class became very differently situated in their intermediation on behalf of the workers, and with the sometimes violent political differences between the Congress and Communist supporters in the 1960s, this again changed significantly. The point to recognise, however, and of no surprise probably for many observers of forms of organisation, particularly by the poor (and with similarities in Bombay for example), is that sustained organisation often takes the form of alliances, including entry points into the dominant political and cultural terrains.

But the form such organisation takes has of course implications – and a longer-term view may present a rather different picture from a shorter-term one. While perhaps essential in terms of organisation of the working poor during the colonial period, the intermediation from the start had close political affiliations and these worked out strongly after Independence.[12] The Congress–Communist differences were particularly relevant, and workers' interests subordinated to party and electoral interests, but much more fractionalisation occurred within both camps. Between the late 1930s and mid-1960s, these differences or factions had been well managed and played off against each other by employers.

From the end of the 1960s, with the rise of the communists in West Bengal, this changed radically. The political agenda of the Left Front explicitly prioritised the countryside, reflecting the party's ideology, strength, and democratic calculus (which was partly reversed during the 1990s). During the 1970s, the employers' association felt themselves rapidly losing the control that they had previously taken for granted:[13] wage structures, delinking wages from productivity, and increased security of work all became part of the victory of workers' organisation, but at a time when the industry went into a serious decline, with decreasing employment, increasing irregularity of employment through the phenomenon of 'lock out', and general instability and uncertainty to the detriment of workers who experienced the recent workers' victory as increasingly hollow.

As indicated, within one factory large numbers of trade unions could be encountered even around 1990, despite the great 'offensive against workers' (Roy 1992), and the history of wage negotiations suggest that a fair amount of bidding occurred between the different unions (also, as described further, unions often were part of patronage networks through which jobs were obtained). It seems that the factions were largely driven by political differences rather than the result of growth of organisation within the ranks. This led to great progress in workers' conditions, but the gains were temporary, and – as described further – for an increasingly small part of the labour force. This illustrates, perhaps, a familiar – theoretical and probably practical – dilemma of intermediaries contributing greatly to the capacity of workers to organise, while at the same time making such organisation less sustainable or at least subject to a variety of motives and incentives.

Do structures determine organisation? Patterns of recruitment and migration

This second part of the chapter looks at how functioning of trade unions has been influenced by the nature of recruitment and employment of labour. Two main characteristics, both of which, too, have been studied well in the historiography of labour and featured frequently in contemporary writings, are the fact that workers were migrants and the personalistic character of recruitment.

First, while the very first jute mills near Calcutta employed mostly local, Bengali labour, the employers quickly moved on to employ migrants, mostly from (current) Bihar and Uttar Pradesh, with considerable numbers from Orissa, Andra Pradesh, and Madhya Pradesh. In the literature, the nature of this shift towards migrant labour has been disputed: according to some this was the result of a shortage of local labour; according to others – and this argument has been made particularly strongly for other parts of India – it was an employers' strategy to reduce the likelihood of workers' organisation. For the Calcutta jute mills, there is limited evidence that such a strategy was actively employed, and the change from local to migrant labour may have been the result of a very rapid expansion in the labour market, combined with the pre-existence of active migration patterns from many of the areas of recruitment (de Haan 1994: Chapter 4).

While the reasons for the increase in migrant labour in itself may be important for the workers' organisation (as SEWA currently perceives, too), the main argument here is around the implications of the nature of migration and labour recruitment. Crucially, the pattern of migration was, and to a large extent has remained, circular. Rather than entire families moving to the industrial area, typically single male migrants moved (as sex ratios for urban industrial areas showed), leaving families behind,[14] maintaining very close links with their villages and returning frequently.

Ever since this pattern of migration emerged, it manifested itself in various convenient and inconvenient ways for employers. It was often thought that this made workers less committed to the workplace, and responsible – particularly in the early decades of the industry – for high rates of labour turnover. The close links with the village also gave rise to a seasonal shortage of workers, as migrants left the city in large groups, particularly during the summer months.[15] On the other hand, it also proved to be very convenient, in particular during major economic crises as in 1931, when following the 1929 slump, lots of jobs were cut and workers moved en masse back to the rural areas without signs of protest; they disappeared, as Labour Commissioner Gilchrist observed, as snow for the sun.

The outlook of workers interviewed (de Haan 1994) gave a rather different perspective of this pattern of migration from the one that emerges from the radical historiography. Many workers returning to the village needed no explanation, and answers included exclamations like 'What to do? My house is there!' Many said that they go when there was a 'need' or 'work': marriage, an emergency, taking care of the land (land disputes being a reason for prolonged absence), education of the children and so on. Visiting the family was a key reason for going to the village, for one or two months per year, quite often longer, and frequently beyond the allowed period of leave (and that medical certificates could be bought was a public secret).

What, then, are the implications of this pattern of migration for forms of organisation? Just as this could be both convenient and an irritant for employers, for trade union organisation this provides both an advantage and a challenge – but it is likely to impact upon the form of organisation. As highlighted above, unorganised militancy was quite common in the early years of the industry, and the option of exit appears to have been exercised quite frequently (with the changing labour market situation and increasing surplus of labour, presumably, this has changed, as discussed further). Strikes could be maintained longer, because workers would go home – evidence suggests that this phenomenon that existed in a 1929 strike still existed in a strike in 1992. On the other hand, the dual existence of the workers makes it more difficult to organise workers on a sustained basis, and many a trade union organiser has shared the concerns of the employers about the 'lack of commitment' of the migrant worker to the industry and urban area.[16] In any case, in understanding the specific form of this form of organisation, the complexity of both material livelihoods and the (inter-related) social-cultural orientation needs to be taken into account.

The pattern of migration is closely intertwined with the second key characteristic of labour recruitment and employment. Labour relations have invariably been characterised as personalistic (and employment practices in the 1920s sometimes as chaotic). Relations between management and labour were extremely hierarchical (backed up by repressive colonial power), personified through a range of intermediaries, typically the Bengali labour clerk and the notorious *sardar*.[17] The latter played a significant role in shop-floor management but particularly in the recruitment of labour, especially during the early years of the industry when there was a premium on bringing additional new workers in, and when labour turnover was high. There is also evidence that the sardars exercised control over the replacement of workers, perhaps particularly the system of *badli* labour (temporary workers, particularly significant during the annual period when many workers left). Successive changes in labour management practices and legislation have half-heartedly and largely unsuccessfully tried to dispense with this role.

How trade unions related to the sardars has not been subjected to systematic investigation. It is almost inevitable, however, that trade union organisation to a large extent followed the existing networks of which sardars were a central part. As argued extensively elsewhere (de Haan 1994: 73ff.), sardars were not just a creation of employers in the absence of 'modern' labour management – though they certainly fulfilled an important function – but also part of the social network that created the environment in the industrial area, and linked living space including in rural areas to the work place. Social networks were, and have remained – though labour market conditions have changed significantly as described further – key to obtaining jobs. And certainly for the period for which we have first-hand information, it was clear that trade union leaders, at least at lower levels, did play an important role in the distribution of available jobs; trade unions were, in fact, part of a closed-shop system, though not necessarily based on formal membership.

A story that emerges, thus, is about the importance of 'external' factors for the forms organisations are likely to take. In this case, both the migratory nature and continuing rural–urban links, and the personalistic character of recruitment, have exercised a great influence, sometimes enhancing the potential for organisation (as unions derived strength from the role of union leaders in labour recruitment), sometimes weakening it and sometimes making the process of organisation less equitable. How the structures that originated early on impacted the longer-term history of organisation is the subject of the next section.

Structures: economic fluctuations shape organisation

While patterns of recruitment and labour control, as argued earlier, influenced the form of organisation a great deal, economic busts and booms and changes in labour markets and job opportunities have continuously changed the conditions for, and dynamics of, trade union organisation. We referred to some of these changes earlier in the chapter, and in this section we deal with this question more systematically. It may be appropriate to divide the long history of the industry and the accompanying history of labour organisation into three periods:

1   expansion until the 1920s
2   relative stability until the 1960s
3   a period of turmoil and decline since then.[18]

Up to the late 1920s, the demand for labour was generally thought to outstrip supply. This perception was perhaps not quite accurate, and partly just the common employers' complaint, but from both the official records that showed high labour turnover and oral testimonies of workers suggesting that getting a job was very easy, one may conclude that workers were in a relatively advantageous position – (even though there is little evidence that the high demand for labour resulted in significant increases in wages in fact, real wages appear to have been fairly stable until the late 1960s).

During this period, forms of organisation remained fairly fluid. On the one hand, workers did show much militancy, voted with their feet, and unmediated forms of protest occurred frequently. On the other hand, attempts by organisers from outside were fairly new, and took place in a relatively repressive environment. And the gang leaders played an important role for the workers, but to a large extent the premium was about bringing more people in. The relatively fluid nature of the organisation that existed was, arguably, demonstrated in the severe economic crisis of 1931: large numbers of jobs were cut, but very little protest emerged (in fact, the event did not feature in the workers' memories) and workers appear to have chosen for an option of exit, going back to their villages.[19]

The decades after 1929–31 appear to have been a long period of relative calm. The industry adapted to the 1929 Depression, with restrictions in production and some attempts of rationalisation during the 1930s. With the outbreak of the war, the industry became more profitable. In the period immediately after Independence and Partition, it had to cope with the fact that its supply of raw jute had been cut off but production levels remained high and if anything increased. Labour legislation did, however, change radically after Independence.

Rationalisation during the 1950s implied a reduction of jobs (women lost out in particular, as discussed in the next section). We know, perhaps, too little of the role of trade unions during this period, particularly how they reacted to the changed labour market. What we do know is that radical union leaders like Indrajit Gupta continued to be concerned about the lack of stable organisation. The outside organisers now found themselves in a very different political circumstance: while mill ownership and management remained in the hands of foreigners and Marwaris, government officials were not as clearly on their side as they were before Independence (though this does not necessarily mean they were more favourably disposed to the migrant worker).

From the little evidence we have for the period of the 1950s and 1960s, it appears that corporatist principles predominated within the industry. Labour legislation – which in this period started to prescribe hiring and firing procedures, for example through a ruling that rationalisation should not lead to dismissals – was the result of government intervention (and sometimes had to be 'explained' to workers). Works Committees were introduced and employers saw this as the main institution for negotiating rationalisation. It is significant, and perhaps need to be seen in the context of the lack of stable trade union organisation, that very few strikes or other forms of protest emerged while many jobs disappeared. Jobs were becoming more secure, labour conditions improved marginally, but the benefits were for an increasingly smaller number of workers.

The crisis of the industry that started in the mid-1960s had a number of reasons: decline in exports, imposition of an export duty, and withdrawal of foreign capital. Significant for the analysis here is how labour conditions changed during this period. As was highlighted, from 1965 onwards strikes suddenly became much more common (taking the industry by surprise), wages started to increase significantly, and employers started to resort to 'lock-outs' where previously they tried to change production levels through, at least on paper, negotiated compromises.

Some of the employers, in a similar way in which they used to blame outsiders for unrest, now blamed 'inter-union and intra-union rivalries'. While one does not need to accept this employers' view, there is something paradoxical about the events after the mid-1960s and how these differed from the period before. The increased militancy started to occur at the same time as the crisis of the industry deepened. Moreover, demands and protests were often not related to the most serious aspects of the crisis; for example, unions appeared to have been completely powerless against the phenomenon of strikes. The strikes and workers' victories around 1970 did not feature in the oral histories of workers we interviewed; rather, they saw it as a period of unrest, indiscipline, and murders.

During the period of fieldwork in the 1990s, factionalism and political domination were central characteristics of labour organisations. Titaghur Jute Mill, for example, was said to have 14 unions – CITU, INTUC, and AITUC, all three closely affiliated to the main political parties being the strongest. From interviews, it was not difficult to conclude that unions were not popular, that workers at best approached them for direct benefits of help (for which, they were likely to have to pay small bribes). And as before, trade unions were closely involved in the recruitment of workers (and in effect operated a closed-shop system), who would become members of unions to get a job, and had close links with labour contractors.

Thus, at one level, the form of labour organisation was successful, as the workers, through whatever the dominant political alliance was, have been able to obtain benefits. But at the same time, it seems to have brought in a certain distance between the developments in the industry and demands voiced by organisations, and political motivations (i.e. not directly linked to the industry) arguably have dominated the long-term interest of the industry (rather than leading to a demise of unions). There was certainly nothing inevitable about this pattern, but it appears that the dominant form of organisation has made it vulnerable to developments taking the turn it took. In the process, and this is illustrated in the next section with reference to female labour, the benefits were obtained for an ever-smaller number of workers.

Women in the industry and trade unions

This last section of the chapter focuses on the conditions that have led to a limited representation of women in unions. This is, of course, partly related to the small percentage of women in the industry, but this is not the main story, and in fact what needs explanation is the decline of female labour during this century, and the role that trade unions have played in this.

In the early stages of the jute industry, a fairly large number of women joined the industry (though not nearly in the same proportions as modern export-oriented industries in Bangladesh and elsewhere). There were geographical differences, as described extensively elsewhere. Initially, a fairly large number of Bengali women were working in the mill (Table 4.2). Over time, the substitution of local labour seems to have affected women too. Among the migrants, comparatively more women from Andhra Pradesh and southern Orissa than from Bihar and Uttar Pradesh worked in the industry. It is not entirely clear whether this pattern was present so strongly from the start of the industry in the late nineteenth century, but it certainly developed fairly early on. The *differences* among migrant communities do not appear to have been determined by patterns of recruitment within the industry, though the level of female employment and particularly its decline from the 1930s onwards had a much more unified force behind them (and has arguably led to a spreading of notions restricting mobility of women).

It is important to reflect on the reasons for the decline of female employment. The precondition was created by the development of a surplus of labour, which started with the crisis of 1931, but did not immediately take on a structural nature because of large fluctuation on both

Table 4.2 Female labour in the jute industry, 1912–71

Year	Women (number)	Percentage of total workforce
Bengal		
1912	31,329	15.7
1920	44,545	15.9
1930	52,144	15.9
1935	37,749	14.3
1940	36,640	13.9
1945	38,789	13.7
West Bengal		
1950	35,944	13.6
1955	22,375	8.9
1960	9,419	4.4
1962	8,700	3.0
1971	–	2.5

Sources: Until 1960 IJMA figures; the 1962 and 1971 figures are from the Ministry of Labour, Labour Bureau, 1973.

sides of the labour market during the 1930s and 1940s. The first piece of female-specific legislation, introduced in 1891 – which prohibited night work by women, made maternity leave compulsory, and limited their working day to 11 hours – had little effect because of infractions and the government's practice of exempting particular mills. Further 'protective' legislation was introduced during the 1920s and 1930s, but again this legislation did not result directly in the exclusion of women. It was only in the 1950s that employers started to argue that legislation had made female employment costlier, and that the restrictions on carrying weights and on working in specific occupations made it a problem to employ women.

Legislation was largely a result of official concerns about the welfare of women – rather than the result of organised protest. From the 1920s, female labour became defined as a 'problem', including because of their 'irregular' lives and because of the fact that many men left their wives in the villages and presumed temporary alliances in the industrial area. This official concern, thus, provided the rationale for legislation – but it may also have functioned as legitimation for the exclusion of women later on. Employers during colonial times had successfully lobbied to defer introduction of Maternity Benefit legislation; after Independence when they had less clout, at least the timing of effective implementation may have been a reflection of employer preferences, probably unopposed by trade unions.

Another factor responsible for the disappearance of women was the rationalisation of production during the 1950s. Employment decreased by almost one-third in ten years: in 1948 there were 315,000 workers in the industry, and in 1961 a low of 197,000 was reached. But the rationalisation was not gender-neutral: whereas before, employers had not objected to women working, they now considered them unfit for factory work, especially when new (high-speed) machines were introduced. In the 1960s, there was an explicit drive to reduce the number of female workers in the mills of Thomas Duff & Co., for example, with its chairman arguing that some mills 'could do a lot better' in getting women to resign (the official records emphasised natural attrition and voluntary retirement, and shifts in production were used to speed up the process).

What was the reaction of trade unions to the decline of female labour? For sure, as described by Leela Fernandes (1999: 185–90), there were occasions that unions formally included demands from women, but these never reached high priority, or were even raised during tripartite negotiations. Also, and mirroring the earlier paradox of militancy without sustained organisation, women have displayed considerable degrees of militancy. 'Gherao', plus embarrassment of male officials, have been common strategies. But the militancy and protests of women have not been integrated systematically in the working of trade union organisation, and hostility appears to have existed on both sides, with women workers not being willing to succumb to the discipline of trade unions (maybe because they had the experience of their specific demands being sidelined in the process of negotiations), and on the part of unions who felt that women were less amenable to, less understanding of, long-term benefits.

Exclusion of women had at least three aspects, illustrating how, over time, the organisation of workers became increasingly confined to an ever smaller group, increasingly male. First, women hardly ever (if at all) became trade union leaders (as there were no opportunities for women to become *sardars*) – the role of Ms Das Gupta would not be an exception to this as she was not a worker herself (even if she did have much appeal to workers). Second, the demands of women were never an important part of the demands of the male-dominated unions, even when there was considerable amount of spontaneous protest. Third, the unions did not oppose and often have been instrumental in the displacement of women from the industry,[20] themselves reinforcing a notion of the male breadwinner, which possibly became stronger as the twentieth century developed. (Sen 1999).

The development of the notion of breadwinner has been core to the gendered patterns of access to employment, and how this has been reflected in trade union organisation. It may well have been reinforced by at least some women who agreed that sons or other male relatives should replace them and seeing this as a status elevation; others may have been reluctant but unable to withstand the combined pressures of unions, families, and employers. Further, male workers may have 'sacrificed' supplementary income (from women) to attain upward status mobility (as many workers suggested by responses like 'only women from destitute families work'). Finally, while it has not been uncommon for trade unions to request jobs for women, this was typically only because they had become widowed or otherwise were single heads of households.

It is important to understand the complexity of this development of a breadwinner ideology. With jobs being part of personalised networks of recruitment (job as property, with same gendered characteristics as other form of property), and increasingly scarce, trade unions have been an important instrument in the exclusionist policy of formal sector employment.

Organisations of the poor: concluding thoughts

This chapter has described the history of a particular form of organisation in a particular set of circumstances: boom and bust of a major industry, with outsiders playing an important role in organisation of workers, and the increasing exclusiveness of the organisation. This concluding section tries to bring the description back to thinking about conditions for organisations by and for the poor. To do so, it may be helpful to use a framework proposed by Fox in a research in Mexico (quoted in Bebbington *et al.*, 2006), asking the question, 'how civil society "thickens"?'

A first pathway through which this can happen is referred to as state–society convergence, in which reformist officials within the state facilitate the emergence of autonomous forms of organisation (including in corporatist forms in the two decades after Independence). As we have seen, this has played a very important role in the case of trade union organisation, but it also proved a two-edged sword, and the long-term view adopted in this chapter brings out some of these dynamics. On the one hand, outsiders were essential in organisation and gave the organisation an enormous amount of strength, particularly in the more repressive environment of the colonial periods; on the other hand, arguably it made the organisation more vulnerable to a variety of motives, not always in the interest of the broad set of people they represent, as was arguably demonstrated from the late 1960s onwards.

The second pathway centres on collaboration between external and local civil society actors. Again, coalitions played an important role in the formation of trade unions. The 1990s' wave of global alliances in a sense was not new, as trade union members from the UK and elsewhere did take up the case of workers in Calcutta, and international communism did lend much weight to the organisations – be it that this may have been largely indirectly, through political parties, which as we have seen have contributed to factionalism within workers' organisation.

The third pathway distinguished by Fox is bottom-up mobilisation, and this remains a core issue in trying to explain the long-term trends of workers' organisation. A key theme throughout the century, affecting the entire labour force in the 1920s and women in particular during the 1950s, has been the paradox of militancy and lack of sustained organisation. In circumstances that provided ideal ground for mass organisation, the channelisation of mobilisation was essential – a feature that seems to remain central for many organisations of the poor (perhaps, particularly the working poor, because of employers' class interest. However, the *form* in which protests were channelled has been equally crucial for the development of the organisation, and the strategic choices made have led to processes of exclusion, as well as a direction that has tended to marginalise long-term workers' interests (at the cost of, e.g. electoral interest).

Part of the dynamics has been the marginalisation of women. Unions have not been directly or uniquely responsible for this, as decline of employment was part of a complex process, and women would not have raised one single voice. But neither have unions been able to incorporate the interest of women as workers. Over time they have come to represent the immediate interest of an increasingly small work force, increasingly composed of men, with women employed in exceptional circumstances only, for example when no other breadwinner is available.

In conclusion, we would like to point to what may be considered the largest dilemma of trade unions in countries that are marked by an 'informal sector' comprising about 90 per cent of the labour force, and in contexts of de-industrialisation of sectors in which trade unions traditionally have had the largest foothold: can they broaden their interests and objectives in a way that make them more representative for larger sections of the poor population? The history of organisation among organised workers indicates that they have become increasingly exclusionary, suggesting that a radical change in orientation would be required before they would take on a broader role. While SEWA has filled an enormous gap in organising workers, mostly women, outside the traditional sphere of labour organisation, their continuous efforts for recognition highlight the difficulty in achieving such a change. The role of unions has become increasingly restricted to defending the interests of an ever-smaller group of workers, usually men, and the roles of union leaders and *sardars* seemed to have become increasingly intertwined. A key question that emerges, therefore, is whether unions would be able to lift themselves out of this squeeze, and innovate to become representative of a wider section of the urban (and therefore also the rural) population.

Notes

1 SEWA grew out of the Textile Labour Association, India's oldest and largest union of textile workers. Available online at: sewa.org/aboutus/index.htm.
2 This draws, in particular on our jointly edited volume, A. de Haan and S. Sen, 1999, and our respective PhDs finished mid-1990s.
3 The classic text on this is M.D. Morris in the *The Cambridge Economic History of India*, 1983.
4 Quoted in Dipesh Chakrabarty (1989: 116), the main critique of Marxist labour historiography in West Bengal.
5 For similar perspectives see Basu (1994), and – with a comparative perspective, Cox (1997).

6 Chakrabarty (1989: Chapter 4). After Independence, much higher figures started to be quoted, but these are notoriously unreliable, as trade unions, generally do not maintain membership registration. Many people told us that they joined unions or parties from which they expected to get an advantage. Some said that they had paid donations to all unions to avoid their anger, that they supported the strongest union, and that workers are opportunists.

7 As an indication of this fluidity, I observed that between 1991 and 1993, the influence of BJP politics in the industrial area – which has by and large been spared communal conflicts – appeared to have increased.

8 Modernisation of labour relations included attempts to abolish the role of intermediaries in shop-floor management and, in particular, in recruitment of labour (known as 'sardars'); their role is described further.

9 It may be important to emphasise that much of the description is based on official records, that very few oral and written testimonies of workers exist, and that we are thus, as Chakrabarty put it, forced to read between the lines to get an understanding of the world of workers and their organisation. My own research focused on oral history, but this remains limited too, for example highlighted in the common statement that things were better in the past.

10 Chakrabarty 1989: 131. Penal Code 144 (of 1860) was frequently imposed by authorities to ban demonstrations, to reduce 'public nuisance' (www.righttowater.org.uk/pdfs/india_cs.pdf), and is still frequently used in the context of labour unrest.

11 In a number of cases protests revolved around cultural-religious issues, for example related to recognition of religious holidays. While the living and working environment has remained to a large extent segmented, along regional, ethnic and religious lines, with a few exceptions, trade unions did not organise along such lines.

12 In this context, the discussion of hierarchy is central. Most studies, Chakrabarty's (1989) in particular, stress that the Indian working class has been characterised by a strong hierarchical culture. Industries like jute have been organised in a hierarchical fashion, trade unions have not operated on democratic principles, and the workers' 'cultures' were thought to be equally hierarchical.

13 Interestingly, while the history of trade union organisation is well studied for the colonial period, the more recent period is not well documented; much of my information on this is based on employers' records; see de Haan 1994: Chapter 7.

14 The pattern of migration varied somewhat across regional and perhaps, religious communities, as in the case of my own field research where there was much higher incidences of family migration among migrants from southern Orissa and Andhra Pradesh. But across communities, female migration did occur (de Haan 1994, Fernandes 1999, Sen 1999).

15 Some debate exists for the reason of this annual exodus; while some have argued that this was related to seasonal agricultural activities, I concluded that the return has been mainly during the festive and marriage season, and if anything, after the main harvest. But in any case, it is important to emphasise that rural and urban lives form an integrated phenomenon from the perspective of the worker.

16 For example, a union leader said that workers are only interested in earning money to take it back home. This has been observed in research on unions elsewhere in India too.

17 Das Gupta (1981) has highlighted the central importance of the sardari system – and linked to that the importance of personal ties – till 1937, when the first labour officers were introduced; Chakrabarty (1989: 19ff.) emphasises that a

large part of the sardar's authority was based on fear, and the use of naked physical force; see further Goswami (1985) for a description of the role of intermediaries.

18 Details and references on changes in the industry can be found in de Haan 1994: Chapter 7.

19 A 70-year-old retired female worker from Andhra also said that there were no unions in the past: *paelle union kaha raha?*, *khali bara sardar, laine sardar, e sab hai* (where were unions in the past? There were just the bara sardar, line sardar, all that was there; see de Haan 1994).

20 Fernandes 1999: 185. Our observations also suggested that local union leaders were largely in favour of reservation of jobs for men. Moreover, the illegal practice of illegally employing 'voucher' workers – usually women – in the place of ghost workers has been actively condoned by unions.

Bibliography

Basu, S., 'Workers Politics in Bengal 1890s–1929. Mill Towns, Strikes and National Agitation', Ph.D. thesis, University of Cambridge, 1994.

Bebbington, A., Dharmawan, L., Fahmi, E. and Guggenheim, S., 'Local Capacity, Village Governance, and the Political Economy of Rural Development in Indonesia', *World Development*, 34, 11, 2006, pp. 1958–76.

Chakrabarty, D., *Rethinking Working-Class History. Bengal 1890–1940*, Delhi: Oxford University Press, Delhi, 1989.

Cox, A., 'Rationalisation and Resistance: The Imperial Jute Industries of Dundee and Calcutta, 1930–1940', Fellowship Dissertation, University of Cambridge, 1997.

Das, A., 'Outside Intervention in Jute Mill Strikes – Howrah 1870 – 1930', in: A. De Haan and S. Sen (eds), *A Case for Labour History*, KP Bagchi & Co., Calcutta, 1999.

Das Gupta, R. 'Structure of the Labour Market in Colonial India', *Economic and Political Weekly*, November 1981, Special Number, pp. 1781–806.

Das Gupta, R., (ed.) 'Poverty and Protest: A Study of Calcutta's Industrial Workers and Labouring Poor, 1875–1899', *Labour and Working Class in Eastern India. Studies in Colonial History*, Calcutta: KP Bagchi & Co., 1994.

Fernandes, L., 'Displacing Women Workers on the Margins of Working Politics in the Jute Mills', in: A. de Haan and S. Sen (eds), *A Case for Labour History. The Jute Industry in Eastern India*, Calcutta: KP Bagchi & Co., 1999.

Goswami, O., 'Multiple Images: Jute Mill Strikes of 1929 and 1937 Seen Through Others' Eyes', *Modern Asian Studies*, 21, 3, 1985, pp. 547–83.

de Haan, A., *Unsettled Settlers. Migrant Workers and Industrial Capitalism in Calcutta*, Rotterdam: Verloren, 1994.

de Haan, A. and S. Sen (eds), 1999. *A Case for Labour History. The Jute Industry in Eastern India*, Calcutta: KP Bagchi & Co., 1999.

Morris, M.D., 'The Growth of Large-Scale Industry to 1947', in: *The Cambridge Economic History of India*, Vol. 2, Cambridge: Cambridge University Press, 1983, pp. 553–676.

Roy, B., 'Jute Mill-Owners' Offensive Against Workers', *Economic and Political Weekly*, 5 September 1992, pp. 1893–4.

Sen, S., *Women and Labour in Late Colonial India. The Bengal Jute Industry*, Cambridge: Cambridge University Press, 1999.

5 China as a world factory

New practices and struggles of migrant women workers

Pun Ngai

Introduction

The rise of China as a "world factory" signifies a new century of surplus labor drawn from rural China to fuel the global economy. Since the early 1990s, we have witnessed a surge in the relocation of transnational corporations (TNCs) to China from all over the world, especially from Hong Kong, Taiwan, Japan, the USA, and Western Europe. More than 100 million peasant-workers have been working for TNCs, either directly owned or joint-ventured by big brand-name American and European companies, or in their Chinese production contractors and subcontractors. With China's entrance into the World Trade Organization (WTO), capital from manufacturing industries, high-tech sectors, and financial business further poured into China, creating a hegemonic discourse in the West that Chinese workers have increasingly stolen jobs from Western labor markets. There are, however, increasing concerns emerging amongst non-governmental organizations (NGOs) as well as academic circles about globalization and labor conditions in post-socialist China. In spite of the increase in transnational codes of conduct, practices at the company level, and legal mobilization of labor at the societal level, precarious labor regimes in China are still prevalent (Chan, 2001; Lee, 1998; Pun, 2005a; SACOM, 2005). Globalization and "race to bottom" production strategies adopted by TNCs work against the improvement of labor relations in China through new legal or institutional practices and employment relations, and the changed nature of ownership (Pun, 2005b). Instead, new global production regimes and capital–labor relations produce employment systems which are still highly precarious, generating huge hidden costs that Chinese women workers carry while creating a huge social force ready to resist and challenge the existing social order. How would migrant women workers understand themselves collectively in terms of class and gender identity? Could they be organized as a new worker-subject newly emerged in post-socialist China? At the crossroads of China's incorporation into global capitalism, what are the new forms of labor organizing and women empowerment?

This chapter hopes to examine these timely questions drawn from a ten-year-struggle of a local NGO, *The Chinese Working Women Network* (CWWN), which started its projects in Shenzhen since 1996. Situated primarily in the special economic zone (SEZ) of Shenzhen, CWWN struggles to survive together with migrant women workers who desperately look for civil society space in urban China for labor protections. Set up in 1996, CWWN is a non-profit NGO with the mission of promoting betterment for the lives of Chinese migrant women workers. It endeavors to fight for labor and gender rights, and promote grassroots empowerment and social justice in China. Because of the great difficulties associated with organizing migrant workers at the workplace level, CWWN roots itself in the migrant labor communities and attempts various organizing projects to organize workers outside the traditional trade union model. Limitations, shortcomings, and lack of genuine political space for women's participation far extend the achievement of the empowerment projects. Because of the difficulties related to survival as a local NGO in China, CWWN must spend a great deal of effort in ensuring its sustainability as an organization, which affects CWWN's ability and power to organize labor.

China's accession into WTO

The acceleration of the global manufacturing process after China's entrance into the WTO has contributed to a dual process that underlies the making of a new Chinese working class. First, the global process shatters China's old socialist pattern of industrial ownership and previous workforce composition, the latter of which has constantly been under restructuring since the mid-1990s. In 1981, the state-owned enterprises (SOEs) produced three-quarters (74.76 percent) of the national gross industrial output while the collective-owned enterprises, which had functioned as subsidiaries of state firms, generated another 24.62 percent of national gross industrial output (Lee, 2005:4). The SOEs' decline in industrial significance became even more drastic when economic reform deepened in the 1990s. By 1996, 11,544 units of SOEs had declared bankruptcy (Lee, 2003:74). The national importance of the state-owned and state-controlled firms, in terms of total industrial output, dwindled to only 18.05 and 10.53 percent respectively, in 2001. With regard to the number of industrial employees in SOEs, the 1990 *China Statistical Yearbook* states that, in the same year, there were 43.64 million staff and workers, constituting 68.42 percent of the national total of industrial employment. The neo-liberal ideology borne by the WTO's deepening involvement in market competition and corporate consolidation has contributed to massive lay-offs of state and collective workers in the new millennium. The once provisioning and paternalistic socialist employment systems have acceded to the market forces of demand and supply. As privatization, mergers, and bankruptcies changed the face of Chinese work units, or *danwei*, the number of industrial workers in SOEs remained, until 2002, a mere 15.46 million persons, making up only 41.46 percent of the total industrial employment in China.[1]

Alongside the state-initiated transition to the market economy was a sharp rise in jobs in private, foreign-owned, and joint-venture enterprises that now dot the coastal cities of China. The formation of a new working class of internal rural migrant laborers, or the *dagong* class (Pun, 2005a), in contrast to the Maoist working-class, has been taking shape in contemporary China. Since the late 1970s, the de-collectivization project has generated a massive labor surplus from rural areas. At the same time, the central government has facilitated an unprecedented surge in internal rural-to-urban migration by partially relaxing some of the restrictions of *hukou*, or the household registration system. Most TNCs (of Hong Kong, Taiwan, South Korea, Japan, the United States, and European countries) and their subcontractors recruit millions of peasant-migrants in export-led SEZs. Until the early 1990s, it was consensually agreed that the number of floaters[2] was about 70 million nationwide. The Fifth National Population Census of China, in 2000, estimated that there were over 120 million internal migrant workers in cities, while other estimates range from 100 to 200 million persons (Lavely, 2001:3). This variation is explained by the varied definitions of *migrant worker* adopted by the government and non-state organizations, which take into account the temporal and spatial dimensions of internal rural-to-urban migration (see also Solinger, 1999; Liang and Ma, 2004; Gaetano and Jacka, 2004).

Women constitute a significant proportion of the rural migrant population in contemporary China. The development of SEZs across China, similar to the development of corresponding establishments in most other developing economies, was based on a massive harnessing of young workers, in particular of unmarried women (see Lee, 1998; Pun, 1999; Gaetano and Jacka, 2004). By 2000, female migrant workers accounted for about 47.5 percent of China's internal migrant workers (Liang and Ma, 2004). In Shenzhen, they recently made up about 65.6 percent of all migrants (Liu, 2003).

These rural migrants have been identified as temporary residents who work in a city and who lack a formal urban *hukou*, an urban registry status that confers upon urban residents the entitlement to stay in the city and enjoy welfare and protection there (Solinger, 1999). The old but still existing *hukou* system helps to create exploitative mechanisms of labor appropriation in Shenzhen as well as in other Chinese cities. The maintenance of the distinction between permanent and temporary residents by the *hukou* system facilitates the state's shirking of its obligation to provide housing, job security, and welfare to rural migrant workers. China's overall economy, while it needs the labor of the rural population, does not need the city-based survival of that population, once demand for rural-to-urban migrants' labor power shifts in either location or emphasis. This newly forming working class is permitted to form no roots in the city. Still worse, the *hukou* system, mixed with labor controls, is the specific modality of power that constructs the ambiguous identity of rural migrant labor and that simultaneously deepens and obscures the economy's exploitation of this huge population. Do the state and the society regard the temporary laborers as workers or as peasants? The difficulty that one faces in responding to this question not only exemplifies the ambiguity that surrounds the status of rural migrant labor but also facilitates industry's appropriation of rural migrant labor and precludes the Chinese state's full recognition of rural migrant labor as labor. Hence, this subtle and multi-faceted marginalization of a vast swath of the labor supply has created a contested, if not a deformed, citizenship that has disadvantaged Chinese migrant workers attempting to transform themselves into urban workers. The term *mingong* ("peasant-workers" or temporary workers) blurs the lines of identity between peasant and worker (Pun, 2005a).

The contention here is that this process of proletarianization got underway when the Chinese socialist state, while it allowed rural migration to meet the needs of global capital and national development, constrained and contained the formation of this new working class. Furthermore, urban governments do not provide housing, education, and other environmental infrastructure to the temporary residents. Migrant workers themselves are not rightful citizens; moreover, the workers' family members are barred from living in the particular industrialized city unless they too can find a job there and acquire the status of temporary worker. Thus, local governments and foreign enterprises that profit from these migrant workers can, at the same time, avoid any welfare-related burdens that would otherwise strengthen the workers. In short, the cost of labor reproduction is borne by the rural society.

To better grasp the extraordinary dislocation at hand here, let us consider this specific feature: migrant labor is distinguished by its transient nature. Normally, a worker, especially a female worker, will spend three to five years working as a wage laborer in an industrial city before getting married. Rural communities have long exercised – and have long been expected to exercise – the extended planning of life activities such as marriage, procreation, and family. As in other developing countries, the process of proletarianization in contemporary China relies heavily on the changing subsistence mode of agricultural production.

The dormitory labor regime

Because official and unofficial structures prohibit this newly formed working class from building its own community in urban areas, the burden of the daily reproduction of labor is left to the factory. This shift in responsibility creates what we refer to as China's "dormitory labor regime," which contributes to a specifically exploitative employment system in the new international division of labor. As millions of migrant workers pour into industrial towns and cities, the provision of dormitories for the accommodation of these workers remains a *systemic* feature of glob-ally producing enterprises. Irrespective of industry, location, or nature of capital, Chinese migrant workers – whether they are male or female, single or married – are accommodated in dormitories within or close to factory compounds in China. We theorize this phenomenon as the "dor-mitory labor regime" to capture the recurrence of dormitory factories as the hybrid outgrowth of both global capitalism and the legacies of state socialism (Pun and Smith, 2005). In light of China's incorporation into global capitalism, I and my colleague aim to examine the dormitory labor system, not only as a form of labor management but also as a platform for labor solidarity, labor resistance, and the emergence of new employment relations. While this use of dormitory labor is specific to the context of contemporary China, its impact on global production especially in terms of labor control and labor resistance is far-reaching.

In China, what is noteworthy in the opening up of the country to global production, starting with the Shenzhen Special Economic Zone in 1981, is the emergence of the provision of dormitories on a systemic basis. The employers' provision to workers of dormitory-themed accommodation has extended to the majority of production workers and is the norm. The existence of China's dormitories is therefore more *systemic* than *contingent*. Moreover, dormitory accommodation in China fits neither the paternalis-tic mold identified in the West nor the "managerial familism" in Japan, nor yet again the firm as a "total institution" of the pre-reform Chinese state enterprise. This is because contemporary China's dormitories house mainly single workers for short-term employment, and hence little accom-modation functions for the long term: the dormitory precludes a pro-tracted relationship between the individual firm and the individual worker. Moreover, the Chinese dormitory labor system applies to com-panies irrespective of product characteristics, seasonality, location speci-ficities, or employer preferences.

Most important, it is not the case in China that the enterprises provide employees with accommodation, using it to buy labor loyalty or to retain scarce skills. Rather, the dormitory labor regime in China ensures princip-ally the short-term capture of single migrant workers, which maximizes the use of labor services during the working day. The ensured "capture" represents a new mode of production – one that accounts for both a spe-cific overabundance of rural labor and the economic integration of China into the global assembly line.

The apparent recurrence of this old form is, in fact, the hybrid outcome of global capitalism and state socialism, reinvigorated through foreign-invested firms and local states in a globalizing economic context. Virtually, all foreign-invested companies use dormitories, whether rented from local authorities or provided privately within the enterprise. Each of these companies aims to capture youthful migrant labor, particularly female workers for short sojourns to the factory. This capture, in turn, creates an infrastructure for sustaining China's precarious employment systems.

Exploitation of labor

As I mentioned, the dormitory labor regime stems from the incorporation of global manufacturing production into China's socialist system, all of which is steeped in the new international division of labor. One characteristic of China's foreign-invested manufacturing plants is the housing of workers in dormitories attached to or close to a factory's enclosed compound. Such dormitories are communal multi-story buildings that house several hundred workers. Rooms are shared, typically between anywhere from eight to 20 workers per room. Washing facilities and toilet facilities are communal and are located between rooms, floors, or whole units, such that living space is intensely collective, with no area, except that within the closed curtains of a worker's bunk, available for limited privacy. But these material conditions do not explain the role of the dormitory as a form of accommodation – as a living-at-work arrangement. Central to the dormitory form is a *political economy* that governs the grouping of typically single, young, female workers. Separated from family, from home, and from routine, these workers concentrate in a workspace and submit to a process of homogenization. And insofar as their connection to the firm is short term and contractual, the alienation of labor derives from significantly more than either labor's deficient ownership of product or labor's deficient control of production skills. Workers in dorms live in a system that alienates them from their past and that replaces a customary setting with factories dominated by unfamiliar others, languages, foods, production methods, and products.

Under the dormitory labor regime, management within the foreign-invested firms appears to have exceptional controls over the workforce. In short, the *dormitory labor regime* operates according to the following seven strategies:

1   An absolute lengthening of the workday: a return to an absolute, not relative, surplus-value production.
2   A suppression of wage-increase demands: an elevated circulation of labor makes it more difficult for workers to engage in collective bargaining, in general, and to demand wage increases, in particular.
3   Easy access to labor power during the workday: a just-in-time labor system for just-in-time production profits quick-delivery order and distribution systems.
4   Daily labor reproduction: control of the reproduction of labor power operates in the factory (accommodation, food, travel, social and leisure pursuits within a production unit).

5   Compression of a "worklife": ten years compress into five years owing to excessive work weeks and to the production-based use of chiefly young workers.
6   Direct control over the labor process: limited formal consensual controls characterize workers' bargaining power, while a system of labor discipline imposes penalties – such as fines for effort bargaining – on workers.
7   State and non-market interventions: external and internal state actions that restrict labor mobility affect the overall labor process.

These specific characteristics of China's dormitory system, and the wider exploitative labor regime of which they are examples, have undermined any pro-labor policies proposed by the central government. In recent years, the central government has instituted new regulations that govern, for example, the minimum wage and working hours. The stated goal underlying these regulations is a unified legal framework for the protection of all workers from inhumane treatment. On May 28, 1993, the Standing Committee of the Shenzhen People's Congress passed *The Regulations on Labor Conditions in the Shenzhen Special Economic Zone* so as to institutionalize the labor recruitment system and to govern labor relations at both the enterprise-level and the city-level.[3] The notable feature of these regulations is the provision of important labor protections, including those concerning minimum wage, work hours, and social insurance for internal migrant workers citywide. However, precisely in the course of these government-initiated labor reforms, at least two broad concerns surfaced: first, labor policies and labor regulations are unevenly implemented at local levels and hence protection for workers is seldom enforced; second, state and collective workers have been hard-hit by economic restructuring, and the phenomenon further exposes the lip-service that government pays to labor. Concurrently, as flows of private and foreign capital increase to coastal cities and to SEZs, pronounced competitiveness has taken hold among TNC factory suppliers and local enterprises, each trying to lower the costs of their just-in-time production while trying to raise the quality of their products. This trend has become especially pronounced since China's accession into the WTO.

In view of the working and living conditions that characterize the rural migrant workers in South China, the Guangdong Federation of Trade Unions (GDFTU) issued an investigative report in 1994, stating that all the 127 surveyed foreign-invested enterprises had violated the national labor laws by imposing excessive working hours on their workers (Sun, 2000:179). The report's findings should not come as a surprise, insofar as Taiwanese-invested enterprises (to draw from only one example) wield a militaristic style of management (Chan, 2001:46–56). Corporal punishment, physical assaults, body searches, and other unlawful labor abuses are commonplace. Factories under South Korean ownership are also notorious for their adoption of harsh labor discipline and management practices: managers beat female workers on the shop floor, force them to publicly kneel down, and the like (Chan, 2001:56–63).

When I compared the current working conditions with the working conditions in the 1990s, I found little improvement. For instance, the past ten years have witnessed persistently low wage levels. Another report released by the GDFTU in January 2005 shows that, in Guangdong, the average monthly wage of 11.6 million peasant workers was only 55 percent of the average monthly wage of state and collective staff and workers. In other words, a majority (or 63.2 percent) of the peasant workers earned between 501 and 1,000 yuan a month. Most alarming was the finding that, despite unprecedented economic growth, the overall 12-year increase of Guangdong's wage level for migrant workers amounted to a mere 68 yuan.[4]

Nevertheless, the minimum wage in Shenzhen used to be the highest among those of all China's cities. The wage level of the Shenzhen SEZ between 1997 and 1998 was 420 yuan, compared to Shanghai City's 315 yuan and to Beijing City's 290 yuan.[5] In Table 5.1, we see the Shenzhen government's annual adjustment of the minimum-wage standards, which covers the period from 2000 to 2006 and which takes into account inflation and the cost of living.

However, production workers in Shenzhen industrial towns often receive basic monthly pay that totals about 400 yuan, far lower than the legal standard. Including overtime payment, the earnings of production workers ranged approximately between 600 and 1000 yuan a month. Deductions for costs such as dormitory rent, water, and electricity, and social insurance could amount to nearly 100 yuan a month. And if no canteen were available, and if a dormitory prohibited cooking, workers had to incur the much higher cost of eating out. Given the combination of pitiful income levels with onerous living expenses, most of the women workers we interviewed, complained about their below-subsistence

Table 5.1 Legal minimum wage of Shenzhen City, 2000–6

Year	Shenzhen SEZ (yuan)	Outside the Shenzhen SEZ (yuan)
2000–1	547	419
2001–2	574	440
2002–3	595	460
2003–4	600	465
2004–5	610	480
2005–6*	690	580

Source: Shenzhen's labor and social security bureau.

Note
* The effective date of the legal minimum wage level was 1 July 2005. In previous years, the adjustment was set on 1 May, International Labor Day.

income, which sometimes results from illegally low wage rates. In recent years, this problem of underpay has triggered collective actions by production workers in South China.

In terms of working hours, the Chinese Labor Law, in effect as of 1 January 1995, stipulates that a five-day workweek should not exceed 40 hours and that overtime work must be limited to a maximum of 36 hours a month. However, almost all the enterprises in South China have failed to observe these regulations, and an average work day often lasts between 12 and 13 hours, six to seven days a week. When the production deadline approaches, management sometimes reduces lunch and rest breaks to merely 30 minutes. To cope with the increasingly just-in-time production schedule, management often requires workers to work nonstop into the morning. In extreme cases, they are forced to work for 48 hours straight. Total working hours in a week can thus add up to between 90 and 110 hours (SACOM 2005). Of course, with demands like these, housing in factory dormitories serves an essential role by ensuring round-the-clock availability of labor power.

Under such work-related pressures, women workers suffer from a variety of occupational illnesses that include menstrual disorders, back pain, headaches, deterioration of eyesight, fatigue, and respiratory problems. The situation is compounded by poor ventilation on the shop floor, which is overwhelmed with toxic chemicals. Weaker female workers sometimes faint at their work station, an occurrence that is especially common during the hot summers. Employers provide no paid sick leave, despite the fact that most employees contribute their share to social insurance – the central insurance fund contributed to by both employers and employees at the city level. Paid maternity leave, also required by law, is likewise a neglected, although basic, benefit.

An examination of collective-bargaining power reveals that almost no trade unions operate in foreign-invested factories or private enterprises, despite the stipulation in Article 10 of the Trade Union Law (2001) that any enterprise with 25 employees or more should establish a *jiceng gonghui weijyuanhui*, or grass-roots trade union committee under the auspices of the All-China Federation of Trade Unions (ACFTU), and despite the stipulation in Article 7 of the Labor Law (1995) that workers shall have the right to join and organize a trade union in accordance with the law. And if an official trade union operates in a workplace, the union's functioning is often confined to entertainment and welfare activities such as the organizing of balls and parties during festival days. My in-depth interviews and everyday discussions with production workers revealed, in fact, that none of them had any idea about the organization and function of trade unions. Should there be strong disagreements with regard to wages and overtime work, workers either turn to their immediate shop floor supervisors for settlement of the issue or quit the job. Collective bargaining through trade unions is unheard of among many production workers.

Community-based labor organizing

It is under this global production context in which precarious employment and infringement of labor rights were prominent in China, that CWWN, a Hong Kong NGO, came into being and rooted its base to the industrial zones of South China. Started by organized women factory workers in Shenzhen, the first SEZ of China, CWWN has no choice but work with local official departments by using a community-based organizing model. Set up in 1996, CWWN stands as a non-profit NGO with the mission of promoting betterment for the lives of Chinese migrant women workers. It endeavors to fight for labor and gender rights, as well as promote grassroots empowerment and social justice in China. Because of the great difficulties of organizing migrant workers at the workplace level, CWWN is rooted in the migrant labor communities and attempts various organizing projects to organize workers outside the traditional trade union model.

The CWWN now operates on several fronts, including ongoing projects launched by the Centre for Women Workers, Women Health Express (WHE), Occupational Health Education Centre in Shenzhen and three industrial towns in the Delta. With an aim to provide comprehensive empowerment programs for Chinese women workers, we conduct training workshops on labor and gender rights for enhancing labor conditions in the workplaces. We also organize cultural and educational activities to enrich their social lives and encourage self-help solidarity. In addition to these continuous projects, we encourage workplace training, research exchanges, and experiences sharing among concerned groups on women workers.

For almost ten years, the pioneering CWWN has sought to empower women migrant workers in Guangdong Province's manufacturing hub, the Pearl River Delta, through diverse grassroots programs dealing with occupational health and safety, labor rights, and gender equality. CWWN has also launched factory dormitory organizing initiatives and founded cooperatives for women workers.

Working quietly but consistently in places where these predominately female migrant workers labor, eat, sleep, shop, and recreate, CWWN has reached out and sunk deep roots into this community of working women.

One of our most successful and unique programs has been CWWN's mobile van project, Women Health Express (WHE), which reaches approximately 3,000 migrant workers each month. The project was launched in view of the grave need to empower China's migrant women workers, and the van was reconstructed from a 17-seat mini bus. It contains a small medical clinic, library, and cultural function center with a television set, VCD, and speakers for educational lectures in open areas. This project is affiliated with the Guangdong Province Prevention and Treatment Centre for Occupational Diseases. WHE began operating in the industrial areas of Pearl River Delta in 8 March 2000; the project reached over 80,000 women workers by the end of March 2002 and served 35,000 migrant workers in 2004.

This van functions as a mobile service centre to disseminate information on occupational health and safety, as well as to train workers to assert their basic rights. First launched in 2000, the van has been promoting CWWN's objectives through education and training, workers' organizing, legal advice, health consultancy, and advocacy. The van is currently operating within three industrial towns in South China, with regular contact hours and venues.

We seek to speed up the integration of local women workers into CWWN programs – particularly the mobile van project – so that mainland organizers and active women workers can assume a more integral role in planning and organizing our projects. Jointly carried out with the Chinese migrant workers in South China, the four major projects of CWWN are:

1   The Centre for Women Workers
2   The Women Health Express – the mobile van project
3   The Concerned Group for Chinese Injured Workers
4   Community Occupational Health Education Centre.

The major problems and concerns of the women workers in the Pearl River Delta can be distilled into three areas.

1   labor rights
2   occupational health and safety
3   women's rights for independence and self-determination.

These become the major areas covered by CWWN. For the daily operation of projects, CWWN have established the following objectives:

- To increase women migrant workers' awareness of community and occupational health and safety issues, especially regarding the prevention of occupational diseases and women's health;
- To provide information and training on labor and employment rights, especially on the regulations concerning occupational health and safety and social insurance;
- To offer basic health services like simple physical examinations and occupational disease referrals;
- To develop mutual aid and concern groups so as to reinforce migrants' awareness of labor rights, occupational health and safety, and women's rights;
- To enrich the social and cultural lives of women workers.

The Centre for Women Workers

The Centre for Women Workers was established in 1996 to provide a platform for organizing Chinese migrant women workers in the SEZ of Shenzhen. Major organizing work includes labor rights education, protection against workplace sexual discrimination, sexual health education as well as training for returned migrants. With accumulating frontline experiences in the past few years, we are determined to form self-organizing networks among migrant women workers in the dormitories. The Centre has developed rapidly into a comprehensive dormitory organizing a workers' training base for the migrant labor in South China.

The Centre offers women workers with interactive programs that tailor to their learning needs. We also train volunteers to organize nearby dormitories and develop mutual support networks. Our work initiatives include running small group discussions on labor rights, reading, handicraft making, movie sharing, photography, singing, drama, and so on. Through these diverse cultural forms, women workers are provided a forum to express themselves and articulate their collective identity as migrant women workers.

With the suggestion made by women workers, in May 2004, CWWN decided to establish the Centre for Women Workers in Bao'an district, a huge industrial hub close to the Shenzhen international airport. The Centre, opened in November 2004, functions as a multi-functional activity room and a training room. In normal times, workers can come here for reading, learning, and making friends. This year, more cultural activities like listening to music, singing, performing drama, and reading books have been included to display the life of women workers as a group. The Centre is favored by many women workers; since its opening, it has accepted 140 members and served for 1,118 person-times. Women workers are very enthusiastic about taking part in the activities held by the new Centre, which is still in its infancy.

As many women workers have to work long hours and could not participate in the Centre, we have to reconsider our organization work in order to reach them at the dormitories. Building up a solid dormitory organizing network becomes one of urgent needs with the aims of offering networking, training, and activities to women workers in the dormitories, and helping them form mutual aid groups among themselves in their dormitories.

Organizational and educational work is developed in the dorm area – primarily among women workers – to promote awareness of labor rights, occupational health and safety, and feminist consciousness. Thus far, we have built up eight dormitory networks. Since dormitory organizing is often carried out in late hours around 11:00 p.m., in order to get in touch with the women workers who have to work overtime at night. Each time the organizers have to divide into small groups with one or two workers working at the visited factories, and this enables the workers to bring the organizers into their factory dormitories. Our method of organizing is diversified. In one factory we usually divide workers into different groups: those who have just come to Shenzhen; those who have worked for half a year; those who enjoy particular recreational programs, and so on. According to their need we have designed different talks and sharing programs. For those who have just come to Shenzhen but work in different factories, we have compiled information on how to get used to the working life in Shenzhen as well as an introduction to the minimum wage in Shenzhen. We also encourage the workers to visit each other and expand their social networks.

For those who already have some social relations in Shenzhen, the organizers would start sharing some experience on how to improve their working conditions. Over the years, there are dormitory network groups which organize women workers and initiate them to communicate their requirements regarding salaries and facilities to the management personnel. In one factory, for example, by signing together, 500 women workers succeeded in asking for an increase in their basic salary and overtime fee, thereby improving working conditions. They also asked for a one-room-one-telephone plan after the factory agreed to install telephones. Furthermore, we also established libraries in four factories and trained volunteers to assist in management. In order to cope with women workers' working time, we have tried to hold trainings in their dorms from time to time.

Mobile van project – the Women Health Express

With the launch of the mobile van project, the Women Health Express, CWWN has attempted to further apply the community-based organizing model in the industrial towns of Pearl River Delta. Three industrial areas – Baocheng, Xixiang, and Fujong – were identified as suitable places for carrying out the mobile van project. The WHE parks at specific spots every Tuesday, Thursday, and Sunday from 5:00 to 10:30 p.m.

During each visit, the van uses exhibition boards, distributes handbills, and sets up a facility for broadcasting group discussions on issues of interest to women workers. Usually, a single topic will be chosen for each session. We have designed handbills on 14 topics and 60 exhibition boards. New leaflets and exhibition boards on topics such as workplace injury, occupational disease, how to handle labor disputes cases, and sexual health will be produced.

There is a book corner (mini library) on the van, with more than 300 copies of books and magazines available for borrowing. This serves as a good resource to enrich women workers' cultural life.

Advice and counseling on labor law issues are offered to women workers in different contexts to assist them in analyzing and resolving problems they are facing. Law students from area law schools, supervised by their faculty, travel great distances to help in this program. We also link up the women workers in need of assistance to the women workers who have overcome similar problems, so that the latter can help the former.

Building up a pool of active and enthusiastic women workers as volunteers for the mobile van is also one of the major purposes. Apart from providing them with a platform for serving other women workers and promoting the van project, this activity also enables women workers from different factories and areas to get to know and support each other. The most active volunteers will be trained as local organizers.

In order to promote women workers' awareness, knowledge, and ability, group discussions are also arranged. The topics include public speaking and communication skills, procedures for conducting simple physical examinations for women, sharing of volunteer experiences, and so on. This primarily targets volunteers, along with active members who have been continuing to borrow books from the van's library for a long period. The group activity usually lasts for 30–60 minutes each time during the service time slots. Women workers seldom take initiative to deal with the problems they encounter, as most were taught to be passive and obedient. The group discussions will help them build up confidence and learn how to present their own ideas, as well as to gain new knowledge on relevant topics.

Social gatherings for volunteers from different service spots are often held on public holidays. Cultural performances, games, competitions, and group discussions are held for the sake of networking the volunteers from different districts and to enrich their social and cultural lives.

The concerned group for Chinese injured workers

Based on the van project, we have trained a team of local organizers in China to help promote the self-organizing of injured workers and advocate public awareness on occupational injuries and diseases in China. Localization is an important agenda for the implementation of this project. We are prepared to learn from the organizing experiences of Hong Kong, Taiwan, and other countries. In the process of localization, we have also networked with many local agents to help support the work of the mobile van. All these localized networks and staff make up the important groundwork for the future development of occupational health and safety rights in China. After providing projects in China for migrant women workers for nearly ten years, our hope is to ensure the empowerment of all migrant workers so that they can work in a healthy, safe, and dignified environment.

Intensive training on legal knowledge and labor organizing has been provided to a group of 12 injured workers in the year 2003–2004, and we finally formed a Concerned Group for Injured Workers by the workers themselves in November 2004. This group makes regular visits to hospitals in the three industrial towns where injured workers with broken arms or deformed bodies are admitted. Most of the workers were neither informed, nor educated about the potential hazards in their working environment, nor aware of the legal rights protection and the entitled compensations. In this regard, with the setting up of this Concerned Group, we hope to ensure the empowerment of migrant workers of their basic labor rights, as well as advocate better occupational health and safety education and protections in China.

The community Occupational Health Education Centre

The Occupational Health Education Centre (OHEC), a project jointly organized with Bao'an Health Department, was set up in September 2004. This Centre strongly believes that education is the best way to prevent occupational diseases and industrial accidents. Our frontline staff operates hot-line consultation services, produces education kits, provides information on occupational health risk assessment, and organizes participatory training workshops for workers at plant level. The goal is to build a training and advocacy center for occupational safety and health in China.

Since there is limited manpower in OHEC, the office time has to be set from afternoon to evening, Sunday to Thursday. Services and activities involve the OSH (Occupation Safety and Health) library, activity room (with a television), consultation, developing support group for fellow workers based on factory, visiting patients, training volunteers, holding Cantonese and English classes (with volunteer tutors), and lending out exercise and recreational equipments. The library is open everyday from afternoon to evening and watched by a volunteer.

So far, the OHEC has developed 31 volunteers, of whom 27 were patients of occupational disease and of whom 14 are still in the hospital. Intensive trainings for volunteers have been held. Main subjects include occupational poisoning and its prevention, labor rights and interests, industry injury rights and interests, current situation of labors in Asian countries, self-recognition, and growth. Through such sets of trainings, volunteers cultivate the capacity for spreading knowledge about OSH as well as labor and industry injury rights and interests among their fellow workers. They also cultivate the capacity for doing duty work, as well as assisting in daily management of OHEC.

In 2005, the Centre took a step forward by setting up a specialized unit of legal support for migrant workers. This unit equips migrant workers with systematic legal knowledge such as protection of labor rights, compensation for injured workers and social securities as stipulated in the Labor Law. Our staff compile relevant policy materials and creates user-friendly training manuals. Audio-visual aids are also employed for educational purposes.

Conclusion

The Chinese Working Women Network (CWWN) is a Hong Kong NGO that has pioneered labor rights advocacy and empowerment for women migrants in Guangdong Province, China, since 1996. It was built from scratch by two members of the staff who experienced labor activists in Hong Kong. We now have three Hong Kong facilitators stationed in Shenzhen and Guangzhou, and ten mainland organizers, all of whom were previously migrant women workers.

As China has become integrated into the global economy, Guangdong Province has rapidly become a "world workshop," providing a huge pool of cheap migrant labor for facilitating global production. More than 120 million peasant-workers have been laboring in the production chains spawned by these TNCs – either in factory owned or joint-ventured by big brand-name American and European companies, or in sweatshops run by their Chinese production contractors and subcontractors. As countless workers are being drawn into this new private industry, old institutions and practices that allowed some measure of industrial democracy in the socialist context have proven ineffectual. New labor laws are not enforced.

In the new post-socialist China, there is little room for grassroots workers' voices or women's empowerment. In spite of new labor laws, government rhetoric about women's rights, and the increase in transnational "codes of conduct," we must report that precarious employment in China still prevails.

However, the young migrant workers who face industrial abuse, injury, and death in the Pearl River Delta are beginning to empower themselves and invoke the rights granted to them on paper by the until-now largely ornamental labor and gender equality laws of China. This trend may prove to be an epochal step toward building civil society and people's voice in mainland China. CWWN's work is aimed at just this target – empowering the grassroots to create demand for workers' rights, particularly among migrant women workers.

Yet, this new rights conscious that is being fostered by CWWN is developing against a backdrop of abuses and hidden costs created by the hastily developed and over-determined global factory chain. With "race to bottom" transnational production strategies adopted by TNCs, labor relations in China are difficult to improve without proper resources and effective strategies.

All in all, CWWN serves an alternative community labor organizing model, outside of trade union system, to fight for labor rights in the export-processing zones of China. It targets at foreign-invested and private companies which rely extensively on the use of internal migrant workers whose basic civil rights and labor rights are seriously violated. In addition to building labor networks through the centre-based organizing and the mobile van project, we also encourage cultural projects to facilitate the migrant workers as a collective to fight for their labor and feminist rights and strengthen workers' solidarity. A Chinese magazine *Voices of Dagongmei* (women workers) is regularly published. A collection of oral stories of migrant women workers is also being compiled to engender common and collective working experience and class consciousness.

"What is the weapon of the weak?" Migrant workers as a collective agent, transcending differences in localities, ethnic origins, gender, age, work positions, and the like, are still capable of empowerment. There is a wide array of strategies and diverse forms of labor organizing which can be distinguished from the conventional trade union organizing model.

Notes

1 See *China Statistical Yearbook*, 2003.
2 The migrant workers who tend to float from one location to another have moved, either in the short term or in the long term, away from their registered place of residence and have done so without a corresponding transfer of *hukou* (the official household registration).
3 *Shenzhen Jingji Tequ Laowugong Tiaoli* [Regulations on Labor Conditions in the Shenzhen Special Economic Zone] (1993) defines *laowugong* (temporary hired labor) as those who work in Shenzhen without local permanent residential household status (Article 2). Hong Kong, Macau, and Taiwan citizens, as well as foreign nationals, working in the Shenzhen SEZ are not governed by the regulations (Article 53).
4 *Yang Cheng Wanbao*, quoted from *Apple Daily*, 22 January 2005.

References

Chan, Anita. 2001. *China's Workers Under Assault: The Exploitation of Labor in a Globalizing Economy*. New York: M.E. Sharpe.

Chan, Anita. 2003. "A 'Race to the Bottom': Globalization and China's Labour Standards." *China Perspectives* 46:41–9.

Chan, Kam Wing and Li Zhang. 1999. "The *Hukou* System and Rural–Urban Migration in China: Processes and Changes." *The China Quarterly* 160:818–55.

Cheng, Tiejun and Mark Selden. 1994. "The Origins and Social Consequences of China's *Hukou* System." *The China Quarterly* 139:644–68.

Dore, Ronald Philip. 1973. *British Factory, Japanese Factory*. London: Allen and Unwin.

Gaetano, Arianne M. and Tamara Jacka (eds) 2004. *On the Move: Women in Rural-to-Urban Migration in Contemporary China*. New York: Columbia University Press.

Honig, Emily. 1986. *Sisters and Strangers: Women in the Shanghai Cotton Mills, 1919–1949*. Stanford: Stanford University Press.

Huang, Ping. 2003. "China's Rural Labor Migrants under Uneven Development." *Social Sciences in China* 24(4):102–17.

Lavely, William. 2001. "First Impressions of the 2000 Census of China." *Population and Development Review* 27(4):755–69.

Lee, Ching Kwan. 1998. *Gender and the South China Miracle: Two Worlds of Factory Women*. Berkeley: University of California Press.

Lee, Ching Kwan. 2003. "Pathways of Labour Insurgency," in *Chinese Society: Change, Conflict and Resistance*, edited by Elizabeth J. Perry and Mark Selden. London: RoutledgeCurzon, pp. 71–92.

Lee, Ching Kwan. 2005. "Livelihood Struggles and Market Reform: (Un)making Chinese Labour after State Socialism." Occasional Paper 2. Available online at: www.unrisd.org, United Nations Research Institute for Social Development.

Liang, Zai and Ma Zhongdong. 2004. "China's Floating Population: New Evidence from the 2000 Census." *Population and Development Review* 30(3):467–88.

Lu, Xiaobo and Perry, Elizabeth (eds). 1997. *Danwei: The Changing Chinese Workplace in Historical and Comparative Perspective*. New York: M.E. Sharpe.

Marglin, Stephen. 1974. "What Do Bosses Do?" *Review of Radical Political Economy* 6:60–112.

Perry, Elizabeth. 1993. *Shanghai on Strike: The Politics of Chinese Labor*. Stanford: Stanford University Press.

Perry, Elizabeth (ed.). 1996. *Putting Class in its Place: Worker Identities in East Asia*. Berkeley: Institute of East Asia Studies, University of California.

Pun, Ngai. 1999. "Becoming *Dagongmei*: The Politics of Identity and Difference in Reform China," *The China Journal* 42:1–19.

Pun, Ngai. 2005a. *Made in China: Women Factory Workers in a Global Workplace*. Durham and Hong Kong: Duke University Press and Hong Kong University Press.

Pun, Ngai. 2005b. "Global Production, Company Codes of Conduct, and Labor Conditions in China: A Case Study of Two Factories," *The China Journal* 54:101–13.

Pun, Ngai and Chris Smith. 2005. "Putting Transnational Labour Process in its Place: Dormitory Labour Regime in Post-Socialist China," a paper presented at the 22nd International Labour Process Conference, 5–7 April 2004, Amsterdam.

SACOM. 2005. "Looking for Mickey Mouse's Conscience: A Survey on Working Conditions of Disney Supplier Factories in China". Available online at: www.sacom.org.hk (accessed on 8 December 2006).

Solinger, Dorothy J. 1999. *Contesting Citizenship in Urban China*. Berkeley: University of California Press.

Sun, Wen-bin. 2000. "Labor Disputes in Shenzhen: The Origin, Pattern and Settlement of Workplace Conflicts," in *Guangdong in the Twenty-first Century: Stagnation or Second Take-off?* Edited by Joseph Y.S. Cheng. Hong Kong: City University of Hong Kong Press, pp. 167–90.

Statistical publications of the People's Republic of China

Guangdong Tongji Nianjian [Guangdong Statistical Yearbook] 2004.

Shenzhen Tongji Nianjian [Shenzhen Statistics Yearbook] 2004.

Zhongguo Laodong he Shehuibaozhang Nianjian [China Labor and Social Security Yearbook] 1994–2004.

Zhongguo Tongji Nianjian [China Statistical Yearbook] 1995–2003.

Labor laws and regulations of the People's Republic of China

Shenzhen Jingji Tequ Laowugong Tiaoli [Regulations on Labor Conditions in the Shenzhen Special Economic Zone] (effective as of 1 October 1993).

Laodong Zhengyi Zhongcai Weiyuanhui Banan Guize [The Regulations on the Handling of Labor Disputes].

Zhonghua Renmin Gongheguo Gonghui Fa [Trade Union Law of the People's Republic of China] (amended and promulgated on 27 October 2001).

Zhonghua Renmin Gongheguo Laodong Fa [Labor Law of the People's Republic of China] (promulgated on 1 January 1995).

Part IV
Cooperatives

6 Waste picker cooperatives in developing countries

Martin Medina

Introduction

Cities in the developing world face two major problems in managing their municipal solid wastes (MSW): insufficient collection and inappropriate disposal. Despite spending 20–50 percent of municipal revenues on the management of MSW, Third World cities collect only a fraction – in many cases less than 50 percent – of MSW generated. Disposal is commonly done by open dumping, often in environmentally sensitive locations such as wetlands and riverbanks.[1] Insufficient collection and inadequate disposal of MSW constitute a source of pollution and pose significant risks to human health and the environment. Due to continuing population growth, urbanization, industrialization, and higher consumption levels, the management of MSW in developing countries is likely to worsen. According to a 2003 UN Habitat report, nearly one billion people live in slums worldwide.[2] If present trends continue, two billion people could be living in slums by 2030. The need for MSW collection in slums in the future, therefore, is likely to put additional strain on cities already unable to serve their current residents.

This chapter analyzes the recycling activities carried out by waste picker cooperatives in developing countries, mostly in Asia and Latin America. The chapter argues that waste picker cooperatives can increase the income of their members, improve their working and living conditions, promote grassroots development, and help improve the management of solid wastes.

Scavenging and appropriate waste management technology

Solutions commonly proposed to the problems of MSW in Third World cities are often centralized, bureaucratic, capital intensive, focused on disposal, and ignore the potential contribution of the informal recycling sector. Industrialized and developing countries differ markedly in terms of income, standard of living, unemployment, consumption patterns, capital available, and institutional capacity. Conventional solutions fail to consider these differences, resulting in less than optimum outcomes.

Experience with the use of compactor trucks, incinerators, material resource facilities (mechanized plants that recover recyclables), and automated composting plants in the Third World has been mostly negative. Despite largely negative experience, over 90 percent of the loans offered by the World Bank for improving the management of MSW in developing countries between 1974 and 1988 were used primarily for purchasing compactor trucks commonly used in the Western world.[3]

The transfer of waste management technology from the developed countries to the developing world is expensive and largely inappropriate for the Third World. Consequently, a new approach is necessary. It can be argued that low-income communities need a radically different approach to the solutions of the developed world: affordable solutions that create jobs, protect the environment, promote community participation, encourage and support the entrepreneurial spirit in the community, and consider the contribution that informal waste pickers can make both to sanitation and to gross domestic product (GDP). Community-based waste management systems take advantage of the creativity and entrepreneurial abilities of individuals who are familiar with their communities. Community-based systems promote investment in locally made collection vehicles and equipment, which are tailored to meet the needs of local conditions. By using locally produced equipment, municipalities do not need foreign currency to acquire imported equipment, which is usually more expensive. Additionally, repair of locally made equipment tends to be easier and cheaper than repairing foreign equipment, because spare parts are readily available. These systems tend to rely on the resources that exist in their communities. Waste pickers can play an important role in community-based waste management systems.[4,5]

Current situation of waste pickers in developing countries

Recycling of MSW in developing countries relies largely on the informal recovery of materials by waste pickers. In cities in developing countries, up to 2 percent of the population survives by scavenging. Waste pickers recover materials to sell for reuse or recycling, as well as for their own consumption.[6,7]

Most studies report that waste pickers constitute the disadvantaged and vulnerable segments of the population. Due to their daily contact with garbage, waste pickers are commonly associated with dirt, disease, and squalor. They are often perceived as a nuisance, a symbol of backwardness, and even as criminals. They survive in a hostile physical and social environment. Scavenging often poses high health risks to the individuals engaged in it. According to a study, waste pickers of Mexico City dumpsite have a life expectancy of 39 years, while the life expectancy of the general population is 67 years.[8] Another study, conducted in Port Said, Egypt, found that the waste picker community had an infant mortality of one-third (one death of an infant under one year out of every three live births), several times higher than the rate for the region as a whole.[9] The prevalence of enteric and parasitic diseases was also higher in the waste picker community than in the region. In Cairo, one in four babies born in the waste picker communities dies before reaching the age of one.[10]

In Manila, more than 35 diseases have been identified in waste picker communities and areas that lack refuse collection and sanitation, including diarrhea, typhoid fever, cholera, dysentery, tuberculosis, anthrax, poliomyelitis, skin disorders, pneumonia, and malaria. The health effects of scavenging on waste pickers deserve careful study. However, serious investigations on this topic are scarce.[11]

Waste pickers' low incomes are often a result of the low prices paid by middlemen. In many cases, middlemen grossly exploit waste pickers. For example, middlemen pay waste pickers in some Colombian, Indian, and Mexican cities as little as 5 percent of the price the middlemen receive for recyclables, see Table 6.1. Thus, opportunities exist for the improvement of living and working conditions of wastepickers by circumventing the middlemen.[12,13]

Scavenging patterns

The recovery of materials by waste pickers in developing countries takes place in a wide variety of settings and can be classified accordingly, as follows:

- Source separation at the household or place generating waste materials: items are reused, sold or given away.[14,15]
- Collection crews sort recyclables while on their collection routes. Open collection vehicles, in particular, offer easy access for the recovery of recyclables from collected mixed wastes. [16,17]
- Informal collectors retrieve recyclables prior to the disposal of the refuse they pick up.[18,19]
- Itinerant buyers purchase source-separated recyclables from residents.[20,21]

Table 6.1 Prices paid for corrugated cardboard along the recovery route

Country	Currency	Price per ton at which		
		Waste picker sells to small merchant	*Small merchant sells to large merchant*	*Large merchant sells to industries*
India	Rupees	100–200	900	1800
Colombia	Pesos (Colombian)	1000	3000	5500
Mexico	Pesos (Mexican)	900	1100	4000

Source: Holmes, J. 1984.

- Waste pickers retrieve materials at the communal storage sites, as well as from commercial and residential containers placed curbside.[22]
- On the streets or public spaces, picking up litter.[23]
- In vacant lots where garbage is dumped as well as in illegal dumps.[24,25]
- In canals and rivers that cross urban areas carrying materials dumped upstream.[26]
- At composting plants.[27]
- At municipal open dumps.[28,29]
- At landfills.[30]

Economic and environmental impact of scavenging activities

Waste pickers are usually perceived as being among the poorest of the poor, and scavenging is considered a marginal activity. Waste pickers tend to have low incomes, but they can obtain decent earnings when they are not exploited by middlemen. The second common perception, which sees scavenging as a marginal activity, is often wrong.

A thorough analysis of the linkages between scavenging and the formal sector has been conducted elsewhere, where it was demonstrated that, for its entire existence, the Mexican paper industry has had backward vertical integration with rag and waste paper collectors. Scavengers, therefore, have never operated in the margins of the Mexican economy.[31]

Despite the lack of data at the national level, various studies have highlighted the economic importance of scavenging activities. In Bangkok, Jakarta, Kanpur, Karachi, and Manila, scavenging saves each city at least US$23 million per year in terms of lower imports of raw materials, and reduced need for collection, transport and disposal equipment, personnel, and facilities. Indonesian waste pickers reduce by one-third the amount of garbage that needs to be collected, transported, and disposed of. In Nuevo Laredo, Mexico, the economic impact of scavenging activities amounted to nearly half a million dollars per month. Waste pickers at the Beijing dump earn three times the monthly salary of university professors. Clearly, scavenging can be a profitable activity when waste pickers are organized and authorities sanction – or at least tolerate – their activities. Scavenging also renders significant environmental benefits: recycling materials saves energy, water and generates less pollution than obtaining virgin materials, see Table 6.2. Further, scavenging reduces the amount of wastes that need to be collected, transported and disposed of, lessening air pollution from fewer dump trucks, and extending the life of dumps and landfills.[32,33] As a result, a strong case can be made that authorities should be supportive of scavengers. However, often public officials consider scavenging to be a problem to be eliminated.

Table 6.2 Environmental benefits from substituting secondary materials for virgin resources (%)

Environmental benefit	Aluminum	Steel	Paper	Glass
Reduction of energy use	90–97	47–74	23–74	4–32
Reduction of air pollution	95	85	74	20
Reduction of water pollution	97	76	35	–
Reduction of mining wastes	–	97	–	80
Reduction of water use	–	40	58	50

Source: Cowles, R., 1986, "Source Separation and Citizen Recycling," in W. Robinson, ed. *The Solid Waste Handbook*. New York: Wiley.

Public policy toward waste pickers

Public policy toward waste pickers in developing countries is often based on the perceptions previously referred to, as well as on the need to minimize the risks to human health and the environment from the handling and disposal of solid wastes. Authorities in developing countries display a wide variety of policies that deal with waste pickers, which can be classified into the following.

Repression

The dominant and prevailing view of scavenging sees it as inhumane, a symbol of backwardness, and a source of embarrassment and shame for the city and/or country. Thus, scavenging is illegal and punishable by law in many Third World cities. Restrictions and a hostile attitude toward waste pickers typify repressive policies.

Neglect

In other cases, authorities simply ignore waste pickers and their operations, leaving them alone, without prosecuting or helping them.[34–36]

Collusion

Government officials sometimes develop relationships of exploitation and of mutual profit and mutual assistance with waste pickers; that is, relationships of political clientelism. Mexico City illustrates a situation of collusion between authorities and waste pickers' leaders. Over the last five decades, a complex structure has developed, involving legal and illegal relationships between waste pickers at the dump, the local bosses known as "caciques", street sweepers, refuse collectors, middlemen, industry, and local authorities. Some of the illegal relationships include the payment of bribes to government officials by the *caciques* for ignoring the *caciques'* abuse of power; the tips that refuse collectors demand from small industries and some households to pick up their waste, and the "sale" of refuse collection routes in wealthy neighborhoods. The *caciques* had close ties with government officials and the PRI (until recently Mexico's long-time ruling party), and the most powerful waste picker boss became deputy representative in the Mexican Congress in the mid-1980s. Waste pickers disguised themselves as peasants and workers in official parades and during PRI and pro-government rallies, and beat up anti-government demonstrators. Thus, the Mexican government got bribes and political support from waste pickers, and waste pickers obtained legitimacy and stability in their operations.[37]

Stimulation

The failure of sophisticated waste management technology in developing countries, as well as environmental awareness, has affected a change of policies toward waste pickers. Recognizing the economic, social, and environmental benefits of scavenging, governments are changing their previous attitude of opposition, indifference or tolerance, to one of active support. Supportive policies range from legalizing scavenging activities, encouraging the formation of waste picker cooperatives (in Indonesia, Brazil, and Argentina), awarding contracts for collection of mixed wastes and/or recyclables (in some Colombian towns), to the forming of public–private partnerships between local authorities and waste pickers (in some Brazilian cities).[38]

Should scavenging be supported?

In many cases policies strive for the elimination of scavenging by enacting bans and by trying to find alternate employment for the waste pickers. Supporting scavenging, particularly the formation of waste picker cooperatives, can result in grassroots development, poverty alleviation, and environmental protection. Repressive, neglectful or collusive policies often have a deleterious impact on waste pickers' working and living conditions. Scavenging in developing countries is caused by chronic poverty, high unemployment, industrial demand for recyclables, and by the lack of a safety net for the poor. None of these factors is likely to disappear in the foreseeable future and scavenging is likely to continue to exist.[39]

Efforts to eliminate scavenging and to encourage waste pickers to engage in other occupations usually fail. Many waste pickers enjoy their occupation because of the money they earn, they do not have a boss, and they have a high degree of flexibility in their working hours. Furthermore, many waste pickers would be unable to find a formal sector job, due to their low educational level, their young or advanced age – many children and older individuals survive by scavenging – and to the difficulty for mothers to perform a paid activity while taking care of their children.

Even if some waste pickers get a different source of income, other poor individuals are likely to replace them, given the widespread poverty and unemployment prevalent in developing countries.[40]

Solid waste management plans and development efforts aimed at eliminating scavenging often worsen waste pickers' standard of living. In Bogota, for example, dumpsite scavenging was common until the late 1980s. After the construction of a sanitary landfill, scavenging was prohibited there. Considered as a success by some, the landfill scavenging ban had a negative impact on waste pickers. It forced them into the streets, where they were forced to contend with the traffic, steer a heavy pushcart, and walk long distances. They had to invest in acquiring pushcarts or horse carts to transport materials; some of them were forced to go into debt in order to purchase a pushcart. Street scavenging requires walking up to eight kilometers a day and sometimes forces wastepickers to sleep on the streets, until they get an acceptable amount of recyclables to sell, before returning to their homes. Since they spend a considerable amount of time walking, their productivity is lower than that of dumpsite waste pickers, and thus the landfill ban lowered their income. Street scavengers also reported being assaulted by street gangs and persecuted by police. In short, the landfill ban had a serious negative impact on waste pickers' income and standard of living. Similar experiences have been observed in other Asian and Latin American cities.[41,42]

Scavenging tends to persist despite efforts to eradicate it. Therefore, a more humane and socially desirable response would help waste pickers achieve a better existence. Supporting waste pickers' efforts to organize themselves, to obtain higher incomes, and to improve their working and living conditions can also make economic and environmental sense.

Formation of waste picker cooperatives

Industries that consume recyclables encourage and support the existence of middlemen between the companies and scavengers in order to assure an adequate volume and quality of the materials. Thus, opportunities arise for the exploitation and/or political control of the waste pickers, since they must sell their pickings to a middleman, who in turn sells to industry. Industry demands a minimum quantity from their suppliers and will not buy materials from individual waste pickers. Additionally, industry usually demands that the materials be clean, baled, crushed, and sorted, processing that the middlemen carry out.

Most Third World waste pickers are poor, given their low incomes and purchasing ability, and their substandard living conditions. Waste pickers are poor largely because of the low prices middlemen pay for the materials they gather. Middlemen usually sell the materials at a high mark up as Table 6.1 illustrates. They often operate in monopsonistic markets (markets where there is only one buyer).

The formation of waste picker cooperatives attempts to circumvent the middlemen and thus pay higher prices to its members. Higher prices, in turn, translate into a higher income and a better standard of living for the waste pickers. Waste pickers can organize themselves in cooperatives in order to bypass the middlemen and break the "vicious circle of poverty." Efforts to promote the creation of waste picker co-ops are common in Asia and Latin America.[43]

Successful waste picker cooperatives in Latin America

Colombia

Colombian waste pickers organized the first national scavenger cooperative movement in the world. The *Fundación Social*, a non-governmental organization (NGO), assisted waste pickers in the formation of cooperatives between 1986 and 2000. Faced with the loss of their livelihoods due to the construction of a new sanitary landfill in the city of Manizales, the foundation helped 150 displaced families to form a cooperative. This effort was successful, and encouraged the foundation to assist waste pickers in other cities also to create cooperatives. In 1991, the *Fundación Social* launched its National Recycling Program, which soon grew to include over 100 waste picker co-ops throughout the country.[44,45]

The foundation awarded grants, loans for specific projects, and provided the co-ops with legal, administrative, and business assistance, as well as free consulting services. In 1998, the foundation donated and made available loans to the co-ops for over US$800,000. With the foundation's support, waste pickers created a national, regional, and local associations of cooperatives. The Bogota Association of Recyclers, for example, represents 24 cooperatives with 4500 members. The National Association of Recyclers provides assistance to any group interested in creating a co-op. The major goals of the association are raising awareness of their problems and how their work benefits society, as well as improving the working and living conditions of Colombian scavengers.[46]

The co-ops represent a wide variety of working conditions: some use pushcarts to transport materials, while others use horse carts or pick up trucks. Some co-ops, such as the *Co-operativa Reciclar* in Cartagena, recover materials at the local dumps. Others follow established routes along city streets, retrieving items from containers placed at the curbside or from materials littered in public places. Still other co-ops take part in source separation programs, collecting recyclables from households, offices, commercial establishments, and small industries, sometimes under formal contracts.[47]

Cooperatives created regional marketing associations, which allow them to sell recyclables at higher prices. Co-op members report a higher standard of living, as well as improvements in empowerment, self-esteem, and self-reliance compared to when they worked individually. Colombian waste pickers recover and sell over 300,000 tons of recyclables each year, mostly paper, glass, scrap metals, plastics, and organics.[48,49]

There are also ten independent cooperatives. *Cooperativa Recuperar*, based in Medellin, is one of the most successful co-ops in Colombia and Latin America. It has over 1000 members, 60 percent of them women. They earn 1.5 times the minimum wage and are affiliated to the Colombian system of socialized medicine. Members can receive loans and scholarships from the co-ops, and can have life insurance and accident insurance. *Recuperar* carries out three types of activities. It offers solid waste services, such as collection of wastes and of source-separated recyclables. The co-op signed a contract with the city of Guarne for collecting, transporting, and disposing of the wastes generated in the town. In 1996, *Recuperar* earned 30 million Colombian pesos and the contract saved the city five million pesos (approximately US$30,000 and 5000, respectively). The co-op operates a materials recovery facility, which recovered 5000 tons of recyclables in 1998. Second, *Recuperar* provides cleaning and gardening services to the local bus terminal, private companies, public spaces, local fairs, and conventions. Third, the co-op offers its members as temporary workers that can be hired by public or private organizations to perform various activities.[50,51]

Brazil

The most dynamic waste picker cooperative movement in the world today exists in Brazil. Brazilian waste pickers, popularly known as "*catadores de lixo*," have formed cooperatives in many cities. In Rio de Janeiro alone, 14 co-ops exist with 2500 members. And in Porto Alegre, waste pickers were incorporated into the city's curbside recycling program, reducing overall costs, and serving 79 percent of the city's 1.1 million residents. Coopamare, one of the most successful waste picker co-ops in Brazil, collects 100 tons of recyclables a month, half of what the recycling program operated by the government in São Paulo collects, and at a lower collection cost. Coopamare members earn US$300 per month, twice the minimum wage in Brazil. By comparison, half of the country's labor force earn less than US$150 a month.[52]

CEMPRE (Compromisso Empresarial para Reciclagem), an industry association, has prepared an educational kit for waste pickers and NGOs to help them in the creation of waste picker co-ops. CEMPRE publishes a monthly newsletter and manages a data bank on solid waste management, as well as a scrap broker hotline that answers questions about recycling. CEMPRE's success has encouraged efforts to create similar programs in Argentina, Costa Rica, Mexico, and Uruguay.[53]

Waste pickers created a national organization, *the Movimento Nacional dos Catadores de Materiais Recicláveis*, with nearly 500 cooperatives and

60,000 individual members. They also have regional associations. The largest and one of the most active is *the Federação das Associações dos Recicladores de Resíduos Sólidos do Rio Grande do Sul* (FARRGS) with 52 cooperatives. The Brazilian Ministry of Environment's National Fund for the Environment actively support cooperatives and provides funding for buildings and equipment for waste picker cooperatives.[54]

Argentina

Even though scavenging has existed in Argentina for over 100 years, in recent years the number of scavengers have increased significantly. The country's 2002 economic crisis caused massive unemployment. The unemployed had few alternatives to make a living. One of those alternatives was scavenging. Consequently, a large number of waste pickers, locally known as *cartoneros*, can be seen on the streets of many cities. In Buenos Aires alone, the number of *cartoneros* has been estimated at 25,000 and the number of people dependent on these activities at 100,000.[55]

The currency devaluation of 2002 made imports – including raw materials – prohibitively expensive. Factories preferred to buy inexpensive waste materials recovered by *cartoneros*. Thus, the economic crisis and unemployment forced people to scavenge, while at the same time provided local manufacturers with a powerful economic incentive for switching to recovered materials. There are currently over 14 *cartonero* cooperatives in Buenos Aires. *Cooperativa El Ceibo*, located in the capital's residential area of Palermo, has received the most attention. The co-op has 102 members, most of them women. They have signed an agreement with the city government to provide services to an area covering 93 city blocks. Co-op members collect recyclables separated by participating residents at their homes. Therefore, the materials are relatively clean and the risks to their health are minimized. Further, source separated materials also command a higher price.[56]

The city of Buenos Aires enacted a law in 2002 legalizing scavenging, recognizing the work of scavengers, and supporting their activities.[57]

Mexico

The *Sociedad Cooperativa de Seleccionadores de Materiales* (SOCOSEMA) that operates in Juarez, on the US–Mexico border across from El Paso, Texas, constitutes one of the most successful waste picker co-ops in Mexico. Today, waste picker cooperative members recover nearly 5 percent of the wastes arriving at the municipal dump: 150 tons of paper, cardboard, glass, rubber, plastics, animal bones, organic material, and metals per day. Until 1975, before the co-op was created, a middleman had a concession to recover the recyclables at the dump, operating in monopsonistic markets, paid low prices for the materials recovered by waste pickers, and, as a result, waste pickers had very low incomes.

In 1975, with the support of the local Mayor and an academic, a cooperative was formed that bypassed the middleman. The impact of the creation of SOCOSEMA was impressive: within a few months after its creation, the incomes of cooperative members increased tenfold. The co-op also receives donations of recyclable materials – largely paper and scrap metal – from the border assembly plants popularly known as "maquiladoras." SOCOSEMA members provide cleaning services to these plants as well for a fee. Co-op members now enjoy higher incomes, participate in training courses and formal education programs sponsored by the co-op, have access to health care and to legal protection. SOCOSEMA has developed good relations with industry, despite initial reluctance to do business with the co-op. Industrial demand for recyclables in Mexico is strong, and the co-op often buys materials from independent waste pickers in order to satisfy the demand.[58]

Over the last few years, the creation of waste picker cooperatives has gained momentum in the region and co-ops have been created in Venezuela, Peru, Ecuador, Guatemala, and Costa Rica.[59]

Successful waste picker co-ops in Asia

Philippines

The formation of waste picker co-ops also has gained impetus in Asia over the last few years. In Manila, the group Women's Balikatan Movement created the Linis Ganda program. In this program, each waste picker – called "Eco aide" – has a fixed route in which he or she purchases source-separated recyclables at households and schools. Eco aides wear green uniforms and use green pushcarts or bicycles. At present, the program includes 897 middlemen organized in 17 cooperatives and approximately 1500 Eco aides. Waste pickers affiliated with the program recover 4000 tons of recyclable materials per month. The typical waste picker earns from US\$5 to \$20 per day, depending on the income level of the community where the Eco aide works. The co-ops can obtain low-interest and collateral-free loans from the Philippine Department of Trade and Industry and from the Land Bank. Linis Ganda plans to start composting operations and biogas recovery from market and slaughterhouse wastes in the near future.[60,61]

India

In Chennai (formerly Madras), EXNORA, an NGO, created a waste collection program in low-income neighborhoods. The program formalized scavenging activities in those areas. Waste pickers were incorporated as waste collectors, or "street beautifiers." Communities obtain loans to purchase tricycle carts to be used as refuse collection vehicles by the street beautifiers. Prior to disposal, the street beautifiers recover the recyclables contained in the collected wastes. Residents pay US$0.30 per month for having their refuse collected. Pick up fees are used to pay back the loans and to pay the street beautifiers' salaries. Today in Chennai, about 900 collection units involving waste pickers exist in slums, as well as in middle- and upper-income neighborhoods. The program has improved public perception of waste picker activities, raised their earnings, reduced littering, increased refuse collection, and contributed to a cleaner urban environment. In the city of Pune, approximately 6000 "rag pickers" formed a cooperative, which in 1995 recycled 25 percent of the waste generated by the city's one million residents.[62] In 2005, SWACHH, the Alliance of Waste pickers in India, was created in order to bring together Indian waste pickers and work to improve their working and living conditions.[63]

Indonesia

Unlike the previous cases that involve industry and NGOs, Indonesia has enacted national legislation in support of waste pickers. In 1992, the then president Suharto declared that waste pickers were beneficial to the country's economy and environment. Now the central government supports the formation of cooperatives of dumpsite and street waste pickers. Private banks have granted loans to waste picker co-ops, and the national government has imposed a duty on imported waste materials, in an effort to encourage the use of recycled materials and increase waste pickers' income.[64]

Lessons learned

How cooperatives work

Scavenger cooperatives must comply with all applicable laws. Many countries have regulations that apply specifically to cooperatives that are different from business regulations. Regulations vary from country to country, but they usually stipulate the required number of members, a minimum working capital, and governance. Cooperatives are commonly seen as a way for individuals to get ahead collectively, to accomplish goals that would be hard to achieve individually. Cooperatives are based on the principles of self-reliance, empowerment, active participation, equality, and democratic governance. These principles are particularly important for waste pickers, given their traditional low status and marginalization by society. However, waste picker cooperatives face both internal and external threats to their existence and success. Internally, their own low educational level, lack of business expertise, cheating and unscrupulous leaders can undermine and ultimately cause the demise of cooperatives. External threats include retaliation from middlemen, industry's reluctance to do business with them, and most importantly, opposition from the authorities, as well as unsupportive public policies.

External support needed

Given the many threats scavenger co-ops have to cope with, external assistance is crucial. In many countries, NGOs have played a critical role assisting in the formation and operation of waste picker cooperatives. Their energy, creativity and familiarity with the local conditions allow NGOs to develop initiatives that have a good chance of succeeding. They can help co-ops obtain loans and grants, or furnish the credit themselves. NGOs also provide essential technical, business and legal assistance to the co-ops.

Newly constituted co-ops are particularly vulnerable, considering that they may have to deal with opposition from the middlemen being displaced. Industry may be reluctant to have their usual supply channels disrupted. And the authorities may covertly hinder the efforts to create a new waste picker co-op if a patron–client relationship exists between particular government officials and the waste pickers.

Timing in the formation of a cooperative

The timing in which a co-op is formed can contribute to its success. A window of opportunity appears during changes of administration, particularly at the local level. A new Mayor, especially a member of a different political party than his/her predecessor, may be more inclined to support a recently formed waste picker co-op in order to demonstrate his/her commitment to the poor and in favor of change. Such an action could improve the Mayor's image, while scoring political points. A mass media campaign, showing the waste pickers' plight, their harsh working and living conditions, as well as the benefits the community receives from their work, may increase public support. Further, a grassroots information campaign can also be conducted among community leaders, schools, and neighborhood associations. This approach has been successful in several Colombian cities.

Threats and opportunities posed by privatization programs

Many cities have privatized, or are in the process of privatizing municipal solid waste management (MSWM) services. This presents both risks and opportunities for waste pickers. Private companies usually do not allow scavenging activities in the dumps/landfills they operate. As sanitary landfills replace open dumps, waste pickers are forced to collect materials on the streets instead. As previously discussed, this can have serious negative impacts on their earnings and standard of living.

However, privatization can provide opportunities for waste picker co-ops. The co-ops can provide services such as collection of mixed wastes/recyclables, street sweeping, composting, and recycling plants. Incorporating waste pickers into formal MSWM programs and awarding contracts to waste picker cooperatives can save cities money while providing a steady income to waste pickers.

Conclusions

Scavenging represents an important survival strategy for hundreds of thousands of poor individuals in developing countries. Scavenging occurs in quite different socio-economic, cultural, and religious settings throughout the developing world, but distinct patterns do exist. Waste pickers are usually poor immigrants from rural areas. The recovery of materials takes place in a wide variety of conditions, from open dumps to garbage floating in canals and rivers. Waste pickers respond to market demand and not to environmental considerations. The underlying factors that cause people to become waste pickers are the poverty resulting form underdevelopment, the inability or unwillingness of individuals to obtain other forms of employment, as well as industrial demand for inexpensive raw materials.

Authorities, development banks, and bilateral development agencies usually do not recognize the social, economic, and environmental benefits of scavenging. Consequently, scavenging is often ignored when designing solid waste management (SWM) policies and plans. Alternatively, when scavenging is considered in SWM plans, one of the objectives is usually its elimination. As long as poverty and industrial demand for materials persist, scavenging is likely to continue to exist. Official efforts to eradicate scavenging have not succeeded and have caused further deterioration in the working and living conditions of waste pickers.

Middlemen perform useful services to industry by sorting and processing of recovered materials, accumulating and selling them in the amounts that industry demands. But middlemen often exploit waste pickers. The formation of waste picker cooperatives can bypass the middlemen and increase waste picker earnings.

Non-governmental organizations can play an important role in organizing waste pickers and in helping them, particularly in the formative and initial stages of their operations. Development banks and other development agencies should actively support scavenging activities in their lending and donor assistance. Waste picker co-ops can achieve a better standard of living for their members, dignify their occupations, and strengthen their bargaining power with industry and authorities. Equally important for a co-op is the support of the local authorities, who can legitimize their activities, award concessions or contracts for the provision of SWM services. Industry can also facilitate waste picker co-ops' activities by purchasing materials from the co-ops, or even taking a more active role supporting the formation of waste picker co-ops, as CEMPRE does in Brazil. Some of the most successful waste picker co-ops in Latin America – *Recuperar* in Colombia and SOCOSEMA in Mexico – have learned that diversification can increase their earnings. Both co-ops also provide cleaning services to cities and private industry. Other successful co-ops add value to the recyclables they gather, by processing the materials and engaging in the production of salable items such as hoses and compost.

Waste pickers can be successfully integrated into formal SWM programs for the collection and recycling of solid wastes, as several cases in Asia and Latin America demonstrate. By supporting waste picker cooperatives, refuse collection could be extended at a low cost, creating jobs, and benefiting low-income communities. Instead of being a problem, waste pickers can be part of the solution to the seemingly intractable problem of collection and disposal of solid wastes in developing countries. Waste picker cooperatives can promote grassroots development in an economically viable, socially desirable, and environmentally sound manner. When supported, scavenging can represent a perfect example of sustainable development.

Notes

1 S. Cointreau, *Private Sector Participation in Municipal Solid Waste Services in Developing Countries*, Urban Management Programme Discussion Paper, No. 13. Washington, DC: The World Bank, 1994.
2 UN Habitat, *The Challenge of Slums: Global Report on Human Settlements 2003*. London: Earthscan, 2003.
3 C. Bartone and C. Oliverira, "A Unit Cost Model for Solid Waste Collection," *Urban Note*, No. UE-1. Washington, DC: Infrastructure and Urban Development Department, The World Bank, 1992.
4 S. Cointreau, *Environmental Management of Solid Wastes in Developing Countries*. Washington, DC: The World Bank, 1983.
5 M. Medina, *Informal Recycling and Collection of Solid Wastes in Developing Countries: Issues and Opportunities*. Tokyo: United Nations University/Institute of Advanced Studies Working Paper No. 24, 1997.
6 C. Bartone, "The Value in Wastes," *Decade Watch*, 1988, 3–4.
7 Medina, *Informal Recycling*, pp. 2–7.
8 H. Castillo, *La Sociedad de la Basura: Caciquismo Urbano en la Ciudad de México*, Second Edition. Mexico City: UNAM, 1990.
9 T. Semb, "Solid Waste Management Plan for the Suez Canal Region, Egypt," in K. Thome-Kozmiensky (ed.) *Recycling in Developing Countries*. Berlin: Freitag, 1982: pp. 77–81.
10 G. Meyer, "Waste Recycling as a Livelihood in the Informal Sector – The Example of Refuse Collectors in Cairo," *Applied Geography and Development*, 1987; 30: 78–94.
11 B. Adan, V. Cruz and M. Palaypay, *Scavenging in Metro Manila*, Manila, Philippines: Report Prepared for Task 11, 1982.
12 J. Holmes, "Solid Waste Management Decisions in Developing Countries," in J. Holmes (ed.) *Managing Solid Wastes in Developing Countries*. New York: John Wiley & Sons, 1984.
13 Medina, *Informal Recycling*, pp. 2–7.

14 M. Medina, "Recovery of Recyclables in Mexico City," *Urban Issues.* New Haven: Urban Resources Institute, 1992: 17–18.

15 K. Kresse and J. Ringeltaube, "How Resource Recovery and Appropriate Technologies Can Cut Costs of Waste Management in Developing Countries," in J. Thome-Kosmienzky (ed.) *Recycling in Developing Countries.* Berlin: Freitag, 1982: 34–47.

16 Castillo, *La Sociedad de la Basura*, pp. 59–67.

17 J. Gonzalez, M. Cadena and M. Suremain, *Estudio Sobre los Circuitos de Reciclaje de Desechos Sólidos en la Ciudad de Bogotá.* Bogota: ENDA America Latina, 1993: 45–67.

18 Meyer, *Waste Recycling as a Livelihood*, 78–94.

19 Medina, *Informal Recycling*, pp. 2–7.

20 C. Furedy, "Resource-Conserving Traditions and Waste Disposal: The Garbage Farms and Sewage-Fed Fisheries of Calcutta," *Conservation & Recycling*, 1984; 7: 181–90.

21 B. Lohani and J. Baldisimo, "Foille et tri à Manille," *Environnement Africain* Dakar, Senegal, 1990, 181–90.

22 E. Ouano, "Developing Appropriate Technology for Solid Waste Management in Developing Countries: Metro Manila Pilot as a Case Study," *International Expert Group Seminar on Policy Responses Towards Improving Solid Waste Management in Asian Metropolises*, Bandung, Indonesia, February 4–8, 1991, p. 13.

23 C. Chapin, "The Rag-pickers of Pune," *The UNESCO Courier.* March, 1995: 18–19.

24 J. Vogler, "Waste Recycling in Developing Countries: A Review of the Social, Technological, and Market Forces," in J. Holmes, (ed.) *Managing Solid Wastes in Developing Countries.* New York: John Wiley & Sons, 1984: 244.

25 G. Mendoza, *Contaminación por Desechos Sólidos en el D.F.*, Mexico City: IPN, 1983: 78.

26 R. Abad, "Squatting and Scavenging in Smokey Mountain," Ateneo de Manila: *Philippine Studies*, 1991; 39: 267–85.

27 Vogler, *Waste Recycling in Developing Countries*, p. 244.

28 Medina, *Informal Recycling*, pp. 2–14.

29 Furedy, *Resource-Conserving Traditions*, pp. 181–90.

30 S. Cointreau and M. de Kaadt, "Living with Garbage: Cities Learn to Recycle," *Development Forum*, January–February, 1991: 12–13.

31 M. Medina, *Scavenging on the Border: A Study of the Informal Recycling Sector in Laredo, Texas, and Nuevo Laredo, Mexico*, PhD Dissertation, Yale University, 1997.

32 J. Baldisimo, "Scavenging of Municipal Solid Waste in Bangkok, Jakarta and Manila," *Environmental Sanitation Reviews* No. 26. Bangkok: Asian Institute of Technology, 1988.

33 Medina, *Scavenging on the Border*, pp. 271–5.

34 E. Waas and O. Diop, "Economie Populaire du Recyclage des Déchets à Dakar," *Environnement Africain*, 1990: 105–28.

35 S. Diallo and Y. Coulibaly, "Les Déchets Urbains en Milieu Démuni à Bamako," *Environnement Africain*, 1990: 159–76.

36 F. Tonon, "Gestion des Ordures Ménageres à Cotonou," *Environnement Africain*, 1990: 79–92.

37 Castillo, *La Sociedad de la Basura*, pp. 75–99; 141–89.

38 M. Medina, *The World's Scavengers: Salvaging for Sustainable Consumption and Production.* Lanham, MD: AltaMira Press, 2007.

39 Medina, *Scavenging on the Border*, pp. 287–301.

40 Ibid.

41 Gonzalez, Cadena and Suremain, *Estudio Sobre los Circuitos de Reciclaje*, pp. 45–67.

42 Medina, *Scavenging on the Border*, pp. 287–301.
43 Fundación Social, *Memorias del Primer Encuentro Nacional de Recicladores*. Bogota: Fundación Social-Programa Nacional de Reciclaje, 1990.
44 M. Medina, "Supporting Scavenger Coops in Colombia," *BioCycle*, June, 1997: 45–7.
45 Fundación Social, *Tecnología, Diseño Industrial y Factores Humanos en el Reciclaje de Basuras*. Bogota: Fundación Social-Programa Nacional de Reciclaje, 1991.
46 M. Medina, "Supporting Scavenger Coops in Colombia," *BioCycle*, June, 1997: 45–7.
47 *Ibid.*
48 Fundación Social, *Memorias del Primer Encuentro Nacional de Recicladores*. Bogota: Fundación Social-Programa Nacional de Reciclaje, 1990.
49 M. Medina, "Supporting Scavenger Coops in Colombia," *BioCycle*, June, 1997: 45–7.
50 G. Jaramillo, "Cooperativa Recuperar: De Basuriegos a Empresarios," *Trabajando Con Desechos: Experiencias Colombianas*. Bogota: Fondo Rotatorio Editorial, 1991.
51 M. Medina, "Scavenger Cooperatives in Developing Countries," *BioCycle*, June, 1998: 70–2.
52 C. Wells, "Managing Solid Wastes in Brazil," *BioCycle*. June, 1995: 53.
53 *Ibid.*
54 Medina, *The World's Scavengers*, 2007.
55 F. Suarez, *Actores Sociales de la Gestión de Residuos Sólidos de los Municipios de Malvinas Argentinas y José C. Paz*, Master's Thesis, Buenos Aires, Argentina: Universidad Nacional, March 2001.
56 C. Reynals, *De Cartoneros a Recuperadores Urbanos*. Buenos Aires, Argentina: Unpublished paper, 2002.
57 Available online at: www.buenosaires.gov.ar/areas/med_ambiente/pru/ley.php (accessed 8 December 2005).
58 Anon, *La Basura y el Medio Ambiente*. Mexico: Premio Serfin al Medio Ambiente. Mexico City: unpublished, 1982.
59 M. Medina, "Scavenger Cooperatives in Developing Countries," *BioCycle*, June, 1998: 70–2.
60 M. Medina, "Collecting Recyclables in Metro Manila," *BioCycle*, June, 1993: 51–3.
61 M. Medina, "Scavenger Cooperatives in Developing Countries," *BioCycle*, June, 1998: 70–2.
62 *Ibid.*
63 Available online at: www.karmayog.com/cleanliness/smseep.htm (8 December 2005).
64 Anon, photo and caption, *The Jakarta Post*, 24 September 1992: 3.

7 Co-operatives and the emancipation of the marginalized

Case studies from two cities in India

Sharit K. Bhowmik

This chapter attempts to examine the role of co-operatives in empowering marginalised sections of the working class. We shall illustrate this with the help of two studies in two different metropolises in India. These are Ahmedabad in Western India and Calcutta (now renamed 'Kolkata') in Eastern India. We will discuss co-operatives formed by waste pickers in Ahmedabad and worker co-operatives in Calcutta. These cases show how marginalised workers of society try to protect their right to gainful employment through collective action.

The process of globalisation through structural adjustment has adversely affected the working class throughout the world. Labour in most developing countries has suffered because restructuring of industry has invariably led to unemployment due to closure of 'unprofitable' industrial units. In India, the Industrial Policy Statement placed before Parliament on 24 July 1991 was in tune with the global process of structural adjustment. This policy is in contrast to the earlier policies in the sense that it openly favours privatisation of industry and trade. It also shows some interest in encouraging worker take-overs. Paragaph 16 of the Industrial Policy Statement reads: 'Workers' participation in management will be promoted. Workers' co-operatives will be encouraged to participate in packages designed to turn around sick companies.' So far this appears as lip-service as the government has taken no step to encourage such co-operatives.

At the same time there are a number of co-operatives that have emerged through the workers' struggle to maintain employment and production. There are some instances of worker co-operatives in tea plantations, mines, and industrial units. The workers of Sonali Tea Estate, a tea plantation employing around 500 workers in the Jalpaiguri district in the state of West Bengal, established the first worker co-operative in the tea industry in 1974. In Tripura, a state in North Eastern India, five tea plantations are being successfully managed by their workers since the early 1980s (Bhowmik 1992). In Dalli Rajhara, near the Bhilai Steel Plant in the state of Chattisgarh in Central India, there are six worker co-operatives operating in the open cast-iron ore mines (Bhowmik 1994). In Calcutta, the capital of the state of West Bengal, there are at least 20 industrial units that are managed by worker co-operatives since the early 1980s. All these co-operatives are surviving with very little or no financial assistance from the government. The fact that these co-operatives have survived for nearly two decades or more without external assistance is itself a measure of their success. We have tried to examine some of these co-operatives in this chapter.

Along with the unemployed, due to closure of industries there are growing numbers of people who come to the urban areas, especially the metropolises, in search of work. These people are driven from the rural areas or from small towns due to lack of any form of livelihood. They have little skills to enable them to compete in the labour market and they search for work in any form to keep off the pangs of hunger. These are the lowest types of the self-employed and they form the bulk of the urban poor. Yet, we can see, as in the case of female waste pickers in Ahmedabad, that they too can improve their living conditions through collective action.

Waste pickers in Ahmedabad[1]

Every metropolis has a section of its population that makes a living by recycling waste. These people are ascribed the lowest status among the urban poor and are also economically, the poorest among the poor. A large section of these waste pickers are women and children. They roam the streets on foot, searching for waste, which they put inside the sacks that they carry. They leave their homes at dawn, walking several kilometres each day so that they can complete their collection by late afternoon. Their work tools comprise a collection bag and a rod to prod and poke through garbage. In their work they are subjected to a number of hazards. They get cuts and bruises from sharp objects and broken pieces of glass or they get skin allergies from the waste chemicals in the garbage. After they finish their collections for the day, they sort out the materials and then sell these to traders. The rates they receive for their collection are very low and these people live on the brink of poverty.

These waste pickers are in fact serving the needs of the city because while working for their livelihood they are cleaning the streets of garbage. Unfortunately, the police and the municipal authorities do not look at them in this manner. They are harassed by the urban authorities and they face frequent threats and even beatings from these officials. The better-off sections in the city regard them as a public nuisance and frequently lodge complaints on them.

The city of Ahmedabad is the capital of Gujarat, one of the prosperous states in the country. This city had a number of large industries but it was especially known as a centre for textile production. The scenario is very different now. Since the past 15 years or so, most of the city's textile mills are being closed, rendering a large number of workers jobless. Many of the wives and children of these workers have been forced to 'take to the streets for waste collection' (SEWA 1999: 56). Like all other large cities, Ahmedabad too has a number of waste pickers who depend on recycling for their existence. Since the past 25 years, the Self-Employed Women's Association (SEWA), based in Ahmedabad, has been organising women waste pickers in the city as one of its activities (ibid.). We shall examine some of the activities of this union in helping this section of the working class.

Origins of SEWA

The origins of SEWA were in the Textile Labour Association (TLA). TLA was started by Mahatma Gandhi in 1918 and later became the main trade union of textile workers in Ahmedabad. In 1968, TLA decided to start a Women's Wing of the union and invited Ela Bhatt to look after it (Rose 1995: 41). The main activity of this wing was to impart training programmes for developing skills of poor women so that they could earn a livelihood. Skill development mainly meant teaching the women sewing on machines, encouraging them to take up activities such as block printing of cloth and garments, dyeing of clothes and so on. Its work was more in the nature of social service. After engaging in these activities for some time the organisers found that the type of activities they were engaged in could only provide partial relief to these marginalised women. What they needed was an organisation that could unite them to collectively fight for their basic rights such as minimum wages, health, education, and so on.

In 1972 the Women's Wing decided to convert itself into a trade union under the Trade Union Act of 1926. This was easier said than done. Though the working women were convinced that they could form a trade union, the Registrar of Trade Unions thought otherwise. The main objection was that there was no relation between employer and employee in an association of the self-employed. It took ten months to convince the Registrar that such an association could well be a trade union (Bhatt 1997: 214). At present, SEWA with its total membership of over 500,000, is the largest registered trade union in the state. Initially SEWA had close links with TLA but these were snapped in 1981.

Besides organising self-employed women workers through trade unions, SEWA promotes co-operatives among its members to cover a variety of services and helps in providing alternative employment opportunities. In 2000, SEWA had sponsored more than 80 such co-operatives covering a wide variety of areas. These include industrial and producer co-operatives and service co-operatives. After forming a co-operative, the union assists its members in developing financial and managerial skills. It organises adult education classes for these women, where, besides learning to read and write, the women are taught about accounts, the objectives of co-operatives among other topics. These activities help in empowering the members to manage their co-operatives through their own resources rather than depend on outsiders.

Unionising waste pickers

One of the first activities of SEWA as a trade union was that of organising waste pickers in the city. SEWA unionised these women so that they could be protected from harassment by the civic authorities. The union provided its members aprons, gloves, shoes, and bags for waste collection. It collected donations initially in order to provide these articles. The aprons and bags are blue in colour and they have SEWA written on them in bold white letters. These essentially become their identity as union members, though they carry their union cards as well. After forming the union, the waste pickers are harassed less often. They are allowed access into several streets where they had been prevented earlier. Their identity as members of SEWA is mainly responsible for this change in people's attitude as they are now seen as a part of a collective.

Harassment and prevention from carrying out their activities are not the only forms of exploitation these workers face. The traders they sell their daily collection to, exploit them by paying them very low prices. The women are very poor and they accept whatever prices the traders pay them, as this is the sole means of subsistence for them and their families. There is no way they can bargain with the traders for better prices; if the trader refuses to accept their goods, they will starve that day.

The union activists of SEWA studied the waste recycling market and found that the demand for waste paper fluctuated over the year. It increased in some part of the year and decreased at other times. The traders increased their profits by storing the waste paper when demand was low and selling them when demand was high. After studying the market fluctuations, the union activists found that the women could get almost double the price when the demand was high. However, these women had neither the space for storing their pickings nor did they have the ability to store their goods over a period of time. Their economic conditions compelled them to sell whatever they had collected each day.

Then, SEWA decided to start a storehouse for keeping the daily collection of these women. They would be paid daily at a fixed rate for their collections. These would be sold through auctions when prices increased. Any profit made from the sale would be distributed among these women as bonus. The union set up the storehouse and all members are eligible to sell their collection daily and they are paid in cash. This scheme proved a success and soon more such storehouses have been set up in other parts of the city.

Co-operatives as alternative employment

The next step the union took was finding alternative employment opportunities or regular earnings for these women. If a section of them could be provided with other types of work then the income of the remaining would increase, as their collections would go up. These new activities could be undertaken by forming co-operatives among the women.

In 1983, SEWA initiated the formation of a co-operative that would take up contracts for cleaning offices and collecting waste paper from them. This co-operative was called Saundariya Mahila SEWA Co-operative. At present, this co-operative has around 500 members. It has contracts for cleaning a number of large offices, academic institutions, and other public buildings. Alongside, the co-operative takes up contracts for removing waste paper from offices. It was able to get contracts from some of the municipal and state government offices for collection of waste paper. The co-operative pays these offices a fixed amount for allowing it to collect the waste paper.

Around 200 members of the co-operative are engaged in these activities. These members get a regular wage for their work. The profits of the co-operative are distributed among all its members. Of late, the co-operative had to face some problems because the state government did not renew its contract for waste paper collection from its offices in 1999. This point is mentioned in SEWA's annual report for 1999. The report also states that Saundariya co-operative was optimistic of renewing its contract with the government offices in the near future. This has been done after the union and the co-operative collectively convinced the higher officers of the state government that the arrangement was mutually beneficial.

Some of the waste pickers were quite skilled at cooking different types of food. The union tried to help them develop their skills so that they could start a commercial venture. In mid-1992, a group of these women started supplying food to the government-sponsored Integrated Child Development Scheme (ICDS). This scheme was started to help the poor in urban and rural areas. The ICDS provides training to pre-school going children. These children are provided a meal at noon.

The group started undertaking contracts for catering food at functions. In 1994, the group formed a co-operative named Trupti Nasta Mahila SEWA Co-operative Society. The co-operative has 130 members, all of whom are former waste pickers. The members undertake contracts for supplying and serving food at weddings, public functions, and other events. At times they are contracted to only serve the food or prepare desserts at these functions. Besides these activities, the co-operative has got contracts to open canteens and tea stalls at offices.

The co-operative organises training programmes for its members on various aspects of food management including nutrition. It also holds programmes on co-operation, education, and literacy. *Trupti Nasta* is one of the more successful co-operative ventures sponsored by SEWA. It has been making profits as its clients appreciate the food it prepares, because it is tasty, comparatively less expensive, and served properly. The co-operative used to operate from the headquarters of SEWA in Ahmedabad. It has now bought its own work space in the city (SEWA 1999: 60).

A number of part-time economic activities for women waste pickers have been organised by SEWA in order to increase their earnings. A section of its members are engaged in shelling peas and pulses in the mornings and they pick paper in the afternoons. Another group of women are engaged in making paper bags and paper stationery.

The success of the two co-operatives of waste pickers in Ahmedabad is mainly due to their strong ties with their trade union, namely, SEWA. First, the union has helped them gain their self-respect as self-employed workers. Second, the members have been able to create alternative employment schemes through co-operatives, which has, in fact, increased their choices.

It may be noted that society in India is ridden with social groups that are ranked on the basis of hierarchy. These are known as castes. Incidentally, the word caste owes its origin to the Portuguese word Casta. Membership of a caste is based on one's birth and as such, one's position in the caste hierarchy is fixed on the basis of the status of the caste one is born into. Hence, even if occupational status of an individual changes one's social status remains unchanged. The waste pickers in most cases belong to castes that are ranked low. The nature of their work, which involves picking recyclable waste from the streets and from garbage bins, is regarded as an unclean occupation by the upper castes. These people perform these activities because they are very poor and they have no other means of subsistence. Hence, they are both socially and economically oppressed and are treated as outcastes among the city dwellers.

Formation of co-operatives has helped these women improve their conditions but the crucial factor is that these are linked with their trade union. The impetus for improving their working conditions came through collective action, after they unionised themselves. This gave them confidence in their own abilities. They were able to enhance their development through co-operatives. Hence we can see that the interlinking of trade unions with co-operatives can become an effective measure for emancipation of the poor and the socially oppressed.

Let us now turn to another type of co-operative and examine how they have contributed to the emancipation of another section of the working class. In the next section, we shall examine the functioning of worker co-operatives in the city of Calcutta.

Worker co-operatives in Calcutta[2]

Calcutta was once a vibrant industrial metropolis famous for its jute mills and engineering factories. Since the late 1960s, the scenario changed sharply. The city witnessed closing of a number of large industrial units. During the 1980s, around 1500 industrial units ceased to function. This made 1,580,000 workers employed in these units redundant. Several more industries are on the verge of closure.

In the midst of this depressing scenario one finds a flicker of hope in the fairly large number of worker co-operatives that exist here. We have identified around 20 such units in and around Calcutta. These are mainly small-scale or medium-scale industries having between 20 and a little over 100 workers each. We shall take up three of these co-operatives for our study.

It is necessary to note some of the features of these cases in order to have a general background. Calcutta is the capital of the state of West Bengal, situated in Eastern India. The state is governed by a coalition of communist and leftist political parties known as the Left Front. The largest, and dominant political party in this coalition is the Communist Party of India (Marxist), CPI(M). This coalition was elected in the elections in 1977 and has continued to be voted into power up to the present (January 2007). The major trade union in the state is the Centre for Indian Trade Unions, CITU, which is regarded as the trade union wing of CPI(M). Trade unions in all the worker co-operatives in Calcutta, including the four cases in this chapter, are affiliated to CITU.

The four co-operatives have been selected after surveying 18 of the existing co-operatives (two of the co-operatives had ceased to function). These include a ship-building unit, a unit manufacturing printing equipment, and a unit manufacturing aluminium cables and electric conductors. Each of these units was functioning very well at one time and was regarded the best in their respective areas of production. We have tried to examine the reasons for the downslide of these companies and how the employees had tried to revive them.

Ship-building co-operative

Situated in the Cossipore area of Calcutta, the East Bengal River Steam Service and Engineering Workers' Industrial Co-operative Society Limited was formed in 1979. The original company was an old enterprise, which originated in the late nineteenth century. It ran a successful shipping enterprise and later started shipbuilding as one of its major activities. From 1965, the company showed a downward slide movement due to various reasons. Some were external factors, relating mainly to its restriction in business with the erstwhile East Pakistan (now Bangladesh) and others concerned with the internal management of the company. It managed to pull along until 1969. Its balance sheet of 1968–69 showed a profit. After that the company started making heavy losses. In September 1976, the owners shut down the company, as its debts were insurmountable. Its labour force, which was once over 1000, was reduced to 91 as most workers left to find other work. Its debtors had filed cases for recovery in the High Court of Calcutta.

After the Left Front was voted into power, the union proposed to the state government that it should declare the company as sick and take over its management. The state government sent a proposal to the central government in 1978 for take-over of the company, but the central government rejected the proposal. The workers' union then requested the state government that they be permitted to run the company. This was accepted, and the state government advised that the workers should form a co-operative so that they could manage the company. The state government's Department of Industrial Reconstruction would help in financing the venture.

The co-operative was registered in November 1979. All 91 workers became its members. The local leaders of the CPI(M) and the CITU assisted the workers in their venture. The secretary of the local committee of the CPI(M) has been the main supporter of this venture. The state government had conceded to the union's proposal mainly because the union was affiliated to CITU and because of the political support of the CPI(M).

Based on the assurance of the state government, the co-operative appealed to the High Court that it be permitted to buy the company. The court agreed to this and ordered that an official assess the company's worth. The price was thus fixed and the co-operative took possession of the company on 30 October 1980. The sale deed was executed in 1981. The state government agreed to provide a loan to the co-operative for buying the company. Production was started in December 1981. A guarantee of Rs.3,000,000 was provided by a nationalised bank (after the state government agreed to act as guarantor) and Rs.400,000 was provided as working capital. This amount was very low and it was not possible for the co-operative to modernise the existing equipment. The co-operative hoped that it could borrow money from the bank for this purpose. They required a guarantee from the state government for this purpose. Unfortunately, when they approached the government it refused to honour its commitment.

The Ministry of Finance had assured the workers at the time of the formation of the co-operative that this was a temporary arrangement prior to take-over by the state government. The workers now realised that the government would neither take-over the shipyard nor would it help the co-operative in developing it. After a series of general body meetings, in which the local CPI(M) leaders too participated, the workers decided that they would have to manage the company on their own. Two major decisions were taken. First, they decided to freeze wages until the financial situation improved. Second, they would increase their productivity as this would reduce costs of production. The co-operative decided to undertake job work (outsourcing) for other companies, mainly ship repairs.

These efforts paid off as the companies that gave them orders for job work were happy with the outcome. Some of these companies were willing to supply raw materials needed for the repair work and at times even gave advances in cash. By 1991, the co-operative had accumulated around Rs.1,400,000 as surplus which it could use as working capital. A major decision taken by the general body of the co-operative during this time was that wages would not increase even after these surpluses were recorded. The workers realised that their future could be secure only if the co-operative had sufficient funds.

Events took a sharp turn in 1991. At that time the Ministry of Surface Transport was looking for a large plot of land for setting up a garage and workshop for one of its corporations, North Bengal State Transport Corporation (NBSTC). The state government suggested that the co-operative give up a part of the land that it held to NBSTC. This could form a rehabilitation package for the co-operative. NBSTC would pay Rs.10,000,000. The Inland Water Transport Corporation of the state government would take over the co-operative and would modernise the dockyard and the workshop. The co-operative would have to reduce its workforce to 50. Only those workers below 55 years would be retained and the others would retire with adequate compensation. The co-operative agreed to this proposal.

Since the workers were assured of take-over by the state government, they decided to be extravagant with the surplus they had accumulated. It paid a high bonus to its members, built new homes for the security staff, and spent large amounts on festivals.

The elections to the state assembly were held in 1992. The Left Front government was elected once again but the minister for surface transport was changed. The new minister wanted to review the scheme. He raised several objections about the location of the land and the cost of acquiring it. The deal was subsequently cancelled. This came as a shock to the workers. They were now worse off than before as they had no working capital to execute their orders. This incident, however, strengthened their resolve to draw on their own strength and not depend on others. They could only depend on the goodwill they had created earlier. Slowly they started getting orders and they gradually improved their position.

I first visited this co-operative in mid-1998. The workers seemed determined to make their venture a success. Most of them were old. Their uniforms were crumpled and worn. However, there was determination on their faces as they worked relentlessly. They did not give any hint of dejection or helplessness when they spoke to me. The white-collar staff, however, were more critical of the situation. They were bitter that the government they had supported, especially the CPI(M), had turned away from them. These people were still hopeful of government take-over. The local CPI(M) leader who provided the external leadership to this endeavour too, had become critical of the government's attitude. All these people believed that the cancellation of the government's earlier proposal was mainly because of corruption. I was told that the deal would not provide any kick-backs to those in power, hence it was abandoned.

The co-operative was unable to employ technical personnel as it was short of funds. It had a consultant who was a marine engineer. This person was once the general manager of the company and he later helped the workers to run the enterprise. He came every alternate afternoon to provide technical know-how. He did not charge any fees for his services as he was a sympathiser of the CPI(M) and he had adequate income through consultancies in other companies. The presence of this consultant and the local CPI(M) leader increased the confidence of the workers as they felt that even in these troubled times they were not alone.

The situation was more or less the same when I visited the co-operative in June 2000. Its financial condition was slightly better and the workers were receiving higher wages. The consultant had helped in bringing more business. The bitterness at the lack of support from the government had increased. However, both the union and the CPI(M) were with the co-operative at the local level. This was the main reason why the members still remained with the union, despite their grievances with the CPI(M)-led government. A major fall out of this situation was that the workers had become self-reliant. They no longer depended on external agencies to take care of their problems. This was the most significant contribution of the co-operative – it had raised the self-confidence of the workers.

Printing co-operative

The Eastern Type Foundry and Oriental Printing Works Employees' Industrial Co-operative Society Limited was started in 1987. The co-operative has 42 workers as its members. The total number of employees of the co-operative is 51, of whom seven are white-collar workers and the rest are blue-collar workers.

This company, known as Eastern Type Foundry and Oriental Printing Works, was established in 1890 and was registered as a joint stock company in 1912. The company manufactured printing material for letterpresses. This technique became obsolete in most parts of the world after off-set printing was introduced. However, prior to this the company was one of the best in its field in the country. Its market was spread all over India and it had export orders from other countries including China, Nepal, and Mauritius. The total work force was then around 500.

Despite changes in printing technology, the company was able to retain its position because it remained the only manufacturer in the field. Letter presses in the country depended on it for their supplies. Its printing press was also known for its high quality and it had orders from leading publishers.

The problems of the company began in the 1960s. These were mainly due to feuds among the members of the family that controlled the company. These people collectively owned a majority of the shares. In the 1970s, the union pointed out several irregularities of the management. Though workers were paid their regular salaries, it was found that funds collected for social security were not deposited with the authorities. These authorities filed cases in the courts for recovery. The management was unable to pay the dues and finally, in 1980, it stopped operations by shutting down the factory. This continued for seven years during which time most of the workers left to seek other work. The union suggested that the workers should form a co-operative which could take-over the company through the help of the government. Thus the co-operative was formed in 1987 with 30 workers who had continued to fight for their dues. The company, meanwhile, went into liquidation and the co-operative, with the initial financial backing of the state government, was able to buy the company.

The co-operative started functioning in 1989. Though it owned the company, it did not have much working capital. However, it was able to get orders for printing and foundry work. Business picked up gradually and the co-operative needed more workers. On the recommendation of the local committee of the CPI(M), 15 temporary workers were taken on. They were made permanent after a year and 12 of them became shareholders. Trouble started soon after this, in 1994. The original workers were old while the new workers were young. The latter demanded that the older workers should retire and make way for younger workers. Moreover, the local committee of the CPI(M) demanded that the party be allowed to use one of the office buildings as its office. The older workers, who too were supporters of the CPI(M), opposed this proposal as they felt that this would encourage the local committee to take possession of the building. This led to strained relations between the CPI(M) and these workers.

The internal problems of the co-operative had been created by the local CPI(M) leaders. The older members were with the CPI(M) and they initially trusted their local leaders. After these events, they became very critical of the party's functioning. They suspected that the local committee wanted them out so that it could fill the co-operative with their own people. At the same time these workers did not turn against the CPI(M) as a party. They voted for its candidates during the elections and they even campaigned for the party. Their problems were mainly with the local CPI(M) leadership. At the insistence of the younger workers at the annual General Body Meeting held in 1997, the Registrar of Cooperatives appointed an administrative officer who superseded the functions of the managing committee temporarily.

The co-operative was still functioning in 2000 and was able to pay wages. It could improve its position if it was able to take up job work through its foundry. However, it lacked working capital. Its press was working but the tension between the old and new workers had affected its efficiency.

Aluminium Cables and Conductors

This co-operative is known as Alcond Employees' Industrial Co-operative Society Limited and was formed by the employees of Aluminium Cables and Conductors Private Limited in 1987. Its total number of workers in 2000 was 150, of whom 35 were office workers and the rest, blue-collar workers. The co-operative had a membership of 265, all of whom were workers in the company but later some left after they got work elsewhere.

The company manufactured power conductors and aluminium cables. It was very well known in its field of production and was regarded as a profitable venture. The demand for its products rose after the state run electricity corporations decided to switch to aluminium high tension wires instead of copper cables. The company had around 500 workers on its rolls and was a profitable concern until the 1970s. It had a large clientele in India and abroad. The factory is in Hyde Road where a number of industrial units are situated.

Alcond started recording heavy losses from 1978. The workers believe that this was due to diversion of the company's financial resources to other investments. In 1983, it closed the factory. The workers' union moved to all quarters in the government and used all types of pressure on the management to re-open the factory. After three years of determined struggle, in 1986, the workers could force the management to re-open the factory. After a fortnight, the factory closed again and this time it was because its financing bank filed a liquidation case to recover its arrears. The union then decided to organise the workers into a co-operative so that it could run the factory.

The government supported the union's move to form the co-operative and it was registered in 1987. At that time, the High Court had ordered that the company be auctioned in order to recover its debts. The state government purchased the company and on 2 December 1989, handed it over to the co-operative. The government also provided loans and raw materials for starting production. Further, it stood guarantor for bank loans up to Rs.45,000,000. The West Bengal State Electricity Board, a state government undertaking, extended its support by placing orders for equipment.

At the time of take-over, the members found that the machines and equipment in the factory were damaged. The co-operative had to spend large sums of money on repair and maintenance. Production could start only in 1990, after seven years of closure. In its first year, the co-operative recorded a loss of Rs.1,270,000 but in the following year it recorded a turnover of Rs.60,000,000 and a net profit of Rs.750,000. The co-operative could employ 300 of the laid-off workers in the first year and another 100 in the second year. What is remarkable is that the workers were able to turn around the company within 18 months of take-over.

The problems of the co-operative started from the subsequent years. In order to meet its orders, the co-operative took loans from the co-operative bank against its share capital. Most of the contracts the co-operative obtained were from state sector undertakings such as the Electricity Boards of the states of West Bengal and Uttar Pradesh. Payments from these organisations were delayed for 12 to 18 months after deliveries were made. Its capital was thus blocked and it could not undertake other contracts as its working capital was exhausted. At the same time, interest on its loans increased. As in the other cases, the state government, which initially agreed to be guarantor for bank loans, backed out. Finally in 1997, it suspended production as it could not get working capital for executing orders. Its resources were exhausted and it was unable to pay wages. Several of its members left to seek work in other places and the co-operative was left with 150 workers.

In June 1998, the co-operative was able to re-start its activities after recovering some of its outstanding dues. It decided not to take up independent assignments by bidding for tenders. Instead, it began undertaking job work for other industrial units. This provided it with some income. By May 2000 it was steadily improving its financial condition but its past experiences had left bitter feelings regarding the state government's attitude. Its problems in this regard are similar to those of the shipbuilders' co-operative. It lost contracts because it was unable to offer bribes to the concerned authorities. Similarly, recovery of dues from the electricity boards was delayed for the same reason. The workers were bitter because despite their political links with the CPI(M), they had to face these problems.

Conclusion: co-operatives and social emancipation

In the previous sections, we have discussed about two types of co-operatives situated in two different cities. Despite the differences there are some common features among these co-operatives. First, all of them were initiated by their trade unions. This aspect was very important for the formation of the co-operatives. The co-operatives of waste pickers in Ahmedabad were initiated by SEWA as a part of its trade union activities. SEWA has a definite strategy of promoting co-operatives as a part of its trade union activity. This is what distinguishes it from other trade unions and also accounts for its success.

The co-operatives in Calcutta too were started by their union, but there is a difference from the approach of SEWA. The trade union leaders had proposed that the workers should take over the units after their managements had shut them. At the same time the position of the unions was ambivalent in the beginning, unlike the positive approach of SEWA. They had favoured the idea of forming the co-operatives and taking over production as an immediate measure of relief. The union leaders were primarily trying to contain the problem of unemployment resulting from the closures, but they also believed that this was a prelude to take-over by the state government. The workers too believed this.

After the initial support, the state government became indifferent to the fate of the co-operatives. This was a result of changes in the Left Front government's orientation. When the Left Front was elected for the first time in 1977, it adopted a pro-labour policy. After 1987, when it was elected for the third time, its attitudes changed. The government then tried to create an atmosphere in the state that would be congenial to foreign investment. It tried to change its image to an investor-friendly government. In this process, the interests of labour were sidelined. The worker co-operatives were victims of the government's new policies. This had created bitterness among these workers as well as the local level trade union leaders who were supporting the co-operatives in their area. As mentioned earlier, the unions to which the workers are members, are affiliated to CITU and their leaders are local level CPI(M) leaders as well. These leaders have been a major source of encouragement to the workers despite the lack of support of the CPI(M)-led Left Front government.

A positive fallout of this situation is that these co-operatives have learned to depend on their own strength for survival, rather than depend on an external agency like the state government. Despite the adversities, these co-operatives have continued to exist. This is true not only of the four co-operatives discussed in this chapter but of the other worker co-operatives in West Bengal as well. Out of the 20-odd co-operatives in Calcutta in the late 1970s and early 1980s, only two of them have been dissolved so far.

In the above discussion, we have to make an exception in the case of the printing co-operative. Here the local level CPI(M) leaders had tried to disrupt the functioning of the co-operative. The original members of the co-operative say that the local CPI(M)/CITU leaders helped in the formation of the co-operative but they changed their attitude later, when they found that the worker-members were opposed to providing a building to house the party office. After this, the local leaders tried to create divisions by instigating the new members against the original members. The latter too were members of the CITU affiliated union but after the ensuing conflicts with the new workers who were inducted by the local union leaders, they became disillusioned with the union and ceased to be its members. In the initial survey of worker co-operatives in the city we came across two similar instances. In these cases, the local CPI(M) leaders who had initiated the co-operatives viewed them as sources for generating funds for the party and for employment of its cadres.

Besides the support of the trade union, another major factor for the existence of these co-operatives was internal democracy. In the co-operatives initiated by SEWA, democracy was not restricted to election of leaders. The union organised training programmes for its members on how to take control of their organisation. This adds to the self-confidence of its members, all of whom belong to socially-marginalized groups.

Two of the co-operatives in Calcutta had internal democracy and the union leaders played a positive role in promoting this. The exception, as discussed earlier, was the printing co-operative. Leaders (elected and those of the trade union and party) met the workers frequently and explained the problems to them. Day-to-day activities and policy matters were handled through consensus. This ensured that all workers would participate actively in the co-operative's functioning.

Co-operative democracy was practised through formal as well as informal means. The formal means was through the General Body Meetings where reports were placed for discussion and policies were finalised. Elections to the Managing Committee (Board of Directors) were held regularly. Elections in the ship-building co-operative were always unanimous. The number of members was few so it was possible for the leaders to try and build a consensus for the posts in the Managing Council. The aluminium cable co-operative had a comparatively larger number of workers and elections were contested. Members of the Managing Committee were changed through elections thereby giving a chance to more members to take part in the decision-making. The informal methods included holding of discussions and trade union meetings to explain to the workers the functioning and financial condition of the co-operative. This method enabled the members to understand the problems of their co-operative. They could also give their suggestions on managing the co-operative.

Democratic functioning became a major problem in the printing co-operative, as the members were divided. The general body meetings of this co-operative invariably ended in chaos as the battle lines between the two groups were clearly demarcated. This weakened the co-operative's democratic functioning.

Another important issue that needs to be discussed is the role of the state. In the case of the waste pickers' co-operatives the state has neither helped nor hindered in their formation. At the same time there were other features such as harassment from local authorities and termination of contracts for collecting waste paper from government offices which can be viewed as negative aspects of state interference. The co-operatives were able to overcome these through trade union action and its goodwill among (honest) sections of the bureaucracy. As a union, SEWA's influence goes beyond membership of waste pickers, and as such, its collective influence is strong. Hence the backing of SEWA as a union was, to a large extent, responsible for easing the adverse situations faced by the women waste pickers.

The situation of the worker co-operatives in Calcutta was more complex. State intervention was necessary for their formation. The backing of the state came mainly because of the political support their unions enjoyed. However after the co-operatives were formed the state's support was withdrawn. The workers were left to fend for themselves. Another feature which surfaces is that of corruption. Besides not getting the promised guarantees for loans, the co-operatives found that they would have to pay bribes to various state agencies for procuring orders and also for collecting payments, after the orders were executed. This was despite the fact that the state government has a rule that preference must be given to co-operatives in procuring orders.

In conclusion, we can say that despite all the problems and shortcomings, these co-operatives have shown that ordinary workers are capable of taking control of the means of production, given the opportunity. The worker co-operatives in Calcutta have, in their limited ways, tried to protect job losses and production through their collective efforts. The determination they have expressed in their endeavours can be seen from the fact that the co-operatives have existed for several years, despite the odds. The waste pickers organised by SEWA in Ahmedabad demonstrate that the poorest and socially marginalised sections can improve their economic and social conditions through the co-operative movement.

Notes

1 The data on waste pickers was initially collected in 1996. I observed the activities of SEWA and its activities among waste pickers. I interviewed union activists, waste pickers, and members of the food catering co-operative (*Trupti Nasta*). I followed their activities over the years and updated my findings.
2 The data on worker co-operatives in Kolkata was collected as a part of a research project on the same topic. This section contains some of the findings. The project was awarded by the Indian Council of Social Science Research (ICSSR) in 1998. I have updated my information during subsequent visits to Kolkata. I am grateful to ICSSR for providing me a grant. The views are my own.

References

Bhatt, Ela 1997, 'SEWA as a Movement' in R. Dutt (ed.), *Organising the Unorganised Workers*. Delhi: Vikas Publishing House.

Bhowmik, Sharit K. 1992, 'Worker Co-operatives in the Plantation System: A Study Of Tribal Tea Plantation Workers in Eastern India', *Labour, Capital and Society*, 25(2). Montreal.

Bhowmik Sharit K. 1994, 'Worker Co-operatives in the Unorganised Sector: An Alternative Strategy' in Sarath Davala (ed.), *Unprotected Labour in India*. Delhi: Friedrich Ebert Stiftung,

NCUI 1969, *Report of the Committee on Principles of Co-operation Appointed by the International Co-operative Alliance* Delhi: National Co-operative Union of India.

Rose, Kalima 1995, *Where Women are Leaders*. Delhi: Sage Publication.

SEWA (1999), *Self-Employed Women's Association 1999*. Ahmedabad: Shri Mahila SEWA Trust.

8   Literacy and internal control of community finance institutions in Cambodia

Brett Matthews

Introduction

This chapter is intended to provide the conceptual basis for an action research project on internal controls in community finance institutions (CFIs) in rural Cambodia. A CFI is defined as "an institution that specializes in delivering financial services and is owned and controlled by its members within a local community." Organizations built with the intention that they meet this definition in future are also classified as CFIs here.

The internal control project is part of a family of projects in CCA's Cambodia program called "Community Finance Action Learning". The purpose of these projects is to trigger a sustainable process of learning and collaboration among local "community finance" practitioners. This will support the emergence of the leaders and capabilities needed to build a national credit union movement.

In February, 2004, an informal working group of domestic and international non-governmental organizations (NGOs) involved in building CFIs in rural Cambodia was formed. Their mutual goal is to improve the quality of the CFIs (see Box 8.1) they are building. Together, they represent 54,000 CFI members in 12 provinces around the country.

The internal control project will address the most obstinate problem practitioners have experienced in building CFIs in Cambodia. High levels of patron–client dependency, combined with very low levels of literacy – especially among women – present challenging internal control problems

---

Quality

A "quality" CFI is defined as one which has the capacity to and will, accomplish the goals its shareholders set for it. In other words, it is capable of translating ownership by poor people, and reward poor people for their risk-taking by meeting their collective needs.

Box 8.1

for CFIs. A list of issues identified by the working group is presented in Box 8.2.

Internal controls are tools, processes and tests that are essential to the sustained, long-term success of all institutions. They are used by shareholders to determine whether the people they have delegated to act for them day to day (such as the executive committee, managers etc.) are carrying out their tasks effectively and honestly. More formally, internal control is the

> plan of organization and all the methods and measures used by a business to monitor assets, prevent fraud, minimize errors, verify the correctness and reliability of accounting data, promote operational efficiency, and ensure that established managerial policies are followed.
>
> (Siegel and Shim, 1987)

This definition is not dependent on cultural context. If those who are risking their money and other resources in an organization cannot control its operations, the organization will eventually fail. And every

---

Selected quality issues in Cambodian CFIs
(From the minutes of the Network workshop, 5 February 2004)

The following quality issues (issues affecting the ability of poor people as shareholders to exercise effective ownership and control of their community finance institutions) were identified by the group:

- lack of auditing systems
- limited reported systems
- lack of trust among people – a preference by people for using the informal sector to save and to borrow
- weak book-keeping capacity – hard to train people in good book-keeping
- members have low capacity and/or are illiterate – easily manipulated by leaders
- traditional village conflict-resolution does not support shareholder rights in CFIs – safety of deposits, roles of management committees, etc.
- people keep their cash to themselves
- monitoring is inadequate or does not happen at all
- no mechanism for 'micro-governance' surveillance – how to police CFIs locally.

Box 8.2

organization in every country requires a structure, assets, operations and managers, and faces very serious risks of error, fraud and inefficiency.

While the problem is universal, the solutions are not. The forms that error, fraud and inefficiency take vary widely depending on local factors like human capacities, organizational culture and attitudes to authority. Solutions also depend on the availability and effectiveness of local dispute resolution mechanisms and the capacities and culture in the national audit system. In short, the types of tests and processes needed to ensure that internal controls are effective can vary widely depending on context.

Effective internal controls must begin with the rights of shareholders. A conceptual framework for shareholder rights is outlined in this chapter. Also, it addresses specific issues in a Cambodian context.

A framework for protecting shareholders' rights

As shareholders, poor rural women have a right to form agreements with each other as members, and with non-members. They have a right to expect those agreements to be kept by all involved ("shareholder rights"). These rights are grounded in the Universal Declaration of Human Rights, for example, in articles affirming the right to own property in association with others and the right to freedom of association.

The collective ownership of organizations (for example, Microsoft) is the foundation of all developed economies. The cooperative approach integrates social justice and democratic practice into this form of ownership. It plays a vital role in the economic and social development of poor and isolated communities, and supports the transformation of desperate, marginalized people into empowered and secure citizens. It is the socially responsible face of capitalism. In the cooperative movement, members and shareholders are the same.

The rights of shareholders begin with their contributions of resources to their collective enterprises. By pooling resources, shareholders expose themselves to the risk of loss – and also to the opportunity for gain (for example, through reduced vulnerability or improved livelihoods). To protect their resources, and their rights to a fair share in the benefits of the enterprise, shareholders form two types of agreements. These can be formal or informal, written or simply understood.

First, shareholders make *agreements of association* covering matters like shared goals, rules for decision-making and ways of selecting and replacing leaders. Then, to help them achieve their goals, shareholders make *operating agreements* that cover matters like issuing a loan, using a member's buffalo or arranging the safe-keeping of cash.

Shareholders risk their resources and livelihoods on the strength of these agreements. A wise group will ensure that someone they trust is responsible for managing these agreements since they capture the essence of shareholders' rights. Shareholders have a right to accountability from these managers. That is, shareholder protection starts with a problem of accountability.

At the center of the practice of accountability is the practice of account-ing: the management, sharing and storage of information about group activities and performance in reaching goals. To enhance confidence in common agreements and in managers, an accounting system must support full participation and full *control* by illiterate women.

Table 8.1 presents a framework for protecting shareholders' rights. The alertness and initiative of shareholders is the first and most important line of defense. However, for shareholders to effectively practice self-defense, they must learn personal roles and interpersonal skills that can be unfamiliar and challenging. Much of the learning must take place outside of formal training, because it involves applying taught principles to a wide range of real situations. But once the learning is complete, the CFI and the whole surrounding village gain a vital intangible asset: experience in building and operating institutions. This can mean the difference between failure and success.

Practitioners can enable shareholder effectiveness by helping them to make realistic, workable agreements and to hold their managers account-able. However, shareholder primacy also means giving groups the "freedom to fail" – essential, if they are to learn and succeed later.

Shareholders – the first line of defense

In order to assert their rights, shareholders must fully understand the details of their agreements with each other and with non-members, not only when those agreements are formed but as circumstances change over time. That is, awareness of rights starts with financial literacy and the ability to manage information – both individually and collectively. An even

Table 8.1 Protecting shareholders' rights

Elements of a protection strategy	Key conditions	
	For shareholder agreements	For operating agreements
Shareholders are of their rights	Financial literacy Participation Record-keeping	Financial literacy Participation Record-keeping
Shareholders assert their rights	Choice of each other Choice of manager Speaking up	Choice of contractors/agents Speaking up Active management
External actors enable the efforts of shareholders	Training rights, literacy Micro-auditors/standards Network operating procedures Quality of arbitration	Training in rights, literacy Network products and services Quality of arbitration

bigger problem among poor women in rural Cambodia is willingness to assert rights. The shareholder rights approach can bring fresh thinking to this issue, including an aspect that is central to the problem of collaboration: patron–client relations.

Internal control and patron–client relations in Cambodia

There have been few studies of patron–client relations in Cambodia, however, it is generally agreed that patronage is important in Cambodian villages. Poor people experience extremely high levels of daily insecurity with regard to food, property rights, employment, and even basic human rights. This leads them to pledge their loyalty to wealthy or powerful local people (patrons). In exchange, patrons use their influence and resources to help clients protect their security. This means that markets for vital village resources like land, labor, livestock and marketing services are not free; transactions are *highly* personalized. In an analysis of "social organization and power structures in rural Cambodia" for the Swedish bilateral agency SIDA, Ovesen *et al.* conclude that:

> certain political conditions are especially conducive to the existence and promotion of systems of patron–client relations. These conditions are the persistence of marked inequalities of wealth, status and power which are afforded a certain legitimacy; the relative absence of effective impersonal guarantees such as public law for physical security, property, and position; and the inability of either kinship units or traditional village community to serve as effective vehicles of personal security or advancement. It is hard to think of a country that fits these conditions as well as Cambodia.
>
> (Ovesen *et al.*, 1996, p. 71)

Given the high level of insecurity in rural Cambodia, patron–client relations have historically played a useful role. But for CFI members as well as practitioners attempting to develop the rural financial sector, they mean major internal control problems. The goal of a CFI is to reduce human insecurity by creating an alternative to the traditional system of village resource allocation. Many patrons – at village level and higher – will see CFIs as competition and resist their development. There are two ways to resist – by killing the CFI, or by disabling it.

Killing the CFI

The first form of resistance involves attempting to kill the CFI by capturing the resources within it. The following example is from a case study from Prek Trop village (Battambang province) by Simmons and Bottomley.

A project committee of three people, including one from a very poor family, was initially appointed to manage all transactions but members (or elements within the membership) decided that all cash should be kept with the Village Development Committee (VDC).... To date, the activity is said to have generated savings of 1,070,000 riels but the actual amount of savings being held by the VDC has been reduced to only 300,000 riels due to an individual loan (well above the loan limit) for dry season rice production. This member now claims that he is unable to pay back this loan because rice destroyed the harvest.

(Simmons and Bottomley, 2001, p. 50)

In this case, poor cash management (storage in the village) opened a door for political maneuvering by a village patron who moved the cash to the VDC. The result was subversion of the lending limit agreed to by the group and deeper poverty for some of the members.

Ironically, by weakening trust and willingness to cooperate between villagers in future, this subversion actually strengthens the reliance of the poor on direct personal relations with village patrons in future. Compounding this problem is the very weak court system in Cambodia, which limits the recourse of CFI members to repayment, compensation or justice, even when the facts are clear.

Disabling the CFI

The second form of resistance involves "disabling" the CFI. Local patrons accept the existence of the group but bring their considerable resources and influence to bear in order to secure control of its resources. Effectively, the group can then be transformed into a new channel for traditional resource allocation.

A 2001 study of the performance of self-help groups that received subsidized loans in Kampong Thom province found "a domination of the funds by the most powerful, or those whose cash needs are the most visible – in particular the men" (Walter, 2000, p. 18). In this case, regular staff visits by the sponsoring NGO keeps the problem manageable. However, should the NGO phase out, this "domination" can lead to a completely disabled institution.[1]

This form of resistance is insidious and hard to measure. Development practitioners may view the result as a success, taking satisfaction in the financial sustainability and longevity of the group. They may miss the contrary signals: loans allocated against the agreed rules of the group, poor attendance at meetings, failing governance systems, and so on.

Token savings' accumulation is the wedge issue, clearly demonstrating the fear – or lack of trust – of CFI members in Cambodia. A recently completed field study by the Canadian Co-operative Association in three Cambodian provinces found that rural households keep substantial savings in their homes. Among 301 CFI member households, average savings in their CFIs represented approximately 6 percent of total savings. The balance, in the form of cash and jewelry, is saved in secret places and locked boxes in and around the home, or in personal ornamentation (Matthews, 2005, pp. 35–6).

Even if the goal of the practitioner is limited to financial service delivery, it should be clear that Cambodia's CFIs are not providing safe or convenient savings services, and in many cases, cannot provide reliable or fair credit services either.

However, the test of success can be widened to include building healthy community-based institutions. These groups can erode the local culture of repayment, stifle democratic leadership, and entrench the prevailing cynicism about collaboration. In short "impact" – on livelihoods, on the very poor, on citizenship, or on any positive scale – is unlikely to be achieved.

Toward institutional sustainability in Cambodia

The history of efforts to nurture CFIs in Cambodia leads to the conclusion that, while financial sustainability is necessary for success, it is insufficient by itself. CFIs must be *institutionally sustainable* (see Box 8.3) as well. The institution must be robust enough, after the NGO phases out, to resist efforts by patrons to secure control and re-establish traditional, personalized resource allocation methods. Only then can CFIs achieve real sustainability, especially a real impact at a household level.

However, evidence from the sector's NGOs indicates that *institutional sustainability is a significantly greater problem than financial sustainability in rural Cambodia.* Many NGOs that have not phased out are hesitating and fearing that the CFIs they have built are too weak to achieve sustainable impact.

For the institution to be sustainable, its members must be ready to stand up for its rules and their rights, and correspondingly to hold their managers and directors accountable. In other words, they have to see themselves as the owners of the CFI. However, this self-perception is very weak.

Institutional sustainability

To achieve impact on member's livelihoods, financial sustainability is not enough. Shareholders must *also* be able to ensure that profit, loans, jobs, offices and other benefits are allocated according to fair, pre-agreed rules. In other words, members must have effective control of the CFI.

Box 8.3

Legacy of pre-mature external capitalization

Throughout the 1990s (and continuing today) international and local NGOs formed hundreds of CFIs and transferred large capital grants to them. Even today, there are almost no CFIs in rural Cambodia funded locally. The few success stories are the exceptions that prove the rule. Initially funded by grants, they have been profitable enough to accumulate some retained earnings and distribute dividends to their members. Because of their external capitalization they, however, have not yet tried to attract local savings or shares in meaningful amounts.

This policy (and legacy) of external capitalization has three adverse implications for internal control:

- It increases the attractiveness of the group as a target local patrons would like to control.
- It limits the members' need to contribute their own capital, reducing their psychological commitment to the group and to individual savings.
- It raises genuinely difficult questions about who owns the funds; questions that are most easily resolved by reference to traditional resource allocation systems.

There is probably no greater pressure that can be put on an infant internal control system than a large external grant. External grants create enormous temptations among CFI shareholders to bend or break shareholder agreements, and many ways of doing this have been documented in rural Cambodia.

A view is emerging in Cambodia that subsidized credit, which is unpredictable in size and timing, can actually reduce the ability of a village to look to its own resources to bring about change. In the words of Meas Nee, a respected local practitioner who has devoted much of his career to developing healthy village-level institutions: "... this dependence on outside assistance is a factor retarding recovery. ... The restoration of local community in the aftermath of conflict depends largely on the local people themselves" (Meas and Healy, 2003, p. 42).

This raises questions about the current mix of donor funds targeting CFI development in Cambodia. A rebalancing away from external credit towards capacity-building activities such as training, technical assistance, and better shareholder facilitation processes is certainly in order.

Awareness of rights and information management

To exercise their rights as shareholders, poor people must have access to the information needed to ensure that their agreements are being kept. In practice, however, shareholders in Cambodia rarely have access to this information.

The 2001 study cited earlier, focused on CFIs promoted by integrated development NGOs in Cambodia. It concluded that:

> [t]he better-off, the more powerful, the most self-confident and men often enjoy greater benefits than others. ... Financial management skills within the groups remain weak, and low literacy levels among members inhibit leadership accountability and rotation, in turn affecting the potential for sustainability.
>
> (Walter, 2000, p. 48)

A major contributing factor is the high levels of illiteracy in Cambodia. According to CARE (an international NGO) Cambodia 48 percent of men and 29 percent of women are functionally literate; lower in the rural areas.

As long as information management requires formal literacy skills, most poor rural women will depend on literate patrons to protect their rights as shareholders. Conflicts of interest between shareholder and family roles are common and managing them is not well understood in traditional Cambodian villages. This situation breeds a high degree of instability and undermines the foundation of internal control. The yawning gap between oral and literate cultures further destabilizes CFI practices of accountability and information management.

Both democratic institutions and financial services present special challenges for primarily oral societies. Model constitutions, savings, loan contracts, policies and others are primarily lists of time-tested solutions to dynamic human problems. The articles and clauses balance the anticipated needs and rights of many stakeholders – shareholders, directors, staff, borrowers, savers and the wider community. They may seem highly abstract and complex in the rural village, where most CFI members have never experienced similar problems.

This complex information is far removed from the adrenalin-pumping (and memorable) calls to action of epic poetry, political oratory or evangelical preaching. Indeed, the only type of communication further removed may well be the account books and financial statements governing day-to-day savings and loan operations.

Micro-credit institutions and information management

Cambodian micro-credit institutions (MCIs) and cooperatives have been very slow to address the challenge of building financial institutions in a predominantly oral setting. The assumption that savings, loans and co-op management and governance are – and must be – paper-based activities, has rarely, if ever been questioned. So practitioners seek out literate villagers to run CFIs, with perverse results. NGOs intending to empower women have handed control to men and other village leaders due to administrative imperatives that heavily favor literacy.

By contrast, the written word is viewed not just with respect but also with some skepticism in oral communities. Walter Ong, a linguist who has studied this phenomenon in many cultures, concludes that in oral cultures "witnesses were *prima facie* more credible than texts because they could be challenged and made to defend their statements, whereas texts could not" (Ong, 2002, p. 95). This attitude was usually accompanied by a healthy recognition that documents could be, and often were, forged or falsified, at the time of their creation or later. [2]

Why must thousands of illiterate borrowers and depositors sign contracts whose terms are vital to their livelihoods, yet are written in opaque phonetic script by MCIs?

Micro-credit institutions long ago determined how to have the borrower agree to a loan (sign with a fingerprint). Why is it so difficult to have her understand what she is signing? Why is it so difficult to offer her the tools she needs to recall the details of the agreement later, when she really needs to?

As CFIs begin to network to benefit from economies of scale in some services, the failure to address the needs of illiterate borrowers, savers and shareholders can lead to an even wider gap between oral and literate worlds, as the example in Box 8.4 illustrates. In this CFI network, as in most in Cambodia, board members are mostly illiterate.

How do practitioners bridge the gap between model constitutions and loan contracts and the needs of oral societies? In the words of Walter Ong, "the only answer is: *think memorable thoughts*. You have to do your thinking in mnemonic patterns, shaped for ready oral recurrence" (Ong, 2002, p. 34; italics mine).

Procedures for SME Loans in a Cambodian CFI Network

"Procedure#1
Submit loan application forms with *thumbprints* of the Board of Directors indicating their approval including te following documents:

- copy of the by-laws of the CFI
- list of members of the Board of Directors and employees
- Savings and Loan Policy
- Aging report
- financial report ant audit report
- list of members waiting for loans
- estimated cost of the project"

Source: Sample SMI lending policy of Cambodian CFI network

Box 8.4

Information management tools for CFIs in oral societies

A list of information management tools that may be useful in Cambodian villages is presented in Table 8.2. There are two categories of tools – those depending entirely on human recall, and those that depend partly on physical records/objects, accompanied by commonly agreed rules of use.

An oral culture is one in which many or most people are unable to read or write. However, orality is more than simply an absence of literacy. Just as blind people can have unusually well attuned hearing, oral cultures can accomplish feats of recall that most of us would consider impossible without recourse to written text.[3]

What shape do memorable thoughts take? In oral societies, transforming uninteresting but important information into a recallable and hence actionable form was the job of the poets. Homer, for example was a "tribal encyclopedia." He "provided all the information necessary for life in tribal Greek society. From Homer the listener could learn how to rig a sailing ship, how to dress for battle, and how to behave in court" (Logan, 1986, p. 102).

Physical actions like gesture, expression and intonation support poetic techniques and recall for both poet and audience. Much information is handed down in storylines – in Genesis a storyline livens up a lengthy and tedious genealogical list – vital to tribal continuity. Music, song and acting can all support recall, as can settings, costumes and props. Religious recitations use sensory effects like incense, candles and architecture.

Written phonetic script is a highly abstract technology – the most sophisticated stage in the evolution of physical record-keeping. But oral societies can and often do use more informal methods to keep physical records. These include physical objects,[4] pictures, symbols and even numbers and charts made from local materials (as proponents of PRA/RRA techniques can attest).

In general, agreements should not be backed up using opaque methods such as formal writing unless there is a compelling need to do so. However, for certain purposes, scribes have played a useful role in pre-

Table 8.2 Information management tools for CFIs in oral societies

Methods based on recall	Methods based on record-keeping
Individual memory	Pictures
Collective memory + agreement	Symbols
Poetic devices (rhythm, rhyme, alliteration, etc.)	PRA/RRA tools
Song	Numbers (including numerical dates)
Story-telling and related devices (heroes, conflict, imagery, etc.)	Physical records (symbolic objects, coloured boxes, etc.)
Music	Scribes (e.g. high school students)
Theatre and related devices (gesture, action, costumes, sets etc.)	

dominantly oral societies. Evidence from Bangladesh suggests that formal record-keeping can be a sustainable para-profession, and that high school educated youth may have a valuable role to play in service delivery (Matthews and Ali, 2002, p. 254).

A surprising range of activities can be managed by CFIs with no written records. ROSCAs (Rotating Savings and Credit Association) rely on group decision-making and collective memory to manage savings and loans. CARE is tapping oral recall methods in Niger, where its ASCAs (Accumulating Savings and Credit Association) are even holding small sums of cash between meetings (correspondence with Hugh Allen, April, 2003).[5] Cash balances, accumulated profit and other key information are repeated and up-dated at each meeting. Individuals are delegated to remember the names of debtors and amounts outstanding.

Record-keeping will continue to be essential, particularly as the scale and scope of CFI operations expand.[6] Now, flexible and contextually sensitive tools are needed to support CFI institution building and financial service delivery. These are analogous to the tools of rapid/participatory rural appraisal, and rely heavily on symbols, relational formatting, group transparency and collective memory.

The CARE Niger program has developed some very simple forms (see Figure 8.1), but they still rely too much on the written word. What they demonstrate very clearly, however, is that the number of concepts that need to be agreed among participants, and reduced to a format that is user-friendly in an oral society, is manageably small.

The essential aspects of the agreements of CFIs are not complex. They can be managed in a way that is friendly and transparent to all users through a mix of recall and record-keeping methods. They can be "guessable" by poor rural women unfamiliar with their meanings. Some may also provide bridges to formal literacy.

Single share value	TShs 500		
Cycle Number	2		
Meeting number	Shares bought per meeting		
4	🌳	🌳	
5	🌳	🌳	🌳
6	🌳	🌳	

Starting number of shares	6
Total number of shares bought this period	7
Total number of shares redeemed during period	0
Net shares end period (to be carried forward)	13

Figure 8.1 Shareholder agreement, CARE Tanzania (source: adapted from *Jozani Savings and Credit Associations (JOSACA)* – CARE Tanzania Training Guide, December 2000).

Much more work is needed, however. Oral methods of mainstreaming rules-based processes such as dispute resolution, the conduct of meetings, selection and accountability of managers, management of relations with shareholders and other stakeholders, loan diversification and allocation, interpreting and changing the rules, and so on are vital to long-term institutional health. Sponsoring NGOs must have staff with the experience and skills to audit these processes effectively ("micro-auditors").

REFLECT: protecting the rights of illiterate shareholders?

> For many difficult years people needed all of their energy to safeguard the survival of their immediate family. Is it time now for the energy to be redirected to the community?
>
> Meas Nee and Joan Healy

REFLECT (Regenerated Freirean Literacy through Empowering Community Techniques) is an approach to adult education, piloted by the British NGO ActionAid in the early 1990s, which fuses the theory of Paulo Frieire and the practice of Participatory Rural Appraisal (PRA). For an introduction to REFLECT, see Box 8.5.

As noted above, shareholders of CFIs must be aware of their rights and they must be willing and able to assert their rights. (There must also be external enabling actors; this problem is addressed in a separate action research study.) While REFLECT has frequently been used in other sectors, it has rarely been applied to the practice of microfinance. However, it offers promise to address the problem of weak internal controls within CFIs because of the following reasons.

- It is rights-based: the motivation to learn is derived from a consciousness of rights and an intention to develop local ways to protect them.
- It respects the principle that shareholders must be the first line of defense in protecting their own rights.
- It can provide a setting for the emergence and development of effective leadership within the group.
- It uses RRA/PRA techniques to consult with CFI members on the problems and opportunities they face related to financial behavior as well as CFI roles, responsibilities, reporting and record keeping.
- It uses situational literacies, combined with other user-friendly methods to support the efforts of non-literate CFI shareholders to establish an open-ended, sustainable institutional framework for protecting their rights.

In a post-conflict setting such as Cambodia, poor people often cannot imagine the possibility of working together in ways that really change their lives. They respect outsiders and accept credit delivered to their villages.

Background on REFLECT

In October 1993, ACTIONAID began a two-year action research project to explore possible uses of Participatory Rural Appraisal (PRA) techniques within adult literacy programmes. This led to the development of the REFLECT approach (Regenerated Freirean Literacy through Empowering Community Techniques).

"Graphics" constructed by literacy participants might include maps of households, land use or land tenancy; calenders of gender workloads, illnesses or income; matrices to analyse local crops, credit sources/uses or participation in local organisations. Initially constructed on the ground, these graphics are transferred to paper (using simple pictures) and are used as the basis for introducing reading and writing in a meaningful context.

By the end of the literacy course, each circle will have produced between 20 and 30 maps, matrices, calendars, and diagrams; and each participant will have a copy of these in their books, together with phrases they have written (so they individually produce a real document). The graphics become a permanent record for communities, giving them a basis on which to plan their own development.

As learners construct their own materials, they take ownership of the issues that come up and are more likely to be moved to take local action, change their behaviour or their attitudes.

Source: Archer & Cottingham, ActionAid, undated.

Box 8.5

But the war and its aftermath have taught them not to trust those in authority. There is no safe or open, democratic space to discuss the issues holding them back from collective action. So they listen respectfully to high-status NGO staff who tell them they must save together to achieve development and self-reliance. And they do save – in large amounts – but only in their own homes. There they lose, on average, about 15 percent of their savings a year (Matthews, 2005, p. 26).

REFLECT is designed to address just such situations. Effectively facilitated, it can support the efforts of identified groups (such as CFI shareholders) to establish shared, transparent, sustainable ground-rules for managing their shared efforts. As a result, it promises to support the efforts of illiterate shareholders to reinforce their institutional roles, rules and accountabilities, with record keeping and reporting systems that are friendly to them.

REFLECT has been used with encouraging results to improve governance, record keeping and accountability in production cooperatives.

In 1999, members of a Salvadoran cooperative farmers' co-op used participatory budget analysis to analyze internal processes in their stagnant co-op. As a result they identified corruption and non-transparency as major issues. After a struggle, they managed to eject the corrupt leaders and set the co-op on a transparent and financially stable footing (Newman, 2000).

In 2000 a failed multi-purpose cooperative in Lethoso was reorganized. With external help REFLECT and other participatory practices were mainstreamed into governance, book-keeping, distribution of profits and other key elements of shareholder control. Transparency was promoted as a vital guiding principle for all cooperative activities. Structures and processes were talked through and put in place to raise and deal with sensitive issues constructively.

As confidence in the governance grew, the members decided to set up a burial benefit fund to which they contribute monthly. "That this scheme was introduced, indicates that members had thought about ways to support each other in the event of a crisis, and furthermore trusted the structure and each other sufficiently to invest their money in it" (Attwood, 2004).

REFLECT is not viewed here as a panacea for the problems faced by the shareholders of CFIs in Cambodia. CFIs that have already fallen under the control of village and commune level patrons are unlikely to be able to reverse their losses (and if they do, it is likely to be a very difficult and painful process).

However, solidarity within the group, combined with strong leadership, are essential elements to success in building an alternative resource allocation system in the village. For example, the self-employed women's association (SEWA) has overcome similar challenges in building cooperatives in rural Gujurat. SEWA invested heavily in developing strong female leadership, which has helped to consolidate motivation and solidarity over the long term (Rose, 1992, pp. 212–14).

Community finance institutions that have not yet lost control of their affairs, but may be at risk of losing control, are promising candidates. So are new CFIs, and those that have shared control with an incubating NGO, but now face phase-out.

In exploring future prospects for their CFIs, members must assess carefully how higher status patrons are likely to react to the emergence of a sustainable CFI in the village. They must reflect carefully, both individually and as a group, on whether their duties to such people can be reconciled with duties to their CFI.

In some villages, the road ahead will be hard, and members must take careful stock of their collective level of commitment in advance. In others, the CFI may not be seen as a fundamental threat to patrons whose hearts seeks the welfare of their villages, and relations can remain cordial. In either case, a careful reflection on options will leave participants with a far clearer understanding of what it will take to build an institution in their village. It will also leave them armed with a more realistic awareness of the personal contribution they can make to a healthy setting for future institutional development in their village.

Notes

1 Even the traditional self-help associations sponsored by pagodas, ostensibly intended to help the poor through the loans of cash and rice, can drift away from their mission. A GTZ report found that "in most cases ... the clientele comprises relatives and associates of the committee members. And of course the families in question were not poor" (Aschmoneit, 1998, p. 10).
2 Ong reports on a dispute between two churches over customs revenues in twelfth-century England, centuries after the introduction of writing. The disputants chose a jury of trusted, elder men who publicly recalled conversations from their youth, with their ancestors, about how revenues were distributed generations before.
3 The Iliad, the Mwindo Epic, the Old Testament of the Bible and the Vedas are examples of the many book-length works initially composed and handed down orally before later being committed to writing.
4 In Cambodia rice is measured by physical record, using a small wooden container (*taou*) and bamboo counting sticks (*tiv*). The method supports both market transactions and loans in rice. It is transparent and user-friendly for illiterate people. The materials are easily made, cheap and locally available.
5 See also Allen, 2002.
6 In the past decade strong evidence has emerged that the Mesopotamians had a working system of record-keeping, accountability and control *before* they invented writing (see Schmandt-Besserat, 1992; Matthews, 2003).

Bibliography

Archer, David and Sarah Cottingham (no date) *REFLECT: evaluating a new approach to adult literacy*. ActionAid: London.

Aschmoneit, Walter (1998) *Traditional self-help associations in Cambodia: how to identify and co-operate with them*. GTZ: Phnom Penh.

Attwood, Gillian (2004) *Participatory Action Learning: lessons learned from a multi-purpose cooperative in rural Lesotho*. University of Witwatersrand: Johannesburg, South Africa.

Grant, William J. and Henry C. Allen (2002) CARE's Mata Masu Dubara (Women on the Move) program in Niger. *Journal of Microfinance*. Fall, 2002, pp. 189–216.

Lim, Peng Heng (2001) *Rural voluntary savings mobilization in Cambodia*. National Bank of Cambodia, Asian Development Bank: Phnom Penh.

Logan, Robert K. (1986) *The alphabet effect*. William Morrow and Co. Inc: New York.

Mattessich, Richard (2000) *The beginnings of accounting and accounting thought: accounting practice in the Middle East (8000 B.C. to 2000 B.C.) and accounting thought in India (300 B.C. and the Middle Ages)*. Garland Publishing Inc: New York.

Matthews, Brett (2003) Towards a shareholder rights approach to rural livelihoods in Bangladesh. *Alternative Finance*. Available online at: www.alternative-finance. org.uk/cgi-bin/summary.pl?id=350.

—— (2005) *Towards safety and self reliance: public trust and community finance in rural Cambodia*. Canadian Co-operative Association: Ottawa.

—— and Dr Ahsan Ali (2000) Ashrai: A savings-led model for fighting poverty and discrimination. *Journal of Microfinance*, 4 (2), pp. 246–60.

Meas, Nee and Joan Healy (2003) *Towards understanding: Cambodian villages beyond war*. Sisters of St. Joseph: North Sydney, Australia.

Newman, Kate (2000) Democratizing cooperatives: Abel's story. *Education Action* #13 (online journal). ActionAid: Available online at: 217.206.205.24/resources/edacthome.htm.

Ong, Walter (2002) *Orality and literacy*. Routledge: London and New York.

Ovesen, Jan, Ing-Britt Trankell and Joakim Öjendal (1996) *When every household is an island: social organization and power structures in rural Cambodia*. Uppsala Research Reports in Cultural Anthropology #15, Uppsala University: Stockholm.

Rose, Kalima (1992) *Where women are leaders: the SEWA movement in India*. Zed Books: London.

Schmandt-Besserat, Denise (1992) *Before writing, vol. I: from counting to cuneiform*. University of Texas Press: Austin.

Siegel, Joel G. and Jae K. Shim (1987) *Dictionary of accounting terms*. Barron's Educational Series, Inc.: New York.

Simmons, Mal and Ruth Bottomley (2001) *Working with the very poor: reflections on the Krom Akphiwat Phum Experience*. Krom Akphiwat Phum: Phnom Penh.

Walter, Alice (2000) *Learning from integrated savings and credit programmes in Cambodia – part 2 field research*. Australian Catholic Relief, Church World Service and Oxfam Great Britain: Phnom Penh.

Part V

Small self-help groups

9 Membership-based indigenous insurance associations in Ethiopia and Tanzania

Joachim De Weerdt, Stefan Dercon, Tessa Bold and Alula Pankhurst

Introduction

This chapter discusses a particular form of membership-based organisation of the poor – a membership-based indigenous insurance association. They are associations of people who have an explicit agreement to help each other in a specified way when well-defined events occur. These institutions are discussed in two rural contexts: of Ethiopia and Tanzania. In both countries, they have gradually evolved into well-structured groups offering insurance to help cover mainly funeral and hospitalisation expenses. This chapter discusses their history, the way they currently operate, their coverage, and their impact. As many of these associations focus on funeral insurance, we discuss briefly some evidence on how they have been affected by the HIV/AIDS crisis.

The literature on risk in development economics has analysed both the extent of risk experienced and the responses to risk in developing countries (for reviews, see Morduch, 1995; Townsend, 1995; and Dercon, 2002). One key response is that households try to reduce the consequences of the risk in their income by a variety of risk-coping mechanisms, including engaging in forms of risk-sharing via informal arrangements. The key empirical papers (such as Townsend, 1994; Grimard, 1997; Ligon *et al.*, 2002) as well as theoretical papers (including Coate and Ravallion, 1993; Genicot and Ray, 2003) focus on "informal" risk-sharing arrangements, which should be understood not only in the sense that they were taking place outside the market place, but also that they were "informal" in that they were not based on well-defined "formal" associations, with formally defined written sets of rules or regulations governing their operation. These institutions are sustained over time on the basis of implicit rules enforced by social norms, so that, once joined, no one is tempted to defect later when they realise that their own contribution is outweighing their personal and social benefits. However, much recent theoretical literature has shown that norms or other rules-based enforcement mechanisms are not necessary for these arrangements to be sustained. In other words, incentive systems within the arrangements can be designed to make the contracts *ex-post* self-enforcing.

There is some work that considers linkages between individuals and households that identify specific people as their insurance partners (Ayalew, 2003; Fafchamps and Lund, 2003; Dercon and De Weerdt, 2002; De Weerdt, 2004). Even so, these contributions do not focus on groups or associations, but largely on bilateral arrangements with a risk-pooling purpose. This chapter goes beyond this analysis by discussing insurance groups; indigenous associations common in developing countries with a specific focus on insurance and with well-defined rules and obligations, in the form of membership rules, specific contributions, and fines related to deviant behaviour. In particular, it discusses membership-based indigenous insurance associations in Ethiopia and Tanzania, based on a unique data set on the functioning of these groups, with matching household level data on the members.

There is a considerable amount of literature on groups and associations in developing countries and their economic impact. However, most of its focus is on their role as "social capital".[1] The purpose or functioning of these groups is less relevant in this literature. Other literature focuses on development initiatives using community-based organisations. One strand is related to health insurance, since many initiatives have developed around voluntary but community-based health insurance (CBHI) schemes (Jutting, 2003; Atim, 1998). Although some of the issues involved are comparable to those related to indigenous insurance groups, a key difference is that CBHI schemes tend to develop with clear linkages to NGOs or specific health facilities.

Discussion on membership-based indigenous insurance associations in existing literature is very limited at present (but see Dercon *et al.*, 2006). In the Ethiopian context, Aredo (1993, 1998) has discussed funeral associations in some detail from an economic point of view. This study is different in that it is directly based on survey data on the functioning and membership of these institutions in a rural setting. There is a limited amount of sociological and anthropological literature on these institutions as well (for example, Pankhurst, 2003). In the Tanzanian context, there appears to be no analysis of these institutions (except Dercon *et al.*, 2006). More generally, Rutherford (2001) has documented the existence of insurance mechanisms for funerals across the developing world. Still, no systematic economic analysis of these institutions can be found in the literature. Although the present analysis is largely economic, it is also informed by anthropological work focusing on the historical context and evolution of the particular format of the institutions.

Many of the groups we discuss are focused on funeral insurance and there are good reasons for this. First, funeral expenditure in much of the developing world is usually large and tends to represent a large proportion of households' monthly income (see for example Roth, 1999; Rutherford, 2001; Cohen and Sebstad, 2003; Coetzee and Cross, 2002). Second, it is also a highly insurable event in these settings. Moral hazard is unlikely to be relevant for insuring a funeral. Given relatively high mortality, it is a common event in families, but still typically with relatively low covariance.

The next section will present the basic characteristics of these groups based on unique survey data in both countries. The insurance cover provided and the basic functioning and history of these groups will be discussed. Section 3 goes on to discuss how different groups in the same location relate to each other and how a localised insurance market emerges. Section 4 discusses issues related to inclusion, exclusion, and impact. Section 5 puts the emergence of these groups in an historical context, while Section 6 looks at the available evidence of the influence of the HIV/AIDS pandemic on these groups. Section 7 concludes.

Basic characteristics

A membership-based indigenous insurance scheme is a locally initiated association of people, who have voluntarily entered into an explicit agreement to help each other when well-defined events occur. We call these organisations indigenous because they have grown from within the community, without any direct outside involvement. We call them membership-based, because the group is completely owned and managed by its beneficiaries. They are voluntary because no one is under strict pressure to become a member of a particular group, definitely not compared to the stricter kinship-based systems.[2]

We have data from two rural contexts, in Ethiopia and Tanzania, where such institutions are prevalent and important in people's livelihoods. First, there are data from a number of communities in rural Ethiopia, studied as part of the Ethiopian Rural Household Survey (ERHS). This survey has been collecting panel data on households and communities since 1989, focusing on 15 communities from across the country.[3] In this study, data are available on funeral societies in those villages. In total, detailed data has been collected on 78 funeral societies in seven villages[4] – about half the number of funeral societies present in these villages. In one village, the data were matched to the households in the household survey, allowing some more detailed analysis. The village in question consists of the communities in Sirbana Godeti, a relatively prosperous village in Oromiya region in central Ethiopia, where about 30 funeral groups were identified, about half of which were studied. Additional data from communities in southern Ethiopia complement this analysis, although for the time being these data are not fully analysed.[5] It should be stressed that some of the detail of the way the organisations function is different across rural and urban Ethiopia, but most of the fundamental characteristics are common across large parts of the country. In Ethiopia, the funeral associations are known as the *iddir* (*e'dir*) – these associations ensure a payout in cash and in kind to their members when there is death in the member's family.[6]

The second context is a village in Kagera Region in Western Tanzania, called Nyakatoke, relatively close to the Ugandan border, near Lake Victoria. A detailed census of all community organisations and informal networks, with an emphasis on insurance-based linkages, was conducted – details are in De Weerdt (2004). Over 40 groups were identified and 20 of these groups were classified as having a prime insurance function and were included in the analysis. The "traditional" funeral society, the *Bujuni* covers the basic funeral insurance, but several groups surround this to give additional insurance. They include seven Women's Associations, themselves united in the *Muungano* (the Union of Women's Groups), four neighbourhood and five religion-based groups.

In strong contrast to informal networks of neighbours and friends, these associations have clearly defined membership lists. By no means do these groups consist of a loose, rapidly changing association of people. Membership is confined to founding members and those applying to become members afterwards. In both contexts, there is a membership fee to be paid if one joins after formation. A number of instances were found where groups have particular restrictions, such as by gender or age. Payments are made when members incur costs related to funerals or hospitalisations (sometimes also other events, see below, p. 162). The payout is conditional on the relationship of the member to the deceased: for example, the payment for the spouse of a member can be different from the payout for a child or for uncles and aunts. Table 9.1 identifies the defining elements of a membership-based indigenous insurance association.

Although payout systems differ widely between the two study areas and per insured event, a unifying element is that they occur in cash, kind, and

Table 9.1 Defining elements of membership-based indigenous insurance associations

Membership-based	Owned and managed by its beneficiaries. There are founding members and there is membership by application. Typically there is a membership fee. Sometimes there are restrictions to membership (e.g. member belonging to a certain religion, has to be above a certain age or has to be a woman)
Indigenous	Grown from within the community, without outside intervention. Different, for example, from a credit group that has formed with the specific purpose of accessing an NGO's credit scheme
Insurance	For well-defined events, there is a payout in cash, in-kind and/or in labour. Often it will also include the use of capital goods (e.g. sheets to make tents for guests)
Association	They are formed explicitly and no one is automatically a member (as is e.g. the case in kinship networks). Clearly defined membership lists

labour. In-kind payouts can be, for example, food, grass for the funeral guests to sit on, or the use of capital goods that the group owns, like big cooking pots or sheets to make covers against the Sun. Contributions in labour are given at the funeral or hospital, but also to catch up with lost days of labour on the farm.

The payout systems are quite refined and in both contexts, there are written statutes, by-laws, and records of contributions and payouts. There will also be rules defining membership procedures, payout schedules, contributions, and also a set of fines and other measures for non-payment of contributions, or for matters such as failure to attend funerals or not contributing enough in terms of labour on these occasions.

Finally, one of the most remarkable findings of the work in these communities was the very large number of membership-based indigenous insurance associations in these communities. In Sirbana Godeti in Ethiopia, a community about 400 households, about 30 *iddirs* were found. In some other villages in Ethiopia, a somewhat more modest number seems to be present but still five or more; but in a number of villages the number of *iddirs* was well above 50. In Imdibir, one of the study villages, the study was able to identify about 80–100 groups, albeit not all just covering the village, but with substantial membership in the village, despite having only a population of about 350 households. In Tanzania, the village studied (Nyakatoke) had a population of 120 households only, but 20 insurance groups were identified. It is obvious from this that people can and usually are members of more than one association – see further for more details.

What type of insurance do these groups provide? All groups in Ethiopia propose funeral insurance. In Tanzania, all but one group provided funeral insurance (the exception being a small group of 18, with only two members from the specific village) and 13 groups provide hospitalisation insurance. Table 9.2 gives the benefits paid out by groups for funerals and hospitalisation (in the scenario wherein the member is sick or dies; this is usually the maximum payout). At relevant exchange rates, the payout for funerals in Ethiopia is $20 (40 per cent of total monthly consumption), while for Tanzania it is $40 (60 per cent of total monthly consumption). The notes in Table 9.2 contain further information on the comparability of these two figures. The average payout for hospitalisation in Tanzania is about $5 per instance, well below the payouts in the case of a funeral, but still significant.

Table 9.3 summarises a number of crucial differences between the two contexts. For example, in Tanzania, the main groups expected members to provide their cash and in-kind distribution at the moment the death is announced. In Ethiopia about 80 percent of the groups were charging a regular contribution, usually monthly, from the members.[7] In the village studied in more detail, all but one *iddir* operated on this principle. In more urbanised contexts, this percentage is close to 100 per cent. Virtu-

Table 9.2 Payouts for funerals (in case member dies) and hospitalisation

	Mean	Standard deviation	Median
Tanzania (in TSh)			
Funeral	31,372	24,796	22,070
Hospitalisation	3856	3461	3000
Ethiopia (in Birr)			
Funeral	206	177	150

Source: Own data.

Note
The mean Tanzanian funeral payouts include TSh26,601 as in-kind benefits. Ethiopia does not include in-kind benefits. Exchange rates at the time of the surveys: $1 = 10 birr and 800 Tanzanian Shillings. Payouts are defined when the member (policy holder) himself or herself dies. If a relative of the member dies, a lower payout will be made. In Tanzania, the funeral benefits would be on average only TSh16,655 if the Muungano is counted as a separate group. However, since being a member of a Women's group implies membership of the Muungano, the benefits of the Muungano are added to the benefits of each specific Women's group.

Table 9.3 Premiums, asset holdings, entry fees and group size in Ethiopia and Tanzania

Ethiopia	Tanzania
Usually, regular contributions in cash (average about $0.16)	Contribution only when the funeral takes place
Cumulative Asset Holding, largely in cash (mean = $190)	Limited assets (durables)
Usually relatively substantial entrance fee (mean = $4 per family)	Relatively limited entrance fee (mean for women's groups = $1)
Mean group size is 84 (median=55)	Mean group size is 24 (median = 18)

Source: Data collected by the authors.

ally, all groups discussed actually pay a monthly or similarly regular contribution (Pankhurst, 2003).

A key consequence of this phenomenon is that some of these groups retain substantial savings. In fact, in the full sample (i.e. including those not charging a fixed regular contribution), asset holdings were on average about 1900 birr ($190), a substantial sum in a country with a yearly GDP per capita of only about $100. Many *iddirs* were found to have much more in terms of accumulated savings; the highest sum reported was about $3000. Obviously, regular membership contributions and group sizes play a role here as well. Average contributions per month per member of the 63 Ethiopian groups charging a regular contribution (either weekly, fortnightly, or monthly) were 1.64 birr per month (the median is one, the range was 0.25–5 birr, the standard deviation is 1.44). Contributions are fixed per member, irrespective of age or family size. Groups in Ethiopia were also charging substantial entrance fees for anyone currently wanting to join: about 42 birr, or 25 times the monthly contribution. Interestingly, about 40 per cent of groups reported setting these entrance fees as a fixed contribution, the rest suggested a formula based on the current assets and property per member. Furthermore, groups in Ethiopia were larger, on average about 84 members, with a median of 55, compared to an average size of 24 (median 18) in Tanzania.[8] Although a few very small *iddirs* were found in Ethiopia, in each of the seven villages the average size is larger than in Tanzania.

The emergence of an insurance market

This section discusses the inter-linkages between groups in the same community and aims to show how a localised insurance market emerges. Some of the surveyed Tanzanian groups make membership conditional on membership of *other* groups in the village. For example, the women's groups are clearly providing supplementary insurance over and above the village level burial society, the *Bujuni* (which is the Haya word for "mutual help"). The women's groups explicitly state this in their statutes: only women from Nyakatoke whose husband is a member of the village burial society may belong. The insurance they offer is meant to cover expenses not covered by the burial society. The neighbourhood and religion-based groups are similarly providing supplementary cover.

The Ethiopian groups, typically, do not have terms of conditional membership and households are usually free to join as many or as few *iddirs*, as they want. Most villages have a number of *iddirs*, largely differentiated in terms of the amount of cash offered in the event of a funeral, and related to this, the regular contribution paid. Although the groups spoken to in Ethiopia clearly emphasise funeral insurance, a substantial number offer other benefits to their members. First, about 64 per cent of groups offer loans to members, provided the funds are available, with clear (and strictly enforced) rules governing repayment. Members have to present a case for obtaining a short-term loan, and the most commonly accepted reasons are additional funeral spending, illness, and destruction of a house. To put it differently, short-term credit is offered to provide additional cover, mainly for shocks. Second, 64 per cent (but not necessarily the same groups as those offering loans), offer other forms of insurance, but the cover offered is clearly dependent on the group. Table 9.4 summarises the types of insurance they offer and it is clear that each group that provides additional cover, offers only a limited set of other benefits such as fire and house destruction insurance. About 30 percent of the groups offering additional cover provide payouts in case of serious illness in one way or another. Note that in all cases no additional premium is charged, but all are included in the basic premium.[9]

Table 9.4 Types of additional insurance offered in Ethiopian *iddirs* (as a percentage of those groups offering additional cover)

Type of insurance	Percentage
Destruction of house	40
Illness	30
Fire	28
Death of cattle	24
Harvest	14
Wedding	14

Source: Data collected by the authors.

The surveyed groups in Tanzania, in contrast, offer a wider variety of insurance products. For example, Bertha's group has 11 members and offers TSh 100, 30 fingers of bananas and three bowls of beans when there is a funeral, while Eles' group has 17 members and offers 3 kg of meat, two hands of bananas, and five bowls of beans.[10]

But groups will differ in more than just the premiums and payouts they maintain. In the Tanzanian context, a woman typically moves to the village of the husband upon marriage. If a funeral occurs in her home village, then it is typically expensive for her to attend it as there are transport costs, contributions, presents, clothes, and others to be bought. Some groups in Nyakatoke extended their coverage to also include funerals on the woman's side of the family. Subscribing to such a scheme will increase a woman's bargaining power vis-à-vis her husband when deciding whether or not to attend a funeral in her home village.

These groups are completely owned by their members and one manifestation of this is how innovations occur. For example, in Tanzania, the main groups expected members to provide their cash and in-kind distribution the moment a death is announced. It usually only takes one day for the group to get organised. This means that on the first day there will be no contributions, but still visitors will start pouring in and they need to be catered for. Therefore some people have organised themselves in *mwatani wabaki* groups that hold stocks of beans (collected after the bean harvest), own some cups and saucers, and have a commitment to be ready to help from the first hours.

Clearly, there is an element of choice of product in these communities and people can express their preferences for different insurance packages. Furthermore, as they are in a very real sense the "owners" and the "beneficiaries" of these insurance schemes, they are guaranteed to be engineered in a way that benefits the members most.

A last example of an innovative insurance market structure comes again from Tanzania. As noted before, there are seven women's groups in this community. After a period of working independently they decided to join in a super-structure called the *Muungano* or the Union of Women's

Groups. The *Muungano* provides a minimum package of insurance when a member is hit by a funeral or a hospitalisation. Outside of this insurance package through the *Muungano*, each women's group is free to add on additional features to the insurance package, but then only for its own members. The *Muungano* does not have individual members, rather each of the seven groups is a member of this super-structure. It is the group rather than the member that is responsible for paying the premium. This means that monitoring and enforcement occurs within groups of 8–20 people, but insurance is obtained from a pool of over 100 people. This, is of course, is very similar to the idea behind group-based lending made famous by the Grameen Bank. The main difference is that in Nyakatoke, it grew completely from within the community without outside interventions aimed at creating these groups.

Inclusiveness and impact

These insurance groups are remarkable not only by their functioning but also on account of their widespread membership. This section looks at what determines membership, how much protection is offered, and how important this insurance is for its members. In the sample of 15 Ethiopian villages (the ERHS), it was found that about 80 per cent of households were members of at least one *iddir*. However, after excluding two villages in the most northern region of Tigray, where, apparently, these institutions are not yet present, membership is virtually comprehensive. They could be found in all the other villages included in the sample and in almost all villages, more than 95 per cent of households were members of at least one group.[11] In one village, Sirbana Godeti, where groups were matched with household data, it was found that households were members of up to eight groups and, on average, a member of between two and three groups. In Tanzania, with data on only one village, about 95 per cent of household were members of the village level Bujuni. Almost all households with a female adult took out additional insurance from one of the seven village women's groups. Overall, households are members of about three groups.

The widespread membership across the population suggests that these groups are quite inclusive. Even though the percentage of people not included is relatively small, it is still relevant to explore who may not be included in these schemes. The Ethiopian data[12] was used to investigate whether membership was affected by socio-economic characteristics. It was found that the probability of membership increased with the age of the head and with household size. This is consistent only with people typically considering joining *iddirs* after they marry and start a family. There was no effect from current living standards.[13] Mariam (2003) suggested that in his sample of 1200 households, mainly in rural Ethiopia, those not members were either newly arrived migrants, who were not yet well established in the area, or those not yet married but already cultivating their own land as an independent family member. In Tanzania, the few not included in any scheme were not significantly different from others. In both contexts, funeral groups were originally based on ethnicity, religion, and kinship, but the large number of different groups available means that there everyone could, in principle, be a member of some group. For Ethiopia, Mariam (2003) added that all *iddirs* in his sample area now state that anyone in the same locality, regardless of religion or socio-economic status, could apply to be members. In Tanzania, qualitative interviews with members and non-members confirmed that once one is willing to adhere to the rules of the group and give timely contributions when the rules so demand, there is likely to be no objection to anyone joining a group.

However, in both cases there is evidence that the extent of coverage is higher for richer households. In both contexts, households can be members of different groups. As a result, people can choose to have more insurance coverage by joining more groups, or by joining groups offering higher insurance linked to higher contributions. This is investigated further in both data sets. In the data on Nyakatoke, an investigation on the coverage taken out by households suggested that the mean funeral coverage was equivalent to about 21 per cent of total yearly household consumption (while health coverage offered was on average about 2 per cent). In Ethiopia, it was not possible to analyse coverage on the full data set, but there is data on total payments over a four-month period in 1997 by households to *iddirs*, which will give a good indication of the coverage they could themselves receive. Table 9.5 reports the result of simple regression analysis, linking the funeral coverage (Tanzania) or total contributions (Ethiopia) to a set of characteristics. For the Tanzanian data, ordinary least squares were used; for Ethiopia, where about a fifth of households did not spend on *iddirs*, a tobit model was used to account for the large number of zero observations. In Ethiopia, the regression controls for community fixed effects, so the focus is on within-village differences. The characteristics used were household size, age of the household head, whether the head had completed primary school, sex of the head and a set of (cumulative) dummies for wealth (based on the overall consumption levels). The Tanzanian data also allow for controls for the location within the village and for the shared genetic stock with other people in the village.

The regression suggests that larger households take out more coverage, which suggests that they respond to the incentives given in the scheme; larger households stand to benefit more from the system. In all groups, the policy covers all members of the household irrespective of total household size. However, there is no extra cost when insuring extra individuals within a household – so it is relatively more advantageous for larger households to join. The other key effect is that the poorer households have significantly less insurance. In the Tanzanian data, the richest 75 per cent

Table 9.5 Determinants of funeral coverage/contributions per household

	Tanzania – total funeral coverage per household (ordinary least squares)		Ethiopia – total contributions per household (tobit model with community fixed effects)	
	Coefficient	p-value	Coefficient	p-value
Household size	4,601.6	0.026	1.452	0.000
Age of household head	272.1	0.471	−0.046	0.193
Primary school completed?	−1,937.0	0.875	−2.794	0.113
Sex of head	−1,265.9	0.933	2.811	0.027
Genetic share* 1000	1,065.2	0.087	–	–
Distance to centre of village	6.5	0.863	–	–
Richest 75 per cent (dummy)	32,741.2	0.040	2.568	0.092
Richest 50 per cent (dummy)	−17,264.6	0.275	2.308	0.109
Richest 25 per cent (dummy)	7,208.1	0.634	3.055	0.039
Constant	62.1291	0.058	−24.602	0.000
R-squared	0.135 (adjusted)		0.0654 (pseudo)	

Note
* Genetic share is defined as the extent of blood relationship with other people in the village; richest 75 per cent is a dummy one if person belongs to the 75 per cent highest levels of consumption per adult; richest 50 per cent and 25 per cent are similarly defined. Note that for the richest 75 per cent, the three dummies will have the value one. The poorest group is excluded. Sample size for Ethiopia data is 1260; for Tanzania 120.

dummy is positive and significant, while no other wealth dummies are significant. The size of the wealth effect suggests that, in Tanzania, the poorer have typically 25 per cent less coverage than the average household does. Similarly, in Ethiopia, contributions systematically increase with wealth, and there is clear evidence of the richest 25 per cent insuring themselves significantly more than the rest.[14]

A further issue is the composition of the groups: who joins what type of group? Is there any evidence of matching or selection in the group composition? Assortative matching is typically considered as a benefit in terms of being able to save on information and enforcement costs – it is often suggested that similar people will find it easier to monitor and enforce contracts (Hoff, 1997; Ghatak, 1999). Nevertheless, analysis of the group composition in the matched data of households and groups in both countries found only limited evidence of matching in terms of wealth. For only one group out of 18 could any clear evidence be found that they are poorer than the others – hardly systematic evidence of matching by wealth. In De Weerdt (2004), this was found to be rather different when investigating pure "informal" linkages between households in the Tanzanian sample (where linkages were defined on the basis of household and individual level questions on "who would you turn to for help?" and "to whom would you give assistance?"). The evidence showed that wealth and geographical distance mattered significantly and strongly in determining these linkages. In other words, this suggests that these more formal organisations can afford to allow people from a more diverse background to become members, presumably, since clear rules and regulations can compensate for some of the informational and enforcement advantages of social and geographical proximity.

Finally, how important are these groups for the households involved? Funeral costs are very substantial – although the full costs are hard to estimate, but definitely a significant proportion of a month's income. In Ethiopia, the average cash payout per *iddir* is about 40 per cent of monthly household consumption, while in Tanzania it is 25 per cent (and the average household in both countries is usually a member of more than one group). So these groups appear to be crucial to allow households to cover funeral expenses. In Tanzania, the average medical bill for households in the sample reporting serious illnesses in the sample is around $5, exactly the same amount as the coverage by just one group. However, one should not forget that, apart from this substantial insurance, much risk remains uninsured resulting in substantial welfare fluctuations and losses – for example, see Dercon and Krishnan (2000) and Dercon and De Weerdt (2002). Dercon and De Weerdt (2002) found that health shocks were causing households to cut back on average about 20 per cent of non-food expenditure in the Tanzanian sample. In Ethiopia in 1994–5, more than 10 per cent of households drifted into poverty directly related to shocks.

History

It may be tempting but completely misleading to consider these insurance groups as age-old traditional institutions. There is no doubt that mechanisms of mutual support would have existed in traditional society, but this does not imply that the currently observed associations are just replicas of these mechanisms. In this section, a brief discussion of the origins of these institutions is presented – more details can be found in Pankhurst (2003) and De Weerdt (2001). The main point in this section is to show that these institutions are best understood as organisational structures developed in interaction with the general socio-economic and political context, and that they evolved in response to changes in this environment.[15] Some of the existing literature on these institutions in Ethiopia appears to take issue with this view, not least with some of the detail involved (Aredo, 1993, 1998). For example, Aredo (1998) suggests that these institutions may even have existed in the nineteenth century – even though there is no clear evidence in written sources on this, and our own investigations in the same field setting as Aredo suggests that the basis for this claim is weak. In any case, much more work is needed to properly settle some of these issues.[16]

In the debate about the origins of the *iddir* in Ethiopia, a number of interrelated issues have been debated. First, is it basically a rural institution transposed in an urban setting or is it an institution that emerged in the context of urbanisation and then spread to rural areas? The answer depends on what *iddir* means. Societies across the world have cultural requirements for burial and some rules of conduct regarding the way co-operation and mutual support is required for funerals. However, the specific way the *iddir* is organised suggests that it emerged in a context of monetisation and literacy, and probably closely linked to urbanisation – and the need to have clearer community links and obligations.[17] The available data suggests that it is an early twentieth-century institution, probably started by migrants and it was initially linked to the Gurage, an ethnic group with a history of migration and trading.[18] The number of *iddirs* increased significantly in the capital, Addis Ababa, during the Italian occupation (1936–40) and they started spreading from urban areas to rural areas thereafter.

There is also little evidence that there has been any outside influence, for example from similar institutions across Africa. If anything, it is likely that they emerged in parallel with similar organisations across Africa and elsewhere. There is also evidence of a complex relationship with the state. Until the 1960s, *iddirs* had been relatively invisible institutions. This changed in the 1960s, when municipal authorities in Addis Ababa and, more generally, the Ministry of National Community Development sought to promote collaboration between *iddirs* and the government. At the same time, some politicians used these associations as platforms for political

purposes. In this period, different *iddirs* became involved in broader development activities. An attempted coup in 1966 partly blamed on an
indigenous migrant association, meant that the state tried to establish
more control over these associations, including *iddirs*. The revolution of
1974 brought the Derg to power, after which the leadership of the *iddir*
was considered reactionary elites and most *iddirs* retreated to focus only
on burial activities, and the formerly strong urban associations were marginalised. Nevertheless, the spread throughout rural Ethiopia clearly continued, while the size of some urban based *iddirs* increased considerably.[19]

In recent years, the EPRDF (Ethiopian People's Revolutionary Democratic Front) government (which came to power after the fall of the Derg
in 1991) has increased its interest to work with associations like *iddirs*. The
Ministry of Health has expressed an interest in working with *iddirs*, most
notably in anti-HIV/AIDS campaigns, while there have been suggestions
to involve organisations such as the *iddirs* in spreading modern agricultural activities. The government has also been interested in organising
iddirs within towns into broader associations. In the same period, certain
NGOs, notably ACORD (Agency for Cooperation and Research in Development), have started to work with , although this remains largely a
limited number of instances or activities. Some *iddirs* have themselves also
started to try to expand their activities. For example, 21 *iddirs* in the west
of Addis Ababa have formed an umbrella association, strictly politically
neutral but focusing on developmental activities.

The experience in Nyakotoke in Tanzania provides another interesting
example of how these institutions evolve in response to changing political
contexts. The village burial society, the Bujuni (meaning "mutual help" in
Haya) is a relatively old indigenous institution. However, it only became
more formalised after 1973, under the impulse of a migrant from another
village, who had suggested making the rules and regulations more
explicit. Some form of mutual cooperation existed similarly among
women, but formalisation came much later. In 1973, as part of the radical
changes instigated by President Nyerere's ruling party, women were
forced to "unite" in formal groups as part of the UWT (the Swahili
acronym for the Union of Tanzanian Women), organised in relatively
large "village" level groups interpreted to include many communities
beyond Nyakatoke, with pressure to set up village shops and other collective institutions via (forced) contributions. The village shop became bank-
rupt five years later and increasingly, the UWT groups became just
political institutions. However, after this experience, some 70 women
decided to set up a group involved in economic activities to raise money
for events such as funerals, births, and hospitalisation, independently of
the UWT and surviving its gradual disappearance. The group did not
survive long and from 1984 factions broke away, and effectively these
groups became the predecessors of the current groups, with a common
element of providing insurance for funerals and hospitalisation. In 1994,

the different women's groups (under the impulse of a recent migrant) formed the *Muungano*, the union of the women's group, integrating the basic minimum funeral and hospitalisation insurance. Since then, the different groups have experienced a relative degree of stability via the *Muungano*. Overall, the groups clearly conform to the idea of an indigenous association, even though they were initially inspired by the formalised activities of the UWT. There is no evidence of any outside involvement in any of the current groups or their predecessors, and linked to the bad experiences in the UWT, they have stayed clear of any political capture even at the local level, steering away from the activities of the ruling party or the emerging opposition. The rules and regulations have clearly evolved over time, moving gradually further away from economic activities towards a clear focus on specific insurance.

The challenge of HIV/AIDS

HIV/AIDS has been ravaging the study area near Lake Victoria in Tanzania for more than a decade, while in Ethiopia, the epidemic is currently expanding at an alarming rate. This section discusses the limited evidence available on the impact of the AIDS crisis on membership-based indigenous insurance associations, particularly those concerned with funeral expenditure insurance.

A priori, HIV/AIDS has brought about a fundamental change in the risk environment faced by groups insuring funeral expenditures. These institutions had been developing in a context of gradually decreasing mortality figures in the decades until the 1990s. The impact of HIV/AIDS has resulted not just in higher mortality, but has also brought about a fundamental change in the mortality risk distribution across the age, and possibly, even the wealth distribution. The result is that the likelihood of the association being asked to contribute to the funeral of a member has increased, putting pressure on the finances and sustainability of these institutions. During interviews in the rural sample of *iddirs* in Ethiopia used in this chapter, *iddir* leaders suggested that HIV/AIDS had only had a limited impact on societies so far. This is likely to be correct: in rural Ethiopia, the epidemic is only now beginning to spread and mortality rates have just begun to increase. Consequently, *iddirs* have not yet had to change their rules. In any case, in recent years, mortality figures in most parts of rural Ethiopia are more likely to have been more affected by the deaths of conscripts of the Ethio–Eritrean war of 1998–2000 and the drought in 2001–2. However, many had sufficient information on HIV/AIDS to report that premiums would have to increase in the future. In the particular study village in rural Kagera in Tanzania, similarly only limited impact of HIV/AIDS on groups providing funeral insurance was reported although, generally, the groups surveyed were well aware of the actual and potential problems involved. They also could report anecdotal evidence on changes in funeral societies' arrangements in some areas linked to HIV/AIDS, for example involving less expensive funerals.

The clearest evidence available on the impact of the crisis comes from Pankhurst and Mariam (2004), based on a survey in urban Addis Ababa on the impact of HIV/AIDS on the *iddirs*. They found that of 120 respondent *iddirs*, 93 per cent reported experiencing an increase in the number of deaths among their members in the last three years. The number of households receiving burial support in the past had been about 20 per group on average, but this average had now increased to about 31. The observed increase in mortality was largely confined to the age group of 15–35 years, consistent with the demographic predictions on the impact of HIV/AIDS. The *iddirs* also reported increases in bankruptcy of other *iddirs*, due to increased mortality, while about a third of *iddirs* had already started to respond to the crisis by increasing contributions or finding alternative ways of increasing income, such as by renting out utensils. Another study (Tesfaye, 2002) found similar consequences and responses due to the crisis. This is also bound to put pressure on the poorer members of *iddirs*. On the basis of the in-depth study of three *iddirs* in Addis Ababa, Shewamoltot (2001) found substantial increases in regular contributions and suggested that some members had already withdrawn from the *iddir* due to the increased financial cost. Other *iddirs* tried to contain the crisis by paying out only half the usual benefit at the time of the death and the other half, conditional on the continuing payment of the membership fee by the surviving family members. Finally, a striking consequence of the HIV/AIDS crisis on the *iddirs* is that, all these studies report that many *iddirs* have taken the lead in HIV/AIDS education of their members – about half the *iddirs* interviewed in 2002 by Pankhurst and Mariam (2004), now provided such information.

This evidence clearly suggests that *iddirs* are likely to come under increasing pressure in the next few years making increased contributions inevitable. The result is likely to be a less inclusive institution, with the poor increasingly less able to contribute. The fact that *iddirs* are responding to the crisis in different ways is encouraging, and suggests that their survival in one form or other may well be possible. In any case, if their important function in the social fabric as a key social protection mechanism is to be maintained, it may become even more important that policy measures are taken to strengthen these institutions.

Conclusion

A membership-based indigenous insurance scheme is a locally initiated association of people, who have voluntarily entered into an explicit agreement to help each other in a well-defined way when well-defined events occur. We call these organisations indigenous because they have grown from within the community. We call them membership-based, because the group is completely owned and managed by its beneficiaries. They were neither established nor developed by anyone but by their own members. They are voluntary because no one is under strict pressure to become a member of a particular group.

Historical analysis from some survey areas in Ethiopia and Tanzania has shown that these groups are not "traditional" – a term that would suggest that these institutions may have existed unchanged for centuries, whereas they are often relatively new creations and have certainly been evolving and changing.

Analysis from a survey of these associations, matched with household data on the members and the population at large has shown that these groups manage to insure a sizeable part of the expenditures attached to at least some shocks. The associations seem to be inclusive, in the sense that anyone who is willing to abide by their rules is able to join, and at least in the areas under study, these groups showed a high prevalence. In most communities we counted several such associations and most households were members of more than one group. When different groups offer different products, it leads to the emergence of a localised insurance market and introduces an element of choice for the households. Unfortunately, despite these attractive characteristics, people are still found to be severely affected by different manifestations of risk.

Finally, we noted that Ethiopian funeral associations are likely to come under increasing pressure in the next few years, if HIV/AIDS makes increased premiums necessary. The result is likely to be a less inclusive institution, with the poor increasingly less able to contribute. A similar story could not be confirmed for Tanzania.

Notes

1 Using Putnam *et al.* (1993), social capital can be defined as referring to features of social organisation, such as trust, norms and networks that can improve the efficiency of society. In particular, the focus is on the external effects of community relations on outcomes of interpersonal interactions: "strong" social capital tends then to be associated with economic success.

2 In Tanzania, there is some social pressure to be part of at least one women's group. Women not part of a group are considered anti-social and uncooperative. Still, they are free to choose which group to join, or even to set up new groups.

3 Details of the overall survey are in Dercon and Krishnan (2003).

4 "Village" is used to mean a Peasant Association. Rural Ethiopia is administratively divided into Peasant Associations, which are a collection of communities.

5 The data on Sirbana Godeti were collected in 2002, but the data on the other villages were only collected from October to December 2003, and are not yet matched to the household data.

6 "*Iddir*" is the generic name. In some areas, other local names are used – such as "kire" in parts of Wollo. They are all referred to as *iddir* in this chapter.

7 Most of these groups would also ask for a fixed additional contribution at the time of a funeral.

8 Mariam (2003) reports even a mean group size of 175 in his sample of 52 *iddirs.*

9 In a study by Mariam (2003) of 52 *iddirs* in mainly rural Ethiopia, similar results were found. The study reports that, besides funeral expenses, insurance and/or credit was also given for house fire (44 per cent) and illness episodes (20 per cent).

10 Groups that have no name are identified by the name of the chairperson.

11 Other surveys confirm the widespread membership. Open-ended questioning on which social organisations households are members of in a sample in South Wollo collected found about 80 per cent of households to be members of at least one *iddir* (Mogues, 2004; Mariam, 2003) reported in his survey of about 1200 households in 40 largely rural communities in Ethiopia that 87 per cent of households were members of an *iddir.*

12 This analysis uses the 4th round of the data (from 1997) which included specific questions on membership. Membership in that round of the data was about 75 per cent – below the estimate from other rounds – possibly due to slight underestimation related to less precise use of the local terms to describe the funeral societies, affecting data collection in two villages (one in Northern Shoa and one in Daramolo). The regressions used a probit model, using community level fixed effects.

13 In particular, current consumption levels are not significant. Land holdings are also not significant, while there is a very small effect from livestock holdings, increasing the probability of being a member, but the marginal effect is very small and only significant at 11 per cent.

14 It is standard practice to have multiple memberships of groups as a means of increasing coverage. Alternatively, it could be asked why they are not choosing to increase contributions in the existing groups to get more coverage. When discussing this with the groups, it was argued that the only feasible group structure is one in which everybody contributes the same, so that coverage is identical among members. Furthermore, it was often hard to find consensus among all members to increase contributions once a group is established so that for a member to obtain higher coverage, the most feasible route would be to also join another group, unless enough people can be found willing to set up a new group with higher coverage, and leave the original group. Membership fees limit the incentives for this behaviour.

15 This does not contradict that these institutions are responses to market failures. Effectively, they are non-market institutions taking on functions that a perfectly working insurance market could perform. But the specific form these institutions take on is still conditioned by the local context.

16 It was striking that no specific literature dealing with these institutions and their possible precursors in more traditional Haya society in Tanzania could be traced.

17 Although this needs further analysis, it is striking that, in the villages covered by the ERHS, villages in less densely populated areas and with poorer infrastructure and market linkages, fewer *iddirs* were found. Furthermore, in one of the two Tigrayan villages where no *iddir* was found, villagers simply stated that this is something for town people and not needed in a (remote) village like theirs where everybody still interacted with everybody else.

18 Pankhurst (2002) presents evidence that the first reported *iddir* was formed by a group of Soddo Gurage traders, and gained legitimacy via a government minister of Emperor Menelik at the beginning of the twentieth century.

19 There are examples of large professional or work-based *iddirs* in urban areas. Note that the spread in urban areas is sufficiently large to imply that the vast majority of urban dwellers will be members of one or more *iddirs*, across social classes. Indeed, even the World Bank's country office has its own *iddir.*

References

Aredo, D. (1993), "The informal and semiformal financial sectors in Ethiopia: a Study of the Iqqub, *Iddir* and Savings and Credit Co-operatives", AERC, Research Paper 21, Nairobi: African Economic Research Consortium.

Aredo, D. (1998), "The *Iddir* Theory and Practice", paper presented at the workshop organised by Ethiopian Society of Sociologists, Social Workers and Anthropologists, Addis Ababa.

Atim, C. (1998), *Contributions of Mutual Health Organisations to Financing Delivery and Access to Health Care: Synthesis of Research in Nine West and Central African Countries.* Bethesda: Abt Associates Inc.

Ayalew, Daniel (2003), Essays on Household Consumption and Production Decisions under Uncertainty in Rural Ethiopia, PhD Dissertation, Catholic University of Leuven.

Coate, S. and M. Ravallion (1993), "Reciprocity without commitment: characterisation and performance of informal insurance arrangements", *Journal of Development Economics*, 40, 1–24.

Coetzee, G. and C. Cross (2002), "Group approaches to financial service provision in rural South Africa", Working paper, 2002-10, Department of Agricultural Economics, Extension and Rural Development, University of Pretoria, Pretoria, South Africa.

Cohen, M. and J. Sebstad (2003), "Reducing vulnerability: the demand for microinsurance", *MicroSave Africa*, Nairobi, Kenya.

Dercon, S. (2002), "Income risk, coping strategies and safety nets", *World Bank Research Observer*, 17, 141–66.

Dercon, S. and P. Krishnan (2003), "Changes in poverty in villages in rural Ethiopia: 1989–1995", in A. Booth and P. Mosley (eds), *The New Poverty Strategies*, Palgrave Macmillan, London.

Dercon, S. and P. Krishnan (2000), "Vulnerability, seasonality and poverty in Ethiopia", *Journal of Development Studies*, 36, 6, August.

Dercon, S. and J. De Weerdt (2002), "Risk-sharing networks and insurance against illness", Centre for the Study of African Economies, Working Paper Series 2002-17.

Dercon, S., J. de Weerdt, T. Bold and A. Pankhurst (2006), "Group-based funeral insurance in Ethiopia and Tanzania", *World Development*, 34, 4, 685–703.

De Weerdt, J., (2004), "Risk-sharing and Endogenous Group Formation", chapter 10 in Dercon, S. (ed.), Insurance against Poverty, Oxford University Press.

De Weerdt, J. (2001), "Community organisations in rural Tanzania: a case study of the community of Nyakatoke, Bukoba rural District", IDS, University of Dar es Salaam and CES, University of Leuven, Belgium, The Nyakatoke Series, Report no. 3.

Fafchamps, M. and S. Lund (2003), "Risk-sharing networks in rural Philippines", *Journal of Development Economics*, 71, 2, 261–87.

Genicot, G. and D. Ray (2003), "Endogenous group formation in risk-sharing arrangements", *Review of Economic Studies*, 70, 87–113.

Ghatak, M. (1999), "Group lending, local information and peer selection", *Journal of Development Economics*, 60.

Grimard, F. (1997), "Household consumption smoothing through ethnic ties: evidence from Côte d'Ivoire", *Journal of Development Economics*, 53, 391–422.

Hoff, K. (1997), "Informal insurance arrangements: an equilibrium analysis", University of Maryland, mimeo.

Jütting, J. (2003), "Do community-based health insurance schemes improve poor people's access to health care? evidence from rural Senegal", *World Development*, 32, 2, 273–88.

Ligon, E., J. Thomas and T. Worrall (2002), "Informal insurance with limited commitment: theory and evidence from village economies", *Review of Economic Studies*, 69, 1, 209–44.

Mariam, D.H. (2003) "Indigenous social insurance as an alternative financing mechanism for health care in Ethiopia (the case of eders)", *Social Science and Medicine*, 56, 1719–26.

Mogues, T. (2004), "Shocks, livestock asset dynamics and social capital in Ethiopia", University of Wisconsin-Madison, mimeo.

Morduch, J. (1995), "Income smoothing and consumption smoothing", *Journal of Economic Perspectives*, 9 (Summer), 103–14.

Pankhurst, A., (2003), "The role and space for *iddirs* to participate in the Development of Ethiopia", in Pankhurst, A. (ed.) *Iddirs: Participation and Development, Proceedings of the Ethiopian National Conference 20–21 December 2001*, Addis Ababa Agency for Cooperation and Research in Development, Addis Ababa, pp.2–41.

Pankhurst, A. and D.H. Mariam (2004), "The *iddir* in Ethiopia: historical development, social function and potential role in HIV/AIDS Prevention and control", *NorthEast African Studies*, forthcoming.

Putnam, R.D. with R. Leonardi and R. Y. Nanetti (1993), *Making Democracy Work: Civic traditions in Modern Italy*, Princeton, NJ, Princeton University Press.

Roth, J. (1999), "Informal micro-finance schemes: the case of funeral insurance in South Africa", ILO, mimeo.

Rutherford, S. (2001), The Poor and their Money, Oxford University Press for India, Delhi.

Shewamoltot, A. (2001), "The socio-economic impact of HIV/AIDS on *iddirs* with particular reference to in Woreda 11", *Senior Essay in Sociology*, Addis Ababa University.

Tesfaye, S. (2002), "The role of civil society organizations in poverty alleviation, sustainable development and change: the cases of *iddirs* in Addis Ababa, Akaki and Nazreth", MA thesis in social anthropology, school of graduate studies, Addis Ababa University.

Townsend, R.M. (1994), "Risk and insurance in village India", *Econometrica*, 2, 3, 539–91.

Townsend, R.M. (1995), "Consumption insurance: an evaluation of risk-bearing systems in low-income economies", *Journal of Economic Perspectives*, 9 (Summer), 83–102.

10 SHG-based microfinance programmes

Can they remove poverty?

Anand Mohan Tiwari and Sarojini Ganju Thakur

Introduction

In India, the self-help groups (SHGs) constitute a widely accepted development strategy for poverty reduction as they are perceived as powerful vehicles for the promotion of microcredit and microfinance, especially for women. While there are some common elements that the SHG[1] model shares with the Grameen model of Bangladesh, such as using 'peer pressure' as a substitute for collateral, in contrast to Grameen, the SHG-based microfinance in India encourages 'self' management and 'self' regulation of the groups' activities.

Self-help groups have proved to be very versatile and their members have successfully taken up both economic and community-related interventions. It provides poor women an opportunity to take decisions involving themselves, their groups and their lives. Savings and credit is normally used as an entry point for formation of SHGs since it gives the members a chance to participate in decision-making and satisfies their short-term credit needs. SHGs can be an effective tool for bringing about women's empowerment. This approach is now increasingly being recognized in designs of recent programmes.

The SHG-based microfinance model in India encourages group members to manage the group's financial affairs and deposit funds in the local bank in the name of the SHG. Members' savings are initially used to issue small loans to needy members. After gaining some experience of credit handling, a SHG deemed 'credit-worthy' is issued a bigger amount of loan by a commercial bank. Members are free to decide the end use of this loan, its purpose and repayment instalment, without any interference of the promoting organization or the bank, since the SHG is directly responsible to the bank for repayment of the loan. The National Bank for Agriculture and Rural Development (NABARD) has offered a basic framework to the nationalized commercial banks for this purpose, which prohibits insistence on collateral and any direct subsidy.

Women-managed SHGs have shown remarkable growth during the last decade in India. It is estimated that over 16 million borrowers, mostly women, are linked with this mechanism (NABARD, 2004). Realizing that they can be a promising tool in capacity building of rural poor, especially women, central and state governments have vigorously supported the SHG-centric models of development which was pioneered by civil society organizations. A significant shift in the conventional SHG-based approach was made through the Rural Women's Development and Empowerment (Swa-Shakti) Project (1998), which recognized poverty as a multidimensional and complex phenomenon and emphasized a holistic role for SHGS. Some second-tier micro-finance institutions have also emerged in the last decade.

This chapter seeks to examine the nature of the impact that microfinance SHGs have on poverty reduction, and also the key factors that can contribute to their improved functioning and sustainability. This issue was felt to be of particular relevance after an internal evaluation commissioned by the Rural Development Department in 2004, pointed out that very few SHGs formed by various agencies are likely to survive after withdrawal of the implementing agencies. This finding led to the present study on the nature of functioning and sustainability of some SHGs formed in Patan district where there are several implementing agencies for SHG-based programmes. After briefly reviewing the literature on relevant issues, this chapter describes four SHGs set up in the last several years in Patan district and then focuses on alternative structures and strategies for poverty reduction, which are being piloted in Gujarat.

Role of microfinance in rural poverty eradication

The focus of this section is to briefly review the current thinking on some of the debates around the issues that our empirical work in Patan district is exploring. Since most SHGs are based on a savings and credit model, this section examines the links between microcredit and poverty reduction and empowerment. The poor are characterized not only by low levels of income, but also by assetlessness, poor access to government services, lack of opportunities for employment, vulnerability, isolation, dependence, a sense of powerlessness and fatalism. In addition, illiteracy, ill-health, gender inequality and environmental degradation are all aspects of being poor. The exclusion of the poor, and poor women in particular, from formal financial services provided by the state can be analysed in terms of exclusions based on relationships of caste, class and gender as well as discriminatory practices of the state.

In the poverty debate, a focus on women is critical for two reasons. First, poverty has a female face and the phenomenon of the feminization of poverty is well established. Not only are there numerically more poor women than poor men, but women also experience poverty in more exacerbated forms than men do. In South Asia men are leaving agriculture faster than women, giving rise to an increasing concentration of women on land. In India, 86 per cent of rural women workers are engaged in agriculture compared with 74 per cent of rural male workers. In addition, 20 per cent of rural households are headed by females (World Survey on the Role of Women in Development, 1999).

Are microfinance programmes reaching the ultra poor?

The impact of micro-credit on poverty is not clear and continues to be highly debated. The basis of many of the programmes is that microfinance institutions which follow the principles of good banking will also be those that most alleviate poverty. A key tenet is that poor households demand access to credit, not cheap credit. Thus programmes can charge high interest rates without compromising outreach. The argument that is commonly made in the microfinance context is that since moneylenders charge high interest rates, microfinance programmes can too. But, while poor households may borrow from moneylenders at high rates, they are generally doing so to meet short-term consumption needs, not to make long-term productive investments. Moreover, although there are some poor households which are able to pay high rates, there are also many borrowers who cannot pay high rates. These latter households tend to be poorer and harder to reach with traditional programmes and they constitute a larger fraction of client bases (Morduch, 2000).

From the perspective of enterprise development, producing and selling goods and services requires more than capital. It requires skills, other materials, information, connections and transportation. Since richer households tend to have more of these inputs, marginal returns to capital are often higher for them than for poorer households. These richer households will be more willing to borrow than the poorer households. Poorer households are engaged in survival level, multiple income generating activities. Undertaking various occupations at the same time allowed them to reduce the risk of income loss when the demand for services or goods of one profession suddenly declines (Lepenies, 2004).

Microfinance can play a role in increasing the income and the household consumption but the very poor may not benefit from it. An influential cross country study by Hulme and Mosley (1996) found that loans produce the greatest percentage increase in the incomes of upper poor and non-poor borrowers who are close to or above national poverty lines. The extreme or core poor, the poorest 50 per cent of those in poverty were not only less likely to participate in microfinance programmes, when they did participate their post-credit incomes were less likely to increase. Moreover, such increases as occurred were often too small and short lived to enable exit from the poverty trap. As the poor are probably more risk averse, they tend to take small, subsistence protecting loans without investing in new technology, fixed capital or hiring of labour.

Social restrictions on women also limit their economic activities

(Hulme and Mosley, 1996 and Lepenies, 2004). In micro-enterprises they own, women work longer hours for less remuneration compared to men. Women's enterprises were also more embedded within the family, relying on family networks for labour and credit. It is also established that enterprises which build on women's traditional skills and occupations have a greater chance of proving viable than those which require training in new skills. Elsewhere, it is shown that economic conditions of the household and women improve, but it takes a long time to get out of poverty. Significant impact on poverty reduction depends on a cumulative loan threshold (Hussain, 1984; Chen, 1984; Bruntrup, *et al.*, 1997 and Zaman, 1999).

It can be concluded that the impact of micro-credit on poverty is not clear. McGuire and Conroy (2000) suggest that access to credit has potential to significantly reduce poverty, but others argue that it has minimal impact on poverty reduction.

While microfinance is meant to reach the poor, there are almost universally acknowledged views that most programmes, despite stated objectives, do not reach the poorest of the poor. One of the reasons is related to the fact that loans which are normally given for self-employment, presuppose some degree of micro-enterprise and the long-term interest of every implementing agency is to see that members quickly start taking loans for income generation activities.

Marguerite Robinson, the author of *The Microfinance Revolution* (2001), has expressed her view succinctly when she wrote, 'I do not want to reach the poorest of the poor, I want to reach the poorest of the economically active. In general, I believe the poorest of the poor are the responsibility of the Ministry of Social Welfare, the Ministry of Labour, private charities and so forth.'

SHGs as an empowerment tool

There are logical associations between poverty and disempowerment because an insufficiency of the means of meeting one's basic needs often rules out the ability to exercise meaningful choice (Kabeer, 1999). Empowerment refers to the processes by which those who have been denied the ability to make choices acquire such ability. In other words, empowerment entails a process of change.

Empowerment does imply transformed awareness. It is a complex process which involves a change in the perception of the women and their relationships. For purposes of this chapter, the vision of empowered women that we would like to use is of women who will[2]

- demand their rights from family, community and government;
- have increased access to and control over material, social and political resources;

- have self-confidence, self-esteem and enhanced awareness;
- be able to raise issues of common concern and take action through mobilization and networking.

The 'SHGs for women's empowerment paradigm' maintains a clear focus on reducing gender inequality and mainstreaming gender in the developmental processes. Savings and credit is looked upon as an entry point, though not treated as an end in itself. This approach essentially recognizes that a 'credit only approach' fails to change the underlying gender relations that place women at a disadvantage. The Indian model is, in fact, regarded as the credit-plus model, wherein savings and credit are the means for group formation and collective action and not the ultimate goal. For women who have been confined to households, their mobilization into a collective, propels them into a more community-oriented entity, which gives them the basis for negotiating, sharing and bargaining at multiple levels – the household, community and government. Such groups give women the strength and self-confidence to resist the exploitation that they face within the household and community. There are innumerable examples of the nature of strength women have acquired after joining a group. Women members of the SHG have shown increased levels of socio-political awareness and empowerment in the community, raised levels of negotiating power and changes in community norms, particularly in terms of changing attitudes to gender expectations (Brahme, personal communications; Dash, 2003).

Empowerment-oriented programmes emphasize the following key aspects:

- Self-help groups, as a concept, need not be equated with savings and credit groups and SHGs can come together even for non-financial purposes.
- Targeted effort needs to be made to include the poorest of the poor women. At times the very nature of the entry point activity involving money alienates the poor.
- Capacity and skill building, awareness generation, access to information, exposure to one's own environment, knowledge regarding government schemes and others encompass a process of helping women gain control and take charge of their lives.
- Group meetings are treated as a forum to address women's concerns and community issues.

It is true that access to credit generates a form of economic empowerment which can greatly enhance a woman's self-esteem and status within the family. In terms of economic empowerment, it was felt that economic power and access to productive resources would weaken traditional gender roles and empower poor women, but the majority of women micro-entrepreneurs could not even earn minimum wages through these borrowings and the available evidence shows that their work loads have increased considerably (Batliwala and Dhanraj, 2004). The increase in income did not result in improved cooking facilities, better access to drinking water or sanitation, or better health care and nutrition. Although participation in microfinance programmes increases women's mobility into certain public spaces, the positive effect of participation on the condition for empowerment is small since the women's access to more remunerative wage employment and mobility into the male dominated public sphere is not increased (Kantor, 2003).

The historical involvement of banks and microfinance institutions in India has ensured that SHGs adopt a minimalist approach and ignore non-financial inputs like literacy, health, awareness, capacity building and skill training. SHGs can become a good forum for women's empowerment provided the nurturing agencies take care to design their interventions to improve the confidence level of members through better participation in SHG meetings and more interactions with external agencies. Through this process, members develop communication skills and are able to put forward their views confidently. By their involvement in decision-making processes, group members are encouraged to participate in bigger decisions affecting them, their family and their community.

Examples of self-help groups in Gujarat

The state of Gujarat lies on the western part of India. It has a population of around 50 million, of which 65 per cent belong to rural areas. The state has strong industrial capabilities with a high concentration of petrochemical, pharmaceutical and textile industries and a long coastline leading to impressive fishing and port infrastructure. Agriculture here is mainly dependent on monsoon and due to recurring droughts, the rural poor, comprising 15 per cent of the population, frequently have to take recourse to government-supported wage employment programmes. Patan district, having 80,000 poor rural households, falls in north Gujarat and comprises some of the most resource-poor blocks of the state.

The SHG microfinance movement has flourished in Gujarat also. It is estimated that over 200,000 SHGs are functioning in the state, with the Rural Development Department alone supporting over 65,000 SHGs. Of these, close to 35,000 SHGs have been linked with commercial banks that have extended credit of approximately Rs.200 million.

Out of a concern for the long-term viability of microfinance SHG's in Gujurat, one of the authors made field visits to a number of groups in Patan district. Selected findings from visits to four groups will be described here to illustrate the diversity of SHG approaches and to consider implications for poverty reduction and women's empowerment in this region.

Swa-Shakti project

The Rural Women's Development and Empowerment (*Swa-Shakti*) Project, which is being implemented in the Gujarat Women's Economic Development Corporation, is a Rs.1910 million project assisted by the World Bank, the International Fund for Agriculture Development and the Government of India. This multi-state project is based on the formation of women's SHGs for their empowerment. It recognizes the important role of civil society organizations in developing group processes. In Gujarat, it covers ten districts.

One of the SHGs formed under this project in May 2002 in village Sabosan was selected for detailed analysis. Each member was saving Rs.50 per month and more than 75 per cent of the members were regularly attending group meetings. The group had started micro-credit activity in January 2003 and had subsequently received a loan of Rs.25,000 from a commercial bank. Members had saved Rs.22,310 and rotated the funds as loans among them. By September 2004, the group had loaned Rs.64,200, out of which Rs.23,700 was still with the members. The repayment rate has been 100 per cent.

Savings were collected and loans issued in the group meeting. The group had not started any other long-term activity. Although the project aims at ensuring convergence with other programmes of the government, not much progress had been made in this regard by the Sabosan SHG. An analysis of its loan portfolio shows an interesting picture: 12 members had obtained 22 loans with six members obtaining Rs.18,000 for medical purposes, six members had obtained nine loans of Rs.31,000 for animal husbandry, three members had got four loans worth Rs.8200 for service sector activities and the remaining two members had obtained loans of Rs.7000 for other activities. Two of these members had taken loans of Rs.9000 and 5500 respectively, for animal husbandry. Three members had taken multiple loans for small enterprises. Overall, 40 per cent of the members had started small enterprises after joining the SHG and an internal assessment of the project revealed income enhancement of Rs.200–1000 per month for individual members.

Watershed development projects

These development projects are jointly funded by central and state governments. Each of these projects aims at livelihood security through watershed development and community mobilization, and has a provision of Rs.3 million per micro-watershed of 500 hectares. Women's SHGs were earlier limited to savings and credit activities and usually did not play any other role in the project. The project is now focusing on the capacity building of SHGs in a systematic manner. Around 300 SHG members were recently trained in the development of kitchen gardens, rainwater harvesting and masonry. Members are also involved in wage employment schemes.

An SHG formed in July 2003 in Malsund village was taken up for further analysis. Each of its members was saving Rs.30 per month and the group had started micro-credit activity after six months of its formation. Until September 2004, three members had obtained loans, out of which two members borrowed Rs.1000 each for purchase of cattle feed and another member borrowed Rs.3000 for starting a grocery shop. Repayments were regular and the first two loans had been re-paid fully. The third member had also paid Rs.1200 by the end of September, 2004. One member was trained in kitchen garden development, which motivated other members to take up this activity. Members agreed that such activities have improved their self-confidence and status within the family. The demand for credit within the group was increasing and the SHG was examining various options for obtaining additional funds from the project and banks.

Swarnajayanti Gram Swa-rojgar Yojana (SGSY)

This scheme comes under the rubric of poverty alleviation programmes which adopt a SHG approach for establishing micro-enterprises in rural areas. The ideology of SGSY stems from the realization that well targeted subsidies are still required by the poor. This scheme provides some revolving loan for on-lending, by good quality groups.

The SHG in Sabosan village was a mixed group formed with 13 members in the year 2000, but presently it was working with ten members, including a woman. Members were mainly involved in dairy activity. Although they joined the group with the sole aim of obtaining a bank loan and taking up some economic activity, the majority of them are now above the poverty line due to SHG's strong linkage with the local dairy co-operative. Every member saved Rs.100 per month and 'bullet payment system' was followed for loan repayment under which the principal amount could be paid at the end of the loan period as long as the interest amount was paid every month. The majority of the loans taken by members from group funds were for medical purposes. In addition to group savings, it had received a revolving fund of Rs.10,000 in March 2001 from the District Rural Development Agency, Patan and Rs.325,000 from the local commercial bank for purchase of milch cattle. The first loan of Rs.162,500 was received in September 2001 and the second loan of a similar amount was received in the year 2002–3. Each member had purchased two milch cattle and joined the village dairy co-operative. Bank instalments were deducted by the dairy co-operative and directly paid to the bank. Village Dairy Co-operative records showed an average monthly income of Rs.700–2425 per member. Majority were earning over Rs.1500 per month from this activity. Some 74 per cent of the bank loan had been re-paid by them as per the schedule, leaving a balance of Rs.90,020 only.

However, with two-cattle units per household, dairying had not yet become the main occupation for members, and income could further increase through a cross breeding programme which would increase the unit size of cattle.

Jeevika project

With the help of a government-sponsored programme called Development of Women and Children in Rural Areas (DWCRA), Self-Employed Women's Association (SEWA) had organized women's groups in a few blocks of the district. These groups focused on women's empowerment with microfinance as one component. SEWA and other groups formed outside DWCRA were later linked with SEWA Bank, Ahmedabad, through a district federation. Subsequently, the state government helped launch a livelihood restoration project (later called *Jeevika*) with the support of the International Fund for Agricultural Development as a response to the earthquake of 2001. Jeevika groups have been nurtured and trained by spearhead leaders trained by SEWA, to promote local leadership. SEWA Bank also organized training on savings and loan management.

A microfinance group in Shergadh village was taken up for further study. This was a four-year-old group with cumulative savings of Rs.30,380 by 33 members. Every member saved Rs.20 per month which was deposited with SEWA Bank, Ahmedabad. Some of the members had also joined a SEWA insurance scheme which arranges medical treatment through government hospitals and also takes care of serious emergencies. Of the ten members who took loans from the group, some of them used it to retire high interest bearing loans taken from money lenders, a few purchased milch cattle, one member purchased a transport vehicle and another started a brick kiln. The group also obtained a loan of Rs.45,000 from SEWA Bank. The majority of members were very confident during the interactions and some have visited other states.

Issues affecting long-term sustainability of SHGs

Experience has shown that a SHG is strengthened by meeting the following six criteria for long term sustainability (Tiwari, 2001): it should establish proper processes, be financially viable, there should be a critical mass of SHGs in the village, it should become part of a larger federation, its members should be involved in some community action and the SHG should be able to access regular schemes of the government.

Establishing proper SHG processes

Some of the basic principles of SHG formation are their voluntary nature, members coming from similar socio-economic background and their formation for a specific purpose. It is also acknowledged that it is easier to mobilize poor women. Once a group is formed, it should meet regularly, members should attend group meetings and they should participate in the decision-making process. To ensure involvement of every member, strategies like rotation of leadership, training of members, decisions taken only in group meetings, maintenance of records by group members themselves, and so on are adopted. Meetings of the SHGs from all four programmes dealt with savings and credit issues only, without discussing other matters like awareness generation, literacy, health, sanitation or issues affecting the lives of poor rural women. In such a situation, meetings can become ritualized and responsibility for maintaining records, collection of savings and repayments, and other services are not shared by all members. For example, the Jeevika group in Shergadh village, although quite old, had not started inter-loaning activity and their participation in income-generation activities appeared limited. In contrast, all the members of the predominantly male SGSY were involved in such activities. Rotation of leadership was not evident in the four sites. This may partially be attributed to lack of literacy and numeracy skills among members and lack of proper capacity building inputs provided to the members.

Financial viability of SHGs

Financial viability does not only comprise generation of surplus of income over expenditure, but also requires putting in place a very good system of audit of group accounts, fast rotation of group funds, mixing 'warm' money with 'cold' money, control over loan defaults, access to external funds and ensuring credit availability to the majority of members. 'Warm' money is defined as the savings and other funds generated directly by the members, whereas 'cold' money is the grant or loan fund obtained from the promoting organization or financial institutions. It has been observed that many SHGs treat both these types of funds differently, leading to lack of adequate concern for the 'cold' money. It is always suggested to mix both so that the members use all funds with sufficient care.

Although the accounts of the SGSY group were not maintained properly, it rotated funds and arranged adequate credit to its members. The SGSY men's group in Sabosan village was able to provide an average loan of Rs.31,000 to its members compared to approximately Rs.5000 each by the Jeevika group in Shergadh village and the Swa-Shakti project in Sabosan village. Every member of the SGSY group had received a loan, whereas 25 per cent and 65 per cent of members could access loans in Jeevika and Swa-Shakti respectively. SGSY also had a very high credit-savings ratio of 6.82 signifying very high capacity to leverage institutional finance, compared to 1.78 for Jeevika and 2.88 for Swa-Shakti. The watershed group's performance appeared poor on these parameters. With increasing financial transactions in these SHGs, the issue of setting up proper audit systems becomes important. None of the four groups appeared to have a reliable audit system at the local level. SEWA routinely gets all the group records to its district federation office to update the entries but this practice makes SHGs perpetually dependent on the promoting non-governmental organization (NGO).

A majority of the first-time income-generating activities started by the women members of SHGs are marked by very low investment enterprises which can be started with existing skills and involve minimal risks. The returns are also low due to tough competition. The enterprises involve very little mobility and are basically part-time occupations which can be terminated at short notice. The first few enterprise related loans to SHG members are in the range of Rs.1000 per member. With the most optimistic scenario, they cannot expect their daily earnings to exceed Rs.25–30 per day based on 3–4 hours of labour. As a result, such earnings can only supplement the family income and cannot become the main source of their livelihood.

Income generation activities started by the three female SHGs were characterized by a low-investment low-risk and low-return cycle. This may be due to the limitations of the promoting organizations in skill enhancement of members leading to limited credit absorption capacity of their members and low total loans to savings ratio in these SHGs. Any impact on rural poverty with this level of investment is doubtful. In contrast to this, the SGSY men's group was able to obtain two doses of credit from banks and promoted animal husbandry with per capita credit of Rs.30,720 and it was the only one of the four which could show a significant increase in the income levels of its members. The presence of a village dairy co-operative helped them in organizing forward linkages successfully.

Involvement in community level activities

SHGs mature faster with awareness generation of members and lively meetings where various non-financial issues affecting women are also discussed. In fact restricting the SHG members to savings and credit activities for a long time appears to be under-utilization of the potential of women's SHGs. Women's groups can be very effective in tackling community level issues like alcoholism, getting work done through government systems, enforcing implementation of basic, sanitation, water supply management, and so on. Involvement in community activities typically requires efforts by highly trained field workers. None of the local groups appeared to be handling larger community issues effectively.

Convergence with other schemes

Since government projects and NGO-based interventions are for a fixed duration, for the SHGs to survive beyond the project cycle, it is necessary that they get linked with ongoing schemes of the government for being able to keep on accessing support in future. The Swa-Shakti project actively encourages such convergence, and the watershed group was involved in developing a village micro-plan by linking to other existing schemes. Convergence efforts by SGSY and Jeevika groups appeared more limited.

Outreach of SHGs

A large number of SHGs in the same village help to promote project philosophy, create a sense of solidarity among members, create a larger forum for taking up community level issues and ultimately safeguard the project from disturbing influences of weaker SHG-based programmes. This also reduces the implementation cost of such programmes. Jeevika and the watershed project have formed a large number of SHGs in their programme villages.

Alternative approaches for poverty reduction

Although the microfinance activities promoted by women's SHGs had shown considerable potential in the beginning of the last decade, many groups have been unable to reap the full benefits of this marvellous tool of social engineering. As we have seen, their effectiveness can be limited with respect to gender concerns, poverty reduction, and social and political empowerment.

With a view to utilize the potential of SHGs and link them actively with livelihood, employment generation and other opportunities, the Rural Development Department in Gujarat has started few interesting initiatives. It also actively supports alternate structures like women's co-operatives in its efforts to address the needs of the poor and ultra poor.

Shramyogi project

Five of the poorest families from every village are being proactively identified under this project to form small groups on the Grameen pattern. After some capacity building of members, various pro-poor schemes are converged with these groups. Participating households had to fulfil certain basic expectations before they become eligible for the financial benefits under the project. State government guarantees 150 days of wage employment, subsidized house, skill training to a family member, five horticultural saplings, and loan for purchase of small cattle. These guarantees, however, are available only if the family ensures schooling of its children, member is free from addictions like alcohol and tobacco, follows small family norms and attends local body meetings. Out of 91,201 families participating in the project, over 28 per cent were female headed, 12 percent comprised of very old members, and 20 per cent had at least one handicapped member. Under this project, 18,084 groups were formed and 59 per cent of these groups were active after second year, which is a good sign considering their status, age and economic level. Out of the surviving groups, over 78 per cent are involved in regular savings, some of them have started offering internal loans (about 5 per cent of active groups) and have sanctioned Rs.5.85 million among them.

Shramyogi project recognizes the need for financial subsidies to participating families, at least during the initial stages. To this end, it has actively converged various individual beneficiary-oriented schemes by generating 3.6 million person-days of wage employment, providing 227,000 horticultural saplings and 37,000 houses. It also provided skill training to 20,000 family members. This approach ensures that the poorest families in the state are not by-passed and after a period of disciplined regime during which they receive other inputs for raising their confidence levels, they can join a newly formed SHG in their village.

Although the state government has launched this ambitious scheme for bringing these poorest families above the poverty line in a timely manner, the implementers are facing certain unique problems that a large number of Shramyogi families were very old and 24 per cent of families had at least one member who was suffering from some serious handicap. The standard approach of linking them with wage or self-employment programmes could not work and it was tried to link them with existing pension schemes, handicrafts production, horticulture and rearing of small cattle. This project raises issues like 'can microenterprises be successfully taken up by the poorest of the poor?' and the role of thorough planning and research in conceptualization of anti-poverty programmes, as the exact profile of participating families was not known before the scheme was launched. They are now trying different approaches for the old and handicapped. This also leads to a larger general question that how well are the microenterprises conceived and implemented? As could be seen in the subsequent study of the animal husbandry project in Kheda district, simple conception and timely inputs can work successfully for tackling poverty.

Shakti Samanvay project

With a view to converging the resources of various development departments for improving overall quality of life indicators in rural areas, an ambitious convergence project is being piloted in a few parts of the state. No separate funds have been provided for this purpose as the participating departments will leverage their existing schemes to implement it.

By dove-tailing existing schemes of health, education, industries, women and child development, Panchayati raj and rural development, this scheme aims to bring about 50 per cent improvement in infant mortality rate, school drop out rate, per capita income of poor rural famil-ies, access to safe drinking water, safe delivery and malnutrition rates. Women's self-help groups and village panchayats will be used as platforms for convergence of individual schemes by creating demand for these schemes.

After formation of SHGs and capacity building of village local body members, the project will encourage creation of resource centres to provide inputs on health, literacy, skill up gradation and enterprise coun-selling to member SHGs. These resource centres will also link their member SHGs with various development departments.

Animal husbandry project in Kheda district

This Rs.380 million project is being jointly implemented by the local dis-trict dairy co-operative called Amul and the Rural Development Depart-ment. It aims at eliminating poverty in some of the backward parts of the district. Although farmers in this district prospered due to dairy develop-ment efforts of Amul, it has, so far, not focused on the poor families. This project aims to leverage the expertise of Amul to bring 7500 poor families above the poverty line. In order to convert animal husbandry into a full time activity, it is proposed to arrange at least three cattle for each poor family. For the first cattle they will get a cash subsidy of Rs.7500, second cattle will be financed through bank credit and the third one will be cross bred, reared by the beneficiary himself. Government of India agreed to provide grant of Rs.115 million, state government will provide Rs.35 million and commercial banks will provide loan of Rs.230 million. The identified poor families will be trained by Amul before linking them with existing village level milk co-operatives. The project will also support con-struction of cattle sheds, development of fodder plots, installation of bulk chillers and bore wells, creation of doorstep artificial insemination facili-ties, mobile diagnostic laboratory, and the strengthening of a training centre.

Amul has guaranteed repayment of bank loans and has also guaranteed an incremental monthly earning of Rs.1994 from each cattle. It will also provide veterinary services and upgrade quality of milk to Codex stand-ards. This is a unique project in which Amul agreed to pay a penalty of 5 per cent of the project cost if any of the above parameters are not met. At the same time an incentive at 2 per cent of project cost will be allowed to Amul if all the parameters are timely met.

By September 2005, the project covered 3900 families with over 90 per cent repayment rate on bank credit of Rs.132.25 million. Participating families have procured 8997 cattle, constructed 2236 cattle sheds, developed 4726 fodder plots and 4822 women participants have been trained. The Project has also deployed 50 mobile artificial insemination units and created 15 new milk chilling units So far, the poor families are earning more than the guaranteed amount from each cattle. This might be the only project involving the poor where bankers are competing to get the business by reducing the interest rate from 9.5 to 7.5 per cent.

Conclusion

An attempt was made in this chapter to describe a variety of approaches and auspices to microfinance development in Gujarat state. There were obstacles to success with respect to poverty reduction and empowerment of women. Among the groups described, the male group SGSY appears to hold the most promise for poverty reduction. The average size of assistance available to the borrower under this programme is much larger than those of the normal microcredit initiatives in India. The Special Projects component of this scheme, which supports the animal husbandry project in Kheda district, provides an avenue for experimentation and ensuring better linkages.

However, implementation of SGSY suffers from many of the same constraints and limitations of the earlier poverty alleviation programmes, and sometimes in the field vitiates the culture of self-help that has already been developed. Efforts have not been made to change the mindset of the functionaries who were earlier delivering target-oriented programmes. It is either riding piggyback on pre-existing groups, or is unable to go through the processes that are required for the establishment of new groups.

The performance of this group raises few interesting questions. What should be the life of a SHG? If it was for the sole purpose of helping members to improve their economic status, then, since majority of the members had crossed the poverty line, should it not be wound up or can it survive in this form in the future? Considering that they could not successfully convert animal husbandry into a full time activity, should not the SHG now provide inputs like training, cattle feed, veterinary services, increasing size of the cattle unit, others? A view on these issues can be made only after studying the performance of these SHGs for some more time.

The rationale for working with SHGs varies from institution to institution, and also from project to project. For some, SHGs are viewed as a way to reduce transaction costs and enhance outreach, for others interested in poverty reduction, it constitutes part of a mandated poverty reduction strategy or it is only an entry point for the broader goal of empowerment and transformation of power relations within society. In the latter case, while emphasizing the need for sustainable institutions, the focus is on social intermediation through a combination of empowerment-enhancing interventions which could include gender awareness, health, education and legal literacy. Mayoux's typology of the three contrasting paradigms in micro-finance and gender namely, of financial self-sustainability, poverty reduction, and feminist empowerment are useful in this regard. It highlights that the rationale for targeting women also varies – at one end of the spectrum is the efficiency-oriented view that women have high repayment rates, while at the other is the more feminist orientation that women need to be socially and politically empowered. Somewhere in between is the recognition of the need to target women, as there are higher levels of female poverty. It is evident from the objectives of the various initiatives that empowerment does not necessarily form part of the stated objectives. If it is used to explain the nature of outcomes, the understanding of the word is so diverse that it can mean anything from simply covering notions of enhanced well-being and expansion of individual choice to the broader notion of transforming gender relations. Moreover, there is no 'one way of doing things' and the implementers will have to keep on experimenting with various models.

Notes

1 A SHG is an informal, homogenous grassroots institution of 10–20 members who self-select themselves and are linked by some form of affinity that binds them together. They meet regularly, with common and shared goals, having established norms and elected leaders. Since the SHG model is now well-known, its basic principles will not be discussed in this article.
2 This is the vision that was developed by the authors for the Indira Mahilia Yojana programme of the Government of India and it encompasses many of the essential factors for such a process.

References

Batliwala, S. and Dhanraj, D., Gender myths that instrumentalise women: a view from the Indian frontline, *IDS Bulletin*, 2004, 35(4), 11–18.
Bruntrup, M., Alauddin, S. M., Huda, A. and Rahman, M., *Impact assessment of the Association of Social Advancement (ASA)*, 1997, Dhaka.
Chen M., *Developing Non-Craft Employment for Women in Bangladesh*, 1984, New York, Seeds.
Dash, A., Strategies for poverty alleviation in India: CYSD's holistic approach to Empowerment through the self-help group model, *IDS Bulletin*, 2003, 34(4), 133–42.
Hulme, D. and Mosley, P. (1996). *Finance Against Poverty, Vol. 1*, 1996, London: Routledge.
Hussain M., *The Impact of Grameen Bank on Women's Involvement in Productive Activities*, 1984, Grameen Bank, Dhaka.
Kabeer, N., Resources, agency, achievements: reflections on the measurement of women's empowerment, *Development and Change*, 1999, 30(3), 435–64.
Kantor, P., Women's empowerment through home-based work: evidence from India, *Development and Change*, 2003, 34(3): 425–45.
Lepenies, P. H., Exit, voice and vouchers: using vouchers to train microentrepreneurs observations from the Paraguyan voucher scheme, *World Development*, 32(4), 2004, 713–24.

McGuire P. B. and Conroy, J. D., The micro-finance phenomenon, *Asia Pacific Review*, 2000, 7(1), pp. 90–108.

Morduch, J., The microfinance schism, *World Development*, 28(4), 2000, 617–29.

National Bank of Agriculture and Rural Development, *Progress of SHG-Bank linkage in India 2003–04*, 2004, Mumbai.

Robinson, M. S., *The Microfinance Revolution – Sustainable Finance for the Poor*, The World Bank, 2001, Washington, DC.

Rural Women's Development & Empowerment Project, *Staff Appraisal Report*, The World Bank, 1998, Washington, DC, p. 20.

Tiwari, A. M., *Tips for Field Workers, Volumes 1 & 2*, Department of Women & Child Development, Government of India, 2001, New Delhi.

World Survey on the Role of Women in Development, United Nations, 1999, New York.

Zaman, H., Assessing the impact of micro-credit on poverty and vulnerability in Bangladesh, The World Bank Policy Research Working Paper 2145, 1999, Washington, DC.

11 Community-level user groups

Do they perform as expected?

Ruth Alsop

Introduction

India's 1992 constitutional amendments and subsequent state acts created policy environments supportive of decentralized governance and management of development activities.[1] In this environment, community-based membership organizations gained increasing popularity as mechanisms for local resource management. The research reported in this chapter sought to enhance understanding of current levels of inclusiveness and effectiveness among community-level groups in rural development projects aided by the World Bank.[2]

Three types of community level user groups for local resource management were studied: the Site Implementation Committees (SICs) of the Uttar Pradesh Sodic Lands Reclamation Project; Village Forest Committees (VFCs) of the Madhya Predesh Forestry Project; and, the Water User Associations (WUAs) of the irrigation component of the Economic Restructuring Program in Andhra Pradesh (see Appendix).

A mixed methods approach was used for data collection that included a questionnaire survey of 2400 user group members and representatives. Both narrative and statistical techniques, including regression estimation, were used for analysis.[3] The enquiry focused on assessing the performance of settlement-level (or, in the case of irrigation water, system-level) user groups. Figure 11.1 outlines the analytic framework.

Findings based on narrative as well as descriptive statistical and econometric analysis suggested that such groups rarely performed as expected.

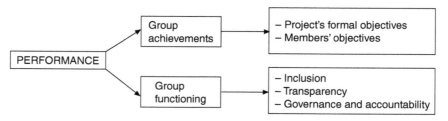

Figure 11.1 Analysis of performance of community level user groups.

Functions related to equitable and short-term delivery of project benefits were effectively undertaken. However, evidence indicated that neither did these organizations function well as democratic entities nor were they likely to operate independent of a project. Overall, community level user groups in the three sectors studied were unsustainable and more likely to act as vehicles for personal gain, rather than for collective action.

Group achievements

Group achievements are examined first by reviewing attainment of project's stated development objectives and then through analysis of respondents' own objectives.

Achievement of formal objectives

Achievement of key objectives as stated in project documentation (see Box 11.1), varied. Overall, 35 percent of respondents stated that their user group's ability to meet formal objectives was good, 28 percent indicated that formal objectives were achieved in a satisfactory manner, and 14 percent said the group had not met its objectives, while 22 percent of members felt they did not have enough information to assess achievements. Ratings varied by project and by objective but in all three states,

---

Uttar Pradesh Sodic Lands Reclamation Project

1   Distribution of inputs (e.g. fertilizer)
2   Creation of site implementation plan (local planning of the project, planning for and arrangements of distribution of inputs)
3   Maintenance of assets created under the project (link drains or items purchased for collective use such as sprayers)

Madhya Pradesh Forestry Project

1   Improved forest protection
2   Management of village development activities
3   Equitable distribution of forest produce

Andhra Pradesh Economic Restructuring Program, irrigation component

1   Effective maintenance of the irrigation system
2   Better water supply
3   Increased agricultural production

Box 11.1 Formal objectives of user groups.

the second and third objectives of the groups were not as well met as the first. For objectives two and three the percentage of respondents unable to make a judgment was high: 30 percent in Uttar Pradesh, 18 percent in Madhya Pradesh, and 36 percent in Andhra Pradesh.

Given traditional social patterns in rural India, regression estimates tested the hypothesis that the excluded or ill informed would be primarily members of disadvantaged, low-caste, or low-income groups.[4] Associations between village-level features and achievement of formal objectives were also investigated.[5] These are reported in the next section.

Uttar Pradesh sodic lands reclamation project

Seventy-seven percent of respondents reported good or reasonable input distribution but 45 percent reported not knowing the site implementation plan and 52 percent knew nothing about assets created under the project, or judged assets to be poorly maintained. Analysis revealed limited association between caste and perceptions of achievement of formal objectives. However, older people and those with smaller holdings felt that site implementation plans were not developed or supported and assets were poorly managed and maintained. Being a long-term group member, regular meeting attendee, group representative, member of multiple organizations and having more intra-group relationships associated with positive assessments of achievement of formal objectives.

More frequent meetings were held with project staff associated with negative evaluations of achievement of formal objectives, unless those meetings were for technical support or sharing inputs. This suggested that members primarily perceived the SIC as a means of accessing technical information and immediate benefits, rather than as a mechanism for establishing long-term cooperation among water user groups.

Madhya Pradesh forestry project

In Madhya Pradesh, tribal people – with forest-based livelihoods – were more satisfied with the performance than older people and those from other backward and scheduled caste households. Scheduled caste respondents and older people knew nothing of, or rated poorly, equitable distribution of forest produce.

Village-level differences indicated that, apart from meeting to share forest produce, frequent contact with project staff improved valuations of user groups. Thirty percent of respondents in Madhya Pradesh also perceived equitable distribution of forest produce to be poor which suggests that meetings associated with product distribution were unproductive or mishandled.

Membership in multiple organizations associated with higher rankings of achievement of formal objectives, but there was an inverse relationship between the number of *external* organizations present in a location and achievement of formal objectives. The density of *locally evolved* organizations[6] positively associated with achievements.

Andhra Pradesh economic restructuring program, irrigation component

The majority of respondents reported that irrigation systems were well maintained. Around half the WUAs surveyed had assisted with the better provision of irrigation water and said this increased agricultural production. Poorer people consistently associated with lower rankings of project achievements.

Asset management, sharing of benefits, and finance reasons were regarded as key WUA activities by most user group members rather than monitoring, capacity building or technical support. "People only come to WUA meetings when there is a problem" (village summaries). Irrigation water, once delivered to a field, became an individual benefit, and it was this rather than collective management that was of primary interest to farmers.

In Andhra Pradesh, a greater density of external organizations and larger number of networks associated with higher assessments of achievement of formal objectives. The last included association with a representative – through work or kinship ties – and participation of other family members in the WUA.

Achievement of members' objectives

The inducements for joining user groups, that respondents describe, rarely coincided with the formal objectives of user groups. In Uttar Pradesh, the most frequently cited member objectives were:

- material goods/inputs
- increased production from own land
- access to information.

In Madhya Pradesh, they were:

- wage labor
- loans
- material goods/inputs.

In Andhra Pradesh, they were:

- material goods/inputs
- increased irrigation water
- increased production from own land.

Among these, only the distribution of inputs in Uttar Pradesh and increased production in Andhra Pradesh matched the objectives outlined in project documentation.

Individual comments (see Box 11.2) clearly indicate that user group members' objectives focused on very specific individualized benefits. In no case did members state that cooperation for the maintenance of collective assets is a reason for participating in the user group.

Expectations of benefits were consistently exceeded in Madhya Pradesh, showed mixed results in Andhra Pradesh, and fell short in Uttar Pradesh. Even in Uttar Pradesh, however, 73 percent of members who expected material goods received them, 76 percent who expected improved production said their expectations were met, and 68 percent said they received the expected access to information.

Expectations did not vary significantly by caste but did vary both by gender and economic position of households. In Uttar Pradesh 75 percent of men but only 53 percent of women respondents expected to benefit from inputs and a higher proportion of men expected better access to information and increased land productivity. In Madhya Pradesh, men were twice as likely as women to expect wage labor and loans from the project. In Andhra Pradesh, 47 percent of male respondents and

---

"SICs should ensure that I always get water and inputs ..." (respondent, Uttar Pradesh). "SIC meetings are linked to the distribution of inputs ... Frequency of meeting fades with the discontinuation of inputs ... The group process is missing" (village summaries, Uttar Pradesh).

"The group is to give families something ... Forest protection will give individual families benefit ..." (respondent, Madhya Pradesh). In Bilaspur, "the forest committee gives labor opportunities, improved irrigation facilities, and construction works" and in Kanker, "food grains are now distributed" (focus groups, Madhya Pradesh).

"In water abundant areas such as the Krishna delta ... farmers do not see there is a need for their participation as long as some people ensure that the physical works are carried out" (village summaries, Andhra Pradesh). "We go to WUA meetings if there is a problem with the water coming to our own fields, not other people" (focus groups, Andhra Pradesh). "Let other people manage general things ... I am interested in my own fields" (respondent, Andhra Pradesh).

Box 11.2 Members' views on user group objectives.

33 percent of female respondents expected increased production from household land. In both Uttar Pradesh and Andhra Pradesh, more men than women anticipated benefit from increased access to information, whereas in Madhya Pradesh this was important for neither.

Differences associated with the poverty rank of a household were less consistent than for gender. In Uttar Pradesh and Andhra Pradesh, proportions of respondents expecting increased returns from their own land ranged from 90 percent in poverty rank one (wealthiest) to 70 percent in poverty rank four (poorest). In Uttar Pradesh, a similar pattern of decreasing expectation as households become poorer was observed for improvements in relationships, access to information, and improvements in irrigation water supplies. The reverse pattern occurred with regard to wage labor opportunities in Uttar Pradesh and Madhya Pradesh. Expectations of other benefits were fairly evenly distributed in Andhra Pradesh as they were in Madhya Pradesh.

Were groups functioning as expected?

User groups in all three projects studied were expected to support equitable inclusion of different groups of stakeholders and to function as democratic bodies overseeing the management of a common, or shared, resource. User groups were expected to continue functioning in this way beyond the life of all projects. Three indicators – inclusion, transparency, and governance and accountability – measured whether or not user groups were operating as expected.

Inclusion

Inclusion was assessed in four ways:

- attendance at user group meetings;
- representation;
- receipt of benefits;
- involvement in group decision making.

Attendance patterns differed by state and were, overall, not encouraging (Table 11.1). The most important reason for non-attendance was lack of information – 40–55 percent of members did not receive prior information about meetings. In Madhya Pradesh and Andhra Pradesh, nearly a quarter of non-attendees had no time to participate in meetings. In Andhra Pradesh, the same percentage had no interest in attending meetings. In Uttar Pradesh, 22 percent indicated that no meetings were held.

In Uttar Pradesh and Andhra Pradesh, poorer and scheduled caste households and women were less likely to attend meetings. In Madhya Pradesh, apart from gender differences, nonattendance did not associate

Table 11.1 Attendance of user group meetings

Project	Percentage of members attending		
	Often	*Rarely*	*Never*
Uttar Pradesh SIC	30	35	36
Madhya Pradesh VFC/FPC	48	24	28
Andhra Pradesh WUA	33	23	44

Source: Individual questionnaires.

with any particular social or economic group. Data analysis clearly showed, however, that representatives participated more in meetings than general members, that those attending *gram sabha* (general village meetings associated with elected bodies) meetings also attended user group meetings, and that there was a strong association between attendance and individual gain. As shown in Table 11.2, representatives were disproportionately male.

In Uttar Pradesh, more representatives belong to poorer households (Table 11.2). In Madhya Pradesh, most representatives belonged to the second richest group and in Andhra Pradesh, the chances of being a representative were higher for the richest households. Women were very poorly represented.

Although the overall pattern was of satisfaction of wants, regression analysis showed that relationship between member characteristics and perceptions of benefits received varied by state. In Uttar Pradesh, "other backward castes" benefited less from inputs or increased production than

Table 11.2 Characteristics of representatives, by state (percent)

Characteristic	Uttar Pradesh	Madhya Pradesh	Andhra Pradesh
Representatives	24.7	15.9	8.6
Gender			
Female	10.4	7.5	8.3
Male	89.6	92.5	91.7
Household poverty rank			
1 – Rich	20.4	22.8	30.0
2	19.4	38.6	13.0
3	28.2	21.3	35.0
4 – Poor	32.0	17.3	22.0
Education			
No formal education	64.1	44.9	52.0
Primary school only	8.7	30.7	22.0
Secondary school	17.8	17.3	15.0
Higher	9.7	7.1	11.0

Source: Individual questionnaires.

scheduled castes. Those with secondary or postsecondary education received better access to information than the uneducated. Small and medium landholders, rather than marginal landholders, and those living in a *kutcha* (unbaked brick or mud) rather than a *pucca* (baked brick or concrete) house, were more likely to receive benefits.

In Madhya Pradesh, representatives were more likely than general members to benefit from increased material inputs. Members with secondary education were less likely than those without education to receive this benefit and large landowners were less likely to receive loans than marginal landowners. Those who had been members of the user group for longer had greater access to loans. Fewer women respondents reported receiving opportunities for wage labor but more women (56 percent) than men (32 percent) reported receiving Village Resource Development Program (VRDP)-related benefits. Wage labor was evenly distributed across poverty ranks, and those with irrigated land were less likely to benefit from material inputs but more likely to benefit from increased access to loans.

In Andhra Pradesh, members in general were receiving the benefits they expected. While medium and large landowners were more likely to benefit from increased availability of irrigation water, the perception of respondents from both these types of households and the poorest households is that, this did not lead to benefits of increased production from their own land. Poorer households gained better access to information but the very poorest quartile had not benefited from increases in quality or reliability of irrigation water supplies.

Important determinants of distributional issues and sustainability of groups or benefits are the power relations operating within groups. Three stages of decision making, as indicators of power relations, were investigated: initiating discussion, participating in discussion, and making final decisions. In Uttar Pradesh, although project staff clearly led discussions, seven out of ten members who attended meetings were involved in discussions. Project staff again played a major role in decision making but members participated in about one-fifth of the cases. Representatives did not exhibit any tendency to control discussions. In Madhya Pradesh, project staff were far less dominant in discussions than in Uttar Pradesh. Usually, chairmen initiated group discussions and finalized decisions. However, more than 90 percent of all group members who attended meetings participated in discussions. Of members who attend WUA meetings in Andhra Pradesh, very few participated actively in any dimension of decision making. Few decisions were ever taken by the group or at meetings, but when they were, the chairman was most active and he discussed decisions with representatives rather than with the WUA as a whole. In all three states, the data show that none of the women interviewed have ever initiated a discussion or made a final decision.

Table 11.3 Members' awareness of finances and transactions (percent)

	Uttar Pradesh		Madhya Pradesh		Andhra Pradesh	
	Aware	Not aware	Aware	Not aware	Aware	Not aware
Availability of funds	8	92	20	80	16	84
Amount of funds	10	90	25	75	18	82
What spent on	12	88	35	65	36	64

Source: Individual questionnaires.

Transparency

Transparency was measured by examining information availability and awareness of group transactions. In all three states, minutes of meetings were not kept or were not accessible to members, and mechanisms of public communication, such as wall posters, were virtually unheard of. Word of mouth, a medium nuanced by power relations, was the most frequently used mode of communication.

In Uttar Pradesh, 14 percent of all non-attendees heard of decisions reached at meetings by word of mouth and 9 percent heard through a member of the project staff. However, 48 percent of members and 68 percent of non-attendees did not hear about the outcome of meetings. In Madhya Pradesh, nearly 25 percent of members and 50 percent of non-attendees had no information on decisions made. In Andhra Pradesh, people most often heard about outcomes by word of mouth. About one-fourth of members had no information on outcomes of meetings.

As Table 11.3 shows, the vast majority of members in each state were unaware of how group funds were structured or used.

Governance and accountability

Information was gathered on members' knowledge of rules for

* conducting group business
* selection of representatives
* holding representatives accountable.

In all three states, awareness of rules for conducting group business was low (Table 11.4) – particularly so, in Uttar Pradesh and Andhra Pradesh.

Table 11.4 Members' knowledge of rules governing group business (percent)

Level of knowledge	Uttar Pradesh	Madhya Pradesh	Andhra Pradesh
Aware of rules	5	34	7
Stated no rules	18	13	42
Don't know	77	53	51

Source: Individual questionnaires.

In Uttar Pradesh, richer households had higher levels of awareness of rules than poorer households (perhaps reflecting different literacy levels), whereas there was no significant difference across poverty ranks in other states. Caste did not play a major role in any state.

Gender differences varied significantly by state. In Uttar Pradesh, there was little difference between the sexes regarding knowledge of rules. In Madhya Pradesh, in contrast, males were twice as likely as females to be aware of rules. In Andhra Pradesh, women were 10 percent more likely than males to be aware of rules.

Group members in Madhya Pradesh and Andhra Pradesh were generally aware of how the chairperson of the group was chosen. They were less aware of selection procedures for other representatives. In Uttar Pradesh, a full two-thirds of respondents had no knowledge even of how the chairman was chosen.

Levels of satisfaction with office holders, by respondents who knew who their representatives were, varied. In Uttar Pradesh 28 percent were satisfied with the chairman and 6 percent were dissatisfied, but 66 percent had no knowledge of the chairman's performance and between 96 and 86 percent had no knowledge of other office holders. Members in the other two states were more familiar with the performance of representatives. In Madhya Pradesh, 74 percent were satisfied with the chairman, 51 percent were satisfied with the vice chairman, and 43 percent were satisfied with the secretary. In Andhra Pradesh, 80 percent were satisfied with the president and 41 percent with the territorial constituency representative. In all cases, those who did not indicate satisfaction stated that they had insufficient knowledge of the representative to comment.

Chairmen were generally to be viewed as performing well. Given the low levels of awareness of the rules for conducting group business and selecting representatives, this implied a high degree of dependence on, and trust in, one individual. This pointed to the need for robust accountability mechanisms but awareness of these mechanisms was extremely low.

When asked if they are aware of any rules they could use if a representative did something that the member disagreed with, the great majority were unaware of such rules (Table 11.5).

In Madhya Pradesh, where awareness was high enough to make follow-up questions meaningful, responses revealed that members rarely took

Table 11.5 Members' knowledge of rules for representative accountability (percent)

Level of knowledge	Uttar Pradesh	Madhya Pradesh	Andhra Pradesh
Aware of rules	4	35	7
Not aware/don't know	96	65	93

Source: Individual questionnaires.

action and preferred to use re-election as the mechanism for displacing unsatisfactory representatives.

Discussion and conclusions

The findings summarized in Box 11.3 highlight the contrasting facts that user groups were perceived as valuable by members, yet were unlikely to realize goals of institutionalization of collective action envisaged in project design. At the project level, this can lead to specific practical recommendations (Box 11.4). However, these conclusions also have broader policy implications for the role of community level user groups in resource management.

The fact that group members were satisfied with their group and with the distribution of benefits even though most did not actively participate in meetings or decision making raises questions over the organization of broad-based user participation in resource management, its ultimate value, and the most appropriate mechanisms for achieving effective local management. The study's findings suggest that either expectations of user groups should be significantly reduced, leading to the potential use of other mechanisms for resource management, or that planning for the use of user groups needed to concentrate more on factors supporting the development of well functioning democratic organizations.

This concluding section therefore focuses on the broader implications of the findings for three aspects of user groups or local organizations, commonly considered critical to decentralized management and implementation of projects: effectiveness, equity, and sustainability.

Effectiveness

Well over half of user group members thought that formal objectives had been met and that groups were effective in managing the resources for which they were responsible. In Madhya Pradesh and Andhra Pradesh, members had pre-project experience of locally evolved systems of collective action. However, formalizing membership in project user groups, legitimizing local governance, and providing some codes of conduct, projects had improved resource management. In Uttar Pradesh, it was unlikely that there would have been reclamation of sodic soil on the scale now found, unless the project and its user groups had been operational.

However, members' favorable perceptions of group performance reflects their past experiences. Typically, these did not lead to high expectations, particularly for equity or long-term sustainability of such collective action initiatives. This, in large part, explains the perceptual gap over objectives between members and those of project designers. Members were concerned with immediate and discrete individual benefits rather than the broader issues of consensus and collective management

On achievements

- Members perceived user groups to be valuable to them and to largely achieve their formal objectives.
- Members' perceptions of the purpose of user groups differed from those of project designers and implementers.
- Members perceived user groups mainly as a means of accessing short-term benefits rather than as a mechanism of cooperation for long-term collective action.

On participation

- Attendance at meetings was low.
- Wealthier people attended meetings more consistently than the poorest in the two states where caste position associated with wealth and education.
- Women's participation in meetings was rare. They were also unlikely to be representatives.
- There was no association between wealth and holding a representative's position.
- A high degree of involvement of project staff in decision making, associated with low levels of member participation in decision making.
- The more highly networked a member, the more likely it was that he or she would participate in value user groups and their achievement of formal objectives.
- Benefits were relatively well distributed among members.
- Members received the benefits they expected.

On transparency

- Information availability about group meetings was poor.
- Members had little knowledge of group finances or financial transactions.

On governance and accountability

- Awareness of business and accountability rules was very low.
- Accountability mechanisms were not used.
- Participation by members in governance was extremely limited.

Box 11.3 Summary of findings.

Data strongly suggest that project designers and implementers need to address the conditions that lead to perceptions of user groups primarily as mechanisms appropriate for channeling of short-term benefits. This is essential if members are to vest in user groups in a manner that supports long-term cooperation over asset and benefit management. Clearly, projects must raise awareness of the importance of long-term cooperation for a continuing flow of benefits in the future, and a sense of ownership must be promoted among rank-and-file members of these groups. Actions to support this would include:

- Improving information availability, both about when meetings are to take place and about what occurs during meetings. This should increase attendance and ownership of group decisions and activities.
- Increasing members' awareness of user group rules and ensuring that those rules function effectively. This would reduce opportunities for corruption or co-option and should increase members' belief in the user group as a mechanism for managing cooperation, rather than just channeling benefits from a project management unit to beneficiaries.
- Taking proactive measures to increase women's knowledge and interest in user group activities and outcomes. If empowerment of women as equal agents in development processes is an objective of projects, this is crucial.

Box 11.4 Response to findings.

prominent in project documentation. Cooperation was regarded as a project requirement and thus a means to ends such as the receipt of fertilizer, seeds, or other inputs. There was little belief that benefit distribution or cooperation would extend beyond the life of the project or without continued support from implementing agency staff.

Members displayed little ownership or individual sense of responsibility for the functioning of the group and project implementers were driven by the incentive system of the project in which they work to meet targets, disburse funds, and demonstrate concrete actions. This resulted in the distribution of project benefits, at the expense of developing members' ownership and understanding of group objectives (Box 11.5).

If interventions were intended only to deliver short-term benefits, community level user groups may not have been the optimal solution to local level resource management. The factors determining decisions to deploy user groups should have been, in part, resource-specific. Different

Uttar Pradesh

"There is lack of clarity about the project and its intentions among farmers ... Project staff interactions have been limited to a few people ... Dissemination of information about the project was concentrated in the main village or hamlet ... The group process is missing ... The concept of a SIC has not worked very well ... People are more interested in water user groups as it is here that financial transactions and other activities take place" (village summaries). "Project staff have played a dominating role in the SIC meetings [and overall] and thus hampered a process of institution building in the SIC. The SIC has not been used as a means to create a participatory approach to implementing the project ... It is used to deliver inputs" (focus groups).

Madhya Pradesh, Bilaspur District

"Forest Department staff have been given total responsibility for implementation ... They run the VFCs ... hence, villagers have little idea about forest related benefit-sharing mechanisms ... [They] have no idea of the rules and regulations of the group or executive committee ... VFCs operate in a mechanical manner, there is lack of innovation" (village summaries). "In discussions on what the VFC should do ... the majority of groups said develop irrigation facilities in the villages, provide better credit facilities, and improve drinking water and electricity supplies. Villagers placed more emphasis on the role of the VFC as an overall development organization and as an opportunity for wage employment rather than forest management" (focus groups).

Madhya Pradesh, Kanker District

"FPCs have been formed very quickly ... The executive committee is formed in a very mechanical way ... Villagers are not consulted when VRDP development works are taken up ... There is little transparency ..." (village summaries). "The most common suggestion for how to improve the FPC is to increase financial assistance to the group which can, in turn, extend financial support to households or generate labor work through construction projects" (focus groups).

continued

Box 11.5 Group development processes and impact.

Andhra Pradesh

"WUAs have been formed in a rapid manner with the result that people are little aware of the functions, roles, responsibilities, and so on. . . . Meetings are only organized when there is some implementation of works" (village summaries). "Suggestions for improvement include specification of the powers of the WUA, better cooperation between and participation in the group by farmers, better awareness of the WUA and the Act, and better collective planning" (focus groups)

Box 11.5 Continued

time commitments and skills were required for the management of different resources: maintaining an irrigation system required frequent clearing and repair of channels on a continuing basis, while forest protection did not call for a high level of ongoing activity. Also, some management activities required a higher level of expertise than others. In some cases, formalizing an existing user group or organizing a new one may have been the most appropriate approach. In other cases, pooling users' funds to hire a commercial contractor would be a more efficient response.

While all the projects studied were effective in certain ways, the capability of the user groups to handle problems independently was questionable. In particular, conflicts arising from scarcity or from attempts to co-opt resources were challenges these groups could not meet. For example, in Andhra Pradesh, when problems arose over equity in water access and use, group members needed recourse to a higher authority. In Uttar Pradesh, equity in distribution of gypsum and fertilizer was contingent on the presence of project staff. In Madhya Pradesh, project staff were considered necessary to "rule" the VFCs. From these experiences, it is apparent that members of user groups expected, and would need, an external backstop.

This requirement was rarely articulated or explicitly addressed in project action plans. User groups were conceived as project-specific entities operating largely in isolation of their local social and organizational context, and as such, were designed to establish relations only with the implementing agents rather than with any other organization. Very few user groups had contact with their local elected representatives or bodies. There was virtually no contact with line departments other than those implementing the project or with other government agencies involved in development activities. In most locations linkages with non-governmental organizations (NGOs) were unrelated to a user group's needs. However, the regression estimation showed a positive association both between the density of different types of organizations present in a location and rating of user groups' value, and between the degree to which a person was networked and his or her assessment of achievement of formal objectives. The results, though, challenged the simplistic view that the greater the overall density of all types of organization, the greater the stock of social capital and the higher the likelihood of having a successful organization. Findings demonstrated an inverse relationship between the number of *external* organizations present in a location and achievement of formal objectives. However, the density of *locally evolved* organizations positively associated with assessments of achievement, suggesting that there was a significant difference between the social capital value of organizations depending upon whether they are externally induced or locally evolved. These findings pointed to the complexity of the concept of social capital and suggested that, formal, government-sponsored organizations did not constitute the right mix of "associations or networks" for improving benefit distribution.

If projects were to establish an entity for management of stocks and flows from local assets, and not just benefit delivery, then implementing agents needed to better assess what degree of responsibility was required of members and which structures and processes were best suited to changing members' vision and developing transparent and accountable local organizations. Formulating realistic objectives for user groups, phasing expectations of achievements, and building in activities and time for user group members to reflect and reassess options for cooperation and management of shared assets and benefits would help achieve these ends.

Ultimately, user groups are unlikely to be of sustained interest to members unless individual and longer-term benefits of cooperation are tangible. Project staff also require sufficient skills, time, and flexibility in objectives to identify the relative importance of different benefits and develop appropriate and phased approaches to achieving and building on outcomes. Entry-point activities have proved useful to developing skills and faith in collective action as have community- or group-level learning and management opportunities, such as local-level monitoring and decision systems. Such strategies may demand either more intense support by project staff or an extension of the time horizon for achieving outcomes.

Equity and empowerment[7]

A striking finding of this study is that, despite the hierarchical social context in which two of the projects were set, distribution of benefits was not biased towards or against any particular social group. This was particularly interesting, since in two states (Uttar Pradesh and Andhra Pradesh), caste position strongly associated with education and wealth – both of which can affect a person's capacity to take advantage of new opportunities. However, this study found no clear overall association between caste and receipt of benefits. This challenged conventional wisdom, and added to other evidence that traditional patterns associated with caste positioning in India are slowly changing. The systematic differences observed, instead associated with gender and the relationship between members' livelihoods and project benefits. A user group was of most interest to members when its activities were closely associated with a household's livelihood portfolio.

While these results reflect reduced associations between caste and the capacity to take advantage of new opportunities, analysis of disaggregated data suggests that the role of project staff was critical to equitable distribution of benefits. In Uttar Pradesh, where project staff dominated user group business, there was a positive association between having small plots of land and receipt of benefits. However, in Andhra Pradesh, where project staff had little to do with WUA operations, poorer households were less likely to benefit from improvements in irrigation systems than richer households. When interventions operate in areas where caste and wealth have traditionally been associated with opportunity, explicit measures to counteract these traditions are required. In Andhra Pradesh, where caste-based power and politics negatively affected WUA functioning, members called for higher levels of input by project staff. In Uttar Pradesh, project staff successfully played the role of "equity police." Whether equity would prevail post-project, without project staff, was questionable.

Empowerment is a concept closely associated with equity, that is, people with lower levels of capacity have to be empowered if a project is to achieve equity outcomes. Project documentation often referred to user groups as the mechanisms for empowerment of project beneficiaries, yet used the term in a manner that left the degree of empowerment of project participants open to interpretation. In addition, claims of empowerment did not take into account the fact that a social system is unlikely to be transformed quickly by the establishment of an externally induced organization or single intervention. Clearly, articulating the nature and degree of empowerment that may feasibly be expected to result from the user group, is essential during project design, as it assists in setting realizable objectives and in defining realistic monitoring indicators.

In the user groups studied, transparency was poor, accountability nonexistent, awareness of the rules of engagement meager, and, in Uttar Pradesh and Andhra Pradesh, participation in group business by members very low. Under these conditions, individual members cannot be said to have been empowered even within the confines of the group's mandate, indicating a need to better plan dissemination and effective use of a group's rules of engagement.

Sustainability

Like empowerment, sustainability is a term as loosely used as it is broadly interpreted. Project documentation consistently failed to specify what was to be sustained, and for how long. While in all three projects, user groups were conceived as both *sustainable organizations* and as mechanisms to ensure *sustainable benefit streams*, documentation did not distinguish these two aspects of sustainability or recognize that, over the course of a project, the activities of groups and the benefits being delivered might change. Greater clarity on the definition and timetable for sustainability would have enabled realistic objectives to be set, appropriate support strategies to be designed, and flexible monitoring indicators to be devised.

The two aspects of sustainability are not necessarily correlated – a sustainable flow of benefits may not always depend upon the sustainability of the organization. Some organizations may be useful as short-term mechanisms to ensure flows of benefits in an initial phase, but it is possible that benefits flows can be sustained later without being hosted by a user group. For example, a savings and credit group whose purpose is to establish good practice and creditworthiness of members so that bank loans can be individually accessed, may be phased out after members qualify for bank loans. In other cases, an induced organization may change its purpose, form, and function, while the initial benefit streams evolve or discontinue. In Madhya Pradesh, for example, the nature of the user group changed when VRDP funds and associated benefit streams became available. This brought increases in levels of attendance along with increased member participation in decision making. In Uttar Pradesh, the SIC was perceived mainly as a source of inputs, principally gypsum and fertilizer. Once soil had been treated and farmers knew how to manage it, their interest in the SIC decreased.

For the projects studied, sustainability of an entity to manage collective resources was appropriate to sustain benefits. Unfortunately, the processes of user group development applied were unlikely to achieve this. Processes of group formation and support activities responded to project staff incentive systems rather than to group needs. Implementing agency staff appeared to operate exclusively, in terms of the time frame and targets of the projects, and project processes provided little incentive for staff to invest in user groups. Moreover, staff often were unskilled in organizational management, lacked the time required to work creatively with local groups, and – sometimes understandably – had basic questions about the need for user groups.

Two questions arise from these findings. First, was it appropriate for these resource management projects to invest in establishing or regularizing groups at all? And second, if a user group was appropriate, how could its development be matched with its objectives and related roles and responsibilities? The lack of correspondence between project design objectives and the objectives of user group members raises fundamental questions over project expectations of these mechanisms of collective action, and suggests that user group roles and functions should have been better reviewed during design. If user groups were essential to achieve project objectives, the role of project staff would be critical. Such staff needed to be well briefed, possess organization-building skills, and be oriented to participatory, client-driven development. In short, unless the process through which user groups were established and developed was given higher priority, there was little chance of them being sustainable.

Summary

For most members, community-level user groups were valuable and achieved their formal objectives. Members' perceptions of the purpose of their group, however, generally differed from those of project designers and implementers. Members tended to be content if they were receiving immediate personal benefits from the project. They demonstrated low levels of ownership of the user group and little interest in, or commitment to, the group as a mechanism for managing cooperation beyond the end of the project.

Attendance at meetings and awareness of meetings, group finances, and the rules of operation was very limited. Indicators of transparency, governance, and accountability were lower than expected. In addition, the inclusion of women in meetings and as representatives was rare. Participation was highest among people who were already well networked. Despite this there was little evidence to suggest that benefits were appropriated by any one social group. The community level user groups studied, appeared to be working well in the short-term delivery of project benefits. Far more doubtful was whether the groups in the three projects would achieve local ownership of the user group and its functions.

Overall, a key question raised by the study was whether user groups could achieve long-term sustainability as independent organizational entities. If user groups were to continue after the life of the projects, either the backstopping function needed to be transferred to another implementing agency (such as local government *panchayat raj* institutions), or resource management projects needed redesigning to accommodate the building of local initiative, responsibility, and accountability. In addition, it was not clear in every case if the sustainability of benefits was dependent upon the sustainability of a user group.

Community level user groups may not have been an appropriate instrument for the local management of the natural resources, in this study. Management requirements differed according to the nature of the resource and communities differed in economic, geographic, social, and cultural terms. A more sophisticated and flexible approach to the design of organizations for local management of resources is called for, during both design and implementation of interventions.

Appendix

Uttar Pradesh: site implementation committee

The site implementation committee (SIC) is a general body of the village. Each household participating in the project, as a member of a Water User Group (WUG), has one male and one female representative in the SIC. The head of Gram Panchayat is the ex-officio chairperson of the SIC, and the local Assistant Manager of the UPBSN acts as the Member-Secretary.[8]

The SIC is the platform for decision-making and implementation of the activities at the village level and acts as a forum for interaction between different project actors. At the time of study, SICs were unregistered bodies. SICs prepare and implement a Site Implementation Plan (SIP) – a micro-plan containing all the activities that are to be carried out in the village as a part of the land reclamation process. The SICs are subsequently responsible for the distribution of agricultural inputs and for post project maintenance of the assets developed under the project , for which it is expected to generate a fund. During project implementation, SICs receive financial inputs from the project for maintenance and management of link drains, main drains, and maintenance and management of drainage network in the village. The SIC also distributes funds to each WUG for construction and maintenance of drains.

A core team – the Executive Body of the SIC – is responsible for executing and monitoring the activities. The core team is constituted from the leaders of the WUGs, a Mitra Kisan (MK – male) and a Mahila Mitra Kisan (MMK – female) who are villagers identified by the SIC to act as animators and as a link between the villagers and the project. The villagers elect these individuals by voting, usually in an open meeting This core group will change if WUGs change leadership, but the MK and MMK usually remain throughout the project period. The SIC is required to meet twice a month during the time of implementation of the project. Post project, the SIC is required to meet quarterly. The SIC has to maintain financial records, minutes of meetings, and records relating to maintenance and management of drains. There are few additional formal rules of the SIC. They are encouraged to develop their own rules and regulations regarding decision-making, change of leadership, meetings, and dissemination of information.

Madhya Pradesh: village forest committees

Three types of village committees are formed under Joint Forest Management (JFM) in Madhya Pradesh:

 i VFCs in degraded and low productive forest areas;
 ii Forest Protection Committees (FPCs) in dense forest areas;

iii Eco-development Committees in national parks and sanctuaries (Government of Madhya Pradesh 2000).

VFCs and FPCs are the user groups included in this study.

VFCs and FPCs are constituted on the basis of a village or hamlet(s) depending on what is most appropriate to existing forms of local organization. The committees are registered with the Divisional Forest Officer (DFO). A Memorandum of Understanding is signed between the Forest Department and the committee. All adult residents are members of the general body of the committee. Each committee is supposed to meet at least once in three months.

The executive committee of the VFC or FPC can comprise 11 to 21 members. The villagers elect a chairperson and a vice-chairperson, one of which has to be a woman. It is recommended that representation of scheduled castes, scheduled tribes, and other backward castes is made proportional to their size of the population in the settlement. A minimum of 33 percent should be women. There should be a minimum of two landless families. All representatives of the Panchayat residing in the village should be ex-officio members. The Beat Guard or Forester is the ex-officio secretary of the executive committee. The term of the executive committee is two years.

Andhra Pradesh: water users associations

The Andhra Pradesh Farmers' Management of Irrigation Systems Act, 1997/98 made Farmers' Organizations (FOs) independent legal entities.

Water users associations (WUAs) constitute the basic unit of an irrigation scheme. Each covers a hydrological unit considered viable for irrigation and manages between 100 to 2000 ha of irrigated area which is divided into four to ten Territorial Constituencies (TCs). The main objectives of WUAs are to ensure distribution of water among users, to maintain irrigation systems, and to enhance agricultural production. The functions of the WUAs (and other tiers) are to prepare and implement plans for improving the distribution of water, regulate water, maintain accounts, carry out social audits, resolve conflicts that may arise over water, assist the Revenue Department in collection of water cess, and liaise with both the Irrigation and Agriculture Department, in order to enhance agriculture.

Water users associations are constituted through elections. Landowners and tenants within the boundaries of a WUA are general members and have a right to vote for the representative of their TC and the President of the WUA. The TC members and the President form the Managing Committee (MC) of the WUA. The term of the MC and its representatives is five years. There is, however, a right of recall of the elected representatives. All decisions related to the management of the irrigation system are to be approved by the General Body of the WUA. The General Body has to meet at least twice a year. The quorum for a general body meeting is one third of the members. Meetings can be postponed if there is no quorum. The subsequent meeting requires no quorum, and resolutions can be passed by the majority of the members present. The MC has to execute the decisions of the General Body (Government of Andhra Pradesh 1997).[9]

Notes

1 The findings of recent research on the performance and factors associated with that of the broader range of organizations found at the district level and below are documented in Alsop 2004, and Alsop and Kurey 2005.
2 In this chapter, user groups are defined as local, membership-based, project-induced organizations whose goal is to facilitate the local management of a collective resource by those who utilize and receive benefits from it.
3 A fuller version of this chapter is available in Alsop *et al.*, 2002. The full research report is available from the author.
4 Regressions were originally run with poverty, caste, and education as independent variables. Concerns over co linearity were addressed by re-running regressions, without the poverty and education variables, and results proved robust to the original specification.
5 Primary associations are based on cross tabulations. Small sample sizes prevent regression analysis of village-level data.
6 "Locally evolved organizations" refers to those that have emerged without external initiative or influence.
7 Empowerment is defined as the capacity of a group or person to make purposeful choice and transform that into desired actions and outcomes. See Alsop *et al.*, 2005 for definition and an analytic framework to understand and measure empowerment.
8 If all the members of SIC agree they may elect another Chairperson than the Gram Pradhan.
9 There is also a provision for WUAs to constitute sub-committees to implement its various functions.

Bibliography

Adato, Michelle, Besley, T., Haddad, L. and Hoddinott, J. (1999) "Participation and Poverty Reduction: Issues, Theory and New Evidence from South Africa." Background paper for *World Development Report, 2001*.

Agarwal, B. (1998) "Environmental Management, Equity and Ecofeminism: Debating India's experience." *Journal of Peasant Studies* 25 (4).

Agrawal, A. and Gibson, C.C. (1999) "Enchantment and Disenchantment: The Role of Community in Natural Resource Management." *World Development* 27 (4).

Alsop, R., Bertelsen, M. and Holland, J (2006) *Empowerment in Practice: From Analysis to Implementation*, Directions in Development Series. Washington, DC: World Bank.

Alsop, R. and Kurey, B. (2005) *Local Organizations in Decentralized Development: Their Functions and Performance in India*. Directions in Development Series. Washington, DC: World Bank.

Alsop, R., Sjoblom, D., Namazie, C. and Patil, P. (2002) Community Level User Groups in Three World Bank-Aided Projects. *Social Development Papers*, Number 40. Washington DC: World Bank.

Cleaver, F. (1999) "Paradoxes of Participation: Questioning Participatory Approaches to Development." *Journal of International Development* 11 (4).

Government of Andhra Pradesh (1997) "The Andhra Pradesh Farmers' Management of Irrigation Systems Act." Department of Irrigation and Command Area Development, Hyderabad.

Government of Madhya Pradesh (2000) Resolution No. F16/4//91/10-2. Forest Department, Bhopal.

Grootaert, C. (1999) "Does Social Capital Help the Poor? A Synthesis of Findings from the Local Level Institutions Studies in Bolivia, Burkina Faso and Indonesia." Washington, DC: World Bank, Social Development Department, Washington, DC.

Johnson, C. (2001) "Local Democracy, Democratic Decentralisation and Rural Development: Theories, Challenges and Options for Policy." *Development Policy Review* 19 (4): 521–32.

Johnson, Craig, Deshingkar, P. and Start, D. (2003) "Grounding the State: Devolution and Development in India's Panchayats." Working Paper 226. Overseas Development Institute, London.

Leach, M., Mearns, R. and Scoones, I. (1997) "Challenges to Community-based Sustainable Development: Dynamics, Entitlements, Institutions." *IDS Bulletin* 28 (4).

Manor, J. (2002) "User Committees: A Potentially Damaging Second Wave of Decentralization." Institute of Development Studies, University of Sussex, Brighton, UK.

Mehta, L. (1997) "Social Difference and Water Resources Management: Insights from Kutch, India." *IDS Bulletin* 28 (4).

Meinzen-Dick, R. and Zwarteveen, M. (1998) "Gendered Participation in Water Management: Issues and Illustrations from Water Users' Associations in South Asia." In D.J. Merrey and Baviskar, S., eds, *Gender Analysis and Reform of Irrigation Management: Concepts, Cases and Gaps in Knowledge*. Colombo, Sri Lanka: International Water Management Institute. Proceedings of the IIMI Workshop on Gender and Water, 15–19 September 1997, Habarana, Sri Lanka.

Oblitas, J. and Peter R.J. (1999) "Transferring Irrigation Management to Farmers in Andhra Pradesh, India." Technical Paper 449. Washington, DC: World Bank.

Ostrom, E., Schroeder, L. and Wynne, S. (1993) *Institutional Incentives and Sustainable Development: Infrastructure Policies in Perspective*. Boulder, CO: Westview.

Poffenberger, M. and McGean, B. eds. (1996) *Village Voices Forest Choices: Joint Forest Management in India*. New Delhi: Oxford University Press.

Schneider, H. (1999) "Participatory Governance for Poverty Reduction." *Journal of International Development* 11 (4).

Tang, S.Y. (1992) *Institutions and Collective Action: Self-Governance in Irrigation*. Oakland, CA: ICS Press.

Uphoff, N., Esman, M.J. and Krishna, A. (1998) *Reasons for Success: Learning from Instructive Experiences in Rural Development*. West Hartford, CN: Kumerian Press.

Watson, G., Jagannathan, N.V., Geltring, R. and Beteta, H.E. (1997) "Water and Sanitation Associations: Review and Best Practices." In A. Subramaniam, Jagannathan, N.V. and Meinzen-Dick, R., eds, *User Organizations for Sustainable Water Services*. Washington, DC: World Bank.

World Bank (1995) "Staff Appraisal Report. India. Madhya Pradesh Forestry Sector." South Asia Department II, Agricultural Operations Division.

—— (1996) *The World Bank Participation Sourcebook.* Washington, DC: World Bank.

—— (1998a) "Project Appraisal Document. The Uttar Pradesh Sodic Lands Reclamation II Project."

—— (1998b) "Project Appraisal Document. Andhra Pradesh Economic Restructuring Programme: Irrigation Component."

—— (2000) "Overview of Decentralization in India", SARD, Washington, DC: World Bank.

—— (2002) *World Development Report 2002: Building Institutions for Markets.* New York: Oxford University Press.

—— (2003) *World Development Report 2003: Sustainable Development in a Dynamic World: Transforming Institutions, Growth and Quality of Life.* New York: Oxford University Press.

Part VI
Campaigning organizations

12 Shack/Slum Dwellers International

One experience of the contribution of membership organisations to pro-poor urban development

Celine d'Cruz and Diana Mitlin

Introduction

This chapter considers the experience of the membership organisations that make up the international network of Shack or Slum Dwellers International (SDI),[1] an international network of national urban poor Federations and their support NGOs. Each federation is made up of local community organisations that are savings schemes (in which women are a majority of participants). Since its inception in 1996, the international network has grown significantly (see Table 12.1). Through an analysis of the experiences of the SDI members, we will identify some successful strategies with regard to the contribution of membership organisations to poverty reduction in urban areas.

It is important to elaborate on the meaning of membership in the context of SDI.[2] SDI specifically seeks to strengthen local groups that address the collective needs of urban poor communities in ways that are inclusive of the poorest residents. Groups develop a recognised identity and draw individuals together in joint activities within a common governance framework. 'Membership' in the savings schemes is defined by participation in savings and other community activities. There is a deliberate effort to avoid formalisation; this advantages the more articulate, literate and higher-income residents who are more familiar with the formal world.

It is equally important to emphasise that the federation leadership does not see the federation as a 'membership organisation' in the conventional sense of an exclusive and defined grouping. In India, where many SDI practices first developed, the precedent to the savings schemes and federations in urban areas were the conventional trade union movements and political parties, both strongly characterised by membership affiliation. Neither was able to address the needs of the urban poor and their strategies appeared flawed to the emerging SDI leadership both because their exclusivity pushed away the poorest (and hence determined their irrelevance to this group) and because such exclusivity prevented the development of a mass movement.

Table 12.1 SDI information – 2005

	Date[1]	Number of settlements where there is a process[2]	Active savers[3]	Savings[4]	Houses built	Land secured (number of families)
India	1986	5000	100,000	$1.2 million	5000[5]	50,000
South Africa	1991	700	30,000	$1.2 million	15,500	23,000
Thailand	1992	42,700	5,000,000	$206 million	30,000	30,000
Namibia	1992	60	10,500	$0.5 million	1000	3700
Cambodia	1993	288	11,300	$145,000	3300	800
Philippines	1994	148	42,727	$631,830	13,388	18,191
Zimbabwe	1995	58	30,000	Z$350 million	650	3500
Nepal	1998	396	3147	$173,402	50	85
Sri Lanka	1998	130	21,506	$29,469	100	2000
Colombia	1999	1	60	$10,000	–	60
Kenya	2000	30	20,000	$5000	38	3500
Zambia	2002	11	6000	$8000	–	–
Ghana	2003	15	5000	$50,000	–	–
Uganda	2003	4	500	$2000	–	150
Malawi	2004	100	20,000	$50,000	222	450
Brazil	2005	5	100	$4000	–	7000
Tanzania	2004	16	1000	$2000	–	–

Notes

1 Date refers to the date at which significant savings scheme activity began, not the date at which federations were first established.

2 This is the most meaningful measure of growth of SDI and the indicator measures settlements in which grassroots activities are taken place to build collective capacity and catalyse people-led development. It has to be recognised that settlements may vary in size from about 100 households to tens of thousands of households. In general, larger settlements are divided into recognised neighbourhoods for daily transactions, and it is the neighbourhoods rather than the settlements that are measured here – nevertheless considerable differences in size remain.

3 The second key indicator of growth is the number of residents (overwhelmingly women) who save on a regular basis and who therefore participate in all savings-related activities.

4 Local currency values converted to the US dollar. Political and economic instabilities in Zimbabwe mean these figures are meaningless and they are not given for this country. Changes in currency due to international trading may distort values.

5 A further 30,000 families in India have been resettled into units not constructed by the Federation as a result of Federation involvement in urban development.

Conscious that the important issues that confront the urban poor are those that affect communities at the city level (for example, evictions, water and other services), the federations sought strategies that brought people together at the community, city and national level. Pavement families in Mumbai may have six to seven members employed in the informal economy and earn a fairly decent family income; however, they live and work in appalling conditions over which they have no control. The federations realised that addressing needs such as secure tenure and basic services requires a politically astute strategy and an all-inclusive position that promotes unity. Individuals determine the extent of their own membership through the level of their participation. There are, inevitably, an inner core of strong savings scheme members in each neighbourhood and a wider outer core of less committed and more hesitant participants who become more involved as they gain confidence in the process or as their personal situation changes. The national federations seek to allow such choices.

An analysis of the experiences of this network requires an understanding of its strategies and activities. Our underlying argument is that the processes used by specific membership organisations are critical to the outcomes that can be anticipated. The chapter will start by describing the growth and strategies of SDI. Subsequent sections look at what has been secured at a local level and analyse factors relevant to SDI's success.

The emergence of SDI

SDI and its strategies emerged from organising approaches used by Indian slum dwellers in the 1970s. In 1975, the 70,000 residents of Janta Colony, north east of Mumbai, were threatened with evictions and organised themselves under the leadership of Jockin Arputham, a local resident. This experience prompted Jockin to form the National Slum Dwellers Federation of India (NSDF). Secure tenure was a central objective; evictions, if unavoidable, should happen in consultation with communities and with an alternative plan for resettlement. The community leaders drew on the main organising traditions that they knew, those of the political parties and trade union movements. They struggled to achieve success and were forced to step back to analyse their failures. Their analysis demonstrated that the movement lacked depth; large numbers could be mobilised for specific events, but there was no continuing activity to keep them engaged.

In 1985, NSDF entered into a partnership with the Society for the Promotion of Area Resource Centre (SPARC), an NGO founded in 1984 in Mumbai, which sought to work with pavement dwellers (Patel and Mitlin 2004). In 1986, NSDF and SPARC together initiated the first pavement women's organisation, *Mahila Milan*. These three organisations created an alliance with the common objective of developing a strategy for housing the urban poor (Patel and d'Cruz 1993). During this period, the main strategies being used to support housing rights by other Asian NGOs were confrontation through demonstrations and legal proceedings. However, there was little follow-up after the initial crisis of demolition. This strengthened the belief of SPARC and NSDF that the affected communities (not the NGOs or politicians) needed to be at the centre of the process. Urban poor communities themselves needed to develop the capacity to identify credible alternatives and to negotiate for such alternatives. The women pavement dwellers working along with SPARC and NSDF began to create a new learning and knowledge that would build such capacity.

In 1991, NSDF was invited to an initiative to organise the poor in the informal settlements of South Africa.[3] The Indians explained that at independence they had been promised a lot by their leaders, but the poor received nothing and were soon evicted by the newly elected government. The message from Jockin was clear '. . . you need to do your own homework and organise yourself to make it easier for your government to deliver houses'. Shack dwellers in South Africa set up savings schemes and initiated regular exchanges between members. In 1994, the South African Homeless People's Federation was formed with 200 savings schemes.

In 1996, leaders from savings schemes in Cambodia, India, Namibia, Nepal, South Africa, Thailand and Zimbabwe came together in South Africa to launch SDI. The links between the communities were already strong due to regular international exchanges. From the beginning, this network believed that the function of its international activities was not to manage local groups but to strengthen local activities by creating a supportive international presence marked by innovation and diversity.

Strategies for change

The aim of SDI is to strengthen communities so that they can initiate, direct and manage change in areas that they themselves have prioritised. Despite appearances, the federations are not primarily vehicles to deliver low-income housing. Ongoing evictions and the scale of insecure tenure lead to the prioritisation of housing. This priority is both practical and strategic (borrowing from the terminology used by Moser 1989). The scale of inadequate housing has been recognised (UN-Habitat 2003), and the consequences for health, well-being and livelihoods are widely acknowledged. At the same time, there is a strategic reason for prioritising shelter. Addressing shelter (including land, infrastructure, services and the dwelling) requires an immediate and continuing collective effort in self-organisation and effective dialogue with local government. Most of the problems faced by the poor require political solutions which can only be achieved if the poor act collectively (Castells 1983). Approaches such as micro-finance create individualised possibilities, may result in increased inequality within low-income settlements (see, for example, Copestake's (2002) analysis of a Zambian programme) and reduce the capacity for collective action. SDI's core organising principles establish the pre-conditions for effective political action by the poor through strengthening inclusive local organisations that, through federating, have the potential to negotiate with various levels of government.[4]

Beginning with the most vulnerable

When SDI groups begin work in a new city, their priority is to identify and organise the very poor and vulnerable groups. Every city has groups of people who are never included in city development plans; these are the pavement dwellers in Mumbai, the homeless and landless groups in South Africa and the scavenger families who live on the dumpsites in Manila. SDI believes that if the strategy is built around the needs, perspectives and capacities of those with higher incomes, it is likely to exclude the very poor. The savings process seeks to ensure that women, often vulnerable, are at the centre of the process. Women's collectives develop and manage systems around savings and loans within the community and control decisions related to money management. These experiences help redefine the relationship between women and the rest of the community. In the past, women have managed their minimal finances at home, and these skills are now transferred to the community level.

Savings and loans

Daily savings is at the heart of the membership (participative) process. Most families have lost the ability to trust their own community, and rebuilding this trust is essential for collective action. Saving together helps families learn to trust one another. The process of savings also embeds practices of accountability and transparency within these local organisa-tions. Managing savings and loans provides the community with new skills and enables the federations to take on new risks and manage complex funds.

> The formula is simple: without poor women joining together, there can be no savings: without savings there can be no federating; without federating, there is no way for the poor themselves to enact change in the arrangements that disempower them.
>
> (Appadurai 2001, 33)

A frequently heard story when SDI initiates savings in any new community is of past leaders running away with the money. The picture that often emerges through in-depth studies of local neighbourhoods or residents' associations is one of male domination, with a major function being to further the incomes and/or political ambitions of the local leader and, at best, partial improvements in the locality (Benjamin and Bhuvaneshari 2001; Peattie 1990; Scheper-Hughes 1992; Thorbek 1991; van der Linden 1997). Such organisations fail to address the needs of some of the more vulnerable groups, notably women. Embedded within existing systems of political patronage, they are designed to secure benefits for a few. The first challenge for SDI is to support local groups to overcome such problems.

Community exchanges as a methodology for learning

The most important vehicle for community learning and knowledge creation is the exchange of information, experience and skills between urban poor communities (Patel and Mitlin 2002). Community exchanges take place at all levels including internationally. Over 60 per cent of those who participate in the exchange visits are women. Exchanges are not a single experience but a series of visits that enable mutual learning. A curriculum based on each community's learning needs is created, and, as a result, knowledge within each community begins to consolidate.

Exchanges between communities draw large numbers of people into a process of learning and change.[5] Exchanges enable the poor to reach out and federate at the city and national level, thereby develop city and national strategies. Exchanges locate the basis of federating within the members of savings schemes and help to avoid it being dominated by, and exclusive to, the leadership. The underlying process is a powerful and critical one. The message is that the poor must learn from, and must depend on, themselves. The NGO leaders step aside from the immediacy of learning, making the poor the agents of change.

Enumeration and the mapping of settlements

National and local governments use census-taking and statistical enumeration to allocate finite state resources. Demographic information provides an objective basis for 'subjective choices' normally determined by 'political processes'. SDI groups have adopted self-enumeration as one of the main strategies. Members gather reliable and complete data about households in their own communities. Hut/shack counts, settlement counts and settlement profiles, and cadastral and household surveys all become powerful tools in mobilising communities. The data generated is used in negotiations for resources such as land, housing, government grants and opportunities for employment.

The collective strength experienced through knowledge derived from these self surveys is empowering and gives people the hope to reach previously unattainable goals. For example, in Dharavi, a slum in Mumbai which is a hub of informal business and houses 85,000 families, the daily cash turnover is Rs.700,000 (US$14,000). Such information makes the urban poor aware of their collective economic power and provides them with a valuable negotiating tool.

House model exhibitions

At large, open-air events attended by housing professionals, government officials and politicians, communities show life-size house models they have designed and constructed. These exhibitions allow the poor (especially the women) to discuss and debate housing designs best suited to their needs. The women furnish the house model with beds, stoves and some basic storage; this enables the women to compare it to the space they presently live in. Federations of the poor dialogue with professionals about construction materials, construction costs and urban services; this process allows communities to redefine their relationship with professionals in their city.

Precedent setting

When savings schemes are strong enough to put forward their own development ideas and options, precedent setting develops. Groups innovate new practices in areas such as land sub-division, water installation, construction of toilet blocks and housing development. These precedents open a dialogue with city officials, demonstrating to senior policy makers and administrators that it is possible to do things differently. Policy change alone is not strong enough, and a 'precedent' that works is what creates the legitimacy needed to bring about change. The process builds trust both within communities about their own capabilities and between the poor and the government. In Kenya, when Pamoja Trust, along with the Federation, constructed the first house model, it set the tone of its initial negotiation with the city. This model prompted the city to assign the Federation the task of constructing 2500 houses in Huruma. The Federation will also construct the first 800 houses to be shifted from railway lands in a recently agreed resettlement process; this agreement emerged from an exchange visit between the Federation in Kenya and Mumbai, India, when officials saw similar resettlement programmes there.

Some successes

The growth of SDI is summarised in Table 12.1 and reflects both national achievements[6] in the mature countries and the appeal of the methodology to other communities and professionals. For the most part, these have been new ventures for community leaders and professionals. However, there have been exceptions, and, in the Philippines, a well-established pro-poor micro-finance group recognised the importance of secure tenure. After exploratory exchanges, the group adopted the SDI methodology and established the Philippine Homeless People's Federation. In Uganda, government officials learnt about the work of SDI through activities in Kenya and asked for capacity-building support in the low-income settlements of Kampala. The challenge for SDI is to continue deepening the success of the more mature and older Federations, whilst at the same time responding to the scale of interest from grassroots organisations and urban development professionals.

Turning to specific outcomes, SDI groups have developed a number of alternatives to evictions. Concerned to find alternatives to existing confrontational strategies that did not result in long-term solutions, the Indian alliance of SPARC, NSDF and Mahila Milan launched a long-term strategy to build community capacities. The pavement women undertook an enumeration about their settlement and began to collect accurate data about themselves to enable a dialogue with the city. The enumerations were compiled in a report that countered a lot of myths about pavement dwellers and educated city officials on how they were different from other groups of slum dwellers.[7] This publication was followed by a survey of vacant lands in the city, showing the potential for resettlement. Through saving, women demonstrated that if government was willing to give them land, they were ready to construct their homes with the funds needed to leverage a housing loan. Affordable and feasible house and settlement design helped actualise these negotiations with practical comments and suggestions. Successes were achieved. By the end of 2005, SPARC and NSDF in India had resettled 50,000 households.

This strategy of building capacity offers city officials the opportunity to look again at the urban poor. The pavement dwellers in Mumbai helped the city officials and politicians reconsider options other than evictions. By 1999, when the railway authorities wished to evict tens of thousands of families living alongside the tracks, the Indian federations were ready with enumeration skills and over 70 per cent of families were already saving daily.

Achievements include the establishment of urban poor funds which make direct investments and bridge finance state subsidies (notably in India and South Africa) to enable people-managed development. SDI groups have experimented with a number of organisational forms of urban poor funds, and in most cases they are located outside of the state.[8] An exception is the Community Organization Development Institute, a state agency in Thailand which provides subsidised loans for housing, land purchase and community revolving funds.

Further success has been achieved in improved regulatory frameworks that reduce the cost of development and facilitate incremental and more affordable approaches. The costs associated with building and land development regulations are considerable, and SDI groups in Africa (notably Kenya, Namibia and Zimbabwe) have sought regulatory reform. Higher-density development, collective infrastructure and extended periods for housing construction all assist with affordability and inclusion. The successes can be illustrated through the experience in Windhoek (Namibia) which, like many Southern African cities, has been growing rapidly in the recent decade. Housing needs are acute, and the City of Windhoek found that it could not respond to the shelter needs of a growing population. Between 1991 and 2001, the Council provided 6000 serviced plots, well below requirements. The Council estimated that only 4 per cent of those living in Windhoek's informal settlements could afford plots with individual household connections. During the late 1990s, there was an evident tension in the Council between a political commitment to provide services, a financial requirement for cost recovery and a high level of professional commitment to managing urbanisation. With this scale of need and limited affordability and in response to a stakeholder consultation process, the Shack Dwellers Federation of Namibia and the Namibia Housing Action Group (NHAG) put forward a development model based around self-help and a new partnership between the poor and the municipality. After discussions with the Federation, the Council designed a system of 'development levels' that define the level of services that is provided. The lowest cost option is a rental plot of $180 \, m^2$ serviced with communal water points; the rental charge is sufficient to cover financing costs for the land investment plus water services and garbage collection. The second lowest cost option is for a group to purchase or lease a block of land, again with communal services. In Windhoek, it costs N\$10,000 to provide individual services to a $300 \, m^2$ plot. Within this policy, Federation groups can supply communal services to $180 \, m^2$ for between N\$2100 and \$3100 and individual connections for N\$3200 and \$4300 (Mitlin and Muller 2004).

The Federating strategies ensure a political presence that consolidates as groups grow stronger. The first step towards achieving voice occurs at a very local level. As one woman member of a savings scheme explained during a review of the loan fund activities of the Shack Dwellers Federation of Namibia: 'Twahangana[9] is good. Before Twahangana, I was silent. I could not say anything. Now I go to meetings. I talk' (Savings scheme member, Oshakati, 12 August 2004).

Central to the process of inclusion is an informal local process that enables the women active in the savings schemes to become leaders. Cleaver (1999) suggests that the formalisation of local organisations may discourage the involvement of the poorest and, in SDI, informal ongoing activities help to ensure that the voice of the least powerful is heard. The first women in SDI, the pavement dwellers in Mumbai, moved from being encroachers in the city to finding an identity for themselves and determining their future in the city as recognised citizens. For the first time, the women experienced the power of being able to sit across a government official's table and negotiate many small victories:

- Health system: the dean from the local hospitals talked to them in their settlements about the policy for health services.
- The women obtained ration cards (enabling access to subsidised food grains). They could not get this in the past due to the fact that they lived on pavements and it was never considered as a fixed address.
- The women talked to senior inspectors from the local police stations about their security rights. It was important for the women to know that they should not be called to the police station after dusk. Many of them complained about their husbands being picked up by the police when they got home late from work. It was part of a routine police exercise to round up a certain quota. It is easiest to pick up the very poor. Today their relationship with the police has changed. The Mumbai Police along with the women's collective have created 'police panchayats' in various neighbourhoods. Mahila Milan is a member of the panchayat, and women leaders solve most petty disputes before they reach the police station.

Growing confidence and skills helped the women tackle the more difficult issue of demolitions. SDI groups are now regularly invited by city officials, NGOs and communities to participate in finding city-level solutions for the urban poor. They have gradually begun to influence decisions at the local, national and the international level. Their critical mass along with their rootedness in the local on a daily basis gives them the strength, wisdom and voice to manage the complexities of this process. At the national level progress has been varied, although SDI has demonstrated considerable adeptness at moving to take advantage of opportunities with international support for national initiatives.

In Cambodia, the urban poor have struggled to establish themselves faced with a history of considerable oppression and rampant redevelopment. Nevertheless, relationship building between the Squatter and Urban Poor Federation resulted in a pledge by the Prime Minister in 2003 to reverse existing policy and favour the improvement of 100 central low-income areas in Phnom Penh (Asian Coalition for Housing Rights 2004). In Zimbabwe, despite very difficult political and economic circumstances, the Federation groups have been able to take advantage of the declining legitimacy of the central state and increasing local political competition to further their interests. As Friedmann and Douglass (1998, 2–3) argue in reference to civil society more generally, these efforts seek to transform (rather than overturn or replace) the state, making it more inclusive and more responsive to its citizens.

The consistent experience of SDI has been that changing agency policy and behaviour requires a critical mass – lots of experiences at a local level that collectively reinforce a new role for these agencies. Scalable solutions designed by the poor often have to contest solutions brought in by bilateral and multilateral agencies. However, over time, Federation strategies have produced credibility and respect as sustained activities demonstrate new solutions that work for city and the poor. SDI will keep responding to strategic opportunities at the centre, but the critical strategy is to build many local experiences and create many local leaders.

Understanding the experience

What do these experiences and achievements indicate about the contribution of membership organisations to urban development and poverty reduction? Four factors appear to be particularly helpful in understanding the contribution of SDI groups to poverty reduction. In each specific locality, these factors may be more or less significant; however, all emerge as being 'necessary' factors if the urban development process is to secure voice, redistribution, and access to housing, land and basic services.

Knowledge and learning

A central component of the SDI process is the recognition that community members learn very differently from the NGOs who work with them and that community learning is imperative to the process. NGOs learn with conventional education strategies: through the written word, seminars, networking and more recently by surfing the web. Formal education trains the professionals to collect information, collate and synthesise it. Community members, often lacking formal education, learn through experiences and collective wisdom. They draw on real-life experiences to understand what works and does not work and what feels right and does not feel right. SDI's experience suggests that they often have particular numeric skills, being more familiar with and street-wise about financial transactions. The prioritisation of knowledge creation and learning capacity within low-income communities is fundamental. The experience of SDI groups is that the emerging solutions only work for the poor if they come from the poor and are refined by the poor through practical experience. Membership, within both local savings schemes and the federations, is critical to that process. Through federations, members gradually consolidate solutions that address the problems they face individually and collectively.

Also important in learning has been the creation of a separate organisational space for women (through savings groups). Traditional leadership is often a couple of male leaders who monopolise information and decision-making. As women organise in a separate space, the traditional leadership is less likely to be threatened; women are not viewed as competition but as having a complementary role. Hence, they are given the space to develop precedents that address their priority needs. The role of the local collective is also essential. In the absence of a collective, women leaders often behave as the conventional men leaders. Collectivising the problem makes it more evident that the only effective solutions are political ones and this requires the community to act together. Once the group understands this, they own the process and begin to build the capacities they need.

Learning and knowledge creation activities at three levels (within the community, between communities, and between the cities and countries) mutually reinforce a process that ensures that the central agency of the poor is able to determine development activities. The focus on local learning enables ideas to emerge and be nurtured so that the activities reflect local knowledge and local commitment. Rather than providing information that is used within an externally driven participatory programme and/or a localised development planning process, knowledge is used to determine choices at the local level. Horizontal exchanges between communities ensure that only one community (in any networked group) needs to take up the opportunities mentioned above (on pages 225–7) as ideas are shared, spread and the exchange provides a catalyst to take learning to the next level. The implications are taken up later in the subsection on federating.

The role of the NGO

The second critical factor is the relationship between the federations and support NGOs. Howes (1997, 597) notes that some NGOs have considerable experience in supporting membership organisations. However, SDI's experience is that the role played by NGOs can be a difficult one.[10] The role of the support NGO is to play a catalytic function to support the federations to claim their own economic, social and political rights. In general, the NGOs manage the finances and take on the administration, helping to create accountability between the two organisations. The NGOs are accountable to the national federation for financial decisions and other choices that affect the federation (and must avoid exercising control), whilst the members are responsible for the finances that they receive. This tension is healthy (despite being difficult). The support NGOs also bridge the gap between development professionals (especially those within the state) and the communities, and this role is extended internationally when dealing with staff in funding and other agencies. They may take the lead when negotiating, if city officials are hostile and are not willing to talk to slum dwellers.

NGO staffs are mostly middle-class professionals who, very easily, fall into their dominant behaviour of providing answers. They like to present themselves as people who know what is best for communities. Such attitudes need to be changed before professionals can serve ordinary people. This is one of the main challenges within this relationship. A further issue is that of donor funding. There is a lot of pressure on NGO staff to give in to donor demands to formalise the community process. The professionals have to 'walk through' the logic of the federation and create a system that works for the members and for the external agencies. They have a double obligation of protecting the federation and meeting the demands from the formal world. A successful outcome can only happen if differences are recognised at the same time as trust is established. There is always a risk that the partnership will break apart, and much patience and courage are needed to find solutions.

As support NGOs take federation ideas that work for the poor and translate them for the formal world, they have to resolve contradictions. At the same time, the relationships are in permanent transition as the federations and savings schemes grow stronger; there is a constant shifting down of tasks as local capacity is developed. This model differs from that discussed by Howes (1997, 601), who suggests that the NGO should move towards a point where they disengage. Within SDI groups, the NGO keeps changing its role, but there is an understanding that it will continue to contribute to the development process. The SDI experience also differs from that researched by Howes (1997, 603) in that prior institutional strengthening of the NGO is not necessary; rather both institutions grow stronger together.

Federating

Whilst some attention has been given to federating (Appadurai 2001; Bebbington 2002; Howes 1997; Mitlin 2004), neither the process nor the outcomes of federating membership organisations has been particularly closely explored in development literature. The experience of SDI suggests that the federating process is significant in changing the nature of the way in which local community organisations function, strengthening their collective identity and taking on responsibility for accumulating knowledge. Thorpe *et al.* (2005) suggest that some of the poorest find it difficult to participate in membership groups and are excluded from many ongoing activities and the benefits they offer. Federations offer a capacity to reflect on such processes and strategies to avoid such processes.

In addition, strong federations change the way city authorities look at their low-income communities – rather than being the 'problem' they have become the 'problem-solver'. A federating capacity opens up new possibilities for a city seeking to upgrade and improve low-income settlements. This is demonstrated by the present resettlement process from the railway tracks in Mumbai, which is being coordinated by SPARC, NSDF and Mahila Milan (discussed in the following sub-section).

The significance of federating at a neighbourhood level can be understood in reference to recent commentaries on the practice of participation in development. Many participatory approaches to development claim to be empowering; however, questions have also been raised about the authenticity of such approaches (Cooke and Kothari 2001). The groups within SDI believe that a participatory development process has to be institutionalised through local groups controlled by their members, which are linked together through a horizontally driven federating process. Activities are then managed through a participatory democratic structure rooted in local organisation. This is the strategy that SDI uses to counter the centralising tendencies referred to recently by Kumar and Corbridge (2002) when they discuss why another participatory anti-poverty initiative has failed. The federative nature is also critical because it has a political agency and identity capable of negotiating with politicians inside and outside of government.

As noted above, many SDI mechanisms have both an immediate material agenda in meeting people's needs as well as a political agenda oriented towards a more ambitious programme of reform, inclusion and redistribution. To what extent can the political agenda of SDI be located within the citizenship agenda that has been promoted by supporters of participation and inclusive governance (Gaventa 2004)? The question is important because it highlights the extent to which the approach of SDI is also concerned to change relationships between state and citizen. In changing this relationship, SDI aims to embed collective action within the process of urbanisation, urban development and urban citizenship rather than supporting an atomised and individualised conception of citizen and state which have previously left the poor and their interests unprotected. This is the theme of the final sub-section.

The significance of citywide strategies

SDI groups are involved in developing new relationships between the urban poor and the city authorities and politicians. Federations, their members and support NGOs work strategically to generate political support and bureaucratic confidence. The role of strongly rooted local organisations is critical in securing political interest and commitment. The default social position for the poor has always been civic invisibility. Federation activities, such as housing exhibitions, provide a means of creating political visibility. The poor gain official recognition and legitimacy for their work through such public events and capture the civic space within the public sphere. However, this public recognition is a small part of more fundamental changes that are sought.

As savings schemes and Federations grow in capacity and scale, they seek to develop initiatives based around precedent setting and the management of state programmes. Groups get involved in water and sanitation provision as well as other local improvements. Despite this work, it is not possible to typecast SDI groups within the category of 'service delivery'. Involvement in services becomes a way of strengthening local organisations and developing strategies that more effectively address the needs of the poor. The objective is both to address material/practical needs and to strengthen political/strategic organisational capacity. What is important for SDI is that the means of securing services is itself a way to strengthen organisational capacity; hence, toilet blocks in which the community manages and maintains the facility are both an efficient way of providing sanitation in dense urban settlements and a community centre which spreads skills and experiences through its operation.

Changing the way business gets done is not always an easy task, especially the precedent setting phase. There are many mistakes that do take place and this makes the process vulnerable to external criticism. The risks and messiness of the process make it easier for city officials and professionals to dismiss the innovation. The first response by external professionals is often 'to throw the baby out with the bath water', as they do not recognise the potential of community strategies to change the way the city does business with the poorest 20 per cent of its population. The failure to manage an innovation is often confused with the potential capacity of the innovation, and the city does not consider how it can assist the process of change. Changing institutional behaviour is always a difficult thing to achieve.

SDI groups seek to identify a political space and then use this space to secure developmental benefits, generally around secure tenure, infrastructure, services and housing, that address immediate needs and build the capacity of the poor to innovate, strategise and negotiate for further benefits. This conceptualisation and reality are not well represented either in present discussions of state and civil society partnerships to provide services or in citizenship. Both discussions are more strongly located within a modern Northern state. Neither discussion fully encapsulates an alternative relationship between citizen and state in which local membership organisations offer alternative development strategies which, when taken up by the state, create new possibilities for citizen action.

SDI groups have been able to create new alternatives from their institutional capacities. Such initiatives broadly fit within what Joshi and Moore (2004, 40) have referred to as institutionalised co-production which is 'the provision of public services ... through regular, long-term relationships between state agencies and organized groups of citizens, where both make substantial resource contributions'. They can be illustrated in the case of Mumbai's recent transport strategy, in which the Federation provided an organisational resource to match state land allocations for resettlement and funds for construction (Patel *et al.* 2002). Mumbai relies on its extensive suburban railway system to get its workforce in and out of the central city; on an average, over seven million passenger trips are made each day on its five main railway corridors. By 1999, nearly 32,000 households lived in shacks next to the tracks at high risk and without water and sanitation; these households reduced the speed of the trains and the capacity of the network. Families lived there because they needed the central location to get to and back from work and could not afford an alternative. Discussions within the Railway Slum Dwellers Federation (to which most of the house-holds along the railway tracks belonged) showed that most wanted to move if they could get a home with secure tenure in an appropriate location.

A relocation programme was developed as part of the larger scheme of the Mumbai urban transport project improving the rail network. The management of the resettlement of 60,000 people was entirely voluntary. Land sites were identified to accommodate the evicted households, and the Federation was given the responsibility for managing the resettlement programme. The resettled people were involved in designing, planning and implementing the resettlement programme and in managing the settlements to which they moved. The huts along the railway tracks and their occupants were counted by teams of Federation leaders, community residents and NGO staffs. Residents' questions about what was being done and how the move would be organised were answered. Maps were pre-pared and each hut was identified with a number. Draft registers of all residents were prepared and the results returned to communities for checking. Households were grouped into units of 50 and the families in each unit moved to the new site together. Identity cards were prepared for all those to be moved and visits were made to the resettlement sites. Then the move took place with some households moving to apartments and others moving to transit camps while better quality accommodation was being prepared.

In this case and in other programmes, the objective is not to work out a way for the state to provide essential services albeit with the financial and organisational support of residents. Rather, it is for the community to work out new ways of developing cities that are inclusive and then to secure state resources to enable the implementation of such solutions at scale. Critically important for SDI is that these processes further strengthen the movement of the urban poor, including its local membership and their capacities such that existing benefits can be maintained and new priorities can be addressed. To this extent, the strategies go beyond 'institutionalised co-production'. Cleaver (2004, 275) recently argued: '[S] surely "empower-ment" and "transformation" require not just the opening up of participatory spaces to debate citizenship, to hold the state to account and so on, but also the more prosaic transformation of everyday life.' SDI seeks to go beyond this dichotomy. The prosaic transformation of everyday life offers ways to empower and to open up participatory spaces; equally the opening of those spaces in turn contributes to the transformation of every-day life. Despite these ambitions, it should also be recognised that there is a frequent tension in such relationships with the state. On the one hand, SDI groups struggle to make state programmes work more effectively for their members within the parameters discussed above (pages 234–5). On the other, the institutions of the state influence the programmes to be less people-centred and locally controlled (see, for example, Baumann and Bolnick (2001) on the experiences in South Africa).

Conclusion

It is possible that the debate on membership organisations will emerge with similar parallels to the debate on participation. First receiving widespread support, criticisms began to emerge based in part on different concepts of participation and what each entails (see, for example, Cooke and Kothari 2001). To anticipate such a debate, it is important that there is an understanding that different forms of membership organisation have different contributions to make to development. Different kinds of processes address different needs, do different functions and have different strengths. In the case of SDI, the process has sought to be inclusive at the local level, drawing in slum or shack dwellers in the settlements and cities where it is active. At the same time, this open process at the grassroots is then focused at the city, state and internationally through a federative structure. This process of federation building is to ensure that the voices of its members are heard and acted upon within agencies involved in local and international policy-making. In a context in which the poor are ignored and representative democracy appears to have lost touch with the concerns of the poorest, SDI develops structures that enable the urban poor who have been involved in local struggles to define and articulate their collective aspirations and vision.

The network seeks to create new possibilities for belonging, an informal equivalent to membership. The multiplicity of levels of organising and federating is a part of the picture: members of the group, the community as a member of a city body, city federations as members of a national federation and the Slum/Shack Dwellers International as a network of national level federations. The large numbers that participate, along with their ability to address the needs of the urban poor on a significant scale, gain the attention of politicians and other middle class in their cities. In the absence of the provision of housing and basic services in any formal political agendas, the federations have filled this vacuum by organising the urban poor at the community level in different cities. The activities promoted at a local level seek to build collective capacity and draw more people into the process by demonstrating the multiple capacities and opportunities of such a collectivity.

SDI's understanding is that membership and citizenship require a transformation in relationships. Out of such a transformation can grow a new conceptualisation of development, one centred on addressing the needs and interests of the poor.

Notes

1 This international network known as Slum or Shack Dwellers International by its grassroots members in Asia and Africa, respectively, reflects the identities with which the urban poor are comfortable.
2 The introductory note for this conference identified political parties, trade

unions and cooperatives as membership organizations that may not be associated with furthering the interests of the poor.
3 Whilst those living in formal areas were organised in 'Civics', informal dwellers had many fewer opportunities.
4 SDI's responsiveness to the needs of the poor has resulted in diverse lending strategies including enterprise development, consumption and emergency needs. However, this is subsidiary to major activities.
5 Face to Face, ACHR available online at: www.achr.net/face_to_face.htm.
6 For more detailed discussion, see Appaduai (2001), Asian Coalition for Housing Rights (2004), Baumann and Mitlin (2003), Patel *et al.* (2002) and Mitlin and Muller (2004).
7 A report published locally: SPARC (1985) – We, the Invisible, a pavement dwellers census.
8 Funds have been established in Cambodia, India, Namibia, the Philippines, South Africa and Zimbabwe. In the last year, Kenya, Nepal and Sri Lanka have also established such funds. In many cases, the capital includes a contribution from the state (national and/or local government).
9 The name of the loan fund in Namibia.
10 As Howes (1997, 602) recommends, all SDI NGOs are national organisations not Northern agencies.

References

Appadurai, A. (2001) 'Deep democracy: urban governmentality and the horizon of politics', *Environment and Urbanization* 13(2): 23–44.

Asian Coalition for Housing Rights (2004) 'Negotiating the right to stay in the city', *Environment and Urbanization* 16(1): 9–25.

Baumann, T. and Bolnick, J. (2001) 'Out of the frying pan into the fire: the limits of loan finance in a capital subsidy context', *Environment and Urbanization* 13(2): 103–16.

Baumann, T. and Mitlin, D. (2003) 'The South African Homeless People's Federation: investing in the poor', *Small Enterprise Development Journal* 14(1): 32–41.

Bebbington, A. (2002) 'Organization, inclusion and citizenship: policy and (some) economic gains of indigenous people's organizations in Ecuador', mimeo.

Benjamin, S. and Bhuvaneshari, R. (2001) 'Democracy, Inclusive Governance and Poverty in Bangalore', *Urban Governance, Partnerships and Poverty Research Working Paper* No. 26, Stage 2 Case Study, University of Birmingham.

Castells, M. (1983) *City and the Grassroots*, London: Edward Arnold.

Cleaver, F. (1999) 'Paradoxes of participation: questioning participatory approaches to development', *Journal of International Development* 11: 597–612.

Cleaver, F. (2004) 'The social embeddness of agency and decision-making' in S. Hickey and G. Mohan (eds) *Participation: from Tyranny to Transformation*, London and New York: Zed Press, 271–8.

Copestake, J. (2002) 'Inequality and the polarizing impact of micro-credit: evidence from Zambia's copperbelt', *Journal of International Development* 14: 743–55.

Cooke, B. and Kothari, U. (2001) (eds) *Participation: the New Tyranny*, London: Zed Books.

Friedmann, J. and Douglass, M. (1998) 'Editors' introduction' in J. Friedmann and M. Douglass (eds) *Cities for Citizens*, Chichester: John Wiley and Sons, pp. 1–9.

Gaventa, J. (2004) 'Towards participatory governance: assessing the transformative possibilities' in S. Hickey and G. Mohan (eds) *Participation: from Tyranny to Transformation*, London and New York: Zed Press, pp. 25–42.

Howes, M. (1997) 'NGOs and the institutional development of membership organizations: the evidence from six cases', *Journal for International Development* 9(4): 597–604.

Joshi, A. and Moore, M. (2004) 'Institutionalised co-production: unorthodox public services delivery in challenging environments', *The Journal of Development Studies* 40(4): 31–49.

Kumar, S. and Corbridge, S. (2002) 'Programmed to fail? Development projects and the politics of participation', *The Journal of Development Studies* 39(2): 73–103.

Mitlin, D. (2004) 'Securing voice and transforming practice in local government: the role of federating in grassroots development' in S. Hickey and G. Mohan (eds) *Participation: from Tyranny to Transformation? Exploring New Approaches to Participation*, London: Zed Books, pp. 175–89.

Mitlin, D. and Muller, A. (2004) 'Windhoek, Namibia – towards progressive urban land policies in Southern Africa', *International Development Policy Review* 26(2): 167–86.

Moser, C. (1989) 'Gender planning in the Third World: meeting strategic and practical gender needs', *World Development* 17(11): 1799–825.

Patel, S. and d'Cruz, C. (1993) 'The *Mahila Milan* crisis credit scheme: from a seed to a tree', *Environment and Urbanization* 5(1): 9–17.

Patel, S., d'Cruz, C. and Burra, S. (2002) 'Beyond evictions in a global city: people-managed resettlement in Mumbai', *Environment and Urbanization* 14(1): 159–72.

Patel, S. and Mitlin, D. (2002) 'Sharing experiences and changing lives', *Community Development* 37(2): 125–37.

Patel, S. and Mitlin, D. (2004) 'Grassroots-driven development: the alliance of SPARC, the National Slum Dwellers Federation and *Mahila Milan*' in D. Mitlin and D. Satterthwaite (eds) *Empowering Squatter Citizens*, London: Earthscan Publications Ltd, pp. 216–44.

Peattie, L. (1990) 'Participation: a case study of how invaders organize, negotiate and interact with government in Lima, Peru', *Environment and Urbanization* 2(1): 19–30.

Scheper-Hughes, N. (1992) *Death without Weeping: the Violence of Everyday Life in Brazil*, Berkeley: University of California Press.

Thorbek, S. (1991) 'Gender in two slum cultures', *Environment and Urbanization* 3(2): 71–81.

Thorpe, R., Stewart, F. and Heyer, A. (2005) 'When and how far is group formation a route out of chronic poverty?', *World Development* 33(6): 907–20.

UN-Habitat (2003) *Global Report on Human Settlements 2003*, London: Earthscan Publications Ltd.

van der Linden, Jan (1997) 'On popular participation in a culture of patronage: patrons and grass roots organizations in a sites and services project in Hyderabad, Pakistan', *Environment and Urbanization* 9(1): 81–90.

13 Membership-based organisations of the poor

The South African tradition

Jan Theron

Crossroads was once a squatter settlement known for factional conflicts and the warlords who presided over the allocation of houses and resources there, in collusion with the apartheid authorities. Now it is integrated into the adjacent townships. The building the most notorious of the warlords once occupied, now derelict, is where Mama N. relocated her crèche and pre-school a few years ago. It belongs to the local authority, and during the day there are 63 children in it, up to the age of six years. There is also a large and flourishing vegetable garden. Produce is sold to the community. To the elderly and sick it is given away.

Mama N. decided to start a crèche and pre-school in 1985, when she learned that there were women in Crossroads desperate enough to abandon their babies on a nearby rubbish dump.[1] At first it was based at her home. Then in 1999 she joined with 15 other crèches and pre-schools to form a co-operative, known as Nosiseko Care Co-operative. Mama N. is its chairperson. It is still going, more than five years later, with the same number of members. Each of them operates a crèche and/or pre-school facility. The largest of these leases premises from the local authority and receives a subsidy from the government. Others operate 'backyard crèches', from their homes. Each member contributes a subscription of R10 a month.

Each member employs between three and six such assistants, called teachers. Strictly speaking, then, the members are employers, in a relationship of power over those who work for them. However the co-operative subscribes to the principle that what each crèche earns should be equally shared between the member and those who work for her.[2] Monthly earnings varied from one crèche to another and from month to month. However, the estimated average income was between R200 and R250 per month.[3] For most of the members, this was the only 'salary' earned by a member of the household. Mama N. herself is part of a household of nine. No-one but her had a job at the time she was first interviewed, and that was still so when I interviewed her again, a year later.

There are a number of reasons the incomes of the crèches fluctuate. People do not require care all the year round, and there are poor parents who cannot afford to pay regularly, or at all. The co-operative regards it as a demonstration of its commitment to the community, in accordance with co-operative principles, that it will accept the children of such poor parents.[4] Doubtless the community has confidence in entrusting their children to a co-operative that displays such commitment. A co-operative is also accountable to the community for the standard of care its members provide in a way an individual operating on her own, or an organisation for profit, would not be. Not that there is any prospect of an organisation for profit offering the same service. There is no profit to be made from this community.

Conceptualising MBOPs

The broad question this chapter seeks to address is whether the notion of a membership-based organisation of the poor ('MBOPs') has practical application in modern-day South Africa. There are some obvious reasons why the concept is attractive: to give the poor a voice through organisations that they belong to and democratically control, and to secure representation of the poor in local and national forums, shaping policy and ensuring accountability. It is also possible that such organisation could enable poor people achieve collectively public goods that the state cannot or does not provide.

Equally, what seems a good idea in theory may be practically difficult to attain, if not misconceived. The first consideration is what form such organisations will take, and how they will be established and sustained. The next consideration is how such organisations will avoid being appropriated: from within, by those wishing to pursue sectional interests, or from without, by political organisations or other interests, or the state. Related to this, any MBOP that is established faces a political dilemma. MBOPs that challenge the status quo are liable to be repressed. On the other hand, MBOPs that restrict themselves to self-help strategies can be seen as enabling the state to evade its responsibilities, by making the poor responsible for their own deliverance.

These are not questions that can be considered in abstract, as the case of the Care Co-operative illustrates. Child-care is indeed the kind of public good that some states provide. There is also a precedent for the local authority in question to do so.[5] A demand that the local authority assumes greater responsibility for care for the very young is certainly legitimate. But who will pursue this demand, if not an organisation that is practically engaged with the problem? In fact, the co-operative can be said to be pursuing this demand by actions such as occupying a building belonging to the local authority and negotiating a lease that can be viewed as representing an indirect subsidy. Now the co-operative intends to negotiate for a direct subsidy from the Department of Social Development. The co-operative has been assisted in these negotiations by the local civic association and sympathetic councillors. Yet neither the civic association nor the local authority is likely to have prioritised child-care as an issue without a push from below.

A co-operative is by definition an MBO. Yet, clearly all MBOs are not organisations of the poor. Even though the members of the Care Co-operative are by any definition poor, that would not seem to be the primary reason to regard it as an MBOP,[6] nor is it merely that the community the co-operative serves is poor. What is paramount is the social and economic need this co-operative fulfils in poor communities. Moreover, it is a need that the co-operative form of organisation is ideally suited to fulfil, for the reasons mentioned. If therefore the notion of MBOPs has practical application, co-operatives should be part of it, because of the function they fulfil, and so too should trade unions. The members of trade unions are not necessarily poor and, in a context of chronic unemployment, may even occupy a position of relative privilege. However, as long as there is a section of the poor that depends on wages earned in an employment relationship, trade unions remain an indispensable organisational form for the poor.[7]

In what follows, I first seek to identify the characteristics of both co-operatives and trade unions that enable them to function as MBOPs. I also identify the limitations of these particular forms and, by implication of MBOPs, in order to explain why they do not always fulfil this function. It follows from this analysis that there is no ideal type of MBOP, which can simply be replicated. There is also no form of organisation that should be regarded as an MBOP by definition. An MBOP is an organisation that functions as such, meeting the social and economic needs of the poor. In the second part of this chapter, I briefly consider what the national experience of MBOPs has been, from a socio-historical perspective, and the current conjuncture. Part three is a survey of actual or possible models of MBOP that have emerged or are emerging in the current conjuncture.

The state of civil society

But is it useful to introduce yet another acronym in debates about the state of civil society in South Africa. In these debates, some emphasise the political interconnectedness of the state and civil society. For this reason, any movement seeking to challenge the hegemony of the state needs a mass-based political party to give it coherence (Marais, 1998, 241–4). It has also been suggested that the inauguration of representative democracy in 1994 has resulted in a withering of civil society in this sense (Seekings, 2000). For others, the state and civil society are often sharply counter-posed (Kotze, 2003; Fakir, 2004). The term 'voluntary' or 'non-profit sector' is sometimes used as an equivalent to civil society in this sense (Pieterse, 1998; Kraak, 2001). Far from withering away, it is suggested that it is larger than generally supposed (Pieterse and Van Donk, 2002).

The voluntary sector is variously characterised as being composed of non-governmental organisations (NGOs) and community-based organisations (CBOs) (Boulle, 1997; Kraak, 2001). In theory, the term NGO should incorporate all forms of non-governmental organisations, including those that are membership-based. In practice, it is common usage to differentiate between trade unions and other NGOs. The co-operative form is more often than not ignored. An alternative formulation, which does acknowledge co-operatives as a distinct form, categorises them as self-help organisations (SHOs). SHOs in turn are a sub-category of group-based organisations (GBOs) (Von Ravensburg, 1998), an equivalent term to CBOs.

The conceptual basis on which the above writers distinguish between NGOs and CBOs is vague, but it appears to relate to perceptions of NGOs as being better resourced, and having a formal legal identity, as opposed to CBOs, which have a more fluid identity, and are a more grassroot form of organisation (Pieterse, 1998; Pieterse and Van Donk, 2002; Kotze, 2003). To this mix, contemporary theorists have added the category of social movements. The term 'social movement' suggests a distinction between an organisation and a form of collective action, or a political campaign. Yet, organisations that are or purport to be membership based are regarded as part of the 'new' social movement in South Africa. This 'new' social movement supposedly arose in the period post-1994, when the adversarial relations between the state and civil society changed (Ballard *et al.*, 2004).[8]

However, what is lacking in the above conceptions is an appreciation of the significance of the distinction between MBOs and organisations which do not have a membership base. What is critical about this distinction is the light it throws on the social basis of organisations and the interests they, in fact, serve, hence the relevance of the concept of MBOPs. Admittedly 'the poor' is an elastic category that can be stretched to accommodate a variety of sectional interests, including those of the not so poor, or the not poor at all. On the other hand, the scale of poverty in South Africa is such that there is no obvious substitute for the term.[9] Certainly, the concept of the working class will not do, given the shifts in its composition and significance over the past decade.

Co-operatives and trade unions as exemplars of membership-based organisations of the poor

In saying that trade unions and co-operatives are forms of organisation that can be utilised by the poor, I do not imply that there is any particular blue-print of a trade union or co-operative that should be adopted. Rather, the argument I seek to advance is that trade unions and co-operatives embody a tradition of organising the poor and disadvantaged. Any endeavour to organise the poor needs to take account of these traditions, because of the considerable experience both these forms of organisation have had in overcoming the organisational and political difficulties inherent in such an endeavour.

I refer to a tradition in this context as a practice or practices constituted by an argument about what it is that an organisation should be, and how it should be constituted (Macintyre, 1985). And although trade unions and co-operatives clearly embody distinctive traditions, it is possible to identify a number of criteria or characteristics that are common to both traditions, and which distinguish them from other forms of organisation. The hypothesis I seek to advance is that these are or should be the characteristics of any organisation that aspires to be an MBOP and embody a tradition of MBOPs. Thus in the tradition of both trade unions and co-operatives:

1   The primary objective is to cater for the socio-economic needs of their members. If the organisation is not seen to do so, it will fail. To do so, however, the organisation requires a mandate from its members that continually has to be renewed. It is the nature of this objective, and the ongoing mandate it implies, that distinguishes these forms of organisation from MBOs having a purely social or cultural objective, on the one hand, or from political organisations, on the other.[10]

2   Both forms of organisation rely on the existence of a well-defined constituency from which membership is drawn ('the membership constituency'). In the case of a trade union, the membership constituency is workers in an employment relationship, more or less broadly conceived. In the case of co-operatives, the constituency is defined by the nature of the enterprise in which the co-operative is engaged.

3   The organisation is financed by the members. In the case of a trade union, this takes the form of a subscription. In the case of a co-operative, this may take the form of either a subscription or a membership share.[11] The method of financing an organisation has of course important implications both for the sustainability of the organisation and for its autonomy.

4   There are clear structures of governance that define, first, the relationship between the members and leadership and, second, the relationship between lower and higher levels of organisation (such as between local or branch and national levels or between primary, secondary and tertiary co-operatives). Thus, the highest decision-making structure in both trade unions and co-operatives is (or should be) the most representative forum of members.

5   There is a strongly developed sense of ownership of the organisation by the members, and of accountability of the leadership to the membership, in sharp contrast to political organisations, in which a sense of accountability and ownership is typically weakly developed or non-existent.

6   Both traditions embody values of co-operation and solidarity. These values are necessary to counter any tendencies for the members for the time being to put their immediate interests above the interests of the constituency from which they are drawn and the long-term interests of the organisation. They, in turn, define a relationship between members and the wider community or polity from which they are drawn, which necessarily has a political character. It is the existence of political values such as those that would differentiate MBOPs from a criminal gang, for example, whose members happen to be poor.

Whether a commitment to such values is rhetorical or actual is of course another matter. Any form of organisation is open to abuse, and it would be boundlessly naive to suppose that merely because an organisation seeks to confine its membership to the poor, or poor people comprise the majority of its members, it will voice their interests. What Michels terms the 'iron law of oligarchy',[12] briefly stated, is that direct democracy in mass-based organisations is impractical, because such organisations necessarily call for a centralised bureaucracy with specialist leadership. The leadership, in turn, has an interest in securing its own permanence and comes to regard the organisation as an end in itself.

Perhaps Michels' argument is over-stated insofar, as it depicts what is properly regarded as a tendency as a law. It is nevertheless incontestable that MBOPs, in particular, are susceptible to this tendency. First, the poorer the members of an organisation are, the wider the gulf in both material conditions and knowledge between members and leadership in an MBOP is likely to be. Second, any organisation with a broad-based membership amongst poor people will necessarily have to reconcile different sectional interests within a notion of the overall good of the organisation, and this, even with the best of intentions, will all too often be the interests of the section that is most vocal or best connected. It follows that any evaluation of MBOPs, and specifically of the extent to which the leadership in fact represents poor members, needs to be grounded in an understanding of the local context, specifically the social and political context, and an understanding as to what legal space exists to promote specific forms of organisations.[13]

Organisation of the poor in the struggle

To understand the social context in which a tradition of MBOPs emerged in the 1970s and more particularly the 1980s, one needs to begin with the controls on the movement of rural people to the urban areas that the apartheid system formalised. These exacerbated an urban–rural divide and tended to relegate the informal economy to peripheries and the rural areas. Apartheid did not simply create a racial hierarchy, with Africans as a race group the poorest. It also created an economic and social divide between urban 'insiders' and rural Africans, as well as, amongst the coloured group, a divide between a relatively privileged middle class and a working class, particularly in the rural areas of the Western and Northern Cape.

The event that more than any other defined the legal space within which a tradition of MBOPs was possible was the 1960 banning of political organisations opposed to white minority rule. Because the membership constituency of organisations representing the African majority, the ANC and the PAC, was overwhelmingly poor, any organisation of the poor would inevitably be seen to be a proxy for the banned political organisations or to be in collaboration with the apartheid regime. This was certainly true of the civic movement that began to emerge in the late 1970s and 1980s, at about the same time as a new generation of trade unions was emerging.

Although sometimes these associations had ambitious schemes to represent residents, by and large they did not feel any need to recruit members, to justify their claims to represent the community. More importantly, almost without exception, they had no presence amongst the poorest sections of the African community: amongst migrant workers living in the hostels and, with the influx of people from the rural areas, amongst the shack-dwellers in areas like Crossroads. The divide between these migrants and recent arrivals, on the one hand, and urban insiders, on the other, was at the root of the factional violence in Crossroads and elsewhere. The apartheid regime repeatedly exploited this division over the years, at the cost of thousands of lives. These were lives that could perhaps have been saved through organisations able to bridge that divide, in struggles over grassroots issues affecting the whole community. As it was, grassroots issues tended to be subsumed in the broader political struggle.

There was a far better understanding of this divide amongst the emergent trade unions, mainly because, in certain areas and certain sectors, migrant workers were an important part of their membership constituency. These trade unions were able to establish relatively effective organisations because, first, there was legislation regulating trade unions, creating legal space despite the lack of political space. Second, because their objective was primarily economic, trade unions did not necessarily constitute a threat either to the state or to the legitimacy of the repressed political organisations. Both these factors also applied in the case of co-operatives, and co-operatives representing poor people were established in the 1980s and 1990s. But these were a far cry from the agricultural marketing co-operatives the legislation catered for. In contrast to the trade unions, which benefited from a degree of ambiguity amongst a business community anxious for reform, co-operatives faced a hostile economic environment with no institutional support. Consequently most of them failed.

The claim that the unions developed a tradition of MBOP is as follows. First, there was no disjuncture between workers in employment and the poor, who depended to a large extent on wages earned in the mines, on farms and in manufacturing for their survival. The membership constituency of the unions was poor, the only section that was not, comprised skilled workers and supervisors, who were mainly white. Second, unions subscribed to the principle that the workers who were their members should be in effective control of their organisation. In doing so, unions also articulated the need for ordinary workers to be part of the political process. In many instances, ordinary workers were elected to high office in such unions.

However, there was a tension in accommodating this need. It necessitated the adoption of procedures such as translating from vernacular into English, and report backs, that community activists perceived as laborious and unnecessary. Initially, this tension was characterised as between the unions, as proxy for the most disadvantaged sections of society, and the community, representing a primarily urban constituency. At the same, the emergent unions were by no means all equally committed to these practices, or impervious to pressure from community activists to adopt a more 'political' approach. The unions that stood closest to the community activists had a weak membership base and were proxies for political organisations. Even amongst unions with a strong membership base, there were differences as to how to strengthen the voice of ordinary members in the union and to bridge the divide between the poorest sections of the working class, who were overwhelmingly unskilled and with close links to the rural areas, and a comparatively sophisticated, urban-based section of the working class. The latter section was becoming increasingly dominant in the emergent unions.

Amongst the unions that formed COSATU, a number of traditions of unionism can be discerned. Of particular importance in this analysis was a tradition that emphasised the importance of the financial autonomy of the union, and the autonomy of the branch or local structure over the head office, or national union. I shall describe this as the tradition of the Food and Canning Workers Union, since it was the primary exponent of this tradition.[14] However, with one other exception, the other emergent unions had, since their inception, relied heavily on donor funding and not on tradition of financial self-sufficiency. Partly as a consequence, most unions favoured a highly centralised structure, in which the branch or local structure was allocated funds (and hence controlled) by the head office. This tradition of organisation from the top down is the one on which the established union movement in post-apartheid South Africa was founded.

The current conjuncture

The trade unions' reward for their support during the struggle was to institutionalise a political role for them and to enact supportive labour legislation. The former took the form of the establishment of a political structure, NEDLAC, in terms of which organised labour and organised business would be consulted about the introduction of socio-economic policy. This can be regarded as representing a form of corporatism, consistent with the tradition of organisation from the top down which unions had opted for.

But for this corporatist project to be credible, it was necessary for government's 'social partners' to be seen as representative of those affected by social and economic policy. One of the ironies about the advent of a democratic government in 1994 is that it coincided with a rapid integration of South Africa into the global trading regime, and the dismantling of protectionist measures. Whether because of the resulting competition, or as a consequence of the restructuring of the capitalist workplace, the basis for this corporatist project was profoundly compromised.

As a result of restructuring, the workplace is less and less a community of workers with different skills, associated in the same physical locality and working for a single employer. Increasingly big business has delegated the role of the employer, particularly in respect of lesser-skilled workers, to intermediaries such as franchisees or temporary employment agencies or service providers of various sorts. These intermediaries can be regarded as proxies for the 'real' employer, which continues to set the terms on which services are provided, ultimately by relying on its ownership of intellectual property rights rather than the means of production.

As a result of job losses attributable to restructuring and international competition, ever fewer persons are in an employment relationship, particularly in the primary and secondary sectors, the traditional membership constituency of the trade unions. The informal economy is burgeoning,[15] and government now speaks of a dual labour market. In the first tier, workers are comparatively well-off and protected by labour legislation. In the second tier, labour legislation is either not applicable, as in the case of those engaged in survivalist activity, or ineffective, as in the case of the employees of intermediaries and other subordinated to big business.

The political ascendance of the unions has thus coincided with their organisational decline, a reality masked only by their increased membership in the public sector, courtesy of the new regime. The creation of a third constituency in NEDLAC to represent the interests of 'the community' by no means ameliorates this situation, for it remains unclear how, practically, the community is to be represented. In any event, corporatism does not encourage the kind of organisation that could credibly do so as much as lobbying in the corridors of power. Given that the organisations represented at NEDLAC also determine what other organisations may be admitted to membership, the arrangement it embodies has elements of a self-perpetuating oligarchy.

Yet, there are also opportunities for the organisations in civil society in the current conjuncture. Along with the integration of South Africa into the global trading system came pressures to curtail government spending and to pare down the role of the state. As a consequence, the state is increasingly constrained to devolve what have hitherto been regarded as its responsibilities to the private sector and organs of civil society. This has accentuated the need for the poor to be represented in civil society if they are to avoid being further marginalised.

At the same time, another irony about the post-1994 dispensation must be noted. Whilst the majority were disenfranchised, the white minority maintained a system of parliamentary sovereignty. However, the form of state South Africa adopted post-1994 was that of a constitutional democracy, with an entrenched Bill of Rights. This system, with the establishment of a Constitutional Court to interpret the Bill of Rights, was initially a concession to white vested interests. However, as well as the traditional civil and political rights, the Bill of Rights recognises a suite of socio-economic rights. These socio-economic rights provide organisations in civil society with a tool to advance a pro-poor agenda.

In the section that follows, I identify five traditions of organisation to which the concept of MBOPs seems to apply and to identify case studies that show both the potential and limitations of MBOPs.

A survey of membership-based organisations

The emergent co-operative movement

My selection of the Nosiseko Care Co-operative as a case study with which to introduce this chapter is not justified by the successes of this form of co-operative, in providing care or related services. Rather, it is to emphasise its potential, particularly in a society riven by AIDS. It is also to raise the profile of the co-operative form, which has been largely disregarded in post-apartheid development discourse.[16] Moreover, in a context in which there is little or no growth in jobs despite the fact that the South African economy is booming, there is often no alternative for the poor but to adopt a self-help strategy.

Government has to some extent acknowledged this, in adopting new legislation for co-operatives, and all indications are that there is a proliferation of new co-operatives of all kinds, alongside the established agricultural co-operatives.[17] These include savings and credit co-operatives, housing co-operatives, consumer co-operatives and co-operatives whose primary objective is to provide employment to their members, which are defined as worker co-operatives in the new legislation. However, these are overwhelmingly primary co-operatives. For the movement to become established, it is necessary for these co-operatives to raise co-operation to a higher level and organise themselves at a secondary or tertiary level.

The case of the Care Co-operative exemplifies both the challenges of raising the co-operatives to this level of organisation and the fragility of the movement.

The members of this co-operative are justly concerned about its future. A large part of their subscription goes towards an affiliation fee. But it is not a co-operative composed of others providing similar services to which it is affiliated, as much as an apex body, seeking to represent co-operatives at the highest level. This body decided to close its Cape Town branch office, believing it would be preferable to centralise its services at its Johannesburg head office. It is a decision that exemplifies the prevailing top-down approach to organisation, probably facilitated by a reliance on donor funding. What exacerbates the members' concern is that the head office officials did not even take the time to meet with them or to discuss the implications of the closure of the local office. 'They were supposed to write letters to us', Mama N. said. 'Now there's nothing. We were just thrown in the desert.'[18]

More worrying is the probability that many emergent co-operatives will never find their way out of the proverbial desert. Precisely because self-help is the only alternative, there is a tendency for groups to constitute co-operatives with no conception as to how to become viable enterprises. Co-operatives are registered solely in the expectation of securing government tenders, or contracts on preferential terms, on the basis that their members are from a disadvantaged background. Others have registered co-operatives as a scam, with precisely the same end in mind, but no intention to operate as a co-operative. This pertinently raises questions as to the role of the state in preserving the integrity of the co-operative form. Yet, all indications are that the role it envisages is a passive one.[19]

It is especially difficult to establish viable worker co-operatives, because of the balance that needs to be struck between creating employment and sustainability, and of reconciling the imperatives of efficient management with democratic control (Philip, 2003). On the other hand, in a context in which the jobs on offer are provided through intermediaries, this form of co-operative represents an alternative to an inherently exploitative model of employment.

Recasting the trade union tradition

The challenge confronting the trade union movement is of a different order. It is how to give organisational effect to values of co-operation and solidarity in a context in which its membership constituency has eroded, and there is growing disjuncture between the first tier of the labour market, where their members are located, and workers in the second tier, who are largely unorganised, even though the itinerant nature of employment in the second tier means that there is also little financial incentive for the established unions to do so.

Rhetoric will clearly not suffice. Rather the tradition of organisation the established trade unions currently subscribe to needs to be revised. A highly centralised form of union controlled from its head office will not easily respond to the challenges of organising workers in the second tier, and workers in the service sector. Such unions need to decentralise, granting local structures greater autonomy. However, the leadership and union bureaucracies have a vested interest in the status quo. Decentralisation not only undermines their power base, but also jeopardises their financial and job security.

An alternative course would be for the established unions to organise workers in the second tier by creating parallel structures for them, such as the establishment of a network of community-based advice centres, where workers in non-standard employment or the self-employed could take their problems. Ironically, this was once a strategy used to organise African workers, before the labour reforms that allowed them to belong to registered unions. If the established union movement does not take some such measures to organise workers in the second tier, the likelihood is that a parallel union movement will emerge alongside it anyway.

To some extent this has already happened. Despite the founding principle of the dominant federation being one union for one industry, there has been a proliferation of small unions post-1994.[20] In part, this proliferation epitomises a perverse consequence of labour legislation's emphasis on employment security. 'Unions' have been established whose sole function is to represent employees in dismissal disputes at the Commission for Conciliation Mediation and Arbitration (CCMA), the official dispute resolution body. In part, it represents a reaction to union bureaucracies that are perceived to be remote from the members. Small locally based unions also operate on lower margins and have more incentive to organise in the second tier. Consequently, they do, in fact, represent some vulnerable workers that the established unions have not been able to organise.[21]

Yet other unions are experimental in form, consciously setting out to extend the notion of the employment relationship that defines the membership constituency of a union. The leading example of the latter trend has been the Self-Employed Women's Union (SEWU), modelled on SEWA in India. Indeed, in targeting self-employed women SEWU can be said to have broken overtly with a premise that defines the membership constituency in terms of an employment relationship. The self-employed were regarded as excluding those who earn a regular wage, and including persons who do not employ more than three others to assist her. Yet SEWU did define itself as a union. Moreover, at a time when most members were street traders, it operated as though local authorities were the employer, in that they determine certain conditions under which self-employed persons operate (Devenish and Skinner, 2004).[22]

But over time the composition of SEWU's membership changed, with a growing proportion engaged in home-based work. In some forms of home-based work, there is an 'employer' putting out work, even though he, she or it may be difficult to locate. Workers contracted through inter-mediaries to manufacture clothing for the formal economy is an example (Godfrey *et al.*, 2005). However, it does not appear the union succeeded in making a link between informal workers such as these and the formal economy. Instead, it focused on more conventional empowerment strat-egies, such as entrepreneurial training and micro-credit facilities for its members (Devenish and Skinner, 2004). This raises the question whether the pursuit of empowerment and trade union-type demands can be recon-ciled within one organisation.

The question remains unanswered.[23] SEWU has now been dissolved. The irony about its dissolution is that it was precipitated by a decision of the CCMA, the effect of which was to order SEWU to reinstate in its employ two dismissed officials. SEWU could simply not afford the cost of the accumulated back-pay consequent to this decision. Thus, an institu-tion that has primarily benefited workers in the first tier of the labour market (the CCMA) has been instrumental in the demise of a significant attempt to address the conditions of workers in the second tier.[24]

Rights-based organisation

Amongst the gamut of organisations that have arisen in the post-1994 period, there are several that can be categorised as issue-bound, in that they are formed to lobby for or mobilise around a specific issue. These organisations may well invoke a concept of membership to legitimate their stance. However, on closer scrutiny membership equates to support, and the issue around which it is formed defines the life-span of the organisa-tion.[25] At the same time, there are organisations of a more permanent kind that can be categorised as lobbying for or formed around certain rights, in a constitutional dispensation in which socio-economic demands may be cast as enforceable rights.

Obviously, the distinction between these two forms of organisation is a fine one. However, I would regard the Treatment Action Campaign (TAC) as an example of the latter. This is because its objective, adequate and affordable treatment for people living with HIV and AIDS, specifically poor people, is framed in a discourse of rights and is not of an *ad hoc* nature. Having said this, it is true that the notion of membership is weakly developed, and that TAC is funded almost entirely by donations (Fried-man and Mottiar, 2004).[26] Perhaps it could not be otherwise, given the degree of destitution of its members.

Another category of rights-based organisations is those formed with the objective of securing rights to land, mainly in the rural areas. Some purport to be membership based, such as the Landless People's Movement (LPM), modelled on the MST of Brazil.[27] Yet the membership constituency of the LPM includes both those wanting secure access to land and those who already have this and want more land (Greenberg, 2004). Within these two broad categories, whose interests are potentially in conflict, there is a range of subcategories, each with particular problems or interests. It is not clear how the competing claims of these groups are to be reconciled within one organisation. Indeed, it has never developed a concept of membership accountability.[28] Thus, the LPM has been described as a 'hybrid between a party-like, hierarchical organisational structure and an agglomeration of grassroots struggles, the latter sometimes spontaneous and sometimes facilitated by the formal structures of the movement' (Greenberg, 2004).

There are other forms of organisation that have emerged in the context of land reform that invoke a notion of membership. The individuals making up groups formed to take legal ownership of land are commonly defined as members, a usage sanctioned by the Communal Property Associations Act, which provides a form of registration for such groups, provided they have an acceptable constitution.[29] This must define who may be a member and adequately protect the rights of members. But how membership is defined (and by whom) is identified as a major source of uncertainty and strife (Cousins and Hornby, 2002).[30] More profoundly, the question this case raises is whether a notion of membership can ever be legislatively imposed.

Membership-based organisations providing financial services

The corollary of high levels of unemployment and the growth of the second tier of the labour market has been burgeoning household debt, and the growth of a substantial micro-lending industry, epitomised by what are commonly known as 'loan sharks'. These are money-lenders who charge exorbitant rates of interest and resort to various dubious practices to secure repayment. The failure of the formal banking sector to make its facilities more accessible to the poor has exacerbated this situation.[31] However, it has been suggested that attempts to reform retail banking are misplaced, and that existing savings and credit networks have far greater potential to alleviate poverty (Baumann, 2001).

There are some such schemes that are workplace based, but a more significant example operating in the formal economy is the savings and credit co-operative movement, operating on the basis of a payroll deduction.[32] But there is a greater variety in the informal economy, which are often described as 'stokvels', although the term has no precise meaning. One form is where the members contribute a fixed amount each month and draw the collective savings of the group after a specified period. There are also schemes where members save for a fixed period of time, or indefinitely. The latter is also the case with burial schemes, another prevalent form of organisation amongst the poor.[33]

The membership of the stokvel is typically small, and female. The constituency from which they are drawn is typically the locality where they stay. All the members are able to meet regularly. This obviates the necessity for more elaborate structures of governance. Of course, the members have little recourse when money is misappropriated, which is a problem that can be attributed to a lack of regulation. On the other hand, members usually have procedures that amount to a form of internal audit. It is suggested that stokvels succeed more often than not, precisely due to a lack of formal regulation and the efficacy of such internal audits,[34] even though success may be defined in terms of intangibles such as a reduction in vulnerability, the development of social assets such as the increased capacity and self-confidence of members (Baumann, 2001). Yet the informality of such schemes must also operate as a constraint. To leverage meaningful resources requires organisation with significant membership. To attain this level of organisation requires the conscious intervention of a leadership, such as will not emerge spontaneously.

The Homeless People's Alliance represents one model as to how to retain the informality of a grassroots organisation while developing the capacity for interventions at a higher level. This alliance comprises an NGO standing in a supportive relation to a federation of community-based savings schemes, whose founding premise is a scepticism as to the capacity of government to prioritise the needs of the urban poor (Pieterse and Kahn, 2004). Savings are primarily utilised to assist members build houses. But when government instituted a housing subsidy for individual households, the Federation negotiated a scheme whereby members could top up the amount of the subsidy, to provide more adequate housing.

The procedures for application for membership of these schemes are supposed to be flexible and mediated by need rather than by rules (Bolnick and Mitlin, 1999, cited in Pieterse and Kahn, 2004). This degree of local autonomy is in refreshing contrast to the top-down tradition that is so prevalent. On the other hand, it suggests that there are no consistent membership criteria. It is also not clear how local autonomy can be maintained when its scheme to assist members in accessing government housing necessitates centralised control.[35] Current indications are that the Federation is in crisis. One of its causes seems to relate to the peculiar difficulty of sustaining informal savings schemes of this kind, in that it failed to articulate a role for the organisation beyond the delivery of houses to those who are for the time being its members.[36]

The civic movement

If there were any one organisation capable of representing the community at NEDLAC, it should be SANCO, a national civic association established in 1992. SANCO claims to be a membership-based organisation, with branches established countrywide.[37] However, it exemplifies the difficulties of sustaining an organisation established from the top down. A resolution to adopt a national system of membership fees in an endeavour to achieve financial sustainability was never implemented. Instead, branches are left to determine their own membership fees (Zuern, 2004). In this instance, the degree of autonomy local branches enjoy must be seen as a product of organisational incoherence.[38] So much so that what the members of the community pay probably represents a tax as much as a membership fee.

It is nevertheless clear that SANCO is a significant presence in certain communities. As Mama N. conceives it, the government's Reconstruction and Development Programme (RDP) that theorists regard as having been abandoned in favour of more conventional economic prescriptions still lives on in her community. 'We are working hand in hand with the RDP', she says, referring to the local development forum on which SANCO is represented. When the co-operative identified a site to which a member operating a backyard crèche might move, it was SANCO that it approached for assistance. SANCO applied to the development forum on her behalf. Her member now has permission to put a container on the site to serve as a classroom. It is hardly a developmental leap forward. However, for the members of the Care Co-operative it is this kind of incremental gain that enables them to keep faith with what it was about the RDP that first caught their imagination.

Conclusions

It would be a fallacy to read the existence of a tradition of MBOPs from the trappings of organisation, such as the existence of structures or loose claims of membership. The concept of membership advanced here is a rigorous one. It would be easy for any member of the Care Co-operative, for example, to define the constituency from which its membership is drawn. By the same token, without reference to a written document, any member could say what a person must do to become a member. Without clear membership criteria, there cannot be proper accountability. In the case of the Care Co-operative, accountability is also sustained through weekly meetings. Poor people especially need to know that they have rights in an organisation before they can assert them.

Similarly, there can be no true accountability in an MBO that is not sustained by the contributions of its members. Such an organisation has no real need of an actual membership. A paper membership will do, provided it satisfies the funders. A consistent theme that emerges from the survey of organisations is the reliance on external funding. External funding, I have suggested, is one of the drivers of a top-down tradition of organisation. It also makes it difficult for an organisation to determine for itself what kind of administrative bureaucracy is sustainable.

Sustainability relates to not only to financial self-sufficiency, but also to an enabling environment, and access to resources. In the case of the Care Co-operative, it was the human resources a branch office provided that were important. The advantage of the model of a local body affiliated to a higher level is its clarity. However, affiliation without accountability is also of limited benefit. The model of an organisation in a symbiotic relationship with an NGO raises the identical problem.

The legal framework within which organisations operate constitutes one aspect of an enabling environment. It is argued that formal regulation represents the kiss of death to organisations of the poor, insofar as are compelled to meet a more formal standard than they are able to attain. However, it is questionable whether informal organisation is sustainable, because its capacity to develop external relations or finance growth must inevitably be constrained by its lack of a formal legal identity (Von Ravensburg, 1998).[39] Moreover, formality can mean consolidating informal practices to which people in any event subscribe.

The argument about what should constitute an MBOP has many elements. It concerns what are the proper objectives of such an organisation. It concerns how the organisation is to be sustained. It concerns how to prevent the organisation from being corrupted. In an overview of this nature, I am only able to draw attention to the complexities inherent in the notion of MBOPs, by raising a series of questions to which there is as yet no definitive answer. In this regard, one must also guard against the fallacy of reading too much from the political stance organisations adopt. An MBOP will necessarily have a political role, whatever its objectives may be. Yet, in large part, the sense of accountability and ownership that MBOPs exemplify is made possible by maintaining as broad a political church as possible. The members of the Care Co-operative come from different political traditions, in a locality where political affiliation was once a matter of life or death in the past.

In the final analysis, membership-based organisation is important because it is less easy to corrupt an organisation in which the members have a strong sense of ownership. The following observation about trade unions is apt in this context '... trade unions are less easily chloroformed and suppressed totally than political parties, because they arise out of the groundwork of the economic system. As long as there are classes ... there will be class conflict' (Anderson, 1967). By the same token as long as there is poverty, there will be poor people struggling for a better life. It would not be realistic to expect the poor to achieve a better life without political organisation. But it could not fail to raise the level of political debate if civil society was permeated by a network of independent organisations, articulating the needs of the poor at both local and national levels in different ways. The fact that I rely on a small local organisation such as the Care Co-operative to invoke this vision suggests that there is much to be done for it to be realised.

Notes

1 Interview, November 2004.
2 Five members were interviewed individually at the end of 2003, with a view to ascertaining the impact of the co-operative on their livelihoods. The interviews were conducted as part of a study on worker co-operatives in the Western Cape conducted for the Department of Labour. See Research report: Workers co-operatives in the Western Cape, Labour and Enterprise Project.
3 This translates roughly to between US $40 and $50 a month.
4 The seventh co-operative principle, as adopted by the International Co-operative Alliance, is headed 'concern for community.' See I. McPherson, Co-operative Principles for the Twenty First Century, ICA Communications, Geneva.
5 The City of Cape Town operates a total of seven nursery schools and crèches. Three are located in the longer established African townships (Guguletu NY6, Langa and Loyiso) and the remainder in traditionally coloured areas.
6 The question arises whether a sports club or cultural society whose members are poor should be regarded as an MBOP. There can be no clear-cut answer, but the social and economic impact of such organisations is likely to be limited.
7 By the same token there are co-operatives whose members are not poor at all. Agricultural co-operatives are a case in point, in the South African context. But that circumstance, I argue elsewhere in this chapter, must be understood in its historical context and does not constitute valid grounds to exclude co-operatives from the scope of an MBOP.
8 In terms of this conception, social movements seem to exist outside of civil society, as a counter-vailing force. Thus, the new social movements are contrasted in this analysis with the 'old' social movements, which is regarded as composed of NGOs, CBOs, the trade unions (as represented by the trade union federation, COSATU) and political organisations (the ANC). In the post-1994 period COSATU, SANCO and NGOs are perceived to be in a collaborative relationship with the government. See Ballard *et al.* (2004, 11).
9 According to the Commission of Inquiry into a Comprehensive System of Social Security for South Africa, otherwise known as the Taylor Commission, between 20 and 28 million persons are estimated to live in poverty, constituting between 45 and 55 per cent of the population.
10 The term 'political organisations' is used here to include political parties.
11 The latter is a form of share that a member is required to take out as a condition of membership, and which cannot be sold to outsiders (as distinct from shares in other corporate entities).
12 R. Michels (1915), 'Political Parties'.
13 The legal space is, at one level, defined by the form of state, and the role assigned by the courts in it. At another level, it concerns the forms of organisation available for poor people to utilise, the benefits a specific form of organisation holds, the likely effect of regulations affecting the form of organisation.
14 The writer was the General Secretary of the Food and Canning Workers Union (FCWU) from 1976 until 1986 and subsequently became General Secretary of the Food and Allied Workers Union. The FCWU was centrally involved in the formation of the Congress of SA Trade Unions (COSATU) and was one of only two of the founding unions that were financially autonomous.
15 There is no satisfactory definition or statistical measure of the informal economy, but in a study conducted by the UNDP the figure for those in formal and informal employment are given as 67.5 per cent and 32.5 per cent of a total of 10,896,420 persons employed in 2002. What is significant about this figure is that the total of unemployed is given as 4,783,502, and that the total of unemployed plus those in informal employment significantly exceeds the

number in informal employment, compared to a situation in 1990, when the number in formal employment was 82.7 per cent of the total employed compared with 19.2 in informal employment, and those in formal employment far exceeded the combined total of the informally employed and the unemployed. See UNDP Report, 2004, Table 3, 238–9. It is also likely that this study underestimates the extent of informal employment, due to a definition of informal employment used in statistical data.

16 This is partly attributable to past failures, and partly attributable to the funders' predilection for promoting small and medium enterprises (SMMEs). However, arguably the past failures of co-operatives to become sustainable enterprises are more readily explicable than the current failure of SMMEs, which is unpublicised and under-researched in this country and elsewhere.

17 According to data provided by the registrar of co-operatives, there were approximately 5000 registered co-operatives in July 2005, with a dramatic uptake in applications for registration.

18 Interview, 24 November 2004.

19 One of the key issues that emerged in deliberations on the new legislation was how prescriptive such legislation should be and whether, for example, co-operatives seeking to register a legal entity should be required to submit a business plan establishing the viability of the enterprise.

20 In 1994, there were 213 registered unions in South Africa. The number of unions (and employer organisations) has steadily grown ever since and was 504 in 2002 according to Department of Labour figures. However, it may be that these numbers will now drop, as a result of amendments to labour legislation introduced in 2002, tightening up on what are perceived to be bogus unions and employer associations.

21 Farm workers represent the most obvious example of vulnerable workers that the established union movement, despite several attempts, has failed to organise into a large centralised union.

22 SEWU was established in 1994, and at its peak, in 2003, it had 4930 members. (Devenish and Skinner, 2004).

23 At the time of writing, there is at least one new initiative that can be seen as an attempt to reconcile the traditional divide between employment and self-employment, and empowerment and trade union-type demands. Women on Farms, a Western-Cape based NGO, has established a union for seasonal women workers. It is also piloting a scheme to establish workers' co-operatives to provide services to farms.

24 To compound this irony, it is probably the case that the emphasis on employment security in the first tier has spurred the growth of a second tier.

25 Examples are the Soweto Electricity Crisis Committee, Concerned Citizens Group and Anti Eviction Campaign, which have mobilised resistance against government attempts to enforce payment for services. The categorisation of this phenomenon as social movements does not seem to raise as many problems as conflating it with organisations of a permanent kind, such as COSATU and SANCO (on the basis of their opposition to certain government policies, notably GEAR, even though both also regard themselves as allies of the ANC) (Ballard *et al.*, 2004).

26 TAC describes itself as a membership-based organisation with 9500 members, and has local, regional and national structures. But there is no clear distinction between members, most of whom do not pay dues, and supporters, volunteers and activists. It appears that some branches of TAC charge a membership fee and others not (Friedman and Mottiar, 2004). The writer was informed by Z. Achmat, the Chairperson of TAC, that it intended to tighten up its membership requirements.

27 The Movimento dos Trabhaladores Rurais Sem Terra (MST) was formed in the 1970s in Brazil.

28 Recently, the LPM decided to formalise membership through the issue of membership cards, both with the object of raising funds from members and achieving greater accountability. But it appears that this decision was never fully implemented on the ground (Greenberg, 2004).

29 Act 28 of 1996. Over 500 communal properties associations (CPAs) have been registered, and CPAs are continuing to be established (Cousins and Hornby, 2002).

30 Cousins and Hornby differentiate between substantive rights members have, such as the right to occupy and use land, and procedural rights, such as the right to participate in meetings where decisions are taken.

31 Pressure on the banking sector to make its services more accessible to the poor has recently resulted in the introduction of a form of low-cost bank account, known as the 'Mzansi account'.

32 SACCOL is a secondary co-operative comprising 32 SACCOs (or primary savings and credit co-operatives) with close to 9000 members.

33 According to an estimate by the National Stokvels Association of South Africa (NASASA), there are 800,000 stokvels, burial societies and savings schemes countrywide, with about 8.25 million members. See ECI Africa, 'Third tier banking report: A review of the capacity, lessons learned and way forward for member based financial institutions in South Africa', 2003, cited in Philip (2003).

34 Interview, O. Van Rooyen, Kuyasa Fund. A procedure where members draw regularly against the savings of the group lessens the need for financial safeguards such as an audit. The need is much greater in a burial society, however, and these are supposed to register in terms of legislation regulating the so-called 'friendly societies'.

35 In 1995, the Federation established a separate Fund capitalised by foreign donors and government, known as the uTshani Fund. Supposedly a 'community-managed revolving loan fund', it serves as a conduit for subsidy transfers from the government to the community, via the savings schemes (Pieterse and Kahn, 2004).

36 Under pressure from members, the federation allowed houses to be built for which there was not adequate finance, or before government subsidies had been secured. In so doing, members may even have forfeited their right to a subsidy, since a household that is already housed is not eligible for a subsidy (Pieterse and Kahn, 2004, 26–7). If this is indeed the case, it would represent an example of the inappropriate resort to self-help.

37 SANCO claims to have 4300 branches. However, this claim is impossible to verify (Zuern, 2004).

38 Even how SANCO branches relate to local structures of the ANC, as well as local government, varies enormously. In one celebrated instance, in Port Elizabeth in 2001, a branch of SANCO even put up its own candidates for local government election (Zuern, 2004).

39 This is possibly because their membership tends to be homogeneous and because they tend to concentrate on the most efficient use of available resources.

References

Anderson, P. 1967. *The Limits and Possibilities of Trade Union Action* in R. Blackburn and A. Cookburn (eds), The incompatibles: Trade Union Militancy and the Consensus, Penguin.

Ballard, Habib, Valodia and Zuern. 2004. *Globalisation, marginalisation and contemporary social movements in South Africa.* Unpublished paper, Conference on social movements, Johannesburg, November 2004.

Baumann, T. 2001. *Microfinance and poverty alleviation in South Africa.* Unpublished Paper, Ray Research and Consultancy Service.

Boulle, J. 1997. *Putting the voluntary section back on the map.* Development Update, 1.

Cousins, T. and Hornby, D. 2002. *Scoping report on communal property institutions in land reform.* Unpublished report for Department of Land Affairs.

Devenish, D. and Skinner, C. 2004. *Organising workers in the informal economy: The experience of the self-employed women's union 1994–2004.* Unpublished paper, Conference on social movements, Johannesburg, November 2004.

Fakir, E. 2004. *Institutional land affairs restructuring, state civil society relationships and social movements.* Development Update, Vol. 5, No. 1.

Friedman, S. and Mottiar, S. 2004. *A moral to the tale: the Treatment Action Campaign and the politics of HIV/AIDS.* Unpublished paper, Conference on social movements, Johannesburg, November 2004.

Greenberg, S. 2004. *The landless people's movement and the failure of post-apartheid land reform.* Unpublished paper, Conference on social movements, Johannesburg, November 2004.

Kotze, H. 2003. *Responding to the growing socio-economic crisis? A review of civil society in South Africa.* Development Update, Vol. 5, No. 4.

Kraak, G. 2001. *The South African voluntary sector in 2001: a great variety of morbid symptoms.* Development Update, Vol. 3, No. 4.

MacIntyre, A. 1985. *After virtue,* 2nd edn, Duckworth, London.

Marais, H. 1998. *South Africa: limits to change,* Zed, London.

Michels, R. 1915. *Political parties.* Reprinted, New York, Dover, 1959.

Philip, K. 2003. *Cooperatives in South Africa: their role in job creation and poverty reduction.* Unpublished paper, SA Foundation.

Pieterse, E. 1998. *Development and community participation: decoding the conceptual 'stock and trade' of the voluntary sector.* Development update, Vol. 2, No. 1.

Pieterse, E. and Kahn, F. 2004. *The Homeless People's Alliance.* Unpublished paper, Conference on social movements, Johannesburg, November 2004.

Pieterse, E. and Van Donk, M. 2002. *Capacity building for poverty reduction,* Dark Roast occasional paper No. 8, Isandla Institute.

Seekings, J. 2000. *The UDF: a history of the United Democratic Front in South Africa 1983–1991,* David Philip, Cape Town.

Von Ravensburg. 1998. *Modern approaches to the production of cooperative self-help in rural developments: implications for South Africa.*

Zuern. 2004. *Continuity in contradiction? The prospects for a national civic movement in a democratic state: SANCO and the ANC in port – apartheid South Africa.* Unpublished paper, Conference on social movements, Johannesburg, November 2004.

14 Informal governance and organizational success

The effects of noncompliance among Lima's street-vending organizations

Sally Roever

The successful representation of poor people on the part of membership-based organizations depends partly on internal governance structures that are responsive to members' needs and aspirations. Among organizations of informal workers, members depend on their leaders to channel their demands and influence government policies that affect their livelihoods, in particular when hostile regulations threaten to prevent these workers from earning a minimal daily income. Yet, not all organizations of informal workers have successfully achieved such influence. While positive examples like the Self-Employed Women's Association in India show that informal workers can successfully represent demands to policy makers, cases of more mixed success abound in other developing countries.

This chapter explores the possibility that organizations of informal workers experience only mixed success because the organizations themselves are run informally. It does so by examining three specific dimensions of informality within Lima's street-vending organizations. First, it examines their *material foundation.* This foundation, which includes formal documentation of the organization's business as well as physical assets, such as an office, budget, and bank account, can contribute to an organization's success, but does not always do so. Second, the chapter examines the extent to which organizations achieve formal *external recognition*, both legal and political. Again, acquiring external recognition can be helpful, but some organizations that lack such recognition have still achieved certain successes. Third, the chapter explores the level of *internal compliance* within organizations, that is, the extent to which leaders and members comply with their organizations' formal internal rules and procedures. It is this last aspect of "informality" that seems to have the most profound influence on the success of the organizations included in this study.

Specifically, the chapter argues that even though membership-based organizations of the poor in theory should have governance structures that make them accountable to their members, in practice, they often lack such accountability. In the case of Lima's street-vending organizations, members often either do not put in place formal democratic governance structures that would ensure accountability or both leaders and members routinely ignore the governing rules and procedures that do exist in the organization's founding documents. These informal practices within an organization can reduce leaders' accountability and credibility in the eyes of the membership; increase the incentives for members to exit the organization in favor of forming new ones; and damage the credibility of leaders in the eyes of external actors, most importantly the policy makers who have a profound influence on poor people's lives.

The empirical base of the study is qualitative. It consists of structured interviews, unstructured conversations, participation in association meetings, attendance at public policy discussions, and more than 100 hours of "hanging around" street markets in dense commercial areas of Lima.[1] The 12 associations included in the study were selected on the basis of convenience and quotas; while they cannot be considered representative of all street-vending organizations in Lima, they should be considered illustrative of some of the challenges facing these poor people's organizations. Some characteristics of the associations included in the study are presented in Box 14.1.

Indicators of "success" for membership-based organizations of informal workers

Existing studies of membership-based organizations in advanced industrial democracies suggest that informal workers are unlikely to form associations at all. These workers are viewed as socially atomized in comparison to formal workers (Jenkins and Leicht 1997); they sometimes lack the physical infrastructure and material resources necessary to build organizations (Roberts 1995); and the very nature of informal work creates intense competition among organization members, so that organization can only take place when all informal workers are threatened equally (Grompone 1991). Yet, informal workers in Lima – particularly street vendors who work in areas of dense commercial concentration – have formed hundreds of organizations across the city. Nonetheless, these organizations exhibit uneven success in terms of producing the sort of democratic effects that would ensure their effective political representation.

This section evaluates "success" among street-vending associations in terms of broader democratic effects attributed to civil society organizations. These positive democratic effects have both internal and external dimensions. For example, internally, Warren (2001) and others suggest that civil society organizations can increase members' personal development or capacity by encouraging them to speak in public, learn civic skills, and access information about community problems. Such individual developmental effects are particularly important for poor people, as associations can empower them to overcome exclusion where other soci-

Name	Location	Products	Size
ACAGOVIC	La Victoria	Sodas and candy	216
AVAMDEGA	La Victoria	Variety	306
Coordinadora	La Victoria	Variety	n/a
ECOMUCSA	Lima-Cercado	Variety	150
FEDEVAL[a]	Metropolitan Lima	Variety	12,000
FENVENDRELP	Nation-wide	Newspapers and magazines	20,000
LV Federations[b]	La Victoria	Variety	4000
FUDDCC	San Martín de Porres	Variety	2500
Herbalists	La Victoria	Herbs, natural products	90
Sr. de los Milagros	La Victoria	Variety	20
UDAMPE	Lima-Cercado	Hardware	1000
20 de Junio	La Victoria	Variety	250

Box 14.1 Twelve street vending associations in Lima.

Notes

a FEDEVAL is a metropolitan-wide federation of street-vending associations that claims to represent about 12,000 vendors in the city. FENVENDRELP and FUDDCC are also federations that are made up of base-level associations, rather than actual members. Thus, the "size" figure in these cases is the number of vendors that the federation claims to represent, rather than the number of actual members.

b "LV Federations" refers to three federations that existed in the district of La Victoria from the mid-1980s to the late 1990s: FEDITAV, CUTASPA, and FEBAINVIC.

etal institutions (such as the education system and the job market) have failed. Membership-based organizations of the poor (MBOPs) might also help poor people overcome exclusion by providing a forum in which members can develop networks, form friendships, and take an active role in discussing important issues, expressing opinions, and making collective decisions. They might also be considered successful if they sustain projects and achieve at least some of their concrete goals over time. In doing so, an organization would overcome the type of reactive orientation that Grompone (1991) says necessarily characterizes larger associations of informal workers.

On the external side, one of the most significant achievements for an MBOP is gaining a "place at the table" in negotiations over public policies that affect their well-being. Gaining a voice in the policy-making process is an obvious way in which poor people may become empowered, though in practice it may happen infrequently. In addition to participation in policy negotiations, an MBOP might be considered successful if it extracts favorable policy concessions, even if it does so through informal channels rather than through institutionalized participation. Finally, we might consider the ability of MBOPs to faithfully represent the voices of their members in the public arena as an important aspect of success. Together, these six factors – three internal to the organization, and three external (see Box 14.2) – constitute a framework for assessing the success of individual MBOPs.

The roots of mixed success among Lima's street-vending organizations

On the basis of the 12 associations included in this study, Lima's street-vending organizations are cases of mixed success. Some of these associations achieve some of the six indicators of success some of the time. No association is entirely lacking in positive democratic effects, nor is any association successful across all six indicators.

What explains this uneven success? On the one hand, vending associations' inability to consistently produce the sort of democratic effects seen among civic organizations in advanced industrial democracies may seem easily explicable. These associations face substantial constraints that more privileged associations do not. Many policy makers are openly hostile toward street vendors because of the public policy problems crowded street markets create; vendors lack the same sort of legal protections that other types of workers enjoy; vendors often have few or no political allies; and relatively speaking, they are resource-deprived, often scraping together budgets only from the meager and irregular donations of their members.

Moreover, it would be easy to assume that informal workers create organizations that are also quite informal, which in turn may limit their effectiveness. Behaviors typically associated with informal economic activity, such as avoiding contact with government authorities, might easily translate into the associational realm. Thus, we might expect informal workers to avoid registering their associations with the authorities, maintaining formal records of their members and activities, and operating their meetings and activities in accordance with formal procedures. This intuitive overlap of informal economic activity and other types of "informal" behavior is reflected in the tendency for some scholars to refer to "informal workers" simply as "informals," implying that informality is a more general characteristic of them as individuals rather than their

Internal dimension	External dimension
Building individual capacity	Gaining access to policy discussions
Fostering expression and debate	Achieving favorable policy
Carrying out concrete projects	Representing voices of the excluded

Box 14.2 Framework for analyzing succes and failure among MBOPs.

working conditions in particular. Along these lines, we might expect informal workers to have informally run organizations that cannot build the type of organizational strength necessary to compete as legitimate players in the political arena.

In fact, however, associations of street vendors in Lima vary substantially in terms of how informal they are. In particular, they vary in terms of three dimensions of informality: their *material foundation*; the extent to which they have been able to achieve *external recognition*; and the degree to which their leaders and members enforce the association's rules and procedures, or *internal compliance*. As the following discussion argues, it is the last of these three factors that has the strongest effect on organizational success among the 12 organizations included in this study.

Table 14.1 summarizes the relationship between each of the three dimensions of informality and the six indicators of organizational success discussed earlier in the chapter. As the table shows, a solid material foundation can help associations facilitate personal capacity building, foster expression and debate, and gain access to policy discussion, but it is not a necessary condition for achieving these results. Rather, it is only necessary for carrying out concrete long-term projects, such as acquiring off-street lots. Achieving external recognition, either legal or political, is helpful for gaining access to policy discussions and extracting favorable policy concessions, but it is necessary only for carrying out projects and representing members' demands effectively. By contrast, internal compliance with the association's governing rules and procedures is either necessary or helpful for all but one of the indicators of organizational success. The following discussion examines each of these relationships, drawing on evidence from the 12 street-vending associations described earlier.

Material foundation

The material foundation of an association has three components: documentation of its existence as an association; resources such as office space,

Table 14.1 Informality and democratic effects among Lima's street-vending associations

	Material foundation	External recognition	Internal compliance
Building individual capacity	✓	−	−
Fostering expression and debate	✓	−	+
Carrying out concrete projects	+	+	+
Gaining access to policy discussions	✓	✓	✓
Extracting favorable policy concessions	−	✓	+
Representing the voices of the excluded	−	+	+

Key
+ Necessary condition; ✓ Helpful but not necessary; − Not necessary.

a budget, and a bank account; and regular activities, most importantly regular meetings of the association's leadership and regular assemblies of the entire membership. In terms of documentation, in order to legally constitute an association, its founders must purchase a Book of Records and write up the association's Act of Constitution specifying when, where, by whom, and for what purpose the association was formed.[2] The founding members must then draw up the Articles of Association, which outline the organizational structure, rights and responsibilities of members, and rules governing the dissolution of the organization and the liquidation of its assets, as well as a set of Internal Regulations specifying procedures for the election of leaders and other internal business. Finally, the association is required to put together a formal Member Registry that includes the names, identification numbers, and signatures of all founding members. In conjunction, these documents form the basis of the association's material foundation. In addition to documentation, this material foundation could also include resources such as office space, some form of income, a budget, and a bank account in the association's name.

Table 14.2 shows the results from interviews asking association leaders about the material foundation of their organizations. Nearly all of them at least had their founding documents in order, and about half maintained an updated member registry. Interestingly, most organizations held regular meetings of their leaders, but only one in four held regular membership meetings. Few were fortunate enough to have office space, half maintained a budget, and just three had a bank account to help manage association funds.

The table thus illustrates substantial variation among street-vending associations in terms of their material foundation. At one extreme is the National Federation of Magazine, Newspaper, and Lottery Vendors of

Table 14.2 Material foundation of 12 street-vending associations, 2002

	Book of records	Updated member registry	Office	Budget	Bank account	Regular meetings (members)	Regular meetings (leaders)
ACAGOVIC	✓	✓	–	✓	–	–	✓
AVAMDEGA	✓	✓	–	–	–	✓	✓
Coordinadora	✓	✓	–	✓	–	–	–
ECOMUCSA	✓	✓	–	✓	✓	✓	✓
FEDEVAL	✓	–	–	–	–	–	–
FENVENDRELP	✓	✓	✓	✓	✓	✓	✓
LV Federations	✓	–	–	✓	✓	–	✓
FUDDCC	✓	✓	–	–	–	–	✓
Herbalists	–	–	–	–	–	–	–
Sr. de los Milagros	✓	–	–	–	–	–	✓
UDAMPE	✓	✓	✓	✓	–	✓	✓
20 de Junio	✓	✓	✓	–	–	✓	✓

Peru (FENVENDRELP). This federation maintains all of its foundational documents, including a Member Registry, which it updates every year with the help of each affiliated local syndicate, in a notarized Book of Records. In terms of an office, it has a government-sponsored Social Assistance Protection House (Casa de Protección de Asistencia Social) that provides the federation's leaders a space in which to hold meetings and other activities. Its budget is financed through its members' sales; by law, 1 percent of the total newspaper, magazine, and lottery sales is deposited into the federation's bank account. The federation's leaders hold regular meetings once a week, and they hold national assemblies about every six months. This is the most "formal" of the 12 associations in terms of the material foundation, and it is also the oldest. AVAMDEGA, ECOMUCSA, and UDAMPE are other associations that have relatively strong material foundations.

The experience of these four organizations suggests that having a strong material foundation is helpful for conducting capacity-building activities, fostering group discussions, and gaining access to the policy process. For each association, regular membership meetings provide a forum in which collective problems are discussed and debated; attendance at these meetings is relatively high, and association leaders have helped facilitate access to information and training for association members, all of which contribute to capacity building. These activities are more feasible for these organizations because they have an office space and budgetary resources that can be devoted to meetings, workshops, and training seminars, and because they are operated according to specific and well-defined rules established in their founding documents. FENVENDRELP has become involved in the policy process over the years, though the other three organizations have struggled to earn the same access.

What makes these four associations stand out from the others, however, is the fact that each has successfully enacted concrete projects that have been sustained over the medium to long term. FENVENDRELP has the best legal protection in that its members are authorized and partially financed by national law, something that no other association enjoys. AVAMDEGA has initiated a project to acquire an off-street lot, and maintains a savings account to which members contribute each day toward the lot's purchase. ECOMUCSA and UDAMPE successfully acquired an off-street lot after several years on the streets through regular, monitored member contributions. Without a material foundation such as an updated member registry, legal documentation of the association, and regular membership meetings, these associations would not have been able to conduct the monetary transactions necessary to acquire private property. Thus, a strong material foundation is a necessary condition for carrying out such projects.

Meanwhile, there are many cases of associations with weak material foundations that still are quite effective at certain aspects of building individual capacity, in particular diffusing important information to their members. Organizations of street vendors that are particularly active frequently issue pamphlets and fliers to educate their members about such issues, hold workshops, and invite speakers from nongovernmental organizations. Street-vending organizations are also quite adept at using "word of mouth" to spread important information about policy changes and impending police harassment. To spread the word beyond their base membership, leaders use a *chasqui* or "runner" system[3] whereby messengers are dispatched to walk from block to block and pass information to the association leader on each block. Because nearly all base-level associations group together vendors on the same street or block, this word of mouth method for diffusing information is widely used and is quite effective.

Associations lacking a strong material foundation can also be effective at facilitating internal discussion and debate. FEDEVAL (the Federation of Street Vendors of Lima) and FUDDCC (the United Front for the Defense and Development of the Commercial Conglomerate Caquetá) offer examples. FEDEVAL's leaders have been quite active in recent years in terms of initiating projects and attempting to revive the federation's organizational strength at the grassroots level, and FUDDCC has initiated several projects in the commercial area of Caquetá. Yet, neither has a strong material foundation. In August 2002, for example, just two of the 11 associations affiliated with FUDDCC had their documents in order and had obtained legal recognition,[4] and the federation lacked office space and funds. FEDEVAL has even less in the way of a material foundation; its leaders were attempting to acquire office space in 2002 but had not yet done so, its meetings were irregular, and it lacked a bank account and formal budget. Thus, while a material foundation is helpful for conducting certain activities, it is only a necessary condition for carrying out long-term projects.

External recognition

Composing the documents necessary for legal recognition is an important step for associations that wish to formalize, but it is not sufficient for actually exercising legal rights. In order to gain formal legal status, an association's founders must have the core documents (Act of Constitution, Articles of Association, Internal Regulations, and Membership Registry) notarized and submit them to an office of the National Superintendent of the Public Registers (*Superintendencia Nacional de los Registros Públicos*, or SUNARP). Once the association is inscribed in the Public Register, it is considered a legally constituted association, with corresponding rights and responsibilities.

In addition to obtaining legal recognition through the Public Register, a street-vending association may also acquire official *political* recognition from a local mayor or city council. In the district of La Victoria, for example, mayors in the 1990s issued occasional Mayoral Resolutions formally recognizing individual street-vending associations.[5] In some cases, local governments recognize them as part of the process of implementing a 1985 metropolitan-wide ordinance, Ordinance 002, which called on municipal governments to work with street-vending associations to solve public space problems. In other cases, recognition came more informally as part of an agreement between an individual association and local officials. Though there is no clear legal framework for issuing and withholding political recognition, obtaining it from the mayor can grant an association legitimacy as a negotiation partner, or protect it from hostile treatment.

Legal recognition and political recognition on the part of state actors thus constitute a second dimension of formality. External recognition makes an association more "formal" in that it in a sense "certifies" the existence of the association in the eyes of government officials. It also confers upon it a certain degree of legitimacy with local authorities. As was the case with material foundation, the 12 street-vending organizations included in this study exhibit substantial variation in terms of whether they have achieved external recognition. Only those with a complete book of records, an updated member registry, and certification through the Public Register are considered to have current legal recognition. As Table 14.3 shows, seven of the 12 had legal recognition in 2002; another two, FEDEVAL and the federations in La Victoria, at one point had legal recognition but have not kept their records or activities current over time. Still fewer enjoy political recognition: ACAGOVIC and AVEMDEGA achieved political recognition in the district of La Victoria, FENVENDRELP is recognized at the national level, and UDAMPE is recognized by the government of Metropolitan Lima, which has been involved at certain points in time with the organization's relocation to an off-street lot.

Table 14.3 External recognition, 2002

	Legal recognition	*Political recognition*
ACAGOVIC	✓	✓
AVAMDEGA	✓	✓
Coordinadora	✓	–
ECOMUCSA	✓	–
FEDEVAL	–	–
FENVENDRELP	✓	✓
LV Federations	–	–
FUDDCC	–	–
Herbalists	–	–
Sr. de los Milagros	–	–
UDAMPE	✓	✓
20 de Junio	✓	–

Achieving external recognition is a more significant contributor to organizational success than a material foundation. ACAGOVIC, AVAMDEGA, FENVENDRELP, and UDAMPE are all organizations that have achieved both legal and political recognition, and these organizations have also been quite successful in producing important democratic effects. ACAGOVIC, an association of soda and candy vendors, is a good example. This association has initiated several successful projects, including one to distribute corporate- and government-sponsored tourist maps of the district with the association's logo and information about its members. ACAGOVIC has also achieved important policy concessions. For example, using its own contacts in the local government, the soda and candy vendors, along with vendors of herbal tea and drinks (*emolienteros*), quinoa, newspapers and magazines, and shoeshiners, successfully negotiated a policy in 2000 that explicitly grants them the right to set up shop on street corners throughout the district. Ordinance 050 of 14 July 2000 granted authorization to these vendors on the condition that they use formal "modules," or stands, with an approved design and their association's logo painted on the side. The policy outlined a specific set of requirements for vendors of these products to obtain authorization, and defined the streets and sidewalks where such vending was prohibited. As the vice president of ACAGOVIC stated in an interview, he considered this a major policy victory for his association, and said that it was not worthwhile involving other groups of vendors. "You have to get your own contacts in the municipality, and negotiate on your own," he said. "We are happy to be formalized."[6] Negotiating this policy concession with the local authorities would not have been possible without legal and political recognition.

AVEMDEGA (the Association of Street Vendors Expelled from Gamarra) is another example of an association that has built success after establishing legal and political recognition. This association occupies a two-block stretch just outside the formal boundaries of the garment district in La Victoria. As its name implies, this association's members formerly occupied space inside of Gamarra before the local government expelled street vendors in March 1999. The majority of AVAMDEGA's 306 members came to occupy their space by "taking the street by assault"; that is, they invaded the street overnight, packed it with their stands and stalls, and from there entered into negotiations with the local authorities. These negotiations resulted in a relatively beneficial agreement with municipal officials. Members of the association were to pay a daily tax called the *sisa* every other day[7]; half the funds would go to the municipal coffers, and half would go into an account that would eventually be used to purchase an off-street lot, to which they would relocate. In exchange for this privileged status, the association would have to guarantee the cleanliness of their blocks, provide space for a fire lane, and provide their own security forces to patrol the streets and protect customers from criminal activity.[8]

FENVENDRELP and UDAMPE are other examples of associations that have been successful in sustaining projects, gaining access to policy discussions, and extracting policy concessions.

Legal and political recognition are important for establishing good relations with local political authorities. Without legal recognition, government officials can easily justify refusing to open policy discussions with individual associations and declare them illegitimate representatives of their members instead. Legal recognition also confers certain collective rights on an association, which again can be very useful in gaining access to the policy forum and avoiding harassment. Political recognition is also especially helpful for extracting policy concessions, as it indicates that the government not only recognizes an association's right to exist but also grants it special status in comparison to other associations within that government's jurisdiction. With legal and political protection, association leaders can focus more on projects and less on organizational defense and survival. Legal recognition can also help reduce the risk associated with initiating projects or campaigns that local authorities may find antagonistic.

While external recognition is extremely helpful for policy issues, however, it is not always absolutely necessary. The constituent associations of FUDDCC are a good example. They have enacted several projects, held lively meetings to discuss important issues, and provided a space for their members to cooperate and coordinate in their work, without having legal or political recognition.[9] The three La Victoria federations (FEDITAV, CUTAPSA, and FEBAINVIC) also illustrate this point, as they experienced a very long lag time between the date on which their organizations were founded and the date on which they actually obtained legal recognition, while in the meantime accomplishing substantial policy concessions. For example, FEDITAV was first formed in 1980, obtained political recognition in 1986, and was not inscribed in the Public Register until 1995. CUTASPA was formed in 1985, received political recognition in 1986, and was inscribed in the Public Register in 1995. FEBAINVIC was founded in 1987, recognized politically that same year, and inscribed itself in the Public Register in 1996.[10] Yet, the federations' most substantial policy victory – achieving an institutional voice through the formation of a Vendors' Social Assistance Fund (FOMA) and Mixed Technical Commission (CTMCA)[11] – occurred in 1993, well before legal recognition had been formally established.

Legal and political recognition are necessary, however, for sustaining many projects over time, and for achieving successful political representation. Projects that require cooperation from municipal governments, transactions with banks, or contracts stall when associations lack legal status. Likewise, without political recognition, municipal governments can create logistical roadblocks for association leaders attempting to enact projects without their support. In addition, without political recognition, leaders have little chance of influencing policy choices and channeling demands effectively, which limits their ability to represent their members effectively.

Internal compliance

A third dimension of informality among associations is the extent to which leaders and members develop, formalize, and enforce internal governance rules and procedures in the day-to-day operation of the association. Among the many rules that make up an association's statutes, two sets of regulations in particular are important for maintaining the organization's smooth internal operation. First, the regulations should clearly outline the rights and responsibilities of association members. The most basic right – and the most basic responsibility – of any association member is to participate in and contribute to the life of the organization. This might require, among other things, equal opportunities to participate in general assemblies, vote in all elections, participate in the election of leaders, and run for office. Members should also participate in the discussion and approval of activities and projects proposed by the leadership, and they should oversee the leaders' compliance with their responsibilities, including managing the budget, maintaining the books, and submitting an annual report. Possible sanctions for noncompliance with members' most basic responsibilities can include fines, suspensions of membership rights, and expulsion.

Second, the internal regulations should specify procedures for a regular rotation of leadership. A typical arrangement is for the general membership to appoint an Electoral Committee, composed of members who are not already on the Directors' Board, to establish the rules for electing new leaders. Among other tasks, this would include maintaining an up-to-date list of members eligible to vote, fixing the date on which elections are to take place, and organizing and overseeing the entire electoral process.

Most street-vending organizations in Lima are characterized by relatively low levels of compliance with their internal regulations and procedures. In some cases, members of the association have given themselves a name, perhaps developed a logo, and elected or appointed a president, but have not drawn up the association's foundational documents, such as the Act of Constitution and Internal Regulations. More commonly, association members have drawn up and filed those foundational documents with the Public Register, but do not actually enforce the rules and regulations governing the association's internal operations. The lack of compliance with these regulations fosters a great deal of discontent and mistrust between leaders and members of these organizations. A common complaint among members is that their leaders take action without consulting with the membership, and a common complaint among leaders is that members are apathetic and do not participate in or help with associational activities. The disjuncture between the actions and attitudes of leaders and members suggests that an important part of these organizations' weakness stems from noncompliance with internal regulations that would structure interaction and cooperation between the two sides.

In particular, the lack of enforcement of members' rights and responsibilities, as well as a lack of leadership rotation within some organizations, seem to be fueling this discontent. In organizations that do not call regular meetings of the general membership, members do not have the opportunity to discuss issues of importance with their peers, nor do they have the chance to give feedback to their association leaders. In addition, when regular meetings are not planned and announced well ahead of time, members say they cannot attend because of family or work obligations. Some members also perceive regular assemblies of the membership as unnecessary or superfluous: as one said, "I only go to the emergency meetings, because you know something important is happening." Thus, it is noncompliance on the part of leaders to exercise their responsibility to call meetings, as well as noncompliance of members with their responsibility to attend, that leads to breakdowns in communication. Though it is standard procedure to include sanctions for noncompliance with responsibilities in any organization's founding documents, I discovered only two organizations, AVAMDEGA and UDAMPE, which actually enforce those sanctions.

Some degree of apathy among an association's members is, of course, quite common, and not at all a problem specific to poor people in general or informal workers in particular. Interestingly, though, some leaders use their status as informal workers to justify the informal way in which they run their organizations. In one interview, a leader excused his association's lack of regular meetings by saying simply that "we are informals," as if to say that it is in informal workers' nature to run their organizations informally and nobody should expect anything different.[12] Other leaders excused the lack of internal compliance with regulations and procedures by saying that the members were not educated or prepared enough to expect internal democracy or take an active role in shaping the association's activities. This sort of disdain for democratic processes inside of these organizations contributes to the distance between leaders and members.

In addition to noncompliance with rights and responsibilities, some organizations also fail to rotate their leadership by holding regular elections. The permanence of the same individuals holding official positions within these organizations can have two deleterious consequences. First, it can create the perception of these leaders as "mafia"-type rulers, both within the organization and outside of it. Second, it creates a stronger incentive for vendors who disagree with the leadership to exit the association in favor of forming a new one, since their "voice" option inside the organization is limited.

These problems seem to be more pervasive at the level of federations than at the level of base associations. FEDEVAL, for example, is attempting to recover from the withdrawal of support on the part of many of its affiliates in past years because of its lack of regular leadership rotation. One leader whose own association has withdrawn from FEDEVAL said that: "its leaders are *mafiosos*," in that they "think they are eternal leaders who own the organizations." But "you cannot deceive people like that," this leader said. "They say the organization is for the people, but it is not."[13] The problem of leadership rotation is especially important for FEDEVAL to overcome, because its leaders' radicalism in the 1980s largely discredited the organization. When policy makers perceive that those same leaders are still heavily involved in the organization, they dismiss the possibility of working with them out of hand.

Federations in La Victoria have likewise experienced tremendously fluid loyalties over the years. Following the dissolution of the FOMA and CTM in that district in 1996, a new "front,"[14] called FUTAVIC, was formed on 4 July 1997 and initially had the support of many associations who feared hostile treatment from the local authorities. However, in most cases, either the support or the association itself dissolved within a few years. Several other new federations followed shortly thereafter, including a new United Front of Agricultural Wholesalers and Retailers, the United Central of Associations of Informal Workers in Perishable Products, the United Associations of Seafood Merchants, and the Promotional Committee of the United Central of Street Vendors of La Victoria.[15] According to Sulmont (1999), this sort of constant dissolution and reconstitution of federations is the result of the struggle for power over the right to speak for the entire sector of street vendors in the district. That struggle, he argues, is conducted for the most part by individuals who occupy leadership positions as a sort of career, rather than ordinary street vendors who rise through the ranks of their organizations by way of democratic elections.

The lack of leadership rotation within some organizations of street vendors means that leaders are difficult to hold accountable by their members. If members are dissatisfied with their leaders' performance, they cannot rely on a new election to provide them with an incentive to perform better. Without regular rotation of leaders, the organization loses legitimacy, and is unlikely to develop the sort of "value infusion" that has helped other types of organizations survive even with very low levels of formality.[16] Likewise, leaders' failure to follow through on regular, formal elections makes their promises less credible to members.

This loss of legitimacy, accountability, and credibility increases the incentives for members to exit and form new associations rather than expressing dissatisfaction directly to their leaders. It thus hinders expression and debate, makes sustaining projects over time impossible, reduces the likelihood of extracting favorable policy concessions, and removes the representative quality of associations when members' voices are not heard equally. In fact, when asked what the most important benefit of their association was in a 2003 survey, only 21 percent of respondents responded "representing my interests."[17] Instead, most association members view their associations as most effective for resolving concrete problems, or providing a forum in which to develop friendship and camaraderie (see Table 14.4). This result may be indicative of the broader failure of street-vending organizations to channel their members' demands into the political process.

The lack of compliance with democratic governance structures and the constant dissolution and reconstitution of vending organizations in Lima both contribute to a negative perception of vending associations. One policy maker interviewed for this project expressed total exasperation with attempts to negotiate with vending leaders, stating that: "every day they demand something different," so that no steady progress can ever be made. Another said that it was not worthwhile to even attempt to incorporate vendor leaders into their policy discussions because of the perception that their associations "appear one day and disappear the next." Without some degree of stability, local officials expect that vending leaders cannot deliver on promises to get their bases to comply with whatever agreements may be reached. Another said that vending associations did not deserve to be consulted about policy because they were "anti-democratic." Thus, the lack of internal compliance within street-vending associations feeds into a difficult cycle that ultimately results in their exclusion from policy discussions.

Figure 14.1 summarizes this dynamic. The degree of internal compliance in an organization is positively related to its internal credibility –

Table 14.4 What is the most important benefit of the association for you?

	%
Resolving problems	41.1
Creating friendships and camaraderie	23.4
Representing my interests	20.6
Delivering benefits	14.2

Source: 2003 Microbusiness Survey.

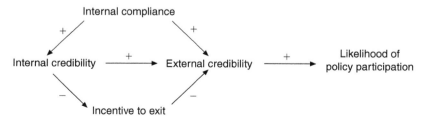

Figure 14.1 Causal diagram: internal compliance and policy participation.

that is, the credibility that leaders have in the eyes of their members. Organizations that have high levels of internal compliance have high levels of internal credibility, and organizations that have low levels of internal compliance tend to have low levels of internal credibility. The extent of internal credibility in an organization, in turn, is inversely related to the incentive for members to exit the organization rather than expressing their voice. For example, an organization with little internal credibility would have a stronger incentive for members to exit, while organizations with high internal credibility would have weaker incentives to exit. Internal credibility is also related to external credibility; policy makers, for example, view associations that lack internal democracy with skepticism. The prevalence of "exit" – that is, the frequency with which members exit their association and form new ones – is inversely related to the association's external credibility. Finally, the external credibility of these associations affects the likelihood that they will be incorporated into the policy making process.

Conclusion

Street vendors remain marginal actors in the Peruvian political system. They constitute nearly 10 percent of the country's urban workforce; they possess substantial disruptive capacity; and they have formed hundreds of associations to defend their workspace, yet, with a few exceptions, they lack the organizational strength to secure an institutionalized voice in the policy process. This lack of organizational strength is not a condition inherent to informal workers, however. Individual cases of organizational success among street-vending associations suggest that these workers have the potential to overcome the odds against them. Their most urgent challenge is to increase compliance within their organizations. Formalizing the internal operation of their associations would increase leaders' credibility, reduce the incentives for members to exit, and enhance vendors' credibility with policy makers. When policy makers view street-vending associations as legitimate partners, they will be more likely to incorporate their voices into policy decisions.

Notes

1 The research was conducted between October 2001 and September 2002 in three districts of Lima: Lima-Cercado, La Victoria, and San Martín de Porres.
2 This discussion of documentation was based on Alternativa (1992) and several copies of associations' founding documents obtained as part of an archive maintained by one of the city's street-vending leaders.
3 *Chasquis* were messengers that Inca rulers relied upon to carry messages to different parts of the Incan empire. Street-vending leaders who spoke of their need to coordinate with other leaders in interviews used the term *chasquis* to describe the runners or messengers they use.
4 Discussion with a FUDDCC leader, 27 August 2002.

5 Examples include R.A. 1060-93-ALC; R.A. 1459-93-ALC; R.A. 0274-95-ALC; and R.A. 0275-95-ALC.
6 Personal interview, 8 June 2002.
7 Paying this tax every other day was a special privilege for this association, as the standard is to pay the tax on a daily basis. I discovered no other organization in Lima that paid only every other day.
8 The streets surrounding the formal boundaries of Gamarra where AVAMDEGA's members and other street vendors work are among Lima's more dangerous in terms of street crime.
9 In the case of FUDDCC, the support of the NGO Alternativa has been very important to the organization's ability to carry out projects.
10 Almanza San Miguel (2004): 2.
11 The FOMA and CTMCA are consultative bodies made up of representatives of street-vending organizations at the district level. The formation of these bodies was required by the 1985 Metropolitan Ordinance 002, but most districts never implemented the ordinance. Thus, their constitution in the district of La Victoria was a major policy victory for federations there.
12 This attitude echoes the assumption in the literature that people who have informal jobs are informal in other ways. But this relationship is not a necessary one, as some associations of informal workers are run quite formally; again, the example of AVAMDEGA demanding that I sign an agreement before seeing their documents illustrates that there are exceptions.
13 Personal interview, 8 February 2002.
14 In this case, the term "front" serves as a term for a sort of "super-federation" that groups together existing federations, which in turn group together existing base-level associations.
15 Almanza San Miguel 2004: 4–5.
16 For an example of an organization that operates informally but does have such value infusion, see Levitsky (1998).
17 The survey, called the 2003 Microbusiness Survey, was conducted among 454 street vendors and micro enterprise owners (see Roever 2005).

References

Almanza San Miguel, José Luis (2004) "Algunos Aspectos del Proceso Histórico de Formación y Desarrollo del Comité Promotor de la Central Unificada de Vende-dores Ambulantes de La Victoria." Unpublished manuscript of a street-vending leader from the district of La Victoria, Lima, Peru.

Alternativa (1992) *Manual para la Obtención de la Personería Jurídica: Asociación Civil sin Fines de Lucro.* Lima: Alternativa.

Grompone, Romeo (1991) *El Velero en el Viento: Política y Sociedad en Lima.* Lima: Instituto de Estudios Peruanos.

Jenkins, Craig and Kevin Leicht (1997) "Class Analysis and Social Movements: A Critique and Reformulation," in John R. Hall (ed.) *Reworking Class.* Ithaca, NY: Cornell University Press.

Levitsky, Steven (January 1998) "Institutionalization and Peronism: The Concept, the Case and the Case for Unpacking the Concept." *Party Politics* 4: 77–92.

Roberts, Kenneth M. (October 1995) "Neoliberalism and the Transformation of Populism in Latin America: The Peruvian Case." *World Politics* 48(1): 82–116.

Roever, Sally (2005) *Negotiating Formality: Informal Sector, Market, and State in Peru.* Ph.D. dissertation, Department of Political Science, University of California at Berkeley.

Sulmont Haak, David (1999) "Del 'Jirón' al 'Boulevard Gamarra': Estrategies políticas y gobierno local en La Victoria-Lima," in Martín Tanaka (ed.) *El Poder Visto Desde Abajo: Democracia, Educación y Ciudadanía en Espacios Locales.* Lima: Instituto de Estudios Peruanos.

Warren, Mark (2001) *Democracy and Association.* Princeton: Princeton University Press.

Part VII

Local power structures and MBOPs

15 Membership-based organizations as a reflection of power structures in rural "community"

Experiences and observations from Sindh Province, Pakistan

Themrise Khan

Introduction

It is almost impossible to imagine development theory and practice without the use of the term "community." The increasing usage of this term can be attributed to the claim that the problems faced by the world's poor need to be addressed by the poor themselves, rather than by those who observe them from a distance, that is, policy makers. To achieve this, the poor need to be organized to be able to accurately identify and suggest solutions to their economic and social woes. This is possibly why the last decade has seen a rapid increase in the number of nongovernmental organizations (NGOs) and community-based organizations (CBOs) in poor countries, all of whom seek representation of the underprivileged and marginalized. These membership-based groups normally work to improve and develop social sectors such as health, education, political empowerment and women's rights, within the "communities" that they choose to represent.

In Pakistan, many of these NGOs and CBOs are local, village-level groups, which survive on the patronage of their organization members, thus making them a classic example of a membership-based organization of the poor (MBOP). There are currently almost 45,000 such organizations in Pakistan, comprised of private, notprofit distributing, self-governing and voluntary organizations, with an estimated membership of about six million.[1] These organizations represent a particular geographical territory, issue, caste group, occupation or demographic group. The underlying assumption in these organizations is that they operate for the benefit of one particular section of society, or as for the purposes of this chapter, for one particular "community." While each of these organizations reflect a different class and type of community, this chapter focuses only on membership-based organizations represented by CBOs in rural villages where a majority of Pakistan's poor reside. It must also be noted that, in Pakistan, most MBOPs are small, grassroots-level organizations, with limited geographical coverage and membership, and there is no organization that could be compared to the size and structure of SEWA in India. Organizations that work on a much larger or national scale such as Rural Support Programmes often are not made up of individual members, but are rather a collective of various groups.

In rural Pakistan, the term "community" takes on a meaning of its own. It is not just a group of people with "common aims and objectives," as the literature so likes to point out.[2] It is a multilayered structure, complete with hierarchies of the dominant and castes of the subservient, a far cry from the universal belief that a community is or has the potential to be a model of uniformity and cooperation. Subsequently, this impacts on how CBOs operate in such areas, especially since most of them are small, grassroots-level organizations, with limited geographical coverage and membership.

The question that arises in this case is that how does such exclusive or limited representation impact on the credibility or objectives of CBOs as a form of MBOPs when the problems of the poor remain common to all social and ethnic groups? Is this an efficient way for CBOs to function, especially given the fact that resources to meet the needs of the poor are already scarce?

In order to be able to answer these questions, it is first important to understand what it is that results in such ethnic and social gaps to form in these institutions. Pakistan is a country deeply embedded with age-old traditions, norms and hierarchies. A typical rural village in Pakistan epitomizes these factors, which dictate the routine norms and practices that govern the survival of its inhabitants. Even within the country, each province embellishes its own set of traditions and hierarchies that set it apart from other provinces. A rural community in the province of Punjab follows a very different pattern of traditional norms than one in rural Baluchistan. But, beneath it all, it is the social and caste hierarchy that controls how members of CBOs interact with each other and those around them.

The argument or hypothesis that this chapter attempts to articulate then is this: traditional power structures are an admitted reality in rural Pakistan and hold great influence over its inhabitants, both male and female. These structures cut across gender, class, caste and wealth. In order to be able to penetrate into this structure, first, it is important to acknowledge its existence and, second, to attempt to use this existing structure to the advantage of all poor and not just a select few. CBOs are seen as the vehicle that can make this a possibility due to their location within and as themselves a part of these power structures. First, this chapter makes some observations about how one can view a "community" within the existing traditional structures of a rural village in Pakistan. Second, it looks into how this can impact upon the presence of MBOPs or, in this case, CBOs within these "communities" and whether such organizations reflect the realities of those that they represent. It does this by

using experiences of various CBOs in rural Sindh Province and the position occupied by them within their respective "communities."

The analysis and reflections presented in this chapter are the outcome
of the author's work with CBOs in various districts of rural Sindh Province
between 1996 and 2002. Visits and interactions with these CBOs were
undertaken in various capacities, which have included project implementation and coordination, data collection and capacity-building initiatives.
All observations, information and findings have been gathered through
numerous field visits to the respective field sites and through informal discussions with the CBO office bearers, members and villagers, both men
and women.

The community: who are we talking about?

In the Pakistani context, Banuri and Mehmood present us with a detailed,
but highly accurate definition of the term by far:

> Define a community on the basis of relative spatial proximity, like a
> village or an urban abadi. This very largely also defines the commun-
> ity in terms of common requirements for social services, like educa-
> tion, health, housing, water, sanitation, roads, energy needs, and the
> environment. It may also define the community in terms of basic
> classes, and therefore employment and income needs.[3]

This definition is one that can be applied all across Pakistan, encompass-
ing both rural and urban areas. It is also one that serves as a benchmark
for the development of CBOs and NGOs as organizations that emerge as a
voice for articulating the social and economic needs of a particular group
of people.

Ian Smillie furthers the view that the community is more than just a
provider of services. The new "community," he argues, is also a way of
organizing the provision of integrating power that many governments now
lack, a way of restoring active citizenship and the participation of individuals in their own future.[4]

The concept of the community taking charge of its own affairs is now a
popular one with the rise of more and more group-based activism. Theorists such as Bookchin, Illich and Schumacher have reasserted the primacy
of small communities taking responsibility for their own condition of life.
Across a range of disciplines, thinking has turned to biology, the nature of
living systems and to principles of self-organization as the only viable way
to cope with change and complexity.[5]

Geoff Mulgan puts forward three basic principles at the core idea of
community: the recognition of people's social nature, scale and the
reassertion of ethics. He says "community is deliberately a different word
from society. In order to be meaningful, it must imply membership in a

human-scale collective, at which it is possible to encounter people face to face."[6] This provides the community with its own individual identity as a living, breathing organism, with the ability to evolve, rather than a static concept only witnessed on paper. Therefore, communities can now be seen as both homogeneous as well as heterogeneous.

The disadvantage of such definitions, however, is that they tend to perhaps overgeneralize the term. First, what needs to be recognized is that communities are fluid and evolving entities whose membership base can increase or decrease based on choice, force or need. Second, a community cannot be represented by just those who tend to be more vocal and vociferous, but by each and every individual residing in it, that is, it must be "inclusive."

This then takes the definitional notion of the term into more complex issues such as territory, caste and class. It is here that the role of CBOs in rural Pakistan can be put into context. For example, a village can be considered as a community by itself. But within that village exist a number of different caste and kinship groups, each a community unto themselves because of their individual histories, backgrounds and class status. Most villages in Pakistan exist within this social state. Furthermore, it is commonly found that even though different communities come together with the same general objectives, they each have very different ideas of how to achieve those objectives. Achieving common ground is not as simple as it is made out to be.

Robert Chambers points out that, within communities, there are many obvious differences. He quotes Alice Welbourn's (1991) four major axes of difference: age, gender, ethnic or social group and poverty.[7] Even within these categories, one can perceive a separate community. Because of such discrepancies between traditional definitions and ground realities, a number of changes have been occurring regarding the way people now look at communities. The conventional notion that those who come together for a common cause are representative of every other member of that cause is now being challenged. Unemployment may be endemic to the world's poor. However, not every poverty eradication initiative may be able to include each and every member affected by poverty, not by reason of geographical or physical outreach, but by reason of social, cultural and economic differences reflective in different "communities."

Multiple identities of "community"

Sindh Province occupies 17.7 percent of Pakistan's land area, ranking third among the four provinces. Geographically, it is divided into three climatic regions: lower Sindh, comprising the Indus River Delta and middle and upper Sindh, which support a harsh and dry climate. Agriculture is the dominant economic activity and 60 percent of land in Sindh is arable and supports the cultivation of rice, cotton, millets, wheat, sugarcane, pulses and bananas, cultivated by large and small landowners, mostly for commercial purposes. Fifty percent of the country's industry is located in the major cities of Karachi, Hyderabad and Sukkur. According to the 1998 census, Sindh has a population of almost 30 million, approximately 50 percent of whom reside in rural areas and is the fastest growing province in the country. Sindh is also the region with the greatest degree of cultural and religious diversity. Its peoples range from Balochis, Punjabis, Pathans and "*mohajirs*" or emigrant Muslims from India, to minority groups, most notably Hindus, Christians and Zoroastrians. According to a survey conducted in 2000, there are approximately 17,000 registered NGOs and CBOs in the province, both in rural and urban areas.

The main contributor of social capital in a rural village in Sindh has been the *biradari* or kinship system. This is what provides a social safety net to the poor in times of need and what defines an individual's identity.[8] These *biradari* divisions come in the form of tribes or castes coming down for generations. Most villages in Sindh are identified by the majority caste group that resides in them, such as the Solangis, Khaskhellis, Talpurs or Ujjans, that is, most households in these villages belong to the same caste group. Here there is open intermixing of men and women. However, some villages are made up of a number of caste groups. In this case, clear divisions are formed and intermixing is not the norm, that is, the Solangi caste does not necessarily mix with the Khaskhelli caste. Women in such villages, for instance, are particularly docile and subdued, as their level of interaction does not even go beyond the confines of their household, let alone to other parts of the same village.[9] Group formation in such circumstances is very difficult.

Using this analysis as a benchmark for our initial hypothesis, we begin with the assumption that a village is a homogeneous entity. However, upon entering the village, one realizes that it is actually made up a number of different groups. These groups are physically divided into neighbourhoods (or *paras* as they are called in Sindh Province), each characteristically different from the other. For example, *para* A consists of rich landowners, *para* B farmers and laborers and *para* C the minority caste. Even though the former two *paras* are made up of the same caste group, they still do not mix with each other due to class differences, or as Welbourn pointed out earlier, because of social and ethnic differences. Similarly, the minority group, even though a part of the same village, is considered a nonentity due to its status as a minority group. It is even physically separated from the rest of the *paras* in the village by being situated in a far corner.

In order to be able to understand how these various levels of "communities" are linked or delinked from one another, one can take the example of community-based organizations or CBOs, who often form a focal point for bringing people together in a village. CBOs in Pakistan are primarily formed as a response by concerned members of a village or urban neighborhood to either a specific issue (health, education, etc.), or for the general uplift of their surroundings. Membership of these organizations is limited to only the village in which the CBO originates, that is, those belonging to one village are normally not members of the CBO of another village and vice versa.

The various perceptions of what a community entails, has had a major impact upon the way these CBOs think and function. To the outsider, it would seem that such organizations often represent their village as a whole, considering that they target generic services such as health, education, sanitation etc. However, it is interesting to note that, in many cases, members of such organizations also belong to one particular and, more importantly, more dominant caste group. In a village where caste is evenly homogeneous, the benefits often reach far. However, where there are multiple castes inhabiting the organization's geographical coverage, the tendency is to veer towards the one closest to the organization's own, as examples in the next section demonstrate.

One cannot and should not generalize from this observation, as cases vary from village to village. However, it has been seen that members of many CBOs often limit themselves to areas that are inhabited by their own caste members, as the chapter further illustrates. The effects of class and wealth also come into play here. If the CBO members belong to a richer caste group, they have less to do with members of a poorer caste or vice versa. Which or whose "community" then do these organizations represent?

On a more academic and theoretical level, such divisions have created multiple levels of hierarchies and subcommunities, which go deep beyond the surface of what a rural settlement has traditionally stood for. Formerly, a village was considered to be made up of a single shared identity, but now it is seen as a constantly evolving entity, made up of a number of varying groups, all with their own individual histories and identities. For instance, in one village, the members of a particular caste group separated themselves from another caste group after facing severe social differences and set up their own new village in the lands across the road. Similarly, an altogether new "village" was created when one particular patriarch decided to move away from his native village to settle on his inherited lands a few kilometers away, followed by members of his extended family. Thus, new "communities" were born.

Hierarchical notions of community

The most obvious forms of community structures are the geographical and physical divisions that constitute a rural village in Sindh Province. This structure begins from the *deh* (administrative unit), filters down to the *goth* (village), further down to the *para* (neighborhood) and finally to the household.

Administratively, the structure operates from top-down. However, if viewed from the vantage point of a community, it moves bottom-up, with the needs of the household and the village being the most important. This is also where the idea for an MBOP takes root. However, class, caste and income have created an inflexible and remote structure within which only the more privileged tend to prosper. This is most apparent in the way the rich treat the poor. It is virtually impossible for a farmer to speak in the presence of a landlord, or for a landlord to have any sort of personal association with his farmers. Similarly, within gender relations, wives of the landlords do not necessarily mix with those of farmers or laborers, even though they may belong to the same caste group. In this regard, a very interesting finding has been that, during the harvest season, women belonging to all levels of households, that is, landowners, farmers and laborers, all work in the fields for wages.

Each class also has its own public space. The *autaaq* (meeting room) of the *wadera* (landlord), for instance, is a very prominent space that is reserved exclusively for the *wadera* and a very select gathering of his acquaintances. Similarly, the government school in the village (if there is one) is a gathering place for many of the social activities conducted by the less "well-off" groups such as farmers or salaried workers. Indeed, even CBOs tend to use school premises after hours as a meeting place for their members or outside visitors.

Certain hierarchies extend even beyond the village. For instance, if a farmer wishes to take a loan from a moneylender in the market, he will need to go through his local landlord for surety. The caste and class hierarchy established in his village dictates which landlord the farmer will go to for assistance. This need not necessarily be the one he works for, as there may be a much larger landlord in the village who is more powerful.[10] The more land a person has, the more powerful he is. In some villages, the *para* of the *wadera* is considered to be the most important as he has the most lands in the village, despite the fact that it may have fewer households than other *paras*.

Whether we accept households, *paras* or villages as one or separate communities, minorities in Pakistan, which include Hindus, Christians, Parsis and so on have always been considered as being located outside the boundaries of Muslim villages. Two cases are stark contrasts in how minorities, in this case low-caste Hindus, have been viewed as separate from the "mainstream" communities.

A tiny hamlet of 14 households makes up a Hindu community whose inhabitants work as *haris* (farmers) on the lands of the neighboring *waderas*. Although the village has a Muslim name in the official records, it is known in the area after its leader from the Bheel caste. A formidable man in his fifties, he has risen the ranks in the eyes of his community. He successfully contested the local elections as a minority candidate and is responsible for handling the *haris* of his local *wadera*. Well respected and well known throughout the *deh*, he has converted his tiny "community" into one that can claim a geographical and cultural identity of its own, despite its marginal status.

Another group of low-caste Hindus has a different story to tell. Their tiny community is located in one of the *paras* of another village that is hardly ever recognized as such by the other inhabitants of the village. Members of the community have to travel far into the desert area to work for daily wages on lands of *waderas*, as there is no work available for them close by. They live under fear of the local landlord and have limited access to facilities for their families, so much so that they complain that the Muslim families in the village do not even let their children use their toilets. Their case exemplifies the concept of communities existing with communities, most of them isolated and forgotten.

Ultimately, it is factors such as caste, religion, occupation and wealth that dictate who manages what and how in a rural village. It also ultimately dictates how membership-based organizations operate in such a complex environment.

Membership-based organizations: ground realities

Once we have established the complex and multilayered structure of rural Pakistan, we can now shed light on the impact that these structures can have on MBPOs and, ultimately, on the lives of their members and beneficiaries. This can be achieved by looking into the functioning of some CBOs in Sindh Province, all of whom work in various areas of social sector service delivery and consider themselves as representatives of their village or "community."

It must be clarified at the outset that the objective of this chapter is not to judge which organization is better than the other, but rather to view the various social and economic factors that condition their attitude and operation. This will enable us to look more closely at MBPOs as evolving entities, rather than just as static service delivery mechanisms. It will also help us to analyze exactly how such organizations and their interventions impact on rural society and economy.

Profiles

The CBOs referred to in this section primarily fit the same profile. Their membership base ranges from 80 to 200 individuals. In most cases, the members are male; however, they do have a small percentage of female members, who are part of what is known as the CBO's "women's wing". By and large, these women belong to the households of the male members. A number of these CBOs are named after the dominant caste of the village (Solangi Welfare Association) or even after the name of the village itself (Jindodero Village Development Organization). There is no written or legal rule that prohibits those of other castes or villages to join the organization. However, even a cursory glance at the membership base of such CBOs makes it apparent that membership is by and large homogeneous, even in multicaste villages.

These CBOs are governed according to a set structure set out under NGO registration laws in Pakistan. They consist of an Executive Committee of office bearers and a General Body membership. Elections are held every two to three years to induct a change of guard and it is compulsory for the CBO to have documented financial accounts.[11] The primary areas of operation of these CBOs range from setting up primary schools, to dispensaries, to micro-credit programs, to providing clean drinking water and sanitation facilities.[12] Most of their finances come from project-related funding provided by either international donors, large national NGOs or through private philanthropy. Membership fees form a very negligible amount of their total revenue.[13]

Findings and observations

Most CBOs in Pakistan have certain similarities that are common to small community-based organizations. There are some major differences in terms of scale and infrastructure. However, the most succinct finding concerns the attitudes of those the organization attempts to serve and even more so, the attitudes of the organization members themselves towards their goals and objectives.

In one single-caste village, it was found that most people thought that the CBO present actually did not cater to their needs, let alone consider them. For instance, there were some non-Muslim families that were living in the village for more than two years, but when questioned regarding the various ethnic and caste groups of the village, members of the CBO omitted to mention them. Similarly, in one *para*, a woman directly addressed some of the members of the CBO saying "you come all the time and write things and leave and we don't get anything. Whatever you get you eat it up yourselves and we get nothing."[14] Members of the CBO chalked this angry response down to an ongoing feud of this family with certain CBO members and clearly showed that they were not part of their beneficiaries.

In discussions with the women of the village, who were made up of a variety of the same caste but poorer class, members of the CBO who were present constantly prompted the other women to respond to the line of questioning. It was later discovered that these women felt intimidated by the CBO members because they belonged to more privileged families in the village. Similar instances have occurred in other villages, especially where minority castes reside. In one such instance, women belonging to a minority non-Muslim caste refused to even speak in the presence of CBO members of their village. Suffice it to say that these women were neither included as members of the CBO nor were the CBO's village development projects such as micro-credit extended to them. When the CBO was asked why this was so, the reply was, "we have approached them, but they are not organized enough to be able to participate in our schemes."[15] The minority group had another story to tell. Apparently, they were not even aware of what the CBO's activities were in the village.

While most of the families in another single-caste village were very forthcoming regarding the CBO's activities, some did not behave well with the CBO Social Organizers. One Social Organizer was asked to leave from a house saying that 'you people come and write down information from us and we get nothing in return. So we won't tell you anything."[16] A number of people from other *paras* indicated that they were not happy with the CBO and made negative remarks about them. Ironically, this was a *para* from where no one was a member of the CBO, as they belonged to a caste different from the CBO's own and thus felt excluded from its activities. One woman remarked, "all those who benefit from them are the President's relatives. Even her workers are related to her." Two CBO Social Organizers turned out to be cousins and the daughters of a CBO office bearer's brother. One Social Organizer is the CBO founder's niece. One member is the founder's cousin's brother-in-law, while the CBO motivator is her cousin's wife. It is interesting to note that, in this particular village, all families belonged to one kinship group. However, the differences occurred in terms of subcastes, occupation and wealth. About 70 percent of the male villagers thought that the CBO did not do anything for the poor and was a one-person show only.[17]

In many projects undertaken by CBOs on behalf of their members and beneficiaries, there is an underlying assumption that these local organizations are the most effective representative of their parent community. In one particular project, which involved bringing together parents and teachers for school improvement, local CBOs were recruited to carry out the task of community mobilization and training. While the CBOs, which were typical membership-based organizations, were fairly successful in bringing together parents and teachers in their own village, they faced a great deal of resistance in other villages of the selected district. It was soon discovered that a CBO may be representative of and recognized by the members of its own organization, community or village, but not in another. Indeed, in those villages that had their own CBOs, the implementing CBOs were viewed to be rivals in "their" territories.[18]

On the other hand, another CBO belonged to yet another village that was made up of multicaste groups. This local CBO was actually a collection of individuals belonging to a less dominant caste group. While members of their own caste in the village were very favorable towards them, others in the village who belonged to higher castes paid them virtually no attention. This proved to be a hindrance to the project at hand, since the objective was to mobilize all parents of the village in school improvement, rather than just a select few.[19]

An analysis of the structures of all these CBOs shows that they are very much the product of their main founders, rather than their membership base as a whole. This serves as a deterrent to the organization's growth needs, among others. In one of the CBOs, for instance, as much as its President and Founder has been the driving force behind the organization, he has inadvertently also been the cause of stagnation for the organization as a whole. Where his confidence and the groups' performance had gained accolades from NGOs and donors alike, the structural development of the organization had remained the same. The reasons for the groups' prominence are related to a number of other social factors as well. Their village is located on the main National Highway, so access to cities and market places is not difficult. It is a homogeneous village, so there is freedom to intermix and social constraints are comparatively fewer than in other villages. But what is missing in this organization is the ability to sustain itself, both financially and structurally.

Similarly, in the CBO working for school improvement, the dominant personality who also headed the project team was a very powerful and politically connected man. He belonged to one of the most powerful clans of the area and was well known throughout the district. This had its own share of pros and cons. While his political power and patronage allowed him to access human and financial resources for his organization, the same power and patronage also posed a threat to other organizations in the area that belonged to smaller and less politically connected clans or kinship groups.

On the other hand, in another CBO, its President and Founder was not the only prominent member of the organization, although he did command most of the attention. A number of others were identified as being very active as well and did not need his guidance to make decisions, although in his presence they do tend to look more toward him for support.

Even above and beyond the idea of representation is that of providing benefits and services. A number of villagers were unhappy with their CBO primarily because they felt it had not done enough for the village. In fact, villagers were more of the opinion that it was only the CBO staff members who were benefiting more than the General Body members. This has been illustrated above (pp. 290–1), but can be further demonstrated by the fact that one particular CBO that was run by a husband and wife team, managed to build a concrete and brick house for themselves out of funds they received for project-related work, with the CBO's offices housed in the ground floor. While the issue is not that the CBO grew from a small village organization to a much larger entity with much more power, it does reflect the fact that this power is more so being used for the benefit of only a few. A further illustration of this observation is that, despite a growth in power and finances, the CBO membership remained the same as it was a few years earlier. So why are new members not joining on?

First, such issues raise concerns about the credibility of the CBO as a fair and representative entity. Second, it raises concerns about exactly how the CBO is functioning in terms of its organizational capacity and decision-making structure.

Are MBOPs the solution?

These examples very appropriately attest to the challenge that CBOs may or may not be the most appropriate representatives of their community. These cases have tried to illustrate the various social and economic factors that condition the responses of organizations that identify themselves to the world on the basis of their membership base. All these organizations have certain commonalities associated with small community-based organizations, such as their internal membership base, legal registration modalities, their limited geographical coverage, their dependence on external sources for revenue generation and so on. While they do differ on grounds of scope and outreach, that is, some CBOs being larger, more exposed and better financially equipped than others, their contribution to their respective villages has to be looked at socially and not just organizationally.

Putting forward a case for membership-based organizations as benefiting the poor, these CBOs have managed to bring forth some exclusive qualities that rural CBOs possess. The most important of these is their ability to mobilize a membership base around a common issue, whether exclusionary or not. Second, because of their membership base that allows the organization to be legally registered, such CBOs are able to access external resources that would otherwise not be accessible to the poor, for example, access to credit, social services, infrastructure, foreign funding and so on. Third, CBOs have managed feed on the hierarchy of rural power structures, on the basis of caste and historical prominence, in order to survive and be recognized both in and outside their village. This combination has allowed these CBOs to successfully operate despite opposition and animosity from within and outside their communities.

This also shows that, instead of looking at CBOs simply from the purview of their organizational framework, one needs to look closer at its location within the society in which it operates. All CBOs used their ties to caste as a way to gradually raise themselves within the social hierarchy of their respective villages, and to be able to provide better services to their members. Thus, while in comparison to more landed castes they may still be less influential, but within their domestic constituencies, they wield great power. Ironically, observations have shown that, in turn, these caste groups have now begun to dominate other more oppressed groups, such as the low-caste and minorities, thus perpetuating the myth of power.

Increased power has enabled some CBOs to obtain funds from international development organizations due in part to improved organizational capacity but also to their leaders' personal networks of social relations. Normally, such personal "networks" would be seen as inappropriate for a professional institution to make use of. However, such actions can be considered justified, if members achieve economic gains. However, where CBOs demonstrate exclusivity in their membership, the result may not be entirely beneficial to the village. For instance, in the case of one CBO, most of the beneficiaries of the organization's projects were the office bearers' own family members and the remaining members primarily belonged to the majority caste group. This brings up the vital question of whether CBOs as MBOPs are representative of just their own "communities" or their village as a whole.

Observations of CBOs in Sindh Province suggest that membership is influenced by a number of factors. In all villages, many nonmembers were of the opinion that the CBO did not fully represent the whole village, but only a select caste and class. For example, one CBO works only in two *paras* of the village, which belong to the landowning class and a majority of its members belong to the *para* of the CBO's founding President. When asked why they were not members of the CBO, villagers responded, "we were not asked to become members"; "they belong to a higher caste" ; "they only associate with their own kind."[20] Similarly, in the case of another CBO, all members belonged to one caste and the remaining population of the village, although aware of the organization's existence, was partly oblivious of its activities.

Similarly, all CBOs were found to be centered around one individual, rather than sharing power with members. That the founding members had retained the main positions within the CBOs governing body since inception showed that members did not have much say in how the organization functioned on a day-to-day basis.

Gender plays an interesting part in this scenario. In development thought, women have always been seen as an independent "community" whose needs and problems require separate and more detailed attention. This has prompted the formation of exclusively women's groups. Despite this fact, however, women belonging to marginalized groups in the village (minority groups) are still excluded from the group's membership, let alone its benefits. This worrying fact continues to raise serious questions about the marginalized (rural poor) further marginalizing the marginalized (the low caste).

Unfortunately, it is factors such as these that pose a risk to the benefits that CBOs and MBOPs can provide to rural economies. CBOs are best aware of how to deal with the complexities of their village. In addition, as legally registered formal organizations, they can act as much needed intermediaries between their community members and those more powerful such as landlords, and even donors.

If looked at in this light, then the role of CBOs becomes a vital element of poverty reduction. Instead of basing funding decisions primarily on the size and purpose of organizations, the emphasis needs to be placed instead on how such organizations can utilize the existing system of social relations and hierarchies within their communities. If CBOs can manage to integrate such traditional systems with more formal organizational frameworks, then they have the potential to be very successful in addressing the complex issues related to poverty.

Conclusion

Complex sets of social relations are what govern rural "communities" in Sindh Province, Pakistan. Going back to Banuri and Mehmood's definition of the term, it is then not so simplistic to be able to define a community in terms of just spatial proximity or common requirements. While these may be useful in identifying an area within which to concentrate efforts for change, they may not necessarily identify the most accurate way in which to bring about change. One particular group in the village may cite education as the need of the hour, despite the fact that a school does exist in their village. However, it is because that school is not accessible to their particular class or caste group that the need arises. If the CBO concerned with the state of affairs in their village belongs to a dominant caste group, they will perhaps be able to address the issue and ensure equal access. However, if members of the CBO are mostly poorer farmers or laborers, then they will either need access to more powerful social representatives, or they will simply come up with their own school, exclusively for their children, thus further pronouncing the caste and class divide. Is this the solution to poverty?

It is questions such as these that MBOPs in Pakistan and ultimately policy makers have to grapple with. While these issues do not have to hamper the generic definitions of community as being a common nucleus for organization and service delivery, they do come into question when one talks about who is advocating for change within them, i.e. membership-based organizations. This is not to undermine or disregard the work of such organizations, but it is important that their inputs be critically analyzed in the context of their social and political surroundings, since these undoubtedly influence their work. Representation need not be limited to farmers and water users' associations, for example, but could include women's groups and minority rights groups.

Social systems exist in all the provinces in both rural and urban areas, albeit with differences in the structures of hierarchies and governance. It is not possible or feasible to assume that the so-called "ripple effect" of development will pervade through an entire region smoothly and uniformly. For practitioners and policy makers, it is vital to recognize and acknowledge the barriers of caste and class, so that there may be more of an opportunity for membership-based organizations to achieve propoor growth. But, before one can come up with ideas for poverty reduction, it is vital to first try and understand these social structures in our evaluation of why poverty exists in poor countries. The answer is not always to rid us of these sorts of relations, but perhaps if we take a closer look into some of the issues above, it may even lie in the institutionalization of these relations. The "community" then just might know what is "best".

Notes

1 A. Ghaus-Pasha, H. Jamal and A. Iqbal, *Dimensions of the Non-Profit Sector in Pakistan*, Karachi: Social Policy and Development Center, 2002, p. 11.
2 See P. Wignaraja *et al.*, *Participatory Development. Learning from South Asia*, Karachi: Oxford University Press, 1998; S.S. Khan, *Poverty Eradication through Community Involvement*, 1997; and T. Banuri, S.R. Khan and M. Mahmood, *Just Development. Structural Adjustment in the 1990s*, Karachi: Oxford University Press, 1997.
3 In T. Banuri, S.R. Khan and M. Mahmood, *Just Development. Structural Adjustment in the 1990s*, Karachi: Oxford University Press, 1997, p. 158.
4 In I. Smillie, *The Alms Bazzar*, London: I.T. Publications, 1995, p. 250.
5 In M. Rahnema, "Towards Post-development: Searching for Signposts, A New Language and New Paradigms", *The Post-Development Reader*, Dhaka: The University Press, 1997, p. 382.
6 Ibid.
7 In R. Chambers, *Whose Reality Counts? Putting the Last First*, London: I.T. Publications, 1997, p. 183.
8 GoP, *Pakistan Participatory Poverty Assessment. National Report*, Islamabad: Government of Pakistan, 2002, p. 77.
9 For a more detailed analysis of MBOPs made up exclusively of female members, see study by T. Khan, NGORC, 1997 (mimeo).
10 For a detailed in-depth study of land tenure systems and rural livelihoods in Sindh and Punjab, see H. Gazdar, A. Khan and T. Khan, 2002 (mimeo).
11 For a detailed explanation of the structure of CBOs in Sindh, see *A Situation Analysis of NGOs in Sindh*, NGORC, 1997.
12 Ibid.
13 Ibid.
14 Personal discussion, Sanghar District, 2001.
15 Personal discussion, Khairpur District, 2001.
16 Personal meeting, Khairpur District, 2001.
17 Various group discussions, Khairpur District, 1996–7.
18 Internal project documentation, Shikarpur District, 1997–9.
19 Ibid.
20 Various visits, Sanghar and Khairpur Districts, 2000–1.

Bibliography

Banuri, T., Khan, S.R. and Mahmood, M. (eds) (1997) *Just Development. Structural Adjustment in the 1990s*, Karachi: Oxford University Press.
Chambers, R. (1997) *Whose Reality Counts? Putting the Last First*, London: Intermediate Technology Publications.
Gazdar, H., Khan, A. and Khan, T. (2002) *Land Tenure, Rural Livelihoods and Institutional Innovation*, a study prepared for Department for International Development, Karachi.

Ghaus-Pasha, A., Jamal, H. and Iqbal, A. (2002) *Dimensions of the Non-Profit Sector in Pakistan*, Social Policy and Development Center, Karachi.

Government of Pakistan, Planning Commission (2002) *Between Hope and Despair. Pakistan Participatory Poverty Assessment. National Report*, Islamabad.

Khan, S.S. (1997) *Poverty Eradication through Community Involvement*, publisher unavailable, Islamabad.

Khan, T. (1997) *Women's Organizations in Social Development. A Study of Women's Groups in NGORC's Two Modules*, NGO Resource Centre, Karachi.

Khan, T. and Rafi, T. (1999) *Partnerships as a "Tool" for Community Participation. Unpacking the Myths*, paper presented at a Conference on "Enhancing Capabilities for Community Participation. Revisiting Practices in Education Development," Karachi.

NGO Resource Centre (1996) *NGOs in Four Divisions of Sindh. A Comparative Analysis*, NGO Resource Centre, Karachi.

Rahnema, M. (ed.) (1997) *The Post-Development Reader*, Dhaka: The University Press.

Smillie, I. (1995) *The Alms Bazzar*, London: Intermediate Technology Publications.

Wignaraja, P., Hussain, A., Sethi, H. and Wignaraja, G. (eds) (1998) *Participatory Development. Learning from South Asia*, Karachi: Oxford University Press.

16 Doing things differently?

The everyday politics of membership-based organisations

Joseph Devine

Introduction

Membership-based organisations of the poor (MBOPs) are not a new phenomenon. However, the interest in the potential contribution they can make to the task of advancing the cause of poor people has recently been renewed, and is growing. The timing of this resurgent interest is worth noting. For the past 15 to 20 years, large amounts of money, resources and energy have been invested in supporting non-governmental organisations (NGOs) throughout the world. However, the anticipated 'associational revolution' (Salamon 1994) linked to NGOs has not occurred and the desired impact at a relevant scale has not materialised. We have therefore entered a period in which development practitioners, activists and scholars have had to revise strategies, and think hard on how, and in which direction to proceed. Part of this revision has led to a renewed interest in organisational forms that were mostly overlooked during the period when NGOs were held to be the *ne plus ultra* of civil society approaches to poverty eradication and development (Kanbur 2001). With a more realistic understanding of the limits of NGO led interventions, the search is now on for new or complementary alternatives. The focus on MBOPs cannot be divorced from this search.[1]

Relationships, poverty and well-being

In a recent exploratory study, carried out in Bangladesh, into people's perceptions of what constitutes a good quality of life, the majority of respondents stressed the significance of their intimate and close social relationships (Choudhury, Camfield and Devine, forthcoming). While this is not a new finding, it is an area that surprisingly has not been explored in sufficient detail. In part, this is because of the tendency, especially within development and poverty studies, to focus exclusively on what people lack in material terms. However, poverty in Bangladesh is as much a statement about the type, quality and experience of relationships that people have, as it is about the lack of material resources. Our appreciation that people can be 'poor in people' (White 1992), or that poverty is a reflection of poor or ineffective relationships (Wood 2003), is therefore undervalued and inadequately understood. Yet, this idea is central to the way people in Bangladesh understand and experience poverty, evidenced in the important distinction they make between *amar kichu ney* (I have nothing) and *amar keu ney* (I have no one). In both cases, people express a situation of poverty and vulnerability. However, while the former indicates a sense of material deprivation, the latter points to a state of vulnerability and hopelessness that is far more profound and debilitating (Devine 1999). 'Not having anyone' is the condition of poverty that people try most desperately to avoid.[2]

In what ways are immediate relationships and social networks significant to the way poor people manage their everyday lives? First, they are used instrumentally to strengthen claims on a range of material goods or services such as employment opportunities (Williams *et al.* 2003), credit (McGregor 1994), medicine and health treatment (Scheper-Hughes 1992), food and daily necessities (Auyero 2000), and even physical protection (Khan 2000). Second, social relationships and networks also hold a deep symbolic value for people in that they offer a structure that gives meaning to their lives. In her analysis of child rights approaches in development, White (2002) talks usefully of a strategy in which individuals extend an 'idiom of belonging' to the people, networks and organisations they most value. In the context of South Asia, this is illustrated, for example, when people bestow family titles such as 'sister' or 'uncle' on people who do not belong to the strict family context. This strategy sets boundaries vis-à-vis the outside, but more importantly it legitimises a process of building 'cross cutting ego-centred linkages' (White 2002: 1098) that produce affective and meaningful relationships between people. These linkages in turn become the basis for the subsequent exchange of goods and benefits, as well as for social action.

The argument of this chapter rests on the premise that the relational milieu constitutes the primary cultural terrain upon which people construct their well-being. The implication of this is that a proper understanding of institutional forms like MBOPs requires us to explore their location and significance within this relational milieu. Using ethnographic insights into a membership based initiative, I will pursue two lines of enquiry. First, I will argue that the success of the initiative lies in the fact that the organisation has become a primary location and expression of agency for poor people. Here I will also explore various dimensions of this agency. Second, I will offer an analysis on the quality of agency by exploring its significance against the background of the relational milieu through which poor people have to negotiate their livelihood options.

The organisation referred to above is called *Shammo*.[3] Although legally registered with the NGO Affairs Bureau,[4] Shammo can be considered an MBOP in at least two important ways. First, Shammo is a membership-based organisation (MBO) by its formal constitution. Its executive committee is made up of members – all of whom were, or are, landless farmers – who retain ultimate control of the organisation. Second, Shammo is an organic institutional form, created from within a community in order to negotiate external and often uneven power relationships. The insights used in this chapter draw mostly on the earlier history of Shammo when its organic nature was most clearly evident.

Shammo – a brief history

The origins of Shammo can be traced back to the mid-1970s when a group of young men established a youth club in their village. Although the main aim of the club was to promote recreational and cultural activities, it also carried out some modest relief and welfare activities. Impressed by the enthusiasm of the youth, the headmaster of the local high school put the leaders in contact with an acquaintance of his, who worked for OXFAM. He in turn visited the club and encouraged the members to move the focus of the organisation away from recreation to helping the poor.

Through their contact with OXFAM, the members of Shammo were invited to meetings and workshops where they were introduced to ideas and practices used by the wider development community. Most of these meetings reflected upon and developed ideas related to conscientisation and mobilisation in which the emphasis lay on the need to understand, identify and confront the structural causes of poverty (Freire 1972). This type of exposure gave Shammo a methodology that fitted their intention to work more with the poor. As a result, they began to organise meetings with poorer landless households and encourage the formation of smaller membership groups known in Bengali as *samities*. This initiative proved to be very successful and the number of *samities* grew rapidly.

The first *samities* were located in villages surrounding an open water body known as 'Boro Bagher Beel'. The Beel was a large lake used mostly for fishing. In 1962, government authorities decided to drain the Beel by digging a canal to a nearby river. As a result, over 820 acres of low-lying agricultural land emerged which legally became *khas* land.[5] Initially, the local elites showed little interest in the land, and encouraged the landless to clear and dredge the whole area so that they could use it for subsistence farming. The task took almost two years to complete. However as soon as the land was ready for farming, the elite leaders forcibly took possession of it and proceeded to divide it amongst themselves. The poor were then obliged to farm the same land as day labourers.

In 1972, the government of Bangladesh issued a number of key presidential orders containing provisions for the redistribution of land such as *khas* among landless households. On that occasion, many of the poor households in the villages surrounding the Beel were officially allotted parcels of land from the Beel,[6] and received the relevant legal documents from the local administrative authority. However, none of those allocated land managed to take possession of what was theirs by right. Instead local elites took advantage of their political position to bypass government orders and carry on using the land for their own benefit. That elites could act in this way reflected the wider political context in which actors at national and local levels colluded to retain de facto if not always *de jure* control over key assets and resources. This constituted an important part of a wider strategy of power accumulation that is captured succinctly in the following observation:

> National politicians and bureaucrats are often themselves large landowners and even if they are not, they depend on rich peasant both for political support and to ensure that the countryside remains reasonably tranquil. To attack the interests of this dominant class would be political suicide for any of the political parties.
>
> (Hossain and Jones 1989: 180)

Poor people 'participate' in this collusion through a complex system of vertically aligned and hierarchically ordered patron–client relationships. This feeds into and reproduces a system of social cohesion based on class relations of dependency (BRAC 1983, Wood 1994). In this environment, the ability of the poor to exercise agency or act collectively is severely constrained. Among other considerations, the logic of patronage demands loyalty from clients more than voice (Hirschmann 1970), and allows a politics of privilege and favour to impose itself on the establishment and implementation of formal rights.

The inability of Shammo's members to pursue their entitlement claims on the *khas* land reflected therefore the fact that, they were mostly dependent for their livelihoods on those who had taken possession of the land. When analysing the causes of their poverty during the early *samity* meetings, members naturally raised the issue of *khas* land and the ease with which the elites had dispossessed them of what was theirs by right. *Khas* distribution and land rights, in general, therefore, became the focus of Shammo's work, and throughout the 1980s, the organisation was engaged in a prolonged struggle over the Boro Bagher Beel.

It is not possible to go into the details of that struggle here. Suffice to say that by the early 1990s, all the land of Boro Bagher Beel had been removed from the control of the elites and re-distributed among landless households. This was a remarkable turnaround and indeed a unique outcome in Bangladesh. Throughout the 1980s, many membership organisations, NGOs and donors had adopted *khas* land distribution as a key component of their development activities.[7] However by the early 1990s, the enthusiasm had waned as a result of a number of factors including a donor shift away from social mobilisation activities (Devine 2003), general frustration at the slow pace of even small gains in *khas* land activities, and the constant threat of violence that accompanied *khas* land struggles. Shammo then was one of the few organisations that remained committed to *khas* land issues. Its success, however, came at a high price. Thus, the organisation's history is littered with incidents of village sieges, false imprisonments, deaths, murders, and many other forms of violence and general harassment.

Enabling new forms of agency

The fact that the members of Shammo managed to take control of the *khas* area and protect the rights of landless households to use the land is in itself an important indicator of success. However, it is neither the only nor the most important indicator. In order to collectively pursue entitlement claims and then defend these against powerful elites, there had to be a change in the configuration of the core patron–client relationship that underpinned the prevailing system of social cohesion. The argument proposed here is that Shammo became the site around which the process of re-configuration occurred. Through this, the organisation effectively became the primary location and expression of a new form of agency for its members.[8] Three key interlinked moments enabled this new form of agency:

1 the construction of a shared identity, sufficiently secure and reliable for members to shift their allegiance away from the domination of elites;
2 the ability to secure tangible improvements for members;
3 the fostering of an utopian space (de Certeau 1984) in which future aspirations and the potential for further reconfigurations of power relations are nurtured (Appadurai 2004).

Belonging and identity

> I am our *samity* leader and so many women [...] come to me when they are in trouble. Many of them are widows and have no one to look after them (*tader keu ney*). I just tell them that I was like that before I joined the *samity*. Of course my life is still hard, but at least now I know that with the *samity* I have people (*amar keu ache*) I can rely on – they are my friends [...]. Other groups and NGOs have started work here but you only see them once a week.
>
> (Rokeya)

The success of organisations like Shammo depends fundamentally on their ability to attract and retain members. Rokeya's words begin to explain why Shammo has been more successful than others in building up its membership base. She portrays Shammo as a friend that can be relied upon, an organisation that is in touch with what is really happening in her life. This sense that the organisation has an affective relationship with its members contrasts in Rokeya's mind with the more distant relationship other associations have with people. In evaluating the organisation, this criteria is given at least as much weight by members as the ability of the organisation to deliver actual material benefits. This is not peculiar to the case of Shammo. Williams *et al.*'s (2003) observation that party workers are valued because they are considered friends and close to the poor, Scheper-Hughes' (1992) findings that patrons are judged to be 'good' because of their nurturant and caring qualities, and Auyero's (2000) discovery of a moral relationship between 'self-sacrificing' brokers and their clients, all confirm the importance attached to an affective relationship that goes beyond the immediate exchange of material resources. This is portrayed in Rokeya's statement that with Shammo, she now has friends to rely on.

There are a number of ways in which Shammo is seen to communicate effectively with the deeper concerns of its members. The most obvious one is the *samity* meetings that take place formally at least once a week but more frequently on an informal basis. Recently, the value given to *samity* meetings in Bangladesh has waned as they are considered time-consuming, difficult to motivate, and vacuous in content and ambition (Hashemi 1990). For Shammo's members, however, the meetings remain important because they offer space and time where people can discuss issues that are important to them, and identify appropriate courses of action. The meetings ensure that there is an active and open link between the organisation and people's day-to-day lives. For those who participate, the meetings also nurture a sense of belonging, identity and support. To use, in reverse, the language and analysis of labelling (Wood 1985), Rokeya's relation to Shammo is one in which she feels more 'person' than 'client' or 'beneficiary', and in which her history and context are acknowledged and not ignored. In other words, the organisation is perceived as 'taking her life seriously'.

Organisations like Shammo have to prove not only that they are friends of their members, but that they can also be relied upon (McGregor 1999). In the case of the struggle over the Boro Bagher Beel, Shammo's success depended on its ability to convince members to openly shift their allegiance from local elites to the organisation. This is a pivotal moment because although it is relatively easy to demonstrate the exploitative and predatory nature of patron–client relations (Shammo's members were already fully aware of this), it is far more difficult to convince people to remove themselves from those same relations, and then to confront them. To shift allegiance from a patron – however exploitative – entails a huge risk calculation and exposes poorer individuals and households to potentially debilitating and long-term insecurity. Therefore, before becoming a member of Shammo, people had to think carefully about their options. If the calculation backfired, members faced the ultimate risk of being left in a situation akin to that of *amar keu ney*, in other words with no one with whom to negotiate the satisfaction of basic and everyday needs.

It is impossible to identify a single event or message that convinced members to shift their allegiance to Shammo. Instead, over time, members gradually gained greater control over aspects of their lives that previously had been dominated by elite patrons. In this process, people's confidence in the organisation grew. This was supported by foundational or catalytic moments achieved through the kind of 'offensive struggles' outlined by Bayat in his study of urban organised groups (Bayat 1997). In highlighting these struggles, Bayat argues for greater recognition of those pro-active initiatives of the poor that 'place a great deal of restraint upon the privileges of the dominant groups, allocating segments of their life chances (including capital, social goods, opportunity, autonomy and thus power) to themselves' (Bayat 1997: 56). In Shammo's case, the 'offensive struggles' usually took the form of direct and conscious action such as open and mobilised campaigns, processions and political vigils, and mass repossession of *khas* land. Securing and then consolidating gains in this way endowed Shammo with a reputation as an organisation that can be relied upon. As this reputation increased, the risk calculations of existing and potential members also changed. This led to membership expansion and also strengthened the commitment of existing members.

Tangible benefits

> It is too late for me to join [Shammo] ... now. I would not get *khas* land because there is little of it left and there are many *samity* members still hoping to get land.... If I had joined Shammo I would be better off. Others in the village have improved. I made a mistake but I thought I was doing the right thing.
>
> (Roton)

I met Roton for the first time in 1997 and have returned to see him on a number of occasions over the intermittent eight years. He is one of the poorest men I have met in my life: landless, homeless, undernourished and always complaining of being physically in pain. I was introduced to him by one of his brothers who was a member of Shammo. The two men had started their adult lives working for the same patron household where their father had worked – a form of inherited clientelism – yet their paths had gone in very different directions. When Roton was asked to join Shammo, he was not prepared to jeopardise his household's security by leaving his patron (with limited resources) to become a member of an organisation that had even less resources. However, by the time I met Roton the situation had changed dramatically. The ability of his patron to mobilise resources had deteriorated significantly while that of Shammo had increased. Roton's brother did join Shammo and had fared much better as a result of his association with the organisation. Although still poor, he owned agricultural land, a house, some livestock, and his children went to school. Neither of the brothers have any doubt that their respective qualities of life are explained by the fact that one became a member of Shammo while the other did not. In what ways then does Shammo help deliver material improvements to its members?

For most of the landless around Shammo's area, securing a stable livelihood source is the primary welfare concern. Although the struggles over *khas* land came to assume symbolic significance, the initial focus on land arose straightforwardly because agriculture was the main source of employment for members. Those who were fortunate and were allocated parcels of *khas* land gained therefore, an important livelihood platform from which they were able to begin accumulating assets. At a minimum, the allocation of *khas* land enables farmers to subsist for a significant part of the year on their own land. Many, like Roton's brother, later managed to generate profit and invest in small business enterprises. However, since the amount of land to be distributed was limited, not all members were fortunate enough to receive *khas* allotments. How then does Shammo help secure tangible improvements for these members?

One of the characteristics valued most by members is that Shammo provides points of access to external bodies or organisations, especially to various institutions of the state. The initial struggle for *khas* land catapulted the organisation and its members into a direct relationship with different institutions and organisations of the polity, especially the Land Ministry.[9] Through this experience Shammo acquired the types of skills, knowledge and contacts that gave the organisation a legitimate 'positional advantage' (Knoke 1990) to exert influence and make claims in key policy areas at national and local levels.[10] Besides successfully mobilising around *khas* land, Shammo's members, for example, have also lobbied to have minimum wages for agricultural labourers and improved working conditions for sharecroppers, to ensure the provision of basic infrastructural services, and to demand a more transparent distribution of government welfare goods and services such as the Vulnerable Group Development cards.[11] By using the organisation's positional advantage to push legitimate claims, Shammo and its members have successfully accessed material resources, goods and services that have had an immediate and positive impact on the livelihood status of the members.

Another way in which members seek to achieve tangible improvements in their lives is through reciprocal help and support. Without over-romanticising the idea, it is clear that Shammo's members care and look out for each other. This is an inflection from the point made earlier about the organisation having to take people's everyday concerns seriously. Members, therefore, also take each others' lives seriously. For this reason, when faced with difficulty, most members seek help in the first instance from fellow members, often through initial discussions in the *samity* meetings. Here Shammo acts as a 'problem solving network' (Auyero 2000) where members can help each other. The kind of problems that members resolve amongst themselves range from satisfying everyday basic needs (financial, medical and so forth) to mediating disputes within or between households, kinship groups, neighbourhoods or villages.

Utopian spaces

> Poor people have to struggle [. . .]. But having my own land makes me happy and makes me think that the fighting and years in prison were worth it. Tomorrow there will be a different struggle and if we stick together Shammo will also win that. And the day will come when there will be no more need for fighting.
>
> (Mahfuz)

Mahfuz was a member of the very first landless *samity*, formed by Shammo. Like many other members, he held on to the idea that one day there would be an 'ultimate victory' of the landless, vindication of the years of struggle, sacrifice and efforts. Mahfuz's words reflect the coexistence in his life of two spheres: the polemological and the utopian (de Certeau 1984). While the former refers to the polemics and conflicts that arise as a result of his association with Shammo, the latter points to a part of his life where aspirations and illusions are nurtured, an almost impregnable area where 'the fatality of the established order can be subverted' (de Certeau 1984: 16–17).

The introduction of the notion of utopia should not be interpreted as some *fuga mundi* fantasy. Aspirations matter, and can be the basis of social action through which people construct their anticipated futures (Appadurai 2004). In other words, they are constitutive of agency. Crucially for the discussion here, aspirations can also be shared. In thinking about how Shammo and its members work towards their anticipated future, I am helped by the distinction between tactics and strategies, offered by de Certeau (1984). The main difference between a strategy and a tactic is that the former requires a figurative 'fixed position' or node that is identifiable, discrete and demarcated. This serves as an autonomous base from which to plan relations with other external agents, events and circumstances. In this instance, people have more control over what they do. A tactic, instead, lacks a fixed position and as a consequence, can only operate on borrowed or imposed terrains. This allows for limited or opportunistic (as opposed to planned) interactions.[12] Here people exercise much less control over what they do.

A good illustration of how Shammo has allowed its members to move from tactical to strategic mobilisation can be seen in its recent engagement with the formal electoral process. Being an MBO with a significant membership base, Shammo has always attracted electoral candidates seeking votes and support. In the early days of the organisation, members were forced to react (i.e. negotiate 'tactically') to demands made by competing candidates. Inevitably, members tried to negotiate with candidates so that once elected they would support the efforts of Shammo to ensure the allocation of *khas* land to the poor. Normally, however, the promises and commitments made by candidates were ignored almost as soon as the elections were over, thus confirming de Certeau's (1984) observation that gains secured through tactical practices tend to be fleeting and are difficult to consolidate. However, as the organisation grew and became more established, its engagement with the electoral process also changed. For example, during the parliamentary elections of 1996, the members of Shammo mobilised in a collective and purposeful way (Devine 2006). This had a very direct impact on the final electoral outcome as the incumbent Member of Parliament (an old adversary of Shammo) was elected out of office and replaced by a candidate that the members had together chosen to support.

The main difference between the 1996 elections and the earlier elections is that the organisation had secured the authority or 'fixed position' that allowed strategic as opposed to tactical planning. The sense of purpose was again evident in the 1997 local elections where for the first time, a significant number of members stood for election. Of the 52 candidates from Shammo, 43 were successfully elected. The importance of this result has to be read in two ways. First, in Bangladesh it is not uncommon for candidates promoted by MBOPs or other pro-poor organisations to present themselves at elections. However, the number of successfully returned candidates tends to be very low (Hassan 1999). By contrast, Shammo achieved a high rate of successfully returned candidates – a result of strategic mobilisation. The second significant feature of the elections is that it demonstrates how Shammo's members were capable of consolidating previous gains to purposively forge new opportunities – a characteristic of strategic practice. The fact that some members now hold political office is therefore part of a wider strategy to further influence areas where new entitlement claims might be pursued. In short, strategic action enables members to create the conditions that will allow them to allocate even more segments of their life chances to themselves (Bayat 1993), and therefore to make their anticipated future more of a reality today.

Agency, hierarchy and dependency

Members have to listen to leaders. If they do not, they will be ignored or even thrown out of the organisation as I was. Other members ... could have defended me but they were frightened. In fact, some worked hard to get rid of me in the hope that they would be benefit in some way. Members are always trying to please the leaders.

(Anjan)

The chapter so far has argued that Shammo has supported a process of change that allows its members to act upon and make better sense of their present and future realities. More specifically, the organisation shapes numerous possibilities for members to deal more 'strategically' with their everyday lives. To the extent that the process changes the fundamental relation that links people and society, it can be seen as constitutive of a new form of agency for Shammo's members. Agency, however, can take many forms and it is therefore important to take the analysis forward by asking about the type and quality of agency that MBOPs like Shammo facilitate.

Anjan's statement alerts us to an important dimension of the organisational politics of Shammo. As the organisation has grown, the social and economic distance between leaders and members has also increased. This is not an observation that should surprise us, as it is one of the key reasons that led Robert Michels to famously argue 'who says organisation says oligarchy'. However, our analysis of pro-poor organisations often struggles to deal with this dynamic because of the prevalence of strong normative assumptions about the collectivist tendencies and democratic inclinations of these organisational forms. As a result, our understanding of MBOPs is impoverished because, as Anjan hints, the relationships nurtured within an organisation condition quite significantly the forms of agency that are then possible to its members. The experience of Shammo offers two important observations in this regard.

First, although Shammo presents itself as an organisation committed to protecting the rights of the poor, in practice, this is underpinned by a logic of preferential behaviour in which the entitlement rights of certain people are privileged over others. This leads to a rather nebulous institutional area where favours and rights intertwine. A good example is that of Roton. On many counts he had very strong entitlement claims (indeed stronger than some who were allocated land) on available *khas* land. Yet, as discussed earlier, he did not receive land simply because he was not a member of Shammo. From this we can conclude that 'being poor' was a necessary but insufficient basis for pursuing entitlement claims on *khas* land with Shammo. As I have argued elsewhere, the key criteria used to determine the final outcome of *khas* land distribution were membership and allegiance to the organisation (Devine 2002).

Naturally, there are arguments that justify the decision to allocate *khas* land only to members. First, this ensured that the land went at least to genuine landless households and this represents a significant pro-poor outcome, and a radical improvement on the *status quo ante*. Second, by distributing the land among members it was easier to monitor its subsequent use and collectively protect it from attacks by elite-led groups. If Roton had received land what was to stop his patron taking control of it again? While all these arguments may be plausible, the point, however, remains that the rights of some were advantaged over others and this has had a direct and immediate impact on people's well-being. Paradoxically therefore, one of the unintended consequences of Shammo's work with landless households is that the livelihood prospects of poor non-members seem to be spiralling into greater insecurity and uncertainty.

The second point to note is that relationships constructed within the organisation are based not on equality but on inequality and hierarchy. This is illustrated well in the case of Anjan, who had emerged as a strong leader of the landless, and was elected chairman of the organisation – a move fully supported by Shammo's leaders. The decision to expel Anjan was taken after he had publicly challenged the leadership on its strategy in relation to the 1996 parliamentary elections. Anjan refused to follow the collective decision of the organisation and ended up 'exercising his right' to campaign publicly for a different candidate than the one chosen by his fellow members. His eventual expulsion was a direct consequence of this public show of disloyalty to the organisation.[13] Anjan's argument is that other members were too frightened to act in their own interests because this meant opposing decisions taken by the organisation's leaders. Members depend on the organisation and are aware that there is a price to be paid for being disloyal. For this reason, some even used the occasion of his expulsion to deliberately make a public show of their allegiance and loyalty to the leaders – a show that hopefully would help gain or protect benefits.

There is then an evolving tension in the relationship between members and leaders. Members are aware of the unequal nature of the relationship, and even strategise around it. Elsewhere, and following Bailey (1970), I have used the idea of 'moral proximity to leaders' to help distinguish between 'core members', 'followers and new recruits' and 'excluded' in the organisation (Devine 1999).[14] These categories imply different types of relationships to the leaders and reflect different degrees of loyalty or attachment. In this way, a social hierarchy of relationships is constructed within the organisation. Importantly, there is correspondence between one's position in the hierarchy and the strength of claims on resources and benefits. Members again are fully aware of this and therefore endeavour to be part of the inner or core group, or at least to have good links with core members. However, if loyalty brings privilege it also brings expectation and obligation. Thus outright confrontation and dissension by core members like Anjan is rare. It is also tolerated less.

The creation and perpetuation of a social hierarchy through which exchanges take place and competing claims, entitlements and obligations are resolved, is of course a key characteristic of the same culture of patronage Shammo originally set out to break down. Notwithstanding its status as a MBOP then, relationships within the organisation are constructed in such a way that nurtures clientelistic behaviour. These observations represent, in effect, an antithesis to the first section of this chapter that described how Shammo facilitates a new form of agency for its members.

Bringing these two sections together produces an intriguing question: is it possible to exercise greater agency from a position that also encourages the persistence of clientelistic behaviour? The question rests on paradox because commentators and analysts have tended to see agency and clientelism as mutually exclusive opposites, the latter an aberration of and an obstacle to the former. In the final part of the chapter I briefly address this question.

Discussion

Shammo is a problematic site of agency. The persistence of characteristics associated with clientelistic practices runs counter to many of the core tenets of the dominant civil society perspective, which makes us think about a range of pro-poor organisations. Clientelism is perceived as a negative form of social action because it atomises people and encourages mechanistic and coercive exchanges between powerful patrons and weaker clients. The task of organisations like MBOPs is precisely to free poor people from these kinds of ties and to facilitate collective action. In short, pro-poor organisations are supposed to de-clientelise and not re-clientelise individuals.

This chapter rests on the premise that the relational milieu constitutes the primary cultural terrain upon which people construct their livelihood and well-being. In the case of Bangladesh, the relational context is replete with different types of networks and support mechanisms that contain patterns of obligation, dependency, expectation and responsibility. For poor people, moving in and between these various networks and relationships is a necessary and routine part of their lives (Auyero 2000). In trying to pursue a more grounded perspective of MBOPs, the chapter attempts to locate their significance against the background of this relational milieu. Methodologically, this approach challenges the tendency to essentialise pro-poor organisations, treating them as if they could or should be isolated from their respective cultural contexts. Substantially, this more embedded analysis leads to the possibility that apparent contradictions (agency and clientelism) may co-exist and indeed be co-constitutive of social action.

A key argument of the chapter is that Shammo has facilitated the creation of a new form of agency through which members secure greater control over increasing parts of their lives. The real challenge, however, is to reconcile this with the finding that through its actions, Shammo might also reproduce patterns of dependency and clientelism. Elsewhere (Devine 2006) I have built on insights especially from social psychology to explore the strength of a synthesis that is captured in the notion of 'autonomous dependency'. Here, I very briefly sketch out the conceptual foundations of that synthesis.

In their research into well-being, Ryan and Deci (2001) argue that individuals need to fulfil three basic needs in order to achieve a good quality of life: autonomy, competence and relatedness. Of the three basic needs the notion of autonomy is acknowledged as the most problematic because of its association with ideas of independence and individualism. This clearly connects with concerns raised here about the reproduction of clientelistic and dependency-inducing behaviour. Building on this initial work, Chirkov *et al.* (2003) reiterate the argument that autonomy is central for well-being but then introduce important definitional distinctions that help take the discussion forward. Autonomy, they argue, is understood as the ability of people to act in accordance with their interests, values and desires. The opposite of autonomy is not dependence but heteronomy, that is, coerced action regardless of values and interests. One of the implications of this distinction is that it is conceivable for individuals to strengthen the ability to act autonomously even in contexts when they are enmeshed in relationships of dependency. Indeed, the authors stretch the possibilities further by arguing that in certain circumstances, individuals may need to lock into further dependency, in order to be better able to act autonomously. Thus, '[o]ne can be autonomously dependent on another, willingly rely on his or her care, *particularly if the other is perceived as supportive and responsive*' (Chirkov *et al.* 2003: 98, emphasis added).

This statement drives at the heart of our analysis of Shammo. The chapter provides evidence that Shammo has been an integral part of a process through which members have moved from heteronomous life circumstances to more autonomous ones. In other words, they are now more able to act in accordance with their own interests, values and desires. However, it is important not to over-idealise the relationship between members and the organisation, for it is founded on complex sets of rules, expectations and obligations. Members are therefore aware that the relationships engendered through Shammo are constrained and unequal, and also that they induce dependency behaviour. Despite this, they continue to preferentially apply the 'idiom of belonging' (White 2002) to the organisation because, as I have shown in the chapter, it is perceived to act in a supportive and responsive way to their everyday concerns and ambitions. This, rather than dependency, is the main criteria members use to evaluate the organisation. The fact that poor people in Bangladesh are trapped in dependent relations is repeatedly made, and more often than not, this is portrayed as a negative condition. The experience of Shammo and its members however suggests that this is only part of a more complex story. When dependency is experienced as supportive, it can also be a source of hope and power that helps establish the types of conditions through which poor people can improve their quality of life and well-being.

Notes

1 Recent interest in Faith- or Religious-Based Organisations is also linked to the widening of the 'civil society approach'.
2 See Scheper-Hughes (1992: 99) for a similar observation.
3 *Shammo* is a pseudonym.
4 Registering with the NGO Affairs Bureau is required of all organisations in Bangladesh seeking foreign funds.
5 *Khas* refers to 'unoccupied land' which the government legally owns but which has not been acquired for specific purposes. There are various sources of *khas* land including accredited lands and land vested in the government as ceiling surplus.
6 Normally households are given approximately one acre of land.
7 In 1987 the government initiated a Lands Reform Action Programme and invited NGOs to manage the programme together with the Ministry of Land (Devine 2002). This was perhaps the first occasion when civil society organisations were allowed to operate at such a high level of the polity.
8 Agency is defined broadly here to refer to that which is constitutive of the fundamental relation that links people and society.
9 Shammo was very involved in the Lands Reform Action Programme (see note 7).
10 See Devine (2002) for a fuller discussion on the relationship between Shammo and the external policy environment.
11 Although not explored here, it is important to note that non-members also enjoy many of the tangible benefits derived from efforts of Shammo's members. The case of minimum wages for agricultural labourers is a good case in point.
12 Put succinctly, 'Strategies scheme; tacticians trick' (Scott 1990: 163).
13 See Devine (2006) for more details.
14 Similarly Auyero (2000) speaks of clients organised in inner and outer circles around key political patrons.

References

Appadurai, A. (2004). 'The Capacity to Aspire' in V. Rao and M. Walton (eds), *Culture and Public Action*. Stanford University Press.

Auyero, J. (2000). *Poor People's Politics*. Durham: Duke University Press.

Bailey, F.G. (1970). *Stratagems and Spoils*. Oxford: Basil Blackwell.

Bayat, A. (1997). 'Un-civil Society; the Politics of the Informal People'. In *Third World Quarterly*, 18 (1): 53–72.

BRAC. (1983). *The Net: Power Structure in Ten Villages*. Dhaka: BRAC.

de Certeau, M. (1984). *The Practice of Everyday Life*. Berkeley, CA: University of California Press.

Chirkov, V., Ryan, M., Kuim, Y. and Kaplan, U. (2003). 'Differentiating Autonomy from Individualism and Independence: A Self-Determination Theory Perspective on Internalization of Cultural Orientation and Well-being'. In *Journal of Personality and Social Psychology*. 84 (1): 97–110.

Choudhury, K., Camfield, L. and Devine, J. (forthcoming). *Poor but Happy – an Exploration of the Cultural Construction of Happiness in Bangladesh*. University of Bath, Well-Being and Development research group. Mimeo.

Devine, J. (1999). *One Foot in Each Boat. The Macro Politics and Micro Sociology of NGOs in Bangladesh*. Ph.D. Thesis. University of Bath, UK.

Devine, J. (2002). 'Ethnography of a Policy Process: A Case Study of Land Redistribution in Bangladesh'. In *Public Administration and Development*, 22: 403–22.

Devine, J. (2003). 'The Paradox of Sustainability: Reflections on NGOs in Bangladesh'. In *ANNALS*, 590: 227–42.

Devine, J. (2006). 'NGOs, Politics and Grassroots Mobilisation: Evidence from Bangladesh'. In *Journal of South Asian Development*, Vol. 1, No. 1.

Freire, P. (1972). *Pedagogy of the Oppressed*. Harmondsworth: Penguin.

Hashemi, S. (1990). *NGOs in Bangladesh: Development Alternative or Alternative Rhetoric*. Mimeo. Manchester: Institute for Development Policy & Management, University of Manchester.

Hassan, M. (1999). *Local Governance Study, Bangladesh*. London: One World Action.

Hirschman, A. (1970). *Exit, Voice and Loyalty*. Harvard University Press.

Hossain, M. and Jones, S. (1983). 'Production, Poverty and the Co-operative Ideal: Contradictions in Bangladesh Rural Development Policy'. In D. Lea and D. Chaudhuri (eds), *Rural Development and the State: Contradictions and Dilemmas in Developing Countries* (pp. 161–85). London: Metheun.

Kanbur, R. (2001). 'Economic Policy, Distribution and Poverty: The Nature of Disagreements'. In *World Development*, 29 (6): 1083–94.

Khan, I. 2000. *Struggle for Survival. Networks and Relationships in a Bangladesh Slum*. Ph.D. Thesis. University of Bath, UK.

Knoke, D. (1990). *Political Networks*. Cambridge: Cambridge University Press.

McGregor, J.A. (1994). 'Village Credit and the Reproduction of Poverty in Rural Bangladesh'. In J. Acheson (ed.). *Anthropology and Institutional Economics*, (pp. 261–82). Lanham MD: University Press of America.

McGregor, J.A. (1999). *Growing NGOs: The Relationship between Donors and NGOs in Microfinance*. Paper presented to the DSA Conference, Bath, 12–14 September 1999.

Ryan, R. and Deci, E. (2001). 'On Happiness and Human Potentials: A Review of Research on Hedonic and Eudaimonic Well-Being'. In *Annual Review of Psychology*, 52: 141–66.

Salamon, L. (1994). 'The Rise of Non-profit Sector'. In *Foreign Affairs*, 73 (4): 109–22.

Scheper-Hughes, N. (1992). *Death Without Weeping: The Violence of Everyday Life in Brazil*. California: California University Press.

Scott, J. (1990). *Domination and the Arts of Resistance: Hidden Transcripts*. New Haven: Yale University Press.

White, S.C. (1992). *Arguing with the Crocodile: Gender and Class in Bangladesh*. Dhaka: University Press.

White, S.C. (2002). 'Being, Becoming and Relationship: Conceptual Challenges of a Child Rights Approach in Development'. In *Journal of International Development*, 14, 1095–104.

Williams, G., Veron, R., Corbridge, S. and Srivastava, M. (2003). 'Participation and Power: Poor People's Engagement with India's Employment Assurance Scheme'. In *Development and Change*, 34 (1): 163–92.

Wood, G.D. (ed.) (1985). *Labelling in Development Policy*. London: Sage.

Wood, G.D. (1994). *Bangladesh: Whose Ideas, Whose Interests*. Dhaka: UPL, Intermediate Technology.

Wood, G.D. (2003). Prisoners and Escapees: Improving the Institutional Responsibility Square in Bangladesh'. In *Public Administration and Development*, 20, 221–37.

17 Voice lessons

Local government organizations, social organizations, and the quality of local governance[1]

Vivi Alatas, Lant Pritchett and Anna Wetterberg

Introduction

Questions about improving the quality of government are more than just academic in Indonesia today; they are pressing, practical questions. Indonesia has long been considered a classic example of a "developmental authoritarian" state – one that fostered economic success and delivered concrete material benefits as a claim to political legitimacy while simultaneously creating institutions through which popular participation in politics was structured, channeled, and, thereby, marginalized (see, among many others, Rao 2004). With a radical decentralization of responsibilities to regional (district) governments underway as of January 2000, continuing economic turmoil, and frequent shifts in national leadership (having only recently completed its first transition to a directly elected president), Indonesia is still in the midst of economic, social, and political change. From the national to the local level, the structures and behaviors taken for granted during the Soeharto/New Order era are being challenged and, in many cases, overturned. This chapter is a snapshot at a point in time of this dynamic and focuses on the role of villagers' social activities in creating more participatory and accountable local governments, and aims to contribute an empirically grounded analysis to inform discussions of the reforms of local governance.

Putnam (1992)[2] argued that, even in a "modern" and "developed" country like Italy, the nature and type of social relationships were the most important determinant of the efficacy of the newly created regional governments. This bold reinsertion of personal and particularistic social relationships into discussions of the performance of public sector bureaucracies resonated powerfully with those battling the dominant approach to economic development. This approach, which relied primarily on a national civil service bureaucracy to deliver technically determined services that meet predetermined "needs" of the population (Pritchett and Woolcock 2002), has been labeled "bureaucratic high modernism" – the view of development as bringing activities under the control and order of the state (Scott 1998) – or "institutional monocropping" – the idea that institutional effectiveness is independent of local conditions (Evans 2003).[3] This backlash against "state centric" approaches has led to an enthusiasm in development circles for new approaches (using terms like "social capital" (Woolcock 1998; Narayan and Woolcock 2000); "beneficiary participation"; "empowerment"; "social funds"; "community development"; and "deliberative development") that aim to engage end-users in decision making.

But an overly simplistic generalization that more "social capital/participation/empowerment leads to better local governance" leaves at least three key questions unanswered. First, which *types* of social activities are beneficial? Second, for *whom* does governance improve? Third, can knowledge of social conditions actually facilitate deliberate action or design that would bring about improvements in government performance?

We examine the empirical link between households' social activities[4] and responses about four elements of the workings of village government: (i) *information* about government activities (two questions), (ii) *participation* in decision making (two questions), (iii) voice and expression of discontent (three questions), and (iv) government responsiveness to local problems (three questions). We make two key distinctions. First, we distinguish the *private* impact of social activities – whether households who are more socially active report higher-quality village government – from the *community* impact of social activities – whether households who live in communities where *other households* are more socially active report higher-quality village government. Second, we distinguish the impact of social activities (e.g. participation in public meetings) that are directly related to *village government structures* from that of other social activities (that are not explicitly related to *village* government). The "endogenous" social activities are further divided into three types: (i) socializing with friends or neighbors, (ii) participating in group activities within a network (usually organized around a specific event, such as harvest or prayer), and (iii) participating in social activities related to organizations (such as farmers' groups, formal religious groups, and credit unions that are distinguished by having a permanent leadership). Both of these distinctions prove empirically important – as the estimated associations of private and community and of social organizations and village government organizations with the proxies we use for governance are frequently not even of the same sign.

Generally the *private* impact[5] of participation in village government activities is positive – households that report more frequent participation in *village* government organizations also report increased access to information about government activities, greater participation in decision making, and higher assessed quality of government responsiveness. However, the *community* impact of such activities appears to be largely negative – households living in villages where *other* households report greater participation in the *village* organizations report, on average, reduced information, reduced participation, less voice and lower rate of government responsiveness. Surprisingly, the *net* impact of increased participation in *village* government organizations appears to be *negative* – so, for instance, even though the household that joins the *village government* organizations is more likely to be informed about the local budget, the "crowd out" effects on other households are sufficiently large that fewer people in the village know about the budget.

On the other hand, broadly speaking, participation in *social organizations* has both positive *private* and *community* impacts on governance. To illustrate, we show that for one of the "voice" indicators (whether a household was involved in a protest action about some village issue), households with higher engagement in social organizations were more likely to be involved in a protest. Even more interesting is that households who lived in villages in which *other* households reported higher engagement in social organizations also were more likely to be engaged in protest. The *net* effect of higher engagement in social activities is generally positive.

We are self-consciously avoiding, for now, the obvious, but loaded and imprecise, term "social capital" and are first just reporting on the empirical outcome of a survey. Households were asked certain specific questions (often with limited possible answers); their answers were recorded; and it is a factual question whether households who reported more engagement in endogenous organizational activities were also more likely to report that they knew about the village budget.[6] What one makes of those empirical facts and how they potentially relate to concepts and theories about the world is another question entirely. Hence the sequence of the chapter is as follows: Indonesian context, data, estimation, findings, and then theory, literature review, and implications all together at the end.

Indonesian context

Before describing the findings, it is necessary to explain certain aspects of the structure of Indonesian government. We only cover the barest basics that are crucial to understanding local governance in Indonesia and to interpreting the findings presented in this chapter. This section draws heavily on the qualitative and ethnographic studies done in connection with the Local Level Institutions (LLI) study. In particular, Evers (1999) is a rich and informative study on local governance in rural Indonesia in the immediate precrisis period.[7]

First, we need to replace the potentially misleading word "village" with the Indonesian term *desa*. A *desa* is fundamentally a *political and administrative* designation, rather than a geographic or social one. Although the term *desa* is often translated as "village," it needs to be understood as a structure imposed on local communities by the central government. A 1979 law designated the existing boundaries of the *desas* to create a complete, homogenous structure for local governance. The resulting geographical units of the *desa*, therefore, do not necessarily correspond to the definition of a "village" as a cluster of living units or to individuals' own perceptions of their basic social reality. Rather, especially in less densely populated areas, a *desa* may contain several widely dispersed clusters of household residences and primary social affiliations may be to these clusters rather than the *desa.*[8]

Second, the structures of *desa* government created in the 1979 law did not consolidate existing practice but rather *supplanted* the existing structures of local leadership. Indonesia, a large and diverse country, has a wide range of ethnic and social groups and a corresponding variety of indigenous forms of governance organizations. Traditional (*adat*) leaders or structures were not formally recognized in the new laws. The new law on local administration created hierarchical structures ranging from the *desa* head (*kepala desa*) and local executive council (LKMD) to a designated official for each group (RT) and subgroup (RW) of households.

Third, in the rhetoric of the 1979 law, the new *desa* organizations were a means of channeling a "bottom up" expression of the popular will, and the law created mechanisms whereby villagers could participate in the planning process and express their development needs. The general perception among villagers and those who worked in rural areas was that reality did not match the rhetoric: the *desa* organizations operated "top down." The *desa* apparatus were widely perceived as a means of co-opting and controlling all social forces at both the national and local levels and of delivering the programs and development priorities determined at the center.

During Soeharto's New Order era, the leadership of the provincial and district (*kabupaten*) governments was appointed by the Ministry of Home Affairs and was dominated by retired (and active duty) military officers. Even though there were local elections, the *desa* leaders had to be approved by and reported to this structure.[9] As the first LLI study showed, at the local level, often a very narrow group controls the *desa* government apparatus in a way that does not always reflect a broad community consensus (Evers 1999).

The resignation of Soeharto in May 1998 put in motion three linked but distinct changes. First, there were (generally) free and fair general elections for the national and regional legislatures. This altered the political landscape from top to bottom, shifting power away from Soeharto's Golkar Party toward now-President Megawati Soekarnoputri's PDI-P and a host of newly established political groupings that were allowed to organize in rural areas. Second, the legislature passed a set of laws that initiated substantial decentralization of government services from the center to districts (mostly by-passing provinces).[10] Third, as the center weakened, there was an expansion in local activity that addressed past and present grievances through both violent [e.g. riots, land seizures, stoning local government offices (and officers)] and more "democratic" means (a free press).

LLI study household data

We are going to estimate the relationship between social activities and the perceptions of *desa* government performance using multivariate regressions. To do that we need to specify (i) the construction of each of the four social variables, (ii) the empirical variables used to measure "governance," (iii) the way we propose to distinguish between private and community impacts of social activities, (iv) the nonsocial variables included in the regressions, and (v) the functional form.

The LLI study is a large, complex research endeavor carried out in 48 *desas* in three provinces (six districts), first in 1996 (LLI1) and again in 2000/2001 (LLI2). The study combined both qualitative and quantitative work on issues related to local governance, including documenting the array of social activities of households. The first round of the LLI study documented that, while little recognized by officialdom, local activities and spontaneous local organizations have flourished at the local level alongside the externally imposed *desa* structures (Chandrakirana 1999; Grootaert 1999). In addition, analysis of the household data from the first round found significant positive coefficient of a social capital index (formed as a function of number of household group activities and their characteristics) in a multivariate regression on per capita consumption (Grootaert 2000). This analysis also provided some evidence of contributions of social capital to reported collective action and evidence of differential effects of different types of groups (Grootaert 1999, 2000).

In the second round of the LLI study, a multimodule household questionnaire collected information from 1200 households (30 households in each of 40 *desas*).[11] The questionnaire included standard modules on (i) demographic information, (ii) the SUSENAS "short-form" consumption expenditures, (iii) household assets, (iv) household shocks and coping strategies. In addition, the survey collected information on two more unique aspects: household social activities and household participation in, and perceptions of, *desa* government.

Measures of social engagement

The survey elicited information on all household social activities – from pure sociability to membership in formal organizations. To capture "sociability," households were asked about the frequency with which they visited and were visited by other households. In addition, each household made a complete list of all its group activities in the past month and their purpose. For each group activity, the household was asked whether this activity was carried out by an organization with a fixed leadership. Group activities that did not involve an organization we call *network* activities, while all others were *organizational.* In addition, the respondent was asked about all groups that any member of the household belonged to, whether the member was "active" and the frequency of participation in those groups in the last three months and the purpose of the group (e.g. religions, production, social service) (Table 17.1).

Finally, the household was prompted about whether any member in the household participated in the activities of the *desa government* organizations. For present purposes, the key distinction is between activities in those organizations that were created as an integral component of *desa government* and all other *social organizations.*[12] Participation in (i) the *desa* legislative council (LMD), (ii) the executive council (LKMD), (iii) official neighborhood organizations (RT or RW), (iv) official women's organization (PKK or *Dasawisma*), or (v) official youth organization (*Karang Taruna*) was counted as engagement in a "*desa* government organization." Participation in all other organizations was classified as "endogenous" social organizations, even though some of these groups did have affiliation with the government (e.g. government-sponsored cooperatives). The distinction is not, therefore, between "government" and "non-government" organizations but between organizations that are *part of the structure of local government* and organizations with other purposes.

We differentiate the impact of the four types of social activities: sociability, network, and *desa* government organizations, and other social organizations (see Tables 17.1 and 17.2). However, within each, we simply add either activity or memberships – that is, there is no weighting within the categories to allow for different organizations to have a stronger or weaker impact in creating "social capital" or to have a stronger or weaker associ-

Table 17. 1 Classification scheme of the four types of social activities

Elements of the questionnaire	Designations of the different social activities		Examples
Visits to and from friends, neighbors, relatives	Sociability		Visits with friends, neighbors
Inventory of all group social activities involving members of the household	Network (activities in groups *without* fixed leadership)		
	Organizational (activities in groups *with* fixed leadership)	*Desa* Government	Community work (*gotong royong*) e.g. *desa* Legislative council (LKMD), *desa* women's group (PKK)
		Social Organizations	Religious organizations, youth groups, credit union, and so on

Table 17.2 Average engagement by any household member in four classes of social activities

District (kabupaten), province	Sociability (number visits)	Network activities (activities in the last month)	Social organizations (number of active memberships)	Desa government organizations (participation in the activities)
Sarko (Jambi)	9.70	4.33	0.387	1.80
Batanghari (Jambi)	10.00	4.35	0.804	1.65
Banyumas (C. Java)	8.81	8.16	0.859	2.17
Wonogiri (C. Java)	7.85	6.51	0.920	2.72
Ngada (NTT)	8.85	4.68	2.060	2.87

Source: Based on LLI2 data.

ation with governance.[13] The problem of how to properly aggregate the observed range of social activities pervades all work on "social capital" and is almost certainly intractable *in principle* (Hammer and Pritchett 2006).

Ten empirical proxies for four dimensions of local governance

The LLI2 instrument also elicited household responses about *desa* government.[14] We used ten specific questions about four dimensions of governance: *information, participation, voice,* and *perceived responsiveness* to local problems.

Information

Households were asked whether they knew about three types of information associated with *desa* government: (i) the development programs operating in the *desa*, (ii) the use of *desa* funds, and (iii) funds available for development projects. If the household knew about "all three," we count them as informed. On average, information was widespread, with between 45 and 50 percent of households having heard about any one of *desa* budgets, use of funds, or development projects and 35 percent having heard of all three (Table 17.3). In addition, all households were asked whether information about these *desa* government activities was "more open" than four years ago. Perhaps surprisingly given the political changes, only 20 percent thought information about all three was "more open" than four years ago.

Participation

Participation in *desa* decision making was assessed by asking households if they participated in planning *desa* programs or if they participated in determining sanctions for abuses by *desa* leaders. In both instances, there

Table 17.3 Percent of households informed about various aspects of *desa* budgets and activity, by region

Region (kabupaten)	Percent of households informed about				All three more open than four years ago
	Use of desa funds	Funds for development projects	Government programs available	All three	
Sarko	52.9	48.3	48.3	35.8	20.8
Batanghari	40.4	47.5	44.1	32.5	19.6
Banyumas	45.8	57.4	69.0	39.6	20.6
Wonogiri	36.4	48.5	52.7	20.9	11.7
Ngada	50.5	41.6	41.3	41.0	26.3
Sample Average	45.2	48.7	51.1	34.0	19.8

Source: LLI2 data.

Note
Average is unweighted.

were three possible responses: no participation, participation by giving opinion before decision was made, and participation in making the decision. About 63 percent reported no participation in *desa* planning, with 20 percent providing an opinion and 17 percent reporting that they participated in the decision making. The process of determining sanctions was more closed, with 80 percent reporting no participation and only 7.4 percent reporting having participated in the decision (Table 17.4).

Voice

To investigate the expression of "voice" in response to problems with *desa* government, households were asked whether dissatisfaction was expressed with the *desa* leadership in the previous year. In 381 cases, households reported that there was expression of discontent with the *desa* leadership. Households that reported an expression of discontent were probed about the outcome: most households reported that there was "not yet" a solution; a third reported a complete or partial solution; and in 4 percent of the cases there was a solution, but then the problem had reemerged (Table 17.5).

If there was no open expression of disapproval, respondents were queried about why not. For the 818 households that said there was no dissatisfaction expressed with *desa* leadership, two very different reasons emerged for the lack of expression of discontent. Roughly three-quarters said that the reason for no expression of discontent was that there was "no problem" (see Table 17.6). In the remaining cases, respondents thought there was a problem but reported a variety of reasons why, in spite of the problem, there was no expression of dissatisfaction: that people were afraid to express their dissatisfaction, that expression of dissatisfaction would not result in a change, or that it was difficult to organize.

From these responses we created three indicators of "voice." One, which we call "protest," is whether anyone in the household was involved in "openly expressing dissatisfaction."[15] The second variable is a dichotomous indicator of lack of effective voice: whether a household reports *no expression* of discontent in spite of a problem with the *desa* leadership.

The third "voice" variable combines the information about problems, expression of discontent, and outcomes to approximate effectiveness. For only those households that report a problem we define a variable with three categories: no expression (category A), expression but no solution (category B), and expression with solution (category C). As these are categories, rather than cardinal numbers, we use ordered probit for this third variable.

Government responsiveness

Households were also asked about a variety of problems facing their *desa* (households were prompted about two "economic" problems, four "social"

Table 17.4 Participation in *desa* decision making

District (kabupaten)	Participation in *desa planning* (%)			Participation in *determining sanctions on desa leaders* (%)		
	None	Provided input	Decision making	None	Provided input	Decision making
Sarko	55.8	29.2	15.0	72.5	18.8	8.8
Batanghari	66.7	24.2	9.2	80.0	16.3	3.8
Banyumas	74.0	19.0	7.0	90.9	7.4	1.7
Wonogiri	79.5	9.6	10.9	94.1	2.9	2.9
Ngada	37.7	20.9	41.4	69.5	10.9	19.7
Sample average	62.7	20.6	16.7	81.4	11.3	7.4

Source: LLI2 data.

Note
Average is unweighted.

Table 17.5 Reported outcomes for households who report there was an expression of dissatisfaction in their *desa*

	Frequency	*Percent*
No solution	222	58.3
Completely successful	84	22.1
Some success	43	11.3
Temporarily successful	16	4.2
Not recorded	16	4.2

Table 17.6 Reasons given by those who report no expression of dissatisfaction with the *desa* leadership

	Frequency	*Percent*
No problem	595	72.9
Was a problem, but afraid to express discontent	120	14.7
Was a problem, but protest would be ineffective	62	7.6
Was a problem, but difficult to organize	17	2.1
Do not know	20	2.4
Other	5	0.5

problems, and four "environmental" problems). If the respondent thought there was a problem, they were asked who, if anyone, had attempted to address those problems, and one of the options was the *desa* government. The frequency with which the government is seen responding to existing problems is a crude indicator of its responsiveness to citizen concerns (see Table 17.7). Using these data in combination with information on household and community participation in different types of organizations, we can analyze variations in *desa* government involvement in addressing community problems.

The dependent variables in the regressions will be these ten governance indicators that are measures or proxies for the four concepts: information (two indicators), participation (two indicators), voice (three indicators), and government responsiveness (three indicators).

Distinguishing private, community, and net impact

In order to distinguish between the *private* consequences of engagement in activities (i.e. those benefits that accrue to the household) and the *community* consequences of such involvement (i.e. the impacts on *other* households), we use the fact that the sampling is by *desa*. We can therefore calculate for each household its own activity and the social activity of all *other* households in the *desa*.

Consider as an example membership in social organizations, for the *i*th household in the *j*th *desa*. We can calculate the number of memberships

Table 17.7 Fraction reporting various types of problems, and for those who report problems, the fraction reporting engagement of *desa* government (*pemerintah desa*) in addressing the problem

Region (kabupaten)	Economic (%)		Social (%)		Environmental (%)	
	Fraction reporting	Desa government responds	Fraction reporting	Desa government responds	Fraction reporting	Desa government responds
Sarko	67.9	7.9	5.8	50.0	50.4	27.2
Batanghari	62.5	3.3	50.0	36.6	55.4	49.6
Banyumas	35.5	16.2	37.2	45.5	59.1	44.0
Wonogiri	19.7	8.5	11.7	21.4	52.3	45.6
Ngada	70.3	29.7	29.3	48.5	94.1	74.6
Average	51.2	13.1	26.8	40.4	62.3	48.2

of the household: O^i, social organization memberships of the ith household.

The average level of social organization membership in the jth *desa* excluding that of the ith household is:

$$O^{-i,j} = \sum_{k=1, k \neq i}^{N^j} O^k / (N^j - 1)$$

Suppose there were a linear, causal relationship between whether household reports it being informed about the *desa* budget and the household's organizational activities and the organizational activities of all* other households in the *desa* (and other variables in the matrix **Z**):[16]

$$Informed_{i,j}[= 1 \ if \ yes] = \alpha + \beta_p * O^i + \beta_s * O^{-i,j} + \Theta Z_{i,j}$$

The *private* impact of the ith household joining one additional social organization on the likelihood that household is informed is β_p.

The impact of ith household joining one additional social organization on all other households in the *desa* is to raise the "*desa* less household" average by $1/N_j$ for each household. The *community* impact of the ith household's increased organizational activity is then β_s/N_j on *each* other household in the *desa*. This could either be zero, if there is no social interaction at all; positive, if the ith household shares information with others; or negative, if the ith household gaining information tends to exclude other households and hence reduces the likelihood that they are informed.

The total number of people in the *desa* informed about the budget is just the sum of the individuals:

$$Informed \ in \ desa_j = \sum_i Informed_{i,j}$$

If we are interested in the net impact on the *total* number of households in the village who are informed, this is the private impact plus the sum of individual impacts:

$$\frac{d(Informed \ in \ desa_j)}{dO^i} = \frac{dInformed_{i,j}}{dO^i} + \sum_{k \neq i} \frac{dInformed_{k,j}}{dO^i}$$

The sum of N_j-1 across those impacts of magnitude β_s/N_j is just $\beta_s * \left(\frac{N_j-1}{N_j} \right)$.

$$\frac{d(Informed \ in \ desa_j)}{dO^i} = \beta_p + \beta_s * \left(\frac{N_j-1}{N_j} \right)$$

The net impact on the number of people in the *desa* informed about the budget associated with the ith household's increased organizational membership is just the sum of the private and community impacts.[17]

The reasons for distinguishing the private, community, and net impacts of social activities will be discussed further in the section on implications, but for now let us just illustrate some of the possible outcomes.

Table 17.8 assumes a positive relationship between organizational engagement and perceptions of *desa* government organizations. We are assuming that households that are more active in social activities are better informed and also participate more in formal decision making. While it would be unusual if participation in the *desa* government organizations had no association with household perceptions of governance, it is possible that engagement in non-*desa* government organizations is unrelated to governance. It is also possible that active engagement in social organizations precludes household participation in *desa* government groups, if these two types of organizations have overlapping and competing functions.

Even assuming there are positive associations between both *desa* government and other social activities and the households' perceptions of local governance, there is the question of whether there are any effects of these social activities on *other* households. There are four plausible conjectures, each of which would lead to a different pattern of results.

1   *No externalities.* A household's perception of "voice" in the *desa* could depend on its characteristics and social activity only and not be affected by other *desa* members' social activity. The community impacts are empirically small, and the net effect is determined by the direction of the private effects.

2   *Zero sum.* Perhaps there is a fixed number of people who participate in decision making or who are informed about activities or who feel there is "voice" and hence improvements for one household within a *desa* come at the expense of another. Or, it could be that as the participation of other households rises, other households' participation falls as the "free ride" on the activities of others. Then, if the private effect is positive, the community effect would be negative of the same magnitude and the net effect zero.

3   *Positive externalities ("crowd in").* It could be that increased information acquired by one household is more likely to be transmitted to another household when the social organizational activity in the *desa* is high. Or perhaps it is easier to organize villagers to act jointly to express discontent with *desa* government performance when there are more social connections among them. In this case, the community effect would be positive and the net effect would be larger than either the private or the community effect along.

4   *Exclusion (more than one for one "crowd out").* It is also possible that members actively exclude nonmembers and as the number of people involved in an organization gets larger, their ability to exclude others becomes stronger. In this case, nonmembers would feel that they have

Table 17.8 Possible patterns of empirical relationships between organizational activity and perceptions of governance

	Desa government organization			Social organizations		
	Private	Community	Net	Private	Community	Net
Private effects on governance only for *desa* government groups; no social linkages	+	0	+	0/–	0	0
Positive private effects of desa and social organizations and …						
No social linkages (zero linkages or externalities of social activities)	+	0	+ (equal to private)	+	0	+ (equal to private)
Zero sum (positive private, negative offsetting community effects)	+	–	0 (private and community offset)	+	–	0 (private and community offset)
"Crowd-in" (positive either) externalities of social activities	+	+	++ (larger than either)	+	+	++ (larger than either)
"Crowd out" (sign (negative externalities of magnitudes) social activities)	+	–	+/0/– (sign depends on magnitudes)	+	–	+/0/– (sign depends on magnitudes)

less information, voice, or participation in decision making as more other people become members.[18] It is possible that the strength of the exclusion effect is stronger than the positive private effect so that the net effect is negative.

Control variables

To estimate the partial associations we control for other variables that may influence household reports of *desa* level governance. For instance, more educated households may both be more likely to be involved in organizational activity and may be better informed about government budgets. The household demographic and economic characteristics included in each multivariate regression are (i) household consumption expenditures (as a proxy for household income), (ii) education of the head of the household, (iii) age of the household head, (iv) whether the head of the household is a government worker, (v) whether the household head works in agriculture, (vi) whether the household is headed by a female, and (vii) size of the household.

We also include a categorical variable for each of the five districts. These are frequently important as there are substantial differences across the regions. Ngada in NTT Province, which is a predominantly Christian province (primarily Catholic), has a markedly different pattern of organizational activity. (In Table 17.2, Ngada has more than twice the level of "social organization" activity of any other region.) Controlling for this difference in levels implies that the effects are estimated only using the differences across households and *desa* within a district.

Functional form

All of the governance indicators except one are binary variables (yes/no), and a probit estimator is used. The marginal effects – the increase in a household's probability of answering "yes" (e.g. "are informed," "did participate") associated with a unit increase in the independent variable – are reported, along with the *p*-levels of the test for the index function coefficient being zero. Our indicator of "effective voice" is a categorical variable with three levels, and hence ordered probit is used. In that case the marginal effect of moving from the second to the highest category is reported, along with the *p*-levels of the hypothesis tests of zero for the index function coefficients. (If the preceding two sentences were not obvious, Annex 1 is a brief discussion of probit and ordered probit estimates and results.[19])

Findings

The raw findings of the regressions are reported in Annex 2. We discuss the findings in three sections, each of which examines the relationships of the governance proxies across the range of independent variables: first, the "control" variables, *sociability* and social *networks*; second, the results for participation in the *desa* government organizations; and finally, the results for social *organizations*.

Household characteristics, sociability, and social networks

Household characteristics

The household characteristics included in the regressions generally emerged with the "expected" signs. Households with higher schooling (significant and positive in five of ten regressions), households with a government worker (positive and significant in five of ten regressions), and household with higher expenditures per person (positive and significant only two of ten) reported higher levels of the governance proxies. Agricultural households had mixed results (e.g. more likely to report government responded to environmental problems but less likely to report the government responded to social problems).

Consistent with qualitative evidence about the tendency of existing mechanisms to excluded women (DFID 2000), female-headed households reported statistically significantly less participation (on both proxies), less voice (on two of three proxies), and less responsiveness of government to economic problems. Older households seem to fare somewhat better than female-headed ones. The older the head of the household, the less likely the household is to report engagement in protest; however, the household is also more likely to report effective voice (perhaps precluding the need for protest).

Regional controls

There were some patterns across the districts. Households in Ngada were more likely to report government responsiveness (two of three proxies) and more voice (two of three proxies). Wonogiri respondents report less information (one of two proxies), less participation (on both proxies), and less responsiveness to social problems. For present purposes these cross district differences are a "control" and we leave the interpretation of these cross district differences to the qualitative work as part of the larger LLI investigation.

Sociability

For the number of visits each household made or received, we did not attempt to distinguish between private and community effects and record private impacts only. We find that in nine of the ten cases, greater sociability was associated with higher levels of the governance proxies – but the magnitude and significance of the effects were quite weak (statistically significant only twice), and the marginal effects were empirically small.

Social networks

The estimated private and community impacts of network activities were quite small. Interestingly, the only case in which participation in social networks is statistically significant for both the private and the community variables is for *desa* government response to social problems. Households with greater network activities reported a greater degree of government response, and those households living in villages with more activity also reported greater *desa* government responsiveness (this is of course controlling for their own level of social network activity). In villages with more vibrant network activities, such as collective harvesting and other *gotong royong* activities, the government may rely on these networks to mobilize villagers in response to problems.

Desa government organizations

Private impacts

The single strongest result to emerge from the regressions is that the household who report higher levels of activity in the *desa* government organizations also report that their household is better informed, more likely to participate, more likely to report effective voice in the *desa* (though the household is less likely to report having engaged in protest), and, for two of the three indicators, more likely to report the government is responsive to local problems. This aspect of the empirical results is more a relief than an inspiration – after all, the *objective* of the *desa* organizations is to provide information and participation in local decisions. It should come as no great surprise that those that participate report they are more likely to be informed about *desa* government activities and participate in decisions. It is reassuring that the data say what we would have expected to be true: crudely put, people who go to meetings about budgets are more likely to know about budgets.

Community impacts

The most striking and original result to emerge from this empirical exercise is that the *community* impact of *desa* government organizations appears to be *negative*. That is, after statistically controlling for both household characteristics (e.g. education, gender of the head) and the household's social activities (including the household's own participation in *desa* government activities), living in a *desa* in which *other* households are more engaged in the *desa* government activities is associated with a household reporting *less* information (both level and change), *less* participation in decision making, *less* voice, and *less* government responsiveness to economic and social problems. While only six of the nine coefficients that support this interpretation are statistically significant at the conventional levels, we regard this as an overwhelming preponderance of the evidence (Table 17.9).[20]

Net impact

With positive private and negative community effects, the net impact of greater involvement by an additional household could go either way. What is truly striking about the empirical results is that, for eight of the ten indicators, the *net* impact is negative.[21] For example, the estimates for information awareness suggest that households who are members of one additional *desa* government organization are 4.1 percent more likely to report knowing all three types of information (and are also more likely to report improvements in transparency). But the community impact is negative, and even larger – where *desa* (less the household) average membership is higher, *each* household is 8.5 percent *less likely* to be aware of local government information. This suggests that one household increasing its participation in the *desa* government organizations (which, at least in rhetoric, were created to channel information) *reduces* the number of households who know about the budget by 4.4 percentage points (13.5 percent). Even though the joining household is much more likely to be aware of the budget, its neighbors are each sufficiently *less* likely to know about the budget that the total number informed is estimated to go down as engagement in *desa* government organizations increases.

Although we do not estimate their precision, the magnitude of the net effects are substantial: increasing average membership in the organizations by one unit reduces the probability of a household being involved in a protest by 42 percent, the likelihood of "effective voice" by 39 percent, and the likelihood of reporting responsiveness to economic problems by 93 percent. What is surprising is that the effect of the *desa* government organizations seems to go beyond a "zero sum" result in which positive private and negative community cancel out. If interpreted causally, these estimates of the net impact suggest the seemingly paradoxical conclusion that an individual joining a *desa* government organization *reduces* the number of people who are informed. Rather than being modes of disseminating information broadly, the *desa* government organizations appear to have disseminated information down the "chain of command" but *not* outside of that chain. Access to *desa* government information and decision-making mechanisms appear to have been closely guarded, with nonmembers increasingly excluded from these resources.

Figure 17.1 summarizes the results from Table 17.1 on the private, social, and total associations (measured as the marginal effects) of *desa*

Table 17.9 Membership in *desa* government organizations and ten proxies for governance

	Predicted probability	Private (household)		Community (village-less household)		Net (sum of the two)	
		Marginal effects (p-level)	Percentage change	Marginal effects (p-level)	Percentage change	Sum of marginal effects	Percentage change
Household informed about three types	0.327	**0.041 (0.001)**	**12.5**	**−0.085 (0.009)**	**−26.0**	*−0.044*	*−13.5*
Household reports all three "more open"	0.186	**0.029 (0.005)**	**15.6**	*−0.036 (0.176)*	*−19.4*	*−0.007*	*−3.8*
Some participation in planning *desa* programs	0.344	**0.067 (0.000)**	**19.5**	**−0.066 (0.058)**	**−19.2**	*0.001*	*0.3*
Some participation in determining sanctions	0.138	**0.031 (0.001)**	**22.7**	*−0.039 (0.103)*	*−28.3*	*−0.008*	*−5.6*
Household involved in protest	0.089	*0.0074 (0.303)*	*8.3*	**−0.045 (0.021)**	**−50.6**	*−0.0376*	*−42.2*
No expression despite problem (positive is less voice)	0.174	**−0.026 (0.013)**	**−14.9**	**0.094 (0.000)**	**54.0**	*0.068*	*39.1*
Most effective expression (problem, voice, solution)	0.236	**0.0427 (0.000)**	**18.1**	*−0.047 (0.124)*	*−19.9*	*−0.0043*	*−1.8*
Economic problems	0.076	*0.013 (.145)*	*16.6*	**−0.083 (0.001)**	**−109.5**	*−0.071*	*−92.9*
Social problems	0.389	*−0.013 (.639)*	*−3.4*	*−0.040 (.623)*	*−10.3*	*−0.053*	*−13.7*
Environmental problems	0.523	*0.028 (.10)*	*5.4*	**134 (0.004)**	**25.7**	**0.163**	**31.1**

Notes

Italicized items are consistent with the hypothesis of positive private effects of *desa* government and either zero sum or "crowd out" community effects. Emboldened items are based on probit coefficients statistically significant at a *p*-level of 10 percent level or lower. See Appendix 2 for a description of the reporting of the probit results.

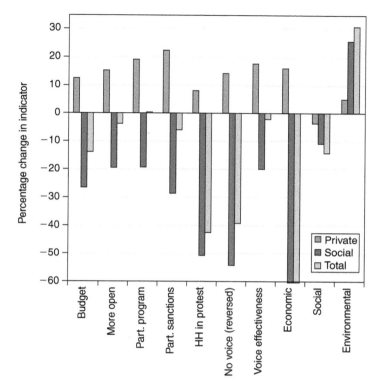

Figure 17.1 Probit regression "marginal effects" of *desa* organizational activity on governance indicators: private, community, total.

governance organization participation and governance indicators. As can be seen, the private effects are consistently positive (nine of ten cases), the community impacts are consistently negative (nine of ten cases), and the sum of the two is consistently negative or essentially zero (nine of ten cases).

Social organizations

The evidence for the impact of social organizations is suggestive but, frankly, damned elusive.

Private impacts

There is evidence of positive impact of social organizations, although it is weaker than for *desa* organizations. For seven of the ten indicators, there is a positive association so that households that participate more in social organizations are more likely to be informed (both indicators), participate in village decisions (both indicators), be involved in a protest, and report the government is responsive to economic and social problems (see Appendix 2). However, only four of the seven estimated effects are statistically significant at conventional levels (and in many cases are *far* from significant). But even though there is no formal connection between social organizations and *desa* government affairs, there is evidence that more engagement generally is associated with more knowledge and participation in *desa* decision making.

Community impact

The evidence for a *positive* private spillover effect of participation in social organizations is decidedly mixed. For half of the indicators, the sign of the coefficient indicates a positive impact. While higher social organization membership of *others in the village* is associated with more expression of voice (the sign is negative because the variable is *not* expressing discontent), it is also associated with *less* participation in determining sanctions. The coefficients are generally empirically small; while a one-unit increase in social organizations is associated with being 30 percent more likely to be involved in a protest and 32 percent less likely to report "no voice," for most of the other variables the impact is much smaller (e.g. less than 10 percent more likely to report "more open") (Table 17.10).

Net impact

Looking across the ten indicators, the *net* effect of social organizations stands in sharp contrast to that of the *desa* government groups. The sum of the private and community impacts indicates that increased activity in social organizations is usually associated with improved governance outcomes. However, for some of the indicators (such as participation in determining sanctions), a negative community impact outweighs the positive private effect. In spite of the mixed results (in terms of both statistical significance and direction of signs), it is worth noting the generally beneficial effects of higher engagement in social organizations. Although they were created for different purposes (e.g.,economic, social, religious), these groups produce better governance outcomes than *desa* government organizations, which were explicitly created to channel information and allow for participation in decision making.

Figure 17.2 summarizes the results. The private effects are generally positive or very small. The community impacts vary widely both in sign and in magnitude. The net effect is "substantially" positive (greater than a 10 percent increase in the indicator) in five cases (more open budgets, more participation in programs, household engagement in protest, expression of voice, and responsiveness to economic problems) and only in one (participation in sanctions) is the association substantially negative.

Table 17.10 Membership in social organizations and ten proxies for governance

	Predicted probability	Private (household)		Community (village-less household)		Net (sum of the two)	
		Marginal effects (p-level)	Percentage change	Marginal effects (p-level)	Percentage change	Sum of marginal effects	Percentage change
Household informed about three types	0.327	−0.0099 (0.495)	5.3	−0.015 (0.651)	−8.1	−0.005	−1.6
Household reports all three "more open"	0.185	**−0.021 (0.071)**	**11.4**	−0.012 (0.663)	−6.5	−0.033	−17.8
Some participation in planning *desa* programs	0.344	**−0.050 (0.001)**	**14.4**	−0.008 (0.832)	−2.2	−0.04	−12.2
Some participation in determining sanctions	0.138	**−0.026 (0.011)**	**18.6**	**−0.042 (0.088)**	**−30.1**	−0.016	−11.5
Household involved in protest	0.089	−0.012 (0.104)	13.5	−0.028 (0.127)	−31.5	−0.04	−44.9
No expression in spite of problem (positive is less voice)	0.174	−0.0054 (0.643)	3.1	**−0.056 (0.037)**	**−32.2**	−0.0506	−29.1
Most effective expression (problem, voice, solution)	0.236	−0.003 (0.763)	−1.3	−0.0143 (0.629)	−6.1	−0.011	−4.8
Economic problems	0.076	−0.012 (0.172)	15.1	−0.011 (0.172)	−15.8	−0.024	−30.9
Social problems	0.389	**−0.047 0.064**	**12.1**	−0.057 (0.453)	−14.7	−0.010	−2.6
Environmental problems	0.523	−0.006 (0.753)	−1.1	−0.034 (0.456)	−6.5	−0.040	−7.6

Notes
Italicized items are consistent with the hypothesis of positive private effects of social organizations and positive community effects; items in boldface are statistically significant at the 10 percent level. Emboldened items are based on probit coefficients statistically significant at a *p*-level of 10 percent level or lower. See Appendix 2 for a description of the reporting of the probit results.

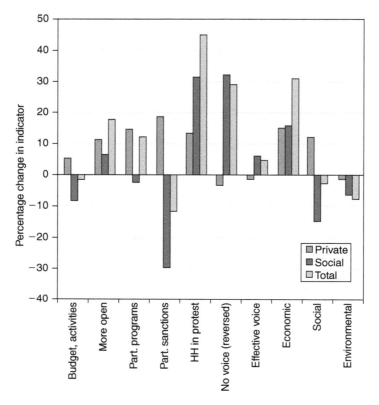

Figure 17.2 Probit regression "marginal effects" of social organization activity on governance indicators: private, community, total.

Regressions on desa aggregates

If we perform the same regressions as *desa* averages, we roughly reconfirm the results on page 335 but also demonstrate the potential losses from focusing exclusively on *desa* aggregated data, even in examining community impacts. Table 17.11 shows OLS regressions of *desa* averages of the three reported voice variables on *desa* averages of the social activity and control variables.[22] In each case, the sign of average social organizational membership is associated with higher expressions of voice. In contrast, average participation in the *desa* government organizations is associated with *less* voice. The magnitudes are roughly comparable with the sum of the two effects reported in Tables 17.9 and 17.10 (see "Total HH" column in Table 17.11) – *desa* government organizations are associated with 51 percent less protest in the averages, while the household data suggest a 42 percent decrease. No expression of discontent in spite of problems is 28 percent more likely when estimated with the averages, 39 percent more

Table 17.11 Regression results of voice variables on *desa* averages (OLS estimation)

	Protest activity			Exists a problem but no expression (positive sign is less voice)			Effective voice		
	Coefficient (p-level)	Percent change, one unit		Coefficient (p-level)	Percent change, one unit		Coefficient (p-level)	Percent change, one unit	
		Aggregate	Total household		Aggregate	Total household		Aggregate	Total household
Sociability	0.003 (0.813)	2.5	–	–0.027 (0.164)	–14.6	–	0.0039 (0.924)	0.4%	–
Network activity	0.015 (0.434)	12.4	–	0.0024 (0.941)	1.3	–	0.026 (0.685)	2.9	–
Desa government organizations	–0.062 (0.081)*	–51.2	–42.2	0.053 (0.350)	28.6	39.1	–0.162 (0.150)	–18.1	–1.8
Social organizations	0.022 (0.642)	18.2	44.9	–0.029 (0.704)	–15.7	–29.1	0.094 (0.524)	10.5	4.8
Control variables	None significant		–	F+, A–		–	Y–, F–		–
Regions	Ngada+			Included, none significant			Included, none significant		
N	42		–	42		–	41		–
R^2 (adjusted R^2)	0.612 (0.388)		–	0.452 (0.135)		–	0.569 (0.311)		–

Source: LLI2 data.

likely from the household data. While the household data suggest only a modest decline in the probability of being in the most effective voice category, the aggregates suggest an 18 percent reduction in "effective voice" (although aggregating to *desa* averages requires treating the categories as cardinal).

There are two large advantages of using the household data over the *desa* averages. First, without the household-level data, one cannot see that the *desa* aggregate impact is a combination of private and community effects. For the *desa* government organizations, a strong positive private effect is generally offset by a more than compensating negative community impact. Second, when using *desa* averages, none of the estimates are strongly statistically significant, almost certainly the combination of attenuation from the reduced signal in aggregated data with the much smaller number of observations.

Interpretation and implications: literatures, theory

The *desa* government organizations imposed by the Indonesian central government, which were ostensibly designed as channels of "participation" to improve local governance, are apparently less effective than social organizations at producing desirable governance outcomes – in fact greater participation appears to *worsen* aggregate outcomes. Less rigidly structured groups (even if sponsored by government) and those that are locally initiated are better able to facilitate broad participation, information sharing, responsiveness, and accountability measures than the "uniform blueprint" groups introduced in the creation of the official *desa* structure.

These findings are *consistent with* an interpretation, based on the LLI fieldwork, that the *desa* government organizations are used as a mechanism of social control. More participation in these groups allows for more effective control of decision making and does not represent a broadening of information, voice, and participation beyond those directly involved. However, the data are *not compelling* for this interpretation as we have no way of technically pinning down the direction of causation responsible for the observed empirical associations.[23]

These empirical findings raise three important issues that relate both specifically to Indonesia and more generally to literatures on social capital, decentralization and local governance, and project design.

In the Indonesian context, there are both issues of project design and of the reform of governance structures. There is a growing, empirically founded consensus that projects that provide local services are more effective when they incorporate the intended beneficiaries in the project.[24] But details matter: how "participation" is structured and through what intermediary organizations makes a difference. Isham and Kähkönen (1999) compared project success in water supply between two types of projects carried out in the same region of Indonesia: the Village Infrastructure Project (VIP) gave the *desa* legislative council (LKMD) final choice of design, while the Water Supply and Sanitation in Low Income Communities (WSSLIC) project facilitated participation through water user associations. Although the WSSLIC user groups may have been predicted as more participatory, the final say for these projects rested with the village head, and in some cases, the village choice was overridden by project staff in the interests of budget and timetable concerns. Even though both projects were intended to be "participatory," the VIP projects in which villagers had greater say operated substantially better, had higher citizen satisfaction (38 percent were "very satisfied" with VIP versus 24 percent in WSSLIC), and had a greater impact on health (54 percent reported improved health in VIP versus 33 percent in WSSLIC).

Qualitative results for the second LLI study indicate that project designs in the research area have grown increasingly participatory. Before 1998, villagers reported only 12 percent of projects giving them a direct say in project-planning decisions. After 1998, they were given the opportunity to participate directly in planning in 22 percent of government projects. There has also been a simultaneous shift in satisfaction with project outcomes (37 percent satisfied or somewhat satisfied with pre-1998 projects versus 50 percent for post-1998 projects) (Wetterberg 2002).

In Indonesia it is recognized that for decentralization to lead to better governance, the preexisting *desa* institutions will have to undergo major changes. Indonesia has embarked on a radical decentralization of power and responsibility to its regions (districts). The success of this decentralization will to a large extent depend on the extent to which changes from top down (creating democratically elected district legislative councils) and bottom up (creating effective *desa* structures) can be integrated.

The qualitative data from LLI2 show that while some modifications to *desa* structures are underway, the direction of change is not yet clear. The main innovation introduced by the decentralization at the village level is an elected council (*Badan Perwakilan Desa* or BPD) that is intended to provide a countervailing force to the often-unchecked power of the village head. Although a small number of villages have seen accountability efforts pioneered by the BPD, most villagers report that the councils' performance has been disappointing and indistinguishable from that of existing *desa* government structures.

These issues in Indonesia reflect more general issues in the literatures on social capital, decentralization, and project design. First, the benefits of decentralization are contingent on being able to structure responsive mechanisms at the local level. As Platteau (2004), Bardhan and Mookerjee (2000) and many others have pointed out, local politics are as much subject to "capture" by elites as those at the national level.[25]

Second, these results reinforce the point that it is the *nature* of social organizations and associational life, not their sheer number or density, that matters. Studies of social capital are often based on the assumption that more ties (or more ties with given characteristics) are inherently better. While denser social organizations of the type that creates relationships of trust among citizens might facilitate collective action and greater efficacy of government,[26] many political outcomes are a zero-sum contest. In these cases, more social organizations can influence the outcome in favor of (or against) a particular group but cannot make everyone better off.[27] Caste associations in India often organize precisely to protect their interests within the village and locality. Wade's (1988) brilliant study of collective action and irrigation in South India showed how villages with superior organizational abilities were able to be more effective in bribing the government officials to allocate them more water than less-well-organized neighboring villages. The present results, showing that different kinds of groups have opposite spillover impacts, reinforce the making of sharp distinctions between types of organizations in their effect on governance outcomes.

Third, these results also raise the difficulty of *using* knowledge about the *existing* empirical associations between social activities and governance to *engineer* improvements in local governance through deliberate institutional innovations or policy action. That is, it might seem that the obvious implications of our empirical results are two-fold: (i) to make local decentralization effective, reforms need to reduce the powers of (or eliminate) existing *desa* organizations and delegate greater powers to, or at least incorporate more in decision making, the social organizations that have positive effects and (ii) to make project implementation more 'participatory' by creating project-specific mechanisms for local input and control. However, while these reactions are on the right track, there are two problems that must be faced. First, well-meaning efforts to create "beneficiary participation" or "user management" in projects must cope with the fact that these new local organizations and institutions do not arise on a blank slate but on top of an already complex pattern of local social organization and activity. Second, discussions about changes in the decision-making scope of local organizations need to be embedded in a coherent theory of the social behavior of individuals as people and organizations will change as conditions change. That is, attempts to exploit the existing beneficial nature of social organizations may well create pressures for the organizations to change their character – if organizations that have beneficial spillover effects are charged with high-stakes decision-making tasks, then the purposive behavior of individuals with respect to the organizations should be expected to change.

Spontaneous social action frequently arises to address problems of collective action – often in face of government failure and "below the radar" of official notice. For instance, Ostrom (1990) has shown that the "tragedy of the commons" is not inevitable. In the right social conditions, collective action can reach stable and sustainable solutions to the problem of "common pool" resources, such as fisheries, water allocations, and irrigation.[28] In Indonesia, the practice of *gotong royong* – common labor to address local problems – long antedates the New Order.

But these type of spontaneous, endogenous solutions are the product of existing physical and economic conditions (e.g. the geographic extent of the "common" pool, the distribution of benefits among users) and social forces. As Fox (1996) illustrates for the case of Mexico, specific constellations of externally imposed government groups and other social organizations have all played roles in shaping current capacities for collective action and particular governance outcomes. Shifts in function in one part of current arrangements are likely to cause both intended and unexpected consequences throughout the system. Attempts to deliberately *create* new local decision-making organizations as an integral part of service delivery have met with both successes and failures. There is a great deal of evidence that changing the delivery of localized services from a "top down technocratic" matter for civil servants to incorporating more feedback from citizens is, in general, associated with more successful outcomes. However, attempts to create "project participation" have also met with – or created – disasters. Uphoff's (1992) account of the *Gal Oya* irrigation project in Sri Lanka details the ways in which things can go wrong – and, later, right. Creating new institutions with decision-making power will inevitably conflict with existing arrangements.

In proposing specific institutional reforms in the structure of local government organizations or project designs (e.g. decision making on investment projects), both the private and social impacts of social capital need to be considered (Bourdieu 1986; Coleman 1990). That is, there is a branch of the social capital literature that emphasizes the *private* benefits to the individual/household of their social connections in obtaining jobs and credit, in marketing arrangements and smoothing income shocks, and even in obtaining benefits from the government (Singermann 1995). In this literature, the individuals act *purposively* to create and maintain social connections because of the benefits the connections provide.[29] The other branch of the social capital literature emphasizes the *social* benefits of social capital and those activities undertaken by individuals perhaps *exclusively* because of the benefits of the activity itself have positive impacts on people besides themselves.[30]

The reason these two have to be considered simultaneously is that changes in the scope of potential benefits of engaging in social activities will change people's behavior in ways that may change the consequences. Take a crude and entirely hypothetical example. Suppose that the data said that information spillovers from *desa* (LKMD) meeting were negative and from mosque attendance were positive. Then one might conclude that if the legally required discussion of the *desa* budget were moved from the LKMD to the mosque (suppose immediately following the weekly service), then this would have enormous spillover effects. But this would not take into account that the people who show up at the LKMD meeting do so (among other reasons) *in order* to learn about the budget – and perhaps because they have a personal interest in budget information. If the budget discussion is moved to the mosque, this changes the incentives of people to attend the mosque – perhaps in ways that reduces the beneficial spillover effects observed from mosque attendance in the existing model.

Conclusion

The social realities of rural Indonesia are complex and rapidly changing. The increasing democratization at the national level and the ongoing decentralization will bring about rapid changes in the power dynamics at the local level. The present empirical result is just one small piece of the critically important puzzle of how to create open, effective, and accountable local governance. This work extends the earlier empirical work demonstrating the "top down" realities of the *desa* administrative structure (Evers 1999) and the vibrancy of local institutions even before the political changes (Chandrakirana 1999). On a broader level, this empirical work extends the literature on "social capital" by demonstrating conclusively that not all local organizations are created equal. Depending on who is doing the organizing, and why, increased participation in local organizations either can be exclusionary and reinforce existing decision-making powers and structures (as appears to be the case for the mandatory government organizations) or can widen the base of voice, information, and participation and increase the responsiveness of local government.

Together they demonstrate the dangers of relying solely on the existing administrative structures to broaden the range of participation, disseminate information more broadly, and increase government responsiveness. As this chapter illustrates, social organizations have an important role to play in creating effective government institutions in Indonesia and in discussions of local governance more generally.

But this chapter also raises a more subtle, troubling, and difficult point. The failures of some attempts to deliver technocratically determined "least cost" or "cost effective" solutions to meet what were perceived to be the population's uniform "needs" highlighted the importance of local institutions and local variability in conditions. This, in turn, led to the recognition that successful development required more than just delivering "goods" – it required the social and political conditions out of which the appropriate collective action could emerge and be supported. This very useful course correction leads to more emphasis on individual and community empowerment, on meaningful participation in decisions, and on the design not just of the development "project" but the development "process." However, people who write and think about issues in these abstract ways face a deep paradox – the trap of discovering and imposing a new universal vision of development on others. Attempts to intervene in the reality of complex historical and social processes are fraught with peril – but so is the alternative.

Appendix 1: A note on reporting of probit estimations

This brief note about probit estimation might clear up some language about the results above. Probit estimation assumes that all that is observed in a binary indicator (yes/no, on/off, zero/nonzero) that is arbitrarily assigned the values 0 and 1. Moreover, it is assumed that the probability of observing 1 is a linear function of some underlying *index function(y^*)*, which itself is a function of the independent (right-hand side) variables (xs):

$$y^* = \beta' * X + \varepsilon, \quad y^* = 1 \text{ only if } y^* > 0$$

where X is an N-by-K matrix (which includes a constant) and β is a K by 1 vector. This implies that, if we assume the error terms are distributed normally.

$$\text{Prob}(y=1) = \text{Prob}(\beta'X + \varepsilon > 0) = \text{Prob}(\varepsilon < \beta'X) = \Phi(\beta'X)$$

where Φ is the cumulative normal distribution. The coefficients of the probit regression are the , of the index function. However, the marginal effect of an increase in one of the independent variables – the change in the likelihood of observing a "1" as x changes – is a nonlinear function of the coefficients and all of the other variables (since the normal distribution is nonlinear). The expression for the marginal effect of one variable, x_1, is

$$\frac{\partial \text{Prob}[y=1]}{\partial x_1} = \phi(\beta'X) * \beta_1$$

where ϕ is the normal frequency distribution. The impact of x_1 depends on the values of X at which it is evaluated. We will report the impact of each variable evaluated at the means of all the variables (including the variable being evaluated). Standard errors and tests of significance of the coefficients are straightforward, while the standard errors of the marginal effects depend on where they are evaluated. Hence we report marginal effects at the means but the *p*-levels not of the marginal effects but of the hypothesis test that the underlying coefficient in the index function (β) is equal to zero.

Ordered probit is a simple extension of probit to multiple categories and thresholds. Unlike a statistical procedure such as OLS that would assume the dependent variable was a cardinal number so that the difference between 0 and 1 was the same as the difference between 1 and 2 or between 4 and 5, ordered probit assumes that the levels are ordered (e.g. 2 is higher than 1) but does not assume that the difference between the categories has any informational content (the categories could be 1, 2, 3 or 1, 20, 24).

The difficulty with ordered probit is in interpretation as even if the underling index function is linear and monotonic, this does not mean that an increase in the independent variable will be associated with an increased probability for all "higher" categories. The algebra is simple (see Greene 2000) and the intuition is that if an increase in an independent variable is associated with "better," then it is unambiguous that the propensity to be in the worst category is smaller and the propensity to be in the best larger, but what happens to all categories in the middle is ambiguous – they could go up or down.

We experimented, and the marginal effects from probit combining two of the categories were similar. For instance, with probit the marginal effect on "some participation" for household membership in *desa* government organizations is 0.067, while the ordered probit marginal effect of moving from "none" to "some" is 0.07.

Appendix 2: Summary of regression results

Independent variables	Information		Participation		Voice			Responsiveness		
	HH informed of 3 types (development funds, use of funds, program availability)	HH reports all 3 "more open" than 4 years ago	Some participation in planning desa projects	Some participation in determining sanctions	Someone in the HH involved in a "protest"	HH reports a problem in desa and no expression of discontent (positive is less voice)	Expression effectiveness – of those who report there was a problem with desa leadership[a]	Desa government responded to economic problems	Desa government responded to social problems	Desa government responded to environmental problems
HH social organizations (private)	0.0099 (0.495)	0.020 (0.071)*	0.049 (0.001)***	0.025 (0.011)**	0.012 (0.104)	0.0054 (0.643)	−0.014 (0.763)	0.012 (0.172)	0.047 (0.064)*	−0.005 (0.753)
Desa less HH social organizations (community)	−0.015 (0.651)	0.012 (0.663)	−0.007 (0.832)	−0.041 (0.088)*	0.028 (0.127)	−0.056 (0.037)**	0.053 (0.629)	0.011 (0.616)	−0.057 (0.423)	−0.033 (0.456)
HH desa government organizations (private)	0.041 (0.001)***	0.029 (0.005)***	0.067 (0.000)***	0.031 (0.001)***	0.0074 (0.303)	−0.026 (0.013)*	0.159 (0.000)***	0.012 (0.145)	−0.013 (0.639)	0.028 (0.100)*
Desa less HH desa government organizations (community)	−0.085 (0.009)***	−0.036 (0.176)	−0.066 (0.058)*	−0.039 (0.103)	v (0.021)**	0.094 (0.000)***	−0.174 (0.124)	−0.083 (0.001)***	−0.040 (0.623)	0.134 (0.004)***
HH Networks (private)	0.016 (0.008)***	0.0083 (0.103)	0.008 (0.228)	0.005 (0.249)	0.0017 (0.629)	0.0083 (0.102)	−0.033 (0.133)	0.003 (0.452)	0.025 (0.045)**	0.002 (0.844)
Desa less HH Networks (community)	0.009 (0.613)	−0.023 (0.120)	−0.005 (0.779)	0.0015 (0.902)	0.0032 (0.754)	−0.0004 (0.971)	−0.048 (0.366)	0.015 (0.283)	0.077 (0.074)*	0.011 (0.670)
N visits HH	0.005 (0.166)	0.006 (0.039)**	0.006 (0.106)	0.002 (0.335)	0.0046 (0.032)**	−0.004 (0.103)	0.0079 (0.516)	0.002 (0.386)	−0.016 (0.032)**	0.001 (0.846)

continued

Continued

Independent variables	Information		Participation		Voice			Responsiveness		
	HH informed of 3 types (development funds, use of funds, program availability)	HH reports all 3 "more open" than 4 years ago	Some participation in planning desa projects	Some participation in determining sanctions	Someone in the HH involved in a "protest"	HH reports a problem in desa and no expression of discontent (positive is less voice)	Expression effectiveness – of those who report there was a problem with desa leadership[a]	Desa government responded to economic problems	Desa government responded to social problems	Desa government responded to environmental problems
Other controls	S+	GW+	S+, F−, GW+	S+, F−, A+, GW+	Y+, O−, A+	F+, O−, A+	S+, F−, A−	Y+, F−, GW+	A−	S+, A+ GW+
Regions	Wonogiri(−)	None	Batanghari (−), Banyumas(−), Wonogiri(−)	Batanghari (−), Banyumas(−), Wonogiri(−)	Ngada(+)	Banyumas (−), Wonogiri (−)	Banyumas(+), Ngada (+)	Batanghari (−), Ngada(+)	Banyumas(−), Wonogiri(−)	Batanghari(+), Ngada(+)
R^2 (or equiv)	0.057	0.058	0.192	0.172	0.131	0.052	0.0585	0.225	0.104	0.116
N	1171	1171	1171	1171	1171	1171	587	597	314	733
Observed p	0.338	0.200	0.372	0.185	0.122	0.186	A, .368; B, .368; C, .262	0.139	0.401	0.518
Predicted p	0.327	0.185	0.344	0.138	0.089	0.174	A, .403; B, .359; C, .236	0.076	0.388	0.523
Estimation technique	Probit	Probit	Probit	Probit	Probit	Probit	Ordered probit	Probit	Probit	Probit
Reported	Marginal effects	Marginal effects	Marginal effects	Marginal effects	Marginal effects	Marginal effects	Coefficients	Marginal effects	Marginal effects	Marginal effects

Notes

The p-levels of the hypothesis that the underlying coefficients are zero are reported in parenthesis. (Note that these are not a test of the marginal effects, which are nonlinear.) p-levels lower than X percent "reject" the hypothesis that the coefficient is zero at that level of statistical significance and the usual levels of 10/5/1 are indicated with one two or three asterisks (*/**/***). Key to control variables: Y, consumption expenditures; F, female-headed household; S, years of schooling; GW, HH head works in government; A, HH head works in agriculture; O, age of HH head in years.

a A, if no expression of discontent; B, if expression but no solution; C, if expression and solution.

Notes

We thank many people who helped in the long course of the LLI2 study and this particular chapter: Scott Guggenheim, Pieter Evers, Kamala Chandrakirana, Robert Chase, Christiaan Grootaert, Michael Woolcock, Sandy Jencks, Jeffrey Hammer, Deon Filmer, Menno Pradhan, and Chitra Buchori provided valuable comments and input during the course of this research. Leni Dharmawan, Erwin Fahmi, R. Yando Zakaria, and their respective regional teams shaped and collected the data. Financial support from the World Bank's Indonesia Country Team, the Research Support Budget, the Norwegian Trust Fund for Environmentally and Socially Sustainable Development, and the ASEM Trust Fund is gratefully acknowledged.

1 Although it should be noted that the book is with Robert Leonardi and Raffaella Nanetti.
2 Of course there is by now an extensive ethnographic literature documenting how, even in authoritarian regimes with no effective formal political opposition, local social organizations and associations both resisted and structured the reality of government action (e.g. Singerman (1995) on Egypt, Seligmann (2002) on Peru).
3 It should be noted that the general term "social activities" includes all group activities that households reported participating in, not that the activities have a "social" purpose. Some, such as water user groups or credit cooperatives, serve primarily economic functions, while others are mixed (e.g. a prayer group that includes a rotating credit scheme as part of its activities).
4 One additional caveat: in discussion of the results below (pp. 323–38) we often use terms like "impacts" or "effects." Since we presently have no technical method that allows us to assert causality – because we cannot rule out reverse causality – this language is not an assertion of causality but merely avoids the pedantic repetition of phrases like "if these partial associations represent causal impacts the effect is . . ."
5 This simple-minded approach to method is not naivety: we have read and considered the critiques of household survey methods, the dangers of attempting to impose empirical clarity on social complexity, and even the dangers of the survey instrument itself as a tool of repression. The household survey was embedded in a larger study that used a range of qualitative techniques to address many of the same questions (Wetterberg 2002).
6 We draw heavily on Evers (1999) because it is the best study, not only because it is part of the Local Level Institutions study, but also because it is among the few studies of the mechanics of local politics. The New Order Indonesian government banned not just the development of political organizations in rural areas but also research on local politics (which could be easily enforced since all fieldwork required official permission).
7 There is a similar distinction in India between a "revenue village" which is a political and administrative unit and a "village" in its sense of a "hamlet" or collection of contiguous residences.
8 The motivations for creating this structure are well beyond the scope of this chapter, but (i) since its birth Indonesia has experienced centrifugal pressures in various regions and the armed forces (from which the New Order leadership emerged) has always considered itself a bulwark of nationalism and stressed the need for central control, (b) without apportioning responsibility, the New Order (Soeharto) government was unquestionably born in social chaos and brutal local violence, an experience no one was anxious to repeat, and (c) the government in this period was "developmentalist authoritarian," anxious to deliver on the concrete benefits of "economic development" *to*

citizens as a means of sustaining legitimacy but less concerned with either local or national mechanisms of "voice" *from* citizens.

9 It should be noted that, as part of the decentralization effort, the 1979 law on village government has been revoked. Change has not been immediate, however, and most of the structures it created still persist throughout the research area (Wetterberg 2002).

10 There were eight less *desas* because one of the districts was in NTT close to East Timor and was not safe for researchers.

11 This is based on the same information (the roster of all group activities) but is a different scheme than that used in analysis of the LLI1 data (Grootaert 1999) that divided groups into nine functional categories by the primary purpose of the group (e.g. production group, religious group, recreation).

12 Other studies of social capital have weighted membership in various organizations by characteristics of the organization thought to contribute to social capital (e.g. horizontal relationships among members, membership inclusive across social categories, frequency of participation); see Narayan and Pritchett (1999), Grootaert (2000).

13 That these are *household* responses should be stressed as a considerable amount of the variation in reported governance consists of differences across individuals, not just differences across villages.

14 The Bahasa Indonesia wording is: *pernah menyatakan ketidakpuasan*.

15 The major problem with the linear specification (of the "index function" for probit) is the lack of interactive effects between the household's participation and the magnitude of participation of others. Strictly speaking, in the form we now estimate the impact of an additional household joining a *desa* government organization on another household is the same irrespective of the level of the household's participation in *desa* activities. In future work we will test for interactive effects.

16 For simplicity we ignore the $N-1/N$ term, which in our samples of 30 per village is near one in any case.

17 This obviously can only be true over certain ranges of participation – as starting from zero participation or nearing 100 percent participation one cannot have the same effect.

18 One aspect of the results yet to be addressed is that the standard errors are not corrected for the possibility of within-cluster correlation of the error terms. This could lead to an overestimate of the precision of estimation and hence an overstatement of levels of statistical significance.

19 Some of the difference is in statistical power, and nearly all of the estimates are imprecise – as is to be expected given the nature of the data and the phenomenon under investigation. For instance, the summary table reports that "*desa*-less household activity" in *desa* government organizations reduces participation in *desa* planning by 19.2 percent ($-0.066/0.344$) and the underlying coefficients' p-level is .058 and hence is "statistically significant" at the 10 percent level. Participation in determining sanctions, on the other hand, is reduced by 28 percent ($-0.039/0.138$) based on a coefficient with a p-level of 0.103 and hence is just barely not statistically significant at the 10 percent level. In our view, making too much of these fine distinctions in p-levels – treating these two as *qualitatively* different because one is modestly below and another barely above some conventional level – is a statistical significance fetish (McCloskey and Ziliak 1996). However, there are also elements of the table in which the p-level is very high – the p-level on "desa-less household" for response to social problems is 0.623, which means even the sign conveys little information.

20 Note that the positive sign for one of the voice indicators (no expression in spite of existing problems) indicates a negative (i.e. detrimental) impact.

21 With the two binary variables, the average is just the fraction of households answering "yes," but with the "effective voice" variable we have to assume (as we did not before) that the categories can be treated as cardinal numbers so they can be averaged.

22 The difficulty is that to do the procedure of "instrumental variables" one needs valid instruments and we have not found a valid and informative instrument for "village less HH" social activity. We attempted using lagged social activities from the 1996 survey as an instrument, but, perhaps surprisingly, the power of the instrument in the first stage was too low and the standard errors on the "social" terms grew very large.

23 The empirical evidence is the strongest for rural water supply (Briscoe and Garn 1995; Narayan 1995; Isham *et al.* 1995).

24 One of the arguments for centralization in the immediate postcolonial era in many locations (Africa, India, Indonesia) was that the power of local leaders was an obstacle and that only through national governments and nonlocal coalitions (e.g. of peasants, labor) could a socially progressive agenda be implemented.

25 Research in the United States has demonstrated connections between ethnic divisions and the quality of public services (Alesina *et al.* 1999). There is also an empirical literature that proposes a link between "trust" and economic performance.

26 There are of course many examples of the negative effects of social organizations. The Ku Klux Klan was an NGO that attracted millions of members to the cause maintaining the privileges of one social group at the expense of vicious, often lethal, suppression of the rights of other citizens.

27 In a particularly telling example of how the "official" sector is (willfully) ignorant of social realities, Ostrom recounts the tale of a delayed irrigation project that planned to provide irrigation to "unirrigated" areas. The delay allowed a closer investigation of the area, which found dozens of fully functional irrigation associations in this supposedly unirrigated area.

28 Glaeser *et al.* (2000) advocate this "economic approach" in which they "analyze the formation of social capital using a model of optimal individual investment decisions" (p. 3).

29 Of course, in every individual, motivations are complex and church attendance may well be correlated with some material benefits or other nonreligious returns (Glaeser and Sacerdote 2002) and yet still be predominantly motivated by belief.

References

Alesina, Alberto, Reza Baqir and William Easterly, 1999, "Public Goods and Ethnic Divisions," *Quarterly Journal of Economics*, 114 (4), pp. 1243–84.

Bardhan, P. and D. Mookherjee, 2000, "Capture and Governance at Local and National Levels," *American Economic Review*, 90 (2), 135–9.

Bourdieu, Pierre, 1986, "The Forms of Capital." In *Handbook of Theory and Research for the Sociology of Education*, ed. John G. Richardson. New York: Greenwood Press.

Briscoe, John and Harvey Garn, 1995, "Financing Water Supply and Sanitation Under Agenda 21," *Natural Resources Forum*, 19 (1), pp. 59–70.

Chandrakirana, Kamala, 1999, "Local Capacity and Its Implications for Development: The Case of Indonesia." World Bank/Bappenas, Local Level Institutions Study, Jakarta.

Coleman, James, 1990, *Foundations of Social Theory*. Cambridge, MA: Harvard University Press.

DFID, 2000, *Sustainable Livelihood Studies: Field Reports*. Mimeo.

Evans, Peter, 2003, "Beyond 'Institutional Monocropping:' Institutions, Capabilities, and Deliberative Development," *Sociologias*, ene./jun. (9), pp. 20–63.

Evers, Pieter, 1999, "Village Governments and Their Communities." World Bank/Bappenas, Local Level Institutions Study, Jakarta.

Fox, Jonathan, 1996, "How Does Civil Society Thicken? The Political Construction of Social Capital in Rural Mexico," *World Development*, 24 (6), pp. 1089–103.

Glaeser, Edward and Bruce Sacerdote, 2002, "Education and Religion," NBER Working Paper 8080, Cambridge, MA: NBER.

Glaeser, Edward, David Laibson and Bruce Sacedote, 2000, "The Economic Approach to Social Capital," NBER Working Paper 7728, Cambridge, MA: NBER.

Greene, William, 2000, *Econometric Analysis*. New Jersey: Prentice Hall.

Grootaert, Christian, 1999, "Local Institutions and Service Delivery in Indonesia," Local Level Institutions Working Paper 5, The World Bank.

Grootaert, Christian, 2000, "Social Capital, Household Welfare and Poverty in Indonesia," Local Level Institutions Study, World Bank.

Hammer, J. and Pritchett, L, 2006, "World Bank Economists and Social Capital: Scenes from a Marriage," in A. Bebbington, S. Guggenheim, E. Olson and M. Woolcock (eds) *The Search for Empowerment: Social Capital as Idea and Practice at the World Bank*. Kumerian Press.

Isham, Jon and Satu Kähkönen, 1999, "What Determines the Effectiveness of Community-Based Water Projects? Evidence from Central Java on Demand Responsiveness, Service Rules, and Social Capital," Social Capital Initiative Working Paper 14, Social Development Family, Environmentally and Socially Sustainable Development Network, The World Bank.

Islam, Jonathan, Deepa narayan and lant pritchett, 1995, "Does Participation Improve Performance? Establishing Causality With Subjective Data, *World Bank Economic Review* 9 (2), pp. 175–200.

McCloskey, Deidre and Stephan Ziliak, 1996, "The Standard Error of Regressions," *Journal of Economic Literature*, 34 (1), pp. 97–114.

Narayan, Deepa, 1995, "The Contribution of People's Participation: Evidence from 121 Rural Water Supply Projects," Environmentally Sustainable Development Occasional Paper Series No. 1, The World Bank.

Narayan, Deepa and Lant Pritchett, 1999, "Cents and Sociability: Household Income and Social Capital in Rural Tanzania," *Economic Development and Cultural Change*, 47 (4), pp. 871–97.

Narayan, Deepa and Michael Woolcock, 2000, "Social Capital: Implications for Development Theory, Research, and Policy," *World Bank Research Observer*, 15 (2), pp. 225–249.

Ostrom, Elinor, 1990, *Governing the Commons: The Evolution of Institutions for Collective Action*. Cambridge, MA: Cambridge University Press.

Platteau, Jean Phillipe, 2004, "Monitoring Elite Capture in Community-Driven Development," *Development and Change*, 35 (2), pp. 225–48.

Pritchett, Lant and Michael Woolcock, 2002, "Solutions When *the* Solution is the Problem," Center for Global Development Working Paper 10, Center for Global Development, Washington, DC.

Putnam, Robert with Robert Leonardi and Raffaella Naneti, 1992, *Making Democracy Work: Civic Traditions in Modern Italy.* Princeton, NJ: Princeton University Press.

Rao, Vijayendru, 2005, "Symbolic Public Goods and the Coordination of Collective Action: A comparison of Local Development in India and Indonesia," Washington, DC: World Bank Policy Research Working Paper No. 3685.

Scott, James, 1998, *Seeing Like a State: How Certain Schemes to Improve the Human Condition Have Failed.* Yale, CT: Yale University Press.

Seligmann, Linda J, 2002, *Between Reform and Revolution: Political Struggles in the Peruvian Andes, 1969–1991.* Stanford, CA: Stanford University Press.

Singerman, Diane, 1995, *Avenues of Participation: Family, Politics, and Networks in Urban Quarters of Cairo.* Princeton, NJ: Princeton University Press.

Uphoff, Norman, 1992, *Learning from Gal Oya: Possibilities for Participatory Development and Post-Newtonian Social Science.* Ithaca, NY: Cornell University Press.

Wade, Robert, 1988, *Village Republics: Economic Conditions for Collective Action in South India.* San Francisco, CA: ICS Press.

Wetterberg, Anna, 2002, "Social Capital, Local Capacity, and Government: Findings from the Second Local Level Institutions Study," World Bank, Washington, DC.

Woolcock, Michael, 1998, "Social Capital and Economic Development: Toward a Theoretical Synthesis and Policy Framework," *Theory and Society*, 27 (2), pp. 151–208.

18 Community-driven development and the Northeast Brazil rural poverty reduction program

Edward W. Bresnyan, Jr, Maria Alejandra Bouquet and Francesca Russo[1]

Introduction

Over nearly two decades, North East (NE) Brazil and the World Bank have been engaged in an evolving experiment in participatory development to reduce rural poverty. From 1986 to the present, some US$1.4 billion have been invested in ten states which comprise the NE region, applying a methodology that has come to be defined as *community-driven development* (CDD).[2] In stark contrast to previous attempts at combating rural poverty in NE Brazil – particularly under the guise of earlier failed integrated rural development schemes – CDD relies on local knowledge and understanding to generate investment options to meet pressing community demands. Having started as an obscure sub-component of a larger set of fairly traditional rural development projects, CDD in NE Brazil has been incrementally modified and fine-tuned into what today arguably represents one of the more effective CDD country programs worldwide, in terms of both its ability to reach the rural poor with investment resources and to generate tangible benefits. Across four successive generations and a cumulative 36 projects, well over 50,000 small-scale community investments have been financed and implemented by some 36,000 community organizations, extending basic services such as rural electrification, safe water and income-generating activities to approximately 1.2 million households, or about seven million individuals.

Yet, strong and vocal critiques of the CDD methodology call into question its purported effectiveness and its ability to generate lasting benefits for those participating in it. First, its participatory nature is believed to be subject to manipulation by local elites, and owing to information asymmetries, can be less efficient in (or worse yet, incapable of) translating community demands into actual investments. Second, given that, in NE Brazil, state-level governments are charged with CDD's overall execution, conflicts and power struggles may arise in the decision-making process that leads up to actual community investments, in that the state may "know better" what communities actually need, thereby annulling the comparative advantage of localized knowledge. Third, the new institutions which form in response to CDD – the myriad community associations through which individual subprojects are identified and implemented, as well as the umbrella project-related Municipal Councils (MC) which are structured to funnel community investment demand and prioritize investment decisions within a given municipality – may only be transient, in that once external assistance is no longer available, they fade into non-existence, since the "game" for which they were created is no longer being played. Similarly, and more broadly, what evidence exists that, beyond the political will to accept CDD as a modality for foreign assistance, state governments are actually making systemic and structural changes in their own budgets and strategies for reducing rural poverty by "mainstreaming" CDD as an effective methodology?

The purpose of this chapter is to trace the origins of and the accumulated experience with CDD in NE Brazil as an example of membership-based organizations for the poor (MBOPs). The next section describes NE Brazil, particularly the rural NE, and the dimensions of poverty there. Sections "Community-driven Development (CDD) and its pre-conditions in NE Brazil," "CDD in NE Brazil (1986–present)," and "MBOPs in NE Brazil: Community Associations and MC" define CDD in the NE Brazil context, discuss its role as a development methodology, and provide the historical background leading up to its adoption as a vehicle for rural poverty reduction in the region, as well as the pre-conditions – internal and external – that facilitated its emergence. The section "The glue that binds: the community subproject" addresses the institutions arising from CDD, the project-related community associations and MC. The section "Lessons learned" addresses the question, "What are the development outcomes achieved by membership-based organizations of the poor (MBOPs) in NE Brazil?" and lays out a set of stylized lessons on the successes, potential for scaling-up and replicability of the CDD experience in NE Brazil. The last section provides concluding remarks and issues for further research.

Background: Northeast Brazil[3]

Brazil is characterized by extreme levels of income disparity, with poverty rates much higher than in other countries with a similar level of per-capita gross domestic product (GDP). In particular, the NE region accounts for some 20 percent of Brazil's land area, yet is home to 48 million people, or 30 percent of Brazil's total population. Poverty is endemic in the region, with 47 percent of the total NE population living on less than US$1 per day. Rural poverty is even more severe: 64 percent of the NE rural population (9.2 million) lives on less than US$1 per day. On a national scale, 49 percent of Brazil's population that lives on less than US$1 per day resides in the NE. For all of rural Brazil, this figure jumps to 64 percent.[4] Among the five major regions of Brazil, the NE ranks lowest in terms of the Human Development Index (HDI) (0.608 compared to 0.764 for all of Brazil). Table 18.1 reports indicators of poverty, income inequality, rural population and HDIs for the NE states.

Table 18.1 NE Brazil, summary indicators, by state (excluding Minas Gerais)

State	Extreme poverty, 2000[a]	Poverty, 2000[b]	Gini (2000)	Total	Rural	Rural (%)	HDI, 2000
Alagoas	55.4	57.2	0.691	2,822,621	902,882	32	0.649
Bahia	52.8	53.6	0.669	13,070,250	4,297,902	33	0.688
Ceará	53.5	54.4	0.675	7,430,661	2,115,343	28	0.700
Maranhão	52.8	56.7	0.659	5,651,475	2,287,405	40	0.636
Paraíba	51.1	52.1	0.646	3,443,825	996,613	29	0.661
Pernambuco	53.2	52.3	0.673	7,918,344	1,860,095	23	0.705
Piauí	51.5	55.0	0.661	2,843,278	1,054,688	37	0.656
Rio Grande do Norte	54.3	52.0	0.657	2,776,782	740,109	27	0.705
Sergipe	49.8	52.2	0.658	1,784,475	511,249	29	0.682

Source: Human Development Atlas for Brazil, United Nations (2004).

Notes
a Percentage of population with per-capita monthly income below R$37.75.
b Percentage population with per-capita monthly income below R$75.50.

Community-driven development (CDD) and its pre-conditions in NE Brazil

What is CDD in the Brazilian context and how did it take hold in NE Brazil? The answer to these questions lies in the confluence of internal transformations occurring in Brazil and the external factors, which facilitated the rise of participatory approaches embodied in CDD.

Failure of Integrated Rural Development schemes

At a 2004 conference which brought together the ten NE states to share their collective experience with CDD, a well-known keynote speaker declared, "State Governments and the international community have been involved in the rural development of NE Brazil for some forty years, and the first thirty years were a resounding failure."[5] A principal component of this failure was the intense devotion to Integrated Rural Development (IRD), which attempted to coordinate and implement (typically at the central government level) a panoply of investment activities designed to reduce rural poverty, build institutional capacity for public service delivery, and create the conditions for improved income-generation, primarily in agriculture. From 1975 to 1987, the Brazilian government committed approximately US$3.3 billion to IRD in NE Brazil, for which it borrowed US$1.4 billion (42 percent of total) from the World Bank. This package of assistance included: (i) the first-generation IRD projects (POLONORDESTE), approved in nine NE states over the 1975–83 period, and (ii) the second-generation projects (NRDP) in the same states, over the 1985–87 period.[6]

The first-generation IRD projects included about a dozen different components. The staples of these projects were agricultural credit (23 percent), land-related activities (16 percent), feeder roads (20 percent), and agricultural extension (14 percent), in the aggregate accounting for 72 percent of total costs (Tendler 1991). To reduce project complexity and focus more exclusively on agricultural production, the second generation IRD projects eliminated health, education, and roads – as well as some smaller components (e.g. micro-enterprise credit, electrification, marketing). Credit (30 percent), extension (24 percent), and a new community-participation component – *Apoio às Pequenas Comunidades Rurais* (Support for Small Rural Communities, or APCR) (16 percent) – accounted for 70 percent of total expenditures under the second generation.[7] Common to both the first- and second-generation IRD projects was a lethargic pace of implementation and significant lags in disbursing resources, partly due to the inflationary crisis in Brazil at the time, but also a function of the complexity in project design, despite its fewer components and activities. These projects also suffered from

i   faulty poverty targeting mechanisms, resulting in significant slippage in benefits;

ii   institutional deficiencies, mainly costliness and inefficiency of agencies, as well as excessive centralization of decision-making;
iii political manipulation associated with entrenched patron-client relations;
iv   inadequate community participation, involvement and capacity building (Tendler 1991).

Decentralization

It is important to recognize that the IRD projects in Brazil began under a centralized military government, where public agencies controlled most development activity. Both participation and decentralization were politically problematic for Brazil during this period in its history. By the mid-1980s, Brazil had returned to democratic rule, and subsequently adopted a new constitution in 1988 that promoted the decentralization of responsibility and resources for implementing development programs from the Federal Government to the states, municipalities and local communities (Van Zyl *et al.* 2000). At the same time, the emergence of the Solidarity program in Mexico launched a World Bank-supported experiment there in CDD that would eventually inspire other countries, including Brazil. Yet, it was the small APCR component in the NE Brazil IRD program that would serve as the prototype for an eventual re-design of the NRDP. In 1993, in agreement with Federal and state Governments and following a study tour of the positive CDD experience in Mexico, the NRDP's project components were dramatically reduced, and the bulk of its remaining resources were reallocated to a scaled-up hybrid of the APCR.[8]

CDD in NE Brazil (1986–present)

The combined effect of the factors discussed in the previous section aided the transformation of the NRDP projects into more participatory CDD vehicles. A lone element of the second-generation IRD projects in the NE – the APCR – performed well enough to make it the centerpiece of the 1993 reformulation effort. A change in project design was implemented, first by devolving direct implementation responsibilities to state-level agencies, typically (but not exclusively) linked to the respective State Secretariats of Planning. This put into practice the principle of *subsidiarity*, in that decision-making and responsibilities should devolve to their most local level of capacity. Second, the NRDP became a community matching grants scheme, founded on local participation in decisions about investment priorities and modes of implementation, with the intent of meeting the expressed needs of rural poor communities. Since governments and central planners had, over the course of several decades, proven to be incapable of reaching the rural poor with basic public services, it was decided that a "role reversal" was in order, with the communities themselves taking on a greater role in deciding what could most improve their quality of life.

The movement from a top-down approach to a bottom-up, participatory, community-based methodology was aided by a favorable policy setting in Brazil – at the Federal and state levels – in the late 1980s and early 1990s. The NE states were painfully aware of persistent failings in the sequential IRD programs over several decades. These failures disposed state governments to a willingness to expend the political capital needed to break with traditional, centralized programming, and move toward a greater reliance on demand-driven processes of investments for poverty reduction. Third, reducing the role of the state – both in terms of size and scope of interventions – was a movement sweeping the developing world in the early 1990s, creating an opening for an expanded role for civil society in poverty reduction.

The results of the reformulated NRDP were impressive: in the three years following its restructuring, the NRDP accomplished 100 percent of its physical implementation targets. Overall, more than 40,000 community associations presented proposals for small-scale investments. Of these, about 18,000 investments or *subprojects* were ultimately financed and implemented directly by these associations, at an average cost of US\$24,000 per subproject and each family had a benefit of about US\$360.

Under the reformulated NRDP, two funding mechanisms for subprojects were available to community associations:

i   *Programa de Apoio Comunitário* (Program for Community Assistance, or PAC), which forged a working relationship directly between the state and the community association;

ii *Fundo Municipal de Ação Comunitária* (Muncipal Fund for Community Action, or FUMAC), which sought to initiate a municipal development context through the formation of a project Municipal Council (MCs), with up to 70 percent of its voting membership being representatives of the community associations residing in the municipality The project coordinating units (PCU) established in each participating NE state were found to be competent in overall project execution, especially in creating awareness of the NRDP among the intended beneficiaries: the rural poor of the NE.

By 1995, and following the successful reformulated NRDP, the NE states began a new generation of CDD, known as the Rural Poverty Alleviation Projects (RPAP). The RPAP retained many of the same mechanisms as the previous NRDP, and sought to expand the number of the project MCs and the emphasis on municipal development. Under the RPAP, project benefits were delivered primarily through two types of MCs (differing in their degree of decentralization of the final decisions on allocating subproject funds, and in their potential to strengthen social capital), and a third non-council mechanism. *FUMAC Councils* (translated loosely as Municipal Community Schemes) were first piloted under the reformulated NRDP. Under FUMAC, the state government delegates decision-making to project-based MCs which deliberate, establish investment priorities, appraise, and vote on community investment proposals. This process is guided by an annual, council-specific indicative budget provided by the PCU which defines the funds available for subproject financing. *FUMAC-P Councils* (Pilot Municipal Community Schemes), a variant of FUMAC, extends decentralization one step further: high-performing FUMACs submit an Annual Operating Plan of subproject investments to the PCU for technical review. Once the POA is approved, the PCU releases funds directly to the FUMAC's bank account. The FUMAC then manages their distribution to community associations with approved investment proposals in the POA, supervises subproject implementation, and is accountable for use of the funds. *PAC* (state community schemes) were the dominant delivery mechanism under the APCR pilot and the reformulated NRDP. Under the RPAP, much greater emphasis was placed on the FUMAC funding mechanism. Under PAC, community associations submit investment proposals directly to the PCU, which screens and approves these proposals, and releases funds to the community association for their implementation. Evaluation shows that, while PAC can be important in the initial stages of CDD, that is, until a municipality has established a FUMAC, it is less effective than FUMAC and FUMAC-P in involving local government and in terms of sustainability and social capital development, and more prone to local political manipulation (Roumani 2004). From 1995 through 2004, World Bank-assisted operations totaling US$625.2 million have been deployed in eight NE states, financing nearly 23,000 subprojects and benefiting over 1.2 million rural households (Table 18.2).[9]

MBOPs in NE Brazil: community associations and MC

The success of the NE Brazil CDD model comes in large part from the perceived advantages of placing intended beneficiaries in the position of identifying, executing, operating, and maintaining those investments which best meet their own needs. Furthermore, by supporting collective action to resolve these needs, so-called "social capital" is both created and deployed in the investment process.[10] Community associations, where interested individuals coalesce around the common goal of expanding community assets and access to basic services (e.g. electricity, safe water, sanitation), are therefore the fundamental building blocks for CDD.

Earlier assessments of IRD in NE Brazil cited the lack of community participation as a chief reason for its failure. In fact, one of the key findings was that, with strong political support at the state level, almost any IRD project component which is *tailored to the immediately felt needs of the*

Table 18.2 Rural poverty alleviation projects – implementation indicators 1995–2004

State	Total project cost (US$ million)	Subprojects	Families benefited (000)	Community associations	Project municipal councils
Bahia	163.4	6608	451.9	3594	354
Ceará	99.6	3056	153.2	2410	139
Maranhão	106.9	3946	184.5	2835	175
Paraíba	79.5	3058	108.4	2458	159
Pernambuco	51.2	1601	136.0	1255	155
Piauí	39.7	1199	70.9	897	170
Rio Grande do Norte	31.6	1697	77.1	1382	132
Sergipe	53.3	1820	62.4	917	71
Totals	625.2	22,985	1,244.4	15,748	1393

Source: Project Management Information System (MIS) data, World Bank.

beneficiaries (emphasis added) can be made to work (Tendler 1991). Sufficient evidence now indicates that development interventions which exclude the active participation of communities are likely to fail, whereas those which seek such participation increase their chance of success (Finstersbusch and van Wicklin 1987; and Narayan 1995). Therefore, building on the success of the APCR component (whose outcome was specifically linked to the strong participation of beneficiaries), its scaling up in the reformulated NRDP and the subsequent RPAP, CDD seeks to engage the participation of citizens and their communities in the development process.

What are these community associations and how do they participate in CDD? Formally defined, community associations under CDD are groups of rural citizens with a common interest and organized into legally-constituted civil organizations (as required under Brazilian law). These associations are not necessarily defined by geographic boundaries, but rather bring together households and individuals that share a mutual objective for improving their quality of life. Community associations are the bedrock of CDD implementation: they identify, prepare, implement, supervise, operate, and maintain their subproject investments, assisted both by technical specialists (whom they contract directly with funds provided in the total subproject envelope) and training made available by the respective project MCs and the PCUs. Even more important, these community associations directly receive and manage the funds required for the execution of these subprojects. Funds are directly transferred from the PCU to the bank account of the respective community association, which is then responsible for contracting all goods, works, and services required to complete the subproject. Upon completion of the investment, the community association submits a simplified statement of accounts to the PCU to verify the proper use of these public funds.

While the community associations are indeed the foundation of CDD in NE Brazil, there is a municipal context in which they operate. Yet and still, it was the desire to break with the historical legacy of political patronage at the local level, combined with justifiable fears as to the potential for manipulation of community associations by strong, and often autocratic, municipal governments, that led to the creation of the project MCs, where broader, more transparent discussions and decision-making could occur. The MC, as such, serves as a means of social control for project activities and community associations. Within any given municipality, community associations choose delegates for seats in the Municipal Council, but in all cases the representation on the Council is approximately two-thirds from community association members, one-third from other elements of organized civil society (e.g. rural workers' union, non-governmental organizations (NGOs), local government), and public sector agencies. In terms of sheer size, most MCs have from 11 to 20 members. Today, about 80 percent of the municipalities in NE Brazil have a project MC established.

The glue that binds: the community subproject

CDD promotes local involvement in public investment decision-making and therefore must provide some reasonable expectation that something tangible will result. Enter the community subproject. Under CDD, community associations can propose almost any investment under the rubric of a subproject, with the exception of a short negative list including the following:

   i Federal or state road repair;
  ii land acquisition;
 iii religious structures;
 iv Federal, state or municipal buildings;
  v investments related to political parties;
 vi Union halls;
vii tobacco production;
viii alcohol production.[11] A maximum cost threshold of US$50,000 is set for each community subproject, though in practice the average cost (since 1995) has been approximately US$25,000.[12] Simplified "rules of the game" – outlined in an Operational Manual for the RPAP – guide the community subproject investment cycle:

- Community Associations determine their local investment priorities and prepare subproject proposals.
- Subproject proposals are submitted to respective project MCs where they are prioritized and approved, based on indicative municipal resource envelopes, as defined by the PCU.
- The PCU technically evaluates approved subprojects and confirms compliance with subproject guidelines before releasing funds to community associations.
- Subproject agreements – signed between the PCU and Community Associations – define the terms and conditions for the funding, execution, ownership, operation and maintenance of the approved subprojects.
- Resources for subproject implementation are transferred directly to the Community Association's bank account.
- Community Associations are responsible for (i) the contracting of goods, works, and services for subproject execution and (ii) the operation and maintenance of all investments. They may also request technical assistance to develop operation and maintenance programs and techniques.

Since 1993 and across three successive generations of CDD, MBOPs in NE Brazil have implemented over 55,000 subprojects (Table 18.3). About 70 percent of these community investments can be broadly categorized as basic socio-economic *infrastructure*, principally rural electrification, water

Table 18.3 Aggregate results, CDD in NE Brazil, 1993–present

	R-NRDP (1993–95)	RPAP (1995–2003)	RPRP (2001–present)	Total
Total project cost (US$ million)	615.6	625.2	171.7	1412.5
World bank lending (US$ million)	338.6	420.6	112.1	871.3
Subprojects implemented	25,000	22,985	7242	55,227
Families benefited[a]	890,000	1,244,477	410,000	2,544,477
Community associations	14,900	19,154	6392	40,446
Water supply				
Investments	2700	7786	2469	12,955
Communities benefited	2250	6528	2469	11,247
Families benefited	110,250	524,108	148,433	782,791
Energy				
Investments	5040	8537	1015	14,592
Communities benefited	4200	7198	1015	12,413
Families benefited	246,960	357,272	55,731	659,963
Productive				
Investments	5893	4887	1298	12,078
Communities benefited	4910	4072	1298	10,280
Families benefited	262,506	414,034	101,779	778,319

Source: Project MIS data, World Bank.

Note

a Includes families which have benefited from more than one community subproject.

supply systems, and sanitation. Another 20 percent of subprojects have been *productive* in nature (e.g., irrigation, manioc mills, agro-processing, tractors), whereas those termed *social,* make up the remaining 10 percent (e.g., crêche, community centers, school rehabilitation).

Targeting of Benefits

Based on project data, each participating community association has implemented, on average, 1.3 subprojects. This raises a fundamental question for interested policymakers: what is the desired balance between breadth of investment (i.e. coverage of the rural poor) and depth of investment (i.e. total project investment per capita)? On a more general level, how are benefits targeted under CDD?

Common to all NE Brazil CDD projects, potential benefits are targeted on three levels:

i   *municipalities* are included in the total project area by the PCU, based on exogenous, transparent criteria, example, HDI, level of rural population;

ii *community associations* self-select into the project, based on need and an understanding of the potential benefits arising from their participation;

iii project *Municipal Councils* prioritize subproject proposals received from community associations, in line with local knowledge of rural poverty and constrained by the resource envelope available for the municipality.

Additionally, participation in the project is limited to associations from communities with up to 7500 inhabitants.

In practice, virtually all municipalities in a participating state were included in the project. Given the finite budget constraint faced by the participating state (i.e. total project cost ceiling), this near-blanket coverage implies that state governments have opted for a focus on breadth rather than depth. This is not surprising in that astute elected officials may perceive that greater political returns are to be had by extending project benefits to as many voters as possible, as opposed to deepening subproject activities, and hence poverty impact, in only a small number of municipalities and communities.

The example quoted here serves as a reminder that CDD does not operate in a political vacuum. In many cases, political imperatives can and do conflict with technical design considerations. Here, it is crucial to bear in mind that one of the primary initial conditions for the success of CDD is the strong political backing from both state and local government. Hence, tradeoffs will inevitably be needed in order to preserve the overall buy-in on the part of these public officials. A question for further exploration would be, whether binding political constraints weaken the effectiveness and impact of CDD, particularly with regard to the potential for widely dispersed, yet uniformly thin investment, at the community level.

Since very few NE Brazil municipalities have been excluded *ex ante* from participating in CDD, what can we say about municipal poverty indicators and their relationship to the level of project resources invested? For example, are those municipalities with *lower* HDIs receiving proportional levels of investment funds under the project? Using HDIs from year 2000, frequency distributions were calculated for various participating NE states and then cross-tabulated with subproject expenditure data – disaggregated by municipality – and finally arrayed in deciles. The resulting paired frequency distributions for two states – Paraíba and Ceará – are given respectively in Figures 18.1 and 18.2.

The data yield several observations with regard to targeting. First, there is overall convergence between the frequency distribution of the HDI and the level of project resources invested, indicating that resources are flowing in concert with an exogenous measure of need. Second, the points at which the curves intersect indicate areas of greater or lesser than proportional investment for a given decile, which can imply either tighter targeting or slippage, respectively. In the case of Ceará, some slippage is present, in that deciles 1–4 (i.e. relatively poorer municipalities) received proportionally less investment funds, while the 5th, 6th, 9th and 10th deciles received relatively more. In Paraíba, a similar slippage occurs, albeit less intense. Given that the overall project is based on a demand-driven model, this may indicate that greater effort is needed to inform those poorer municipalities (and their constituent community

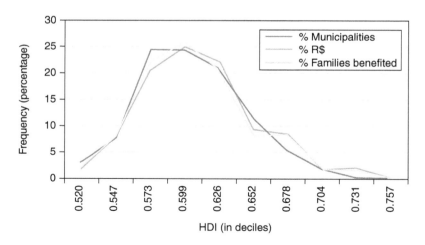

Figure 18.1 Human Development Index (HDI 2000) and CDD investments, 1998–2004 (in Reais), Paraiba (source: project MIS Data, World Bank).

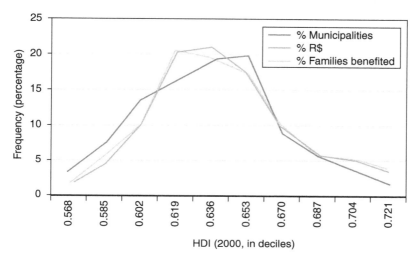

Figure 18.2 Human Development Index (HDI 2000) and CDD investments, 2001–4 (in Reais), Ceará (source: project MIS Data, World Bank).

associations) of how to participate in CDD. It may also be an indication of the ability of better prepared municipalities (i.e. those in the 5th deciles and higher for each state) to organize and demand investment funds under CDD.

While these data shed light on the effectiveness of targeting at the municipal level, they are silent as to the effectiveness of targeting *within municipalities*. World Bank (2003) notes that about 70 percent of families benefited under CDD in NE Brazil have initial household monthly incomes of less than two minimum salaries (about US$300 in 1999 or R$166). Based on an average household size of five in the rural NE, per capita incomes among these families would be slightly more than US$1 per day.[13] Since 1993, CDD in NE Brazil has generated annually about 5,000 community subprojects, benefiting 231,000 families at a per-family cost of US$470. Applying the targeting rate of 70 percent, about 162,000 poor rural NE families have been reached annually by the project, relative to a total of 1.8 million poor families in the rural NE. As such, CDD reaches about 9 percent of the rural NE poor each year with at least one subproject investment. The project therefore reaches about one-eighth of the poor families in the rural NE each year. Over 11 years of CDD experience, subprojects for 1.8 million NE Brazil households were completed. Adjusting for repeat households (i.e. those which benefit from more than one community investment), about 900,000 households (or 50 percent) of the 1.8 million poor households in the rural NE may have been covered through CDD.

Figure 18.3 graphically compares a series of social spending programs in Brazil along four dimensions. First, each "bubble" represents one social spending program. Second, the size of each bubble is proportional to annual per household spending (annualized in the case of investment programs) showing the relative importance of the program to its beneficiaries. Third, the horizontal position of the bubble shows the level of targeting of the program to the bottom quintile of the income distribution. Finally, the vertical position of the bubble shows the reach (i.e. coverage) of the program among the same bottom quintile. Programs in the lower left corner (e.g., pensions, urban services, secondary education, and credit) are poorly targeted and do not reach many of the poor. Programs in the bottom right-hand corner (e.g. land reform) are well-targeted, provide substantial benefit, yet only reach a small share of the poor. Programs near the top left are universally available (e.g. basic health, education, and school lunches). The "ideal" social program is located in the top right-hand corner. These "ideal" social programs are well-targeted and reach a large share of the poor.

Figure 18.3 typifies the trade-off between targeting and reach among the rural poor. As the net is more broadly cast and reach increases, it becomes proportionally more difficult to control benefit slippage. This is the challenge faced when attempting to scale up initially small and well-targeted rural development programs, such as CDD. A second trade-off is

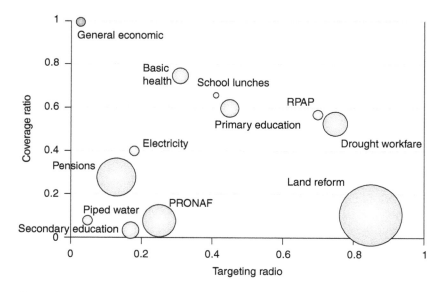

Figure 18.3 Coverage and targeting of selected rural social spending programs. For reference, the impact of distributionally neutral annual growth of 4 percent is shown in the top left-hand corner (source: World Bank (2003)).

also suggested between benefit size and coverage. Expensive programs, like land reform in Brazil (with an average per family benefit of R$4000 or some US$1800) reach only a small number of the poor, while less costly programs, such as the RPAP (average per family benefit of US$434), can afford a larger coverage.

Scale of subproject investments

While the subproject cost ceiling being US$50,000, in practice the average cost has been slightly more than one-half this amount. The first question is, of course, why US$50,000? Procurement rules agreed between the respective state governments and the World Bank – which guide the use of World Bank loan proceeds – have primarily driven the application of this subproject ceiling. Historically, World Bank projects have been associated with large-scale public works. As such, both procurement and disbursement procedures were designed for these large-scale investments, with little or no guidance regarding the smaller investments carried out under CDD (de Silva 2000). Yet, it was clear that arrangements for million dollar works were not appropriate for small-scale works. Second, but just as important, the technical capacity of the new implementing entities – the community associations – was as yet unproven, so the procurement rules would also have to adopt a learning-by-doing approach in step with the innovations embodied in CDD. Community participation was the World Bank's answer: procurement by or on behalf of a community. Here, "community" is defined as "groups of individuals living in close proximity to each other and other social groups, grassroots entrepreneurs or associations able to identify a need and come together to access project funds" (de Silva 2000). As stated in Section 3.17 of the World Bank (2004b) procurement guidelines, "Where, in the interest of project sustainability or to achieve certain specific social objectives of the project, it is desirable in selected project components to (a) call for the participation of local communities in the delivery of services, or (b) increase the utilization of local know-how and materials, or (c) employ labor-intensive and other appropriate technologies, the procurement procedures, specifications, and contract packaging shall be suitably adapted to reflect these considerations."

In determining the appropriate circumstances for community participation, no strict cost threshold exists vis-à-vis the World Bank rules. Therefore, the US$50,000 threshold used for CDD in Brazil can be seen to some extent as the "comfort level" of the World Bank with community participation, beyond which project complexity would dictate adherence to more traditional procurement rules.

Lessons learned

Sustainability

The NE Brazil's experience with CDD has demonstrated that community associations can effectively organize to meet basic needs at a reasonable cost. As for the sustainability of CDD, it must be assessed in at least two aspects: *outcome* and *process*. Outcome sustainability is the extent to which the end product of CDD can be maintained over the long term. Here, the subproject investment is the unit of analysis: what are the assurances that the physical investments undertaken by the community associations will be sustained? More specifically, what are the provisions for adequate operation and maintenance of the newly gained community asset? *Ex ante* arrangements and *ex post* evidence seem to point to a high probability of outcome sustainability.

Prior to receiving funding for their respective subprojects, community associations formally agree to maintain and operate these investments. In fact, once the subproject is completed, community associations receive ownership of the investment, which in itself creates an incentive to maintain the newly acquired asset. A softer element of sustainability is associated with the very act of community residents banding together to meet their collective needs. The effect of this communal effort – combined with the community association's in-cash or in-kind contribution for the subproject – generates a high degree of ownership for the investment and a subsequent sense of responsibility to maintain it.

Van Zyl *et al.* (2000) and World Bank (2003) report that, for a sample of 3633 subprojects implemented from 1997–8, about 89 percent were fully operational in 2000. Furthermore, beneficiary families strongly expressed their satisfaction with the quality of materials used in subproject implementation. Between one-half and three-quarters of the subprojects (varying by participating NE state) were judged by beneficiary families to be adequately sized to meet their needs. Beneficiaries assessed more than 90 percent of all subproject investments as being satisfactory overall.

Analysis of selected productive subprojects also suggests that the investments are generally financially sustainable, in that cost recovery through user fees paid by the beneficiary association is adequate to cover both maintenance and replacement of the original investment long before the end of its useful economic life. Analysis of a sample of 1820 productive subprojects (e.g. farm tractor, irrigation, goat/sheep production, brick production, fisheries, cashew nuts, manioc flour mills, clothes making, dry-land farming), implemented from 1995–8 indicates that 87 percent were fully operational in March 2000. Of 6064 infrastructure subprojects (e.g. rural electrification, water supply, telephone booths, community road rehabilitation, small bridges) funded over the same period, 89 per cent were fully operational.[14] Finally, an analysis of a sample of 239 social subprojects like sanitation, health-related housing improvement and social centers showed that 88 percent were also fully operational in March 2000.

Process sustainability is perhaps a bit more elusive to ascertain. What is the likelihood that the local institutions created and fostered through CDD – the community associations and the project MCs – will survive? Obviously, there is a degree of interdependence between process and outcome sustainability: if a community association succeeds in maintaining its subproject, it may also be more likely to survive and thrive over the long haul. Findings from NE Brazil imply the accumulation of social capital via CDD and its deployment through greater citizen participation in local development planning at the municipal level. Social capital provides citizens with appropriate reasons and motives to act collectively on behalf of their community and encourages a new kind of relationship between the state and the individuals in matters of administration of local public infrastructure – namely, one in which citizens (or civil society) oversee governmental activity and exercise political pressure upon authorities in the interest of the community (van Zyl *et al.* 2000). Furthermore, social capital is also believed to be associated with branching out of these local institutions beyond the World Bank-financed project. Finally, a critical element of process sustainability in the context of CDD is adoption or internalization of the CDD methodology within the formal state and municipal political structures. In practice, this would be denoted by the utilization of project MCs and community associations for channeling public resources for local investments, even after World Bank support wanes, thereby validating the staying power of the CDD model. The state of Maranhão, in NE Brazil, provides a glimpse as to the potential for leveraging the social capital of these community associations and MCs beyond the existing CDD projects.

In 2001, Maranhão was Brazil's second poorest state, both in terms of per capita income and HDI. Applying a poverty line of about a dollar a day, nearly 60 percent of the state population lives in poverty. The lag in education was particularly severe, with the average educational attainment (2.8 years) well below that of both the country and other neighboring NE states. Maranhão is also Brazil's most rural state, and it is in the rural space where HDIs are the lowest.

The state of Maranhão's multi-year investment program (PPA) 2004–7 sets a goal for increasing the state's HDI from 0.647 (in 2000) to 0.700 by the year 2007. Since the 1990s, Maranhão has had a series of competent state governments, and social indicators have increased faster than in most NE states. The state has launched an innovative, decentralized form of government, and has been proactive in attempting to change the culture of Brazil's state and local governments from one of clientelism and patronage, toward more responsible service delivery to its population.

The state's PPA is comprised of six elements: economic integration, competitiveness, transformation of the economic base, social inclusion, construction of a knowledge economy, and environmental sustainability. All programs in the PPA are justified in relation to these six elements. Priority programs are in education, health, water and sanitation, employment generation through local productive clusters, technology, environmental preservation, and public sector management and planning.

The new-generation World Bank-financed CDD project in Maranhão supports the state in its effort to reduce poverty by increasing its HDI by seeking to better align the state's public expenditures with the PPA development priorities, while improving the effectiveness and targeting of expenditures through a mainstreaming of the CDD methodology (World Bank 2004a). The new project will place significantly more emphasis on education, health, culture, natural resource management, and environmental sustainability, as well as take advantage of opportunities to achieve stronger results through coordinated action, including piloting regional subprojects (involving several municipalities) to address environmental issues, and supporting productive subprojects which tackle critical gaps within a broader concept of local production chains (*arranjos produtivos locais*). In sum, the project will attempt to leverage the skills, social capital and institutional arrangements developed under the RPAP project at the local and municipal levels to improve also the relevance, efficiency, environmental sustainability, targeting, and outcomes of non-project investments in rural areas of Maranhão.

Community-driven development in NE Brazil also seeks to stimulate social capital accumulation within a cultural context characterized by traditional forces with opposing political interests. How can CDD succeed in this area? Has it succeeded until now? Studies suggest that the impact of CDD in the process of formation and accumulation of social capital is variable and that this variation is explained by two major factors (van Zyl *et al.* 2000, Rizvi and Costa 2003). The first deals with the endogenous differences that exist at the community level. For example, the best community associations are usually those which have a tradition of collective work (in Portuguese, *trabalho em mutirão*), a characteristic of rural life in NE Brazil. The other relates to differences in potential, in terms of enhancing social capital formation, between the three delivery CDD mechanisms cited earlier for example, PAC, FUMAC, and FUMAC-P.

To assess the degree of community participation in CDD – overall and among the three delivery mechanisms, van Zyl *et al.* (2000) presents a Community Participation Index (CPI) based on a representative sample of community associations that benefited from the reformulated NRDP and the RPAP projects. The CPI considers 15 indicators of social capital, two of which relate to compliance with the project rules of provision of counterpart funding by the beneficiaries (usually 10 percent of the subproject cost) and responsibility of the beneficiary association for subproject operation and maintenance. Two sets of community associations were assessed: (1) 56 associations studied during 1993 and 1994; and (2) 149 associations in 1998–2000. The CPI reflects both the historical progress made with social capital accumulation from the NRDP to the RPAP, and the differences between the three subprograms in terms of community participation and social capital. Results obtained for the CPI are consistent with ethnographic observations made during field studies of both the NRDP and RPAP.

The findings from the CPI show not only the evolution of social capital between the NRDP and the RPAP, but also, the meaningful differences that exist between PAC, FUMAC and FUMAC-P. Communities in the 1993–94 sample (Group 1) had an average CPI of 11.98 (on a scale of 0 to 30). In comparison, the CPI of Group 2 communities, which were visited five to seven years later, is about five points higher, averaging 16.91. More specifically, PAC communities have an average CPI of 11.73, which is marginally lower than that of the NRDP communities interviewed in 1993, but substantially so compared to FUMAC (17.16) and FUMAC-P communities (21.09).[15] These results are a clear indication that FUMAC and FUMAC-P have contributed to enhancing social capital in the participating communities, while very little progress in terms of social capital accumulation took place under the PAC modality. It is also meaningful that the Group 1 sample presents slightly better results than Group 2 in only three of the fifteen indicators:

i   the rate of increase in the associations' membership;
ii   the rate of renewal of members of the associations' boards of directors;
iii the associations' ability to leverage funds from sources other than the NRDP/RPAP.

Considering the context provided by the other indicators of social capital and the huge differences in the averages reached by the two sets of samples and between the delivery mechanisms, it can be argued that, although in 1993, a small proportion of associations were in a better position to get funds from other sources, these funds (and the programs from which they came) were not as able as FUMAC and FUMAC-P to gear up the process of accumulation of social capital.

In response to the larger issue of internalizing CDD within the policy framework of the public sector, the case of the state of Maranhão is a signal that such a move is now underway. Maranhão has linked its medium-term development program to an explicit expected increase in its HDI. Public expenditures specifically budgeted for rural poverty reduction will be allocated and applied using CDD, taking advantage of local participation and consultation through the both community associations and the project Municipal Councils.

However, perhaps the true test of sustainability would take such internalization one step further by building in a fiscal transfer scheme to municipalities for the purpose of financing CDD investments.[16] Fiscal transfers from the federal to municipal government already occur in Brazil under the Municipal Participation Fund (MPF), yet the use of these funds is hamstrung by both fixed and mandatory funding formulas which commit the bulk of these resources *a priori* and the virtual dearth of investment resources within the FPM envelope.

A novel idea taking shape in many NE states is the establishment of a Fund for Poverty Reduction (FECOMP).[17] The revenue for the FECOMP is derived from special taxes levied on luxury items. In Bahia state, annual revenue on the order of R$100 million (roughly US$40 million) is currently available; this amount drastically scales up the resources available for poverty reduction investment throughout the state and, if chosen, extending the reach and depth of CDD with the application of these funds.

Replicability

The simplicity of the CDD model lends itself to wider applicability beyond Brazil, and in fact, strong evidence exists that the model, with necessary adaptations to fit into the local context, can generate equally positive results. In March 2003, the Post-Conflict Fund – a global program funded and implemented by the World Bank – approved a pilot project which sought to test the applicability of CDD in the Haitian context. Interest in CDD arose following a study tour of Haiti public officials to NE Brazil to view "on the ground" the CDD experience.

Some 76 percent of Haiti's eight million people live below the poverty line, with 56 percent in extreme poverty. Nearly 90 percent of poor households and 67 percent of extremely poor households live in the rural areas. Poverty in Haiti is comparable to rates in Sub-Saharan Africa. Haiti ranks 153rd on its HDI (out of 177 countries). Income inequality in Haiti is among the highest in the world, with the poorest and wealthiest 20 percent accounting for 1.5 and 68 percent of incomes, respectively.

At a total project cost of US$1.25 million, the Haiti Community-Driven Development Pilot(HCDDP) was implemented during 2004 in two of Haiti's 137 *communes* (or municipalities): Ouanaminthe (in the *Nord'est* Department) and Anse à Pîtres (in the *Sud'est* Department). The project's components draw quite liberally on the NE Brazil CDD model. Community subprojects (Component 1) were identified by community-based organizations (OCBs, from their French acronym) and later prioritized in representative project commune councils (known locally as *Conseil du Projet de Developpement Participatif*, or COPRODEPs) as a function of available resources under the project. Funding for capacity-building and technical assistance (Component 2) were available to prepare both OCBs and the two COPRODEPs in fulfilling their responsibilities related to subproject execution, monitoring, operation, and maintenance. Finally, project administration (Component 3) finances the incremental costs of the implementing agency, the Pan-American Development Foundation, particularly the installation and equipping of the two decentralized implementation offices (BCT – *Bureau de Coordination Technique*) in the participating communes.

In both Ouanaminthe and Anse à Pîtres, a deep history of community organization was present at project inception. The time when implementation began in Ouanaminthe, some 85 OCBs were identified, of which 46 were determined to meet the criteria for participation in the project. Similarly, in Anse à Pitres, 42 OCBs are active in the project. These OCBs all have obtained legal status, a requirement in order to receive subproject funds. With an average of 50 households each, these 88 OCBs conservatively account for nearly 20,000 individuals or about 20 percent of the combined population in the two communes. Anse á Pîtres formed its COPRODEP in March 2004, while in Ouanaminthe it was constituted in May 2004. COPRODEP membership consists of one representative from each OCB participating in the project, with the balance of membership consisting of public sector representatives, religious organizations, other NGOs, and the municipal government. According to the Operational Manual for the pilot project, 80 percent of the COPRODEP members were potential project beneficiaries. In practice, both in Ouanaminthe and Anse à Pîtres, potential beneficiaries constituted nearly 90 percent of COPRODEP membership.

At the end of October 2004, 44 community subprojects, of which 92 percent have been fully implemented and completed, had been selected through an open, transparent, and democratic process and with strong community ownership and support. These include productive, infrastructure, and social subprojects. More than 100 community associations received capacity-building training and technical assistance to design and implement their projects. Given the strong positive results of this pilot exercise, the scaled up project is now being implemented, at a cost of US$42 million over four years and covering nearly one-half of the municipalities across Haiti (World Bank 2005).

Conclusions

Some two decades of CDD in NE Brazil have shown that simplified approaches based on local participation can make a difference for the rural poor. This chapter has discussed the origins of CDD in Brazil, compared it to earlier integrated rural development projects, and provided a glimpse of the breadth, depth, and scale of investments undertaken through the community associations in the region. Evidence presented indicates that effective targeting results in minimal overall slippage of project benefits, with about 70 percent of families who benefit under CDD having had initial incomes of about US$1 per day. Political buy-in was crucial in getting CDD started in NE Brazil. State governments were favorably disposed to experiment with greater decentralization and the Federal Constitution of Brazil helped to facilitate it. Sustainability of the CDD model appears likely, in terms of both the physical investments and the new institutions – particularly the project MCs – in that effort is now underway to scale up the application of the participatory CDD approach in a broader set of public programs addressing rural poverty. Finally, the simple "rules of the game" guiding CDD in Brazil seem widely replicable, as given by the example of the CDD pilot in Haiti, which is already yielding positive results under quite, different and difficult circumstances.

More effort will need to be devoted to answering some of the questions posed in the introduction to this chapter. CDD, by design, is information-intensive, and the role of the state in facilitating information flows can easily erode into a "supply-driven demand" scenario, especially given the potential for a relapse toward traditional power structures (Tendler and Serrano 1999, Mansuri and Rao 2004). Furthermore, time will tell whether state government remains politically committed to CDD and allow its application more broadly in relevant social programs and respective budgets. Many of the CDD small-scale investments have laid the foundation for basic service provision, a key element of generating greater incomes for the rural poor of NE Brazil. Yet, the linkages of these subprojects to large-scale, complementary investments, which are likely to be implemented by the public sector, is yet to be determined. A greater understanding of the limits to the CDD model would also be of use in helping to build strategic alliances that go beyond the community associations and the MCs.

Notes

1 Opinions expressed are those of the authors and not necessarily those of the World Bank, to which the authors are affiliated. The authors thank Anna Roumani (World Bank) for substantive comments and suggestions in developing this chapter.
2 Throughout this chapter, community-driven development (CDD) projects are those (a) that include intended beneficiaries in their design and management and (b) where communities have direct control over key decisions, including control of investment funds (Mansuri and Rao 2004).
3 NE Brazil is comprised of nine states and the northern section of Minas Gerais.
4 Poverty data from the Brazil National Household Survey (PNAD) for the year 2003.
5 Hans Binswanger, November 2004, João Pessoa Conference.
6 POLONORDESTE is *Programa de Desenvolvimento de Areas Integradas do Nordeste* (Program of Integrated Development for the NE), and NRDP is NE Rural Development Project.
7 *Apoio às Pequenas Comunidades Rurais* (Support for Small Rural Communities).
8 Another facilitating factor for the movement toward CDD were the policy prescriptions widely pursued, chiefly on the part of the multi-lateral lending institutions like the World Bank, which promoted, *inter alia*, the scaling back of the

role of the state, combined with increased privatization. Fukiyama (2004) also points to the changing role of the state in delivering public services, as a result of the so-called "Washington Consensus".

9 Due to fiscal constraints, the NE States of Alagoas and Minas Gerais, which were part of the NRDP, were unable to participate in the RPAP.

10 Social capital can be defined as a stock of knowledge, behavioral practices and attitudes that are held by the members of a social group, which guides the social activities in which they participate, in an orderly fashion or not, so as to resolve a community problem that they identify as a priority (Putnam 1993, van Zyl *et al.* 2000).

11 Some variation in elements of the "negative list" occurs between states e.g. home construction is prohibited in Pernambuco state, yet permitted in Sergipe.

12 This was likely a result, *inter alia*, of a natural rationing of finite resources to benefit the maximum number of households.

13 See Table 5.4 in van Zyl *et al.* (2000) for details.

14 Rural electrification is an exceptional case, in that, following completion, these subprojects are typically transferred to the local electric company, which in turn accepts responsibility for operation and maintenance of the investment, in exchange for monthly service charges assessed to individual families.

15 The difference in longevity between the associations was found to be irrelevant in explaining the variation in CPI results.

16 See, for example, the Mexican municipal transfers as accomplished under *Ramo 33*. Also, Nicaragua, under its National Law no. 463 approved in October 2003, adopted a similar arrangement for financing CDD in its 152 municipalities.

17 In Portuguese, *Fundo Estadual de Combate à Pobreza* (FECOMP).

References

Berthet, R.S. (1996) *Who Knows What's Best for the Poor? Demand-Driven Policies and Rural Poverty in Northeast Brazil.* Masters Thesis: MIT.

Costa, A., Kottak, C. and Prado, R. (1997) "The Sociopolitical Context of Participatory Development in Northeastern Brazil." *Human Organization* 56:2 (138–46).

De Silva, S. (2000) *Community-based Contracting: A Review of Stakeholder Experience.* Washington, DC: World Bank.

Fintersbusch, D. and van Wicklin, W. (1987) "Contribution to Beneficiary Participation to Development Project Effectiveness," *Public Administration and Development*, 7: 1–23.

Fukuyama, F. (2004) *State-Building: Governance and World Order in the 21st Century.* Cornell Ithaca, NY: University Press.

Mansuri, G. and Rao, V. (2004) *Community-Based and -Driven Development: A Critical Review.* The World Bank Research Observer. 19:1 (1–39).

Narayan, D. (1995) *Designing Community Based Development.* Environment Department Papers, No. 7. Washington, DC: World Bank.

Putnam, R. (1993) *Making Democracy Work: Civic Traditions in Modern Italy.* Princeton NJ: Princeton University Press.

Rizvi, A. and Costa. A. (2003) "Can community driven infrastructure programs contribute to social capital?" Findings from the Rural Northeast of Brazil. Mimeo.

Roumani, A. (2004) "Brazil: Community-Driven Development in Rural Communities of the Northeast." A case study from *Reducing Poverty, Sustaining Growth. What Works, What Doesn't, and Why?* Scaling Up Poverty Reduction: A Global Learning Process and Conference. Shanghai, May, 2004.

Tendler, J. (1993) *New Lessons from Old Projects: The Workings of Rural Development in Northeast Brazil.* Operations Evaluation Department, Washington, DC: World Bank.

Tendler, J. and Serrano, R. (1999) *The Rise of Social Funds: What Are They A Model Of?* Department of Urban Studies and Planning, Massachusetts Institute of Technology: Cambridge, Massachusetts.

United Nations (2004). *Human Development Atlas – Brazil.* Brasília, DF: United Nations.

Van Zyl, J., Sonn, L. and Costa, A. (2000) Decentralized Rural Development, Enhanced Community Participation and Local Government Performance: Evidence from Northeast Brazil. Mimeo.

World Bank. (2003) *Rural Poverty Alleviation in Brazil: Toward an Integrated Strategy.* Washington DC: World Bank.

World Bank. (2004a) *Project Information Document: Maranhão Integrated Program: Rural Poverty Reduction Project.* Washington, DC: World Bank.

World Bank. (2004b) *Guidelines: Procurement under IBRD Loans and IDA Credits.* Washington, DC: World Bank.

World Bank. (2005) *Project Appraisal Document: Haiti Community-Driven Development Project.* Washington, DC: World Bank.

Yusuf, S., Wu, W. and Evenett, S. (2000) *Local Dynamics in an Era of Globalization.* Oxford University Press: New York.